WATERFALL LOVER'S GUIDE
PACIFIC NORTHWEST

WATERFALL LOVER'S GUIDE

PACIFIC NORTHWEST

Fifth Edition

GREGORY A. PLUMB

Where to Find Hundreds of Spectacular Waterfalls in Washington, Oregon, and Idaho

MOUNTAINEERS
BOOKS

THIS EDITION IS REDEDICATED TO MY FAMILY MEMBERS
AND NEWLY DEDICATED
TO EVERYONE WHO HAS A LOVE OF GEOGRAPHY.

MOUNTAINEERS BOOKS

Mountaineers Books is the publishing division of The Mountaineers, an organization founded in 1906 and dedicated to the exploration, preservation, and enjoyment of outdoor and wilderness areas.

1001 SW Klickitat Way, Suite 201 • Seattle, WA 98134
800.553.4453 • www.mountaineersbooks.org

© 1983, 1989, 1998, 2005, and 2013 by Gregory Alan Plumb

All rights reserved. No part of this book may be reproduced or utilized in any form, or by any electronic, mechanical, or other means, without the prior written permission of the publisher.

Printed in the United States of America

Distributed in the United Kingdom by Cordee, www.cordee.co.uk
First edition 1983. Second edition 1989. Third edition 1998. Fourth edition 2005.
Fifth edition 2013.

Copy Editor: Laura Shauger
Maps: Gregory A. Plumb
Cover design and layout: Peggy Egerdahl
All photographs taken and prepared for publication by the author unless otherwise noted.

Cover photograph: *North Middle Falls in Silver Lake State Park, Oregon*
Frontispiece photograph: *White River Falls, Columbia Plateau, Oregon*
Backcover photograph: *Pin Creek Falls, Washington*

Library of Congress Cataloging-in-Publication Data
Plumb, Gregory Alan, 1956-
Waterfall lover's guide Pacific Northwest : where to find hundreds of spectacular waterfalls in Washington, Oregon, and Idaho / Gregory A. Plumb. — Fifth edition.
pages cm.
Includes bibliographical references and index.
ISBN 978-1-59485-753-9 (ppb)
1. Hiking—Northwest, Pacific—Guidebooks. 2. Waterfalls—Northwest, Pacific—Guidebooks. 3. Northwest, Pacific—Guidebooks. I. Title.
GV199.42.N68P58 2013
917.9504'44—dc23

2013012829

ISBN (paperback): 978-1-59485-753-9
ISBN (ebook): 978-1-59485-754-6

CONTENTS

THE NORTH CASCADES, WASHINGTON

Bold indicates a five-star area

THE OLYMPICS AND VICINITY, WASHINGTON

MOUNT RAINIER REGION, WASHINGTON

GIFFORD PINCHOT COUNTRY, WASHINGTON

THE INLAND EMPIRE, WASHINGTON

THE COLUMBIA GORGE, OREGON AND WASHINGTON

THE SOUTH CASCADES, OREGON

THE COLUMBIA PLATEAU, OREGON

THE PANHANDLE, IDAHO

CENTRAL WILDERNESS AREAS, IDAHO

THE SNAKE RIVER PLAIN, IDAHO

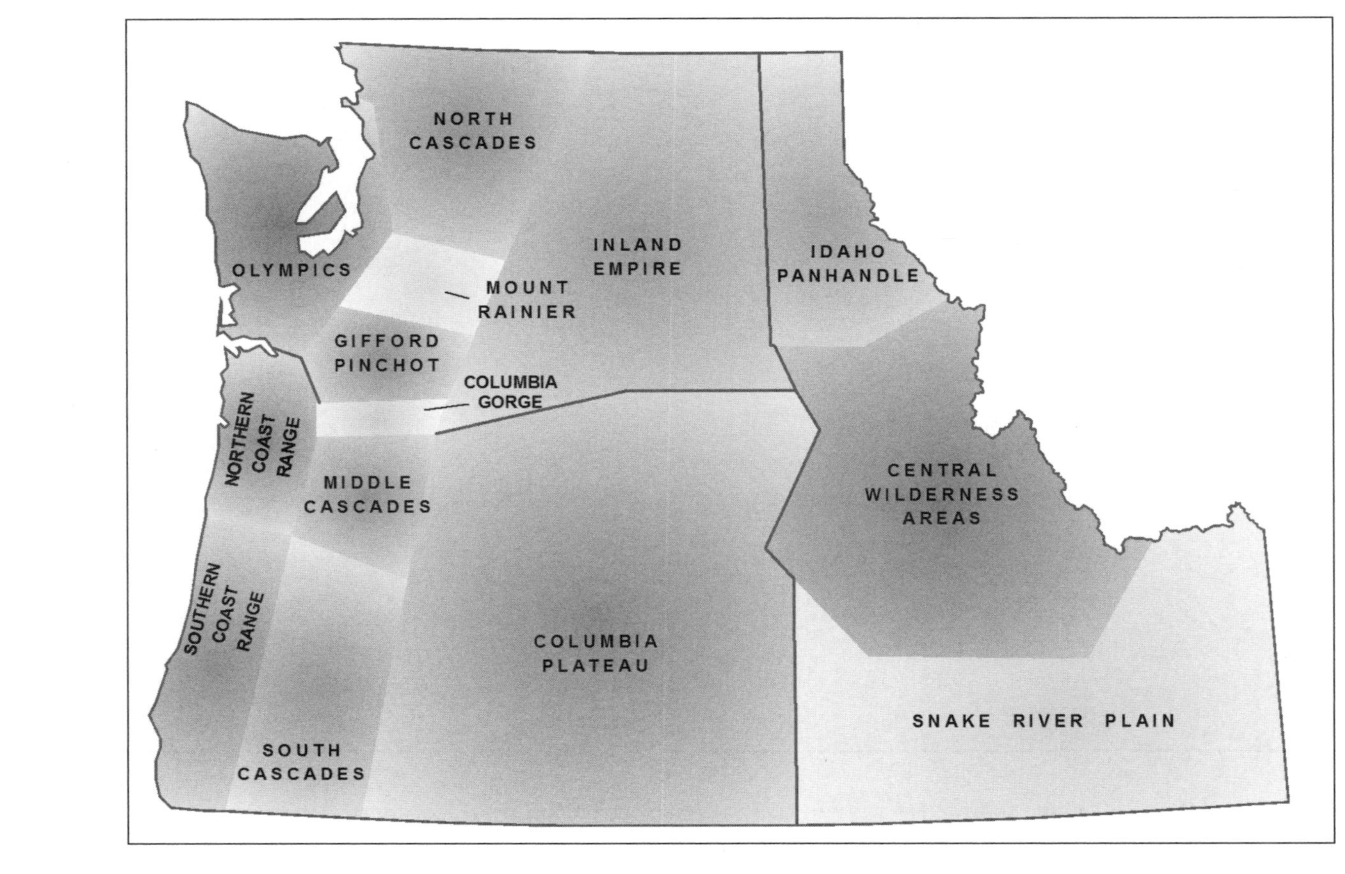

NORTH CASCADES
OLYMPICS
INLAND EMPIRE
IDAHO PANHANDLE
MOUNT RAINIER
GIFFORD PINCHOT
COLUMBIA GORGE
NORTHERN COAST RANGE
MIDDLE CASCADES
CENTRAL WILDERNESS AREAS
SOUTHERN COAST RANGE
COLUMBIA PLATEAU
SNAKE RIVER PLAIN
SOUTH CASCADES

QUICK REFERENCE TO THE WATERFALLS

This chart tallies the number of waterfalls (organized by chapter and section) that possess various characteristics. Falls that are inaccessible to the public are excluded from the tallies.

	Total Falls	New to 5th edition	★★★★★	★★★★	★★★	★★	★	EXPLORE!	Plunge	Horsetail	Fan	Punchbowl	Block	Tiered	Segmented	Cascade	Auto	Trail (easy to fairly easy)	Trail (moderate to hard)	Backpack	Bushwhack	Watercraft	High-Clearance Vehicle
NORTH CASCADES	111	27	4	8	26	43	25	5	9	19	8	8	4	30	11	17	40	23	30	4	12	5	1
1 Newcastle	6	6				2	4		1	1				1	2	1		3	3				
2 Snoqualmie	1		1						1								1						
3 North Bend	6	2		1	1	3	1				2			3		1	3		3				
4 Taylor River	4	1	1		3					1		1		1		1		1	3				1
5 Snoqualmie Pass	4	1			1	2	1		1	1		1		1			2		2				
6 Stampede Pass	2			1	1				1	1								2					
7 Leavenworth	2	1				1	1			1						1	2						
8 Lake Wenatchee	2				1		1					1				1	1	1					
9 Stevens Pass	5	2				5						1			2	2	2	4			1		
10 Alpine Lakes	5			1			4			1				2	1	1		2	3				
11 Index	2				1		1							1		1	2		1				
12 Gold Bar	6	5	1		2	2	1			1				4		1		1	5				
13 Monroe	3	3				2	1			1		2					2				1		
14 Granite Falls	2					1	1			1						1	1	1			1		
15 Robe Valley	4					2	2			1	1			1		1	1	1	1		1		
16 Twin Falls Lake	2			1			1		1	1									2				
17 Boulder River	1					1					1							1					

18	Sauk River	2			1			1					1				1		1			1		
19	Suiattle River	4	1			1	1	2				1			2		1	2		1		2		
20	Sauk Valley	1				1									1					1		1		
21	Mount Baker	1				1				1								1						
22	Bellingham	5	2			1	3		1				1	2	1			2	2					
23	Deming	2	2			2									2					1		1		
24	Maple Falls	1					1										1		1					
25	Nooksack River	3	1		1		1	1		1					1	1		3				1		
26	North Cascades NP	8			1	3	4			1		1			1	4	1	4			4			
27	Ross Lake	9				4	5			1	3	1			4			7	1				1	
28	Rainy Pass	1			1										1				1					
29	Methow Valley	2				1		1							1		1			1		1		
30	Winthrop	3				1	2				1				1	1		1		1		1		
31	Foggy Dew Creek	1					1				1									1				
32	Lake Chelan	8		1			2	1	4		2	1			1								4	
33	Entiat Valley	3				1	2				1			2				3		1				
OLYMPICS		45	12	0	5	7	20	13	0	0	17	2	5	0	11	5	6	13	15	9	1	5	3	0
1	Orcas Island	4					1	3			1	2					1		4					
2	Elwha	2				1	1				2							1		1				
3	Mount Carrie	2					2				1				1					2				
4	Lake Crescent	1			1										1				1					
5	Soleduck	1				1										1				1				
6	Beaver Creek	1				1										1						1		
7	Clallam Bay	5					1	4			4		1					1	1			1	3	
8	Olympic Coast	1					1				1									1				
9	Quinault	5	5			1	2	2			1		1		1	1	1	2	2	1				
10	Enchanted Valley	1			1						1				1						1			
11	Quilcene	2	1				2				1				1			1	1					

	Total Falls	New to 5th edition	★★★★★	★★★★	★★★	★★	★	EXPLORE!	Plunge	Horsetail	Fan	Punchbowl	Block	Tiered	Segmented	Cascade	Auto	Trail (easy to fairly easy)	Trail (moderate to hard)	Backpack	Bushwhack	Watercraft	High-Clearance Vehicle
OLYMPICS (continued)	45	12	0	5	7	20	13	0	0	17	2	5	0	11	5	6	13	15	9	1	5	3	0
12 Dosewallips	3	1		2	1					1				1		1	2		1				
13 Jefferson Peak	2	2		1		1								1		1					2		
14 Lake Cushman	1					1				1							1						
15 Skokomish Valley	1	1				1				1							1						
16 Wynoochee Lake	3	1			1	1	1			1				2			2	1			1		
17 Kamilche	2					1	1							1		1		1	1				
18 Olympia	4				1	2	1					1		1	1	1	1	2					
19 Porter	2					1	1			1		1						1	1				
20 Montesano	1	1				1									1			1					
21 Rainbow Falls SP	1					1						1					1						
MOUNT RAINIER	84	19	3	6	23	31	19	1	13	15	9	5	7	15	6	12	26	22	31	3	10	0	0
1 Sumner	2	2			1	1			1						1		1	1					
2 Carbon River	7			1	2	2	1							3	1	2			6	3	1		
3 Mowich Lake	1		1								1								1				
4 Eatonville	5	2			1	4				1	1	1			2			2	3				
5 Big Creek	2					1	1			2									2				
6 Westside Road	1	1			1				1										1				
7 Nisqually River	12	3	1	1	3	3	4		4	5				1		2	5	4	3		2		
8 Paradise	7	2			2	2	3				2		3	1		1	2	4	2		1		
9 Stevens Canyon	8	1		1	2	3	2		1		2			3		2	5	1	2		1		

10	Upper Ohanapecosh	3				1	1	1			1		1				1	1	1	1				
11	Chinook Creek	6			2	2	1	1					1		2	1	2	1	2	2		1		
12	Cayuse Pass	2					1	1						1	1			1		1				
13	Camp Sheppard	4					1	2	1	1					2			1		2				
14	Rainier Valley	6	4			3	2	1			2	1	1	1			1	2	2	2				
15	Naches	4	1				3	1		1	1			1	1			2	2					
16	Rimrock Lake	7	3	1	1	2	3			3		1	1	1	1			3	1	2		1		
17	Lower Ohanapecosh	5				3	1	1			2	1				1	1	2	1	1		2		
18	Johnson Creek	1					1			1												1		
19	Silverbrook	1					1				1								1					
GIFFORD PINCHOT		**92**	**24**	**3**	**8**	**21**	**38**	**18**	**4**	**15**	**9**	**7**	**7**	**13**	**20**	**6**	**8**	**23**	**23**	**32**	**0**	**12**	**2**	**0**
1	North Fork Cispus River	15	4			4	5	6		2	4	3	2		2		2	6	3	4		2		
2	Walupt Lake	3	3	1		1	1							2	1							3		
3	North St. Helens	14	9			3	5	4	2	3	1	1	1		4	1	1	3	3	5		1		
4	Kalama River Road	2					1	1		1							1	2					1	
5	Lake Merwin	3					3			1	2							1	2			1	1	
6	Kalama Falls	1					1						1						1	1				
7	South St. Helens	8			1	3	3		1	2					5				2	5				
8	Eagle Cliff	7	1		3		2	2		3		1			2		1		5					
9	Lewis River	12	3		1	4	6	1					1	7	2		1	3	2	6		2		
10	Chelatchie	8			1	1	4	2		1	1		2	1	1					8				
11	East Fork Lewis River	7	1			1	3	2	1					3	1	1	1	3	3					
12	Wind River Road	3		1	1	1				1					1	1			1	1		1		
13	Trout Lake	4	2		1	1	2					2				1	1	1	1			2		
14	Mount Adams	3				1	2				1				1	1		2		2				
15	Glenwood	2	1	1		1				1						1		2						

	Total Falls	New to 5th edition	★★★★★	★★★★	★★★	★★	★	EXPLORE!	Plunge	Horsetail	Fan	Punchbowl	Block	Tiered	Segmented	Cascade	Auto	Trail (easy to fairly easy)	Trail (moderate to hard)	Backpack	Bushwhack	Watercraft	High-Clearance Vehicle
INLAND EMPIRE	33	6	1	4	8	16	4	0	1	5	4	3	5	7	3	5	13	10	3	0	5	3	0
1 Spokane	4	2		1	1	1	1								1	3	1	3					
2 Spokane Indian Reservation	2				1	1									1	1	1	1					
3 Lake Roosevelt	2					1	1				1	1					1	1				2	
4 Metaline	2	2			1	1								2				1	1				
5 Boundary Dam	1			1						1											1	1	
6 Park Rapids	1				1									1			1						
7 Colville	3				1	1	1			1	1					1	2				1		
8 Kettle Falls	2				1	1					1		1				1						
9 Northport	2			1		1					1		1						1				
10 Sherman Creek	2					2				2							2				1		
11 Republic	1	1				1				1								1					
12 Conconully	1					1								1					1		1		
13 St. Mary's	1					1								1							1		
14 Nespelem	3				1	2						1		2			1	2					
15 Coulee City	2	1		1		1						1	1				2						
16 Rock Creek Coulee	1					1							1					1					
17 Palouse Canyon	3		1		1		1		1				1		1		1						
COLUMBIA GORGE	74	2	5	6	18	30	15	0	11	18	4	10	4	12	5	6	22	15	32	3	5	0	0
1 Bridal Veil	5		1		2	2			2	1				2			3		2				
2 Multnomah Falls	11	1	1	1	2	4	3		2	2	1		2	2		1	3		7				

3	Oneonta Gorge	5		1	1	2	1			1	3					1		1		3		1		
4	Yeon State Park	2		1		1				1						1			1	1				
5	Tanner Creek	3			1		1	1			1	1			1				3					
6	Eagle Creek	14		1	2	2	4	5		3	1		3		2		3		1	13	3	1		
7	Cascade Locks	4				2		2		1	3								1	3				
8	Wyeth	1				1					1								1					
9	Starvation Creek SP	4			1	1	2				2	1					1	1	2	1				
10	Hood River Valley	3				2	1			1			1		1			3						
11	Mosier	2				1		1			1		1					1	1					
12	The Dalles	2					1	1					1				1	2						
13	White Salmon	3	1				3					1	1	1				2	1					
14	Carson	2					2				1				1				1			1		
15	Stevenson	2				1	1				1			1				1	1					
16	Beacon Rock	2				1	1				1				1					2				
17	Washougal River	6					5	1					2		2	2		5				1		
18	Camas	3					2	1			1		1			1			2			1		
NORTHERN COAST RANGE		23	1	0	2	4	9	5	3	1	2	4	1	2	2	4	4	11	5	3	0	2	0	0
1	Scappoose	1					1									1		1						
2	Beaver Creek	2	1			1		1						1			1	1	1					
3	Olney	2				1	1					1	1					2	1					
4	Jewell	1					1					1						1	1					
5	Wilson River	8				1	2	2	3		1	1			1		2	2	1	1		1		
6	Tillamook	1			1										1				1					
7	Blaine	3				1	1	1			1					1	1	2		1				
8	Dolph	1					1					1										1		
9	Lincoln City	1			1					1										1				
10	Cherry Grove	2					1	1								2		1	1					
11	Falls City	1					1							1				1						

		Total Falls	New to 5th edition	★★★★★	★★★★	★★★	★★	★	EXPLORE!	Plunge	Horsetail	Fan	Punchbowl	Block	Tiered	Segmented	Cascade	Auto	Trail (easy to fairly easy)	Trail (moderate to hard)	Backpack	Bushwhack	Watercraft	High-Clearance Vehicle
SOUTHERN COAST RANGE		36	0	0	1	7	13	6	9	0	2	3	2	4	4	7	5	10	13	4	0	0	0	0
1	Alsea	3					3					1	1				1	1	2					
2	Smith River	1					1							1				1						
3	Central Coast RD	7			1	3	1	1	1			1	1		1	3		1	3	2				
4	Lorane	1					1							1					1					
5	Millicoma River	2				1	1				1					1			2					
6	East Fork Coquille River	4					2	2				1		1		1	1	3	1					
7	Powers	3				2	1				1				1	1		1	1	1				
8	The Wild Rogue	12				1	2	1	8					1	1	1	1	1	2	1				
9	Illinois River	3					1	2							1		2	2	1					
MIDDLE CASCADES		58	7	0	10	15	23	10	0	18	4	6	4	10	6	4	6	17	19	14	0	10	0	1
1	Mount Hood Wilderness	1				1						1								1				
2	Zigzag River	4	1			2	2			1		2					1	2	1	1				
3	Bennett Pass	4	1			1	2	1			1	2					1	2	1	1				
4	Northeast Mount Hood	2			1		1			2								1		1				
5	Oregon City	1				1								1				1						
6	Eagle Creek	2					1	1						1		1			2					
7	Bagby Hot Springs	2					2				1			1				1				1		
8	Silver Falls State Park	11			2	4	4	1		7	1			1	1	1			7	4				
9	Scotts Mills	4	1		2	1	1			2				2				1		3				1
10	Mehama	5	2		1		3	1		4					1			1	2			2		

11	Little North Santiam River	3			1	1	1			1						1	1	2	1					
12	Niagara Park	3	1				1	2			1	1	1					2				1		
13	Marion Forks	4	1		1	1	1	1						2	1		1			1		4		
14	McKenzie River	4			2		1	1					1	1		1	1	2	1	1				
15	Cascadia	3				1	1	1					1		1		1	1		1		1		
16	McDowell Creek Falls County Park	5				2	2	1		1			1	1	2			1	4			1		
SOUTH CASCADES		**82**	**3**	**2**	**6**	**21**	**35**	**13**	**5**	**6**	**8**	**13**	**9**	**6**	**14**	**11**	**9**	**20**	**26**	**28**	**0**	**2**	**1**	**2**
1	Cougar Reservoir	1	1			1					1							1					1	
2	McKenzie Highway	5			1	1	2	1			2	2				1			5					
3	Big Fall Creek	1				1							1					1						
4	Erma Bell Lakes	1				1								1						1				
5	Salmon Creek	4	1				3	1								3	1	3		1				
6	Salt Creek	6		1	1	1	3			2		2			2			1	1	4				
7	Row River	11				4	6		1			4	3		1	2		2	3	4				1
8	Little River	8				4	3	1		2	2	1			2	1		1	1	6				
9	Cavitt Creek	2				1		1					1		1			1		1				
10	Idleyld Park	5	1			2	2	1			1	1		1	2			1	2	2				
11	Steamboat	4				1	2	1			1			1	1	1		2		1		1		
12	Toketee	4		1	1				2	1					1				2					
13	Northeast Umpqua	5			1	1	2	1			1		1	1		1	1	1	3	1				
14	South Umpqua	4					3		1				1		1		1	2	1					
15	Upper Rogue River	6					2	3	1				1	1	1	1	1	1	1	3				
16	Natural Bridge	3					2	1					1				2	1	1	1				
17	Crater Lake NP	2				1		1				1					1	2						
18	Mill Creek	5			2	1	2			1		1			1	1	1		4			1		1
19	Sky Lakes Wilderness	3				1	1	1				1			1					3				
20	Butte Falls	1					1							1					1					
21	Gold Bar	1					1										1		1					

	Total Falls	New to 5th edition	★★★★★	★★★★	★★★	★★	★	EXPLORE!	Plunge	Horsetail	Fan	Punchbowl	Block	Tiered	Segmented	Cascade	Auto	Trail (easy to fairly easy)	Trail (moderate to hard)	Backpack	Bushwhack	Watercraft	High-Clearance Vehicle
COLUMBIA PLATEAU	32	3	2	3	11	10	5	1	2	3	3	2	3	6	5	7	9	9	13	0	2	0	3
1 Tygh Valley	4			1	2	1						1	1	1	1		2	2					
2 Sisters	3	3	1	1		1			1	1	1								3				3
3 Tumalo Creek	6				1	2	2	1	1	1				1	2		3	1	1				
4 Lava Butte Geological Area	3				2	1									1	2	1	2					
5 Cascade Lakes Highway	4				1	2	1				1		1	1		1			4		1		
6 La Pine	2					1	1				1					1	1	1					
7 Newberry Crater	2		1		1									1	1			1	1				
8 Enterprise	4			1	1	1	1			1				1		2		2	2				
9 Wallowa Lake	2				2							1		1					2		1		
10 Ochoco	1					1										1	1						
11 Adel	1				1								1				1						
PANHANDLE	40	15	1	5	13	15	5	1	7	6	6	6	2	3	2	7	6	8	23	0	4	0	6
1 Priest River	3	1				1	2					1				2	2		1				
2 Priest Lake East	5	5		1	3	1				1	1	1				2		1	4		1		4
3 Priest Lake West	3	1		1	1	1				1	1	1					1	1	2				1
4 Pend Oreille	3				2		1			1		1				1		1	1				1
5 Colburn	1					1										1		1					
6 Pack River	1				1					1									1		1		
7 Bonners Ferry	5	3			2	3				1	2			1	1			1	4				
8 Moyie River	1		1											1			1						
9 Boundary Line	2			1	1				2								1		1				

10	Post Falls	2	2			1	1							1		1			2					
11	Prichard	3	3				2	1		3									1	2				
12	Mullan	2				1	1			1		1								2				
13	St. Joe River	2					1		1					1				1						
14	Elk Creek	7			2	1	3	1		1	1	1	2		1		1			5		2		
CENTRAL WILDERNESS AREAS		30	0	1	0	3	21	3	2	2	5	2	4	2	5	4	4	18	0	6	4	2	0	0
1	Selway River	1					1									1		1						
2	Lochsa River	5					3	1	1		1	1			2			4						
3	Warm Springs Creek	1				1							1							1				
4	Little Salmon River	5					2	2	1		1						3	4						
5	Lost Valley	1					1						1					1						
6	Garden Valley	2					2						1	1				2						
7	South Fork Boise River	3				1	2			2	1							2				1		
8	Sawtooths West	5				1	4				2				1	2				1	4	1		
9	Middle Fork Salmon River	1					1							1				1						
10	Stanley Lake Creek	2					2						1		1					2				
11	Sawtooths East	1		1								1						1		1				
12	Ketchum	1					1									1				1				
13	Leesburg	1					1										1	1						
14	North Fork Salmon River	1					1								1			1						
SNAKE RIVER PLAIN		29	1	1	6	7	7	8	0	2	3	1	2	8	1	6	6	18	4	4	0	3	0	0
1	Jump Creek Canyon	1			1						1								1					
2	Hagerman	5	1			1	1	3		1			1	1		2		3	2					
3	Snake Plains Aquifer	3				1		2			1					1	1	3						
4	Snake River Canyon	7		1	2	1	1	2		1	1			1		1	3	5				2		
5	Lava Hot Springs	3					2	1					1	1		1		1	1			1		
6	City of Idaho Falls	1				1											1	1						
7	Swan Valley	1			1							1						1						
8	Henrys Fork	4			1	2	1							2	1		1	2		2				
9	Yellowstone Area	4			1	1	2							3		1		2		2				

PREFACE

Water in its many forms provides some of the earth's most beautiful landscapes. Rivers, lakes, and coasts all offer images of scenic beauty, but undoubtedly, waterfalls are the most impressive of hydrologic features. People have always been drawn to falls as places of wonder, relaxation, and inspiration.

As a youth, my first experience of this sparkling water formation was the popular Tahquamenon Falls in Michigan's Upper Peninsula. The shimmering water of this block-type waterfall naturally tints to a burnt orange during its descent. Our family so enjoyed this waterfall that we began including stops at other falls in our itinerary on vacations "up north." However, we had difficulty finding waterfalls other than those marked by "point of interest" symbols on the state highway map. Even these were not always easy to find.

As an adult, my interest in waterfalls peaked while I was living in northern Idaho in the late 1970s. The Pacific Northwest was a new region for me to explore, and on many trips I discovered waterfalls. After visiting a few, I wanted to see more. Unfortunately, I discovered that no text had been written on the subject. At that point an idea was kindled. The first version of this recreational guidebook was the result.

The publication of this fifth edition celebrates the 30th anniversary of the original book, *Waterfalls of the Pacific Northwest,* and its successor, *A Waterfall Lover's Guide to the Pacific Northwest.* This revision contains information for 768 waterfalls, including accounts of 120 "new" cataracts. Shaded relief has also been added to the maps, which not only is an aesthetic improvement, but also helps orient the reader to the terrain being navigated. Speaking of orientation and navigation, geographic coordinates have been added for travelers to use with their GPS devices.

The complementary website, *The Computer Companion,* has also been updated. This online resource not only includes a color photograph of nearly every waterfall, it also provides hyperlinks to topographic maps and aerial images within which the falls occur. It also contains references for 815 waterfalls not in the book, bringing the grand total to 1583 descents (and forever counting) documented for the Pacific Northwest.

Whether you are a novice or a seasoned waterfall buff, I hope you enjoy using this fifth edition of the guidebook on your explorations.

Opposite: *University Falls, Northern Coast Range, Oregon*

ACKNOWLEDGMENTS

No endeavor of this type can be accomplished without the direct and indirect contributions of others. I am indebted to my wife, Robin, for her continuing understanding and support, as it takes a substantial commitment away from other activities to update a guidebook. Robin also accompanied me on a recent waterfall expedition to the Inland Empire and Idaho Panhandle.

The maps were revised through the resources of the Devon Energy Spatial Graphics & Analysis Lab, Department of Cartography and Geography, East Central University, Ada, Oklahoma. I am grateful to the ECU administration for their support of my publication efforts. The maps were designed electronically using ArcMap/ArcGIS software, a product of Environmental Systems Research Institute. The shaded relief base was derived from US Geological Survey terrain models. Road, trail, and other information were overlain using digital source data including USGS topographic maps and TIGER/Line files from the US Census Bureau.

The most enjoyable part of continually updating this book is, of course, seeking out the waterfalls of the Pacific Northwest! The personnel at the National Park Service and US Forest Service ranger stations were very helpful in providing updated road and travel information. I'm especially grateful for all of the recent trailblazing that has occurred, allowing for more waterfalls to be safely visited.

I'd also like to thank Bryan Swan, Seattle, Washington, and Roger Amundson, Longview, Washington, for helping me seek out several "new" waterfalls that I have added to this edition. Rick Netter, Portland, Oregon, was also very helpful with his email updates on the scores of waterfalls he has visited.

Back at school, ECU cartography majors Jason Melius and Chris Cox performed yeoman's work cross-checking the manuscript maps with the text. Salutations also go out to ECU cartography major Sergio Jimenez-Garcia, originally from Madrid, Spain, for working his Photoshop magic restoring many of my old color slides to publication quality. A special tip-of-the-cap is extended to Joseph Elfelt, Redmond, Washington, for writing his killer GMap4 web app. I'm also very appreciative to everyone at The Mountaineers Books for continuing to believe in this endeavor. I apologize if I've left anyone out.

Lastly, I am grateful to God for placing these magnificent features in the universe and creating us to experience them.

INTRODUCTION

Welcome to the waterfalls of the Pacific Northwest! This book has been written as a field guide to lead you to hundreds of falls in all shapes and sizes. Whether you want an afternoon trip or an extensive vacation, a short walk or a backpacking trek, this guidebook will tell you where to find the cataracts. Extraordinary adventures await you!

But first, some words of warning. The grandeur of waterfalls is accompanied by an element of risk. Accidents can occur at even the most developed locations, particularly when youngsters are left unsupervised or people act unwisely and unduly place themselves in dangerous situations. Worldwide, many persons are injured each year and several die near waterfalls. Such tragedies are almost always due to irresponsible behavior. Think safety first! Here are some basic guidelines:

- Use common sense.
- Closely supervise your children.
- Do not take children on long, difficult, or uncertain journeys.
- Do not stray from observation points or trails in steep areas.
- Never try to climb up or down a waterfall.
- Stay away from sloping, bare (unvegetated) surfaces.
- Know your physical capabilities and do not exceed them.
- Turn back whenever you feel insecure about the route ahead.
- Remember the first guideline.

Erics Falls, Gifford Pinchot Country, Washington

When hiking, remember to carry sufficient water and food. Bringing along the rest of the Ten Essentials (a map, compass, first-aid kit, flashlight, knife, matches in a waterproof container, fire starter, sunglasses, and extra clothes) is also a good idea, especially as the journey's distance increases. Bushwhackers should wear long pants to help protect themselves from scrapes, poison ivy, ticks, and snakes. Refer to other books dedicated to hiking or backpacking for further information on preparation.

You also have ethical responsibilities. Maintain respect for the land, its ownership, and other visitors. Do not litter, and if you encounter a bit of trash, please consider packing it out. Please pay at places charging a fee. While there may be some debate concerning the Northwest Forest Pass, philosophical and otherwise, there are recently constructed roads and trails to waterfalls that would not have existed or been improved if it weren't for the fee system. Lastly, some cataracts may be located on private property, so be considerate when you visit. Heed all "No Trespassing" signs, as landowners may decide not to allow access whenever they choose, even though at one time it may have been granted.

REGIONAL FORMAT

This guidebook is organized into fourteen geographic regions. Use the map on page 11, the table of contents, and the index to help you navigate the book. The regional chapters are further subdivided into smaller areas, or sections, containing waterfalls in relative proximity to one another.

WATERFALL ENTRIES

Waterfalls with a scenic rating of two or more stars are described in complete entries consisting of the following elements:

Name

The name of the falls is considered to be official if it occurs in the federal government's Geographic Names Information System listing or is used by a federal, state, or local agency. A designation of (u) following the name of the falls indicates an unofficial name.

Rating

Each waterfall included in this book has been assigned a rating of one to five stars, which helps you understand quickly how scenic it is. Because of space considerations, descriptions of one-star falls are provided in the online *The Computer Companion* at www.mymaps.com/nwfalls/toc.htm.

★ *Uninspiring:* Probably not interesting except to waterfall collectors
★★ *Modest:* Nice background for a picnic
★★★ *Good:* Scenic feature worth a trip
★★★★ *Very good:* Outstanding scenic feature
★★★★★ *Exceptional:* An awe-inspiring sight

Waterfall Forms

The form listed is the one most representative of the falls. It is not uncommon for falls to possess elements of more than one form.

Plunge: Descends vertically from the stream, losing contact with the bedrock surface

Horsetail: Descends vertically or nearly so, maintaining substantial contact with the bedrock surface

Fan: Similar to the horsetail form, except that the breadth of spray increases downward

Block: Descends from a wide breadth of a river or stream

Tiered: Descends as a distinct series of several falls, with at least two tiers visible from a single vantage point

Punchbowl: Descends from a narrow stream into a pool below

Segmented: Descends in multiple threads, with at least two threads visible from a single vantage point

Cascades: Descends as a series of steps along a dipping bedrock surface. Also includes rapids

Accessibility

The approach to each waterfall is described as follows:

Auto: The falls is next to a road accessible by a passenger vehicle or within a short, quick, and easy walk from such a road.

High-clearance: The falls is located next to a road accessible by a high-clearance vehicle or within a short, easy walk from such a road.

Trail: Reaching the falls requires a walk of somewhere between ten minutes and three hours along an established path or primitive road (in other words, a day hike).

Backpack: Access requires such a substantial hike that overnight or multiple-night camping is recommended.

Bushwhack: Access requires bushwhacking; that is, no developed trail leads to the falls. A strong pair of hiking boots is suggested. The trip is not recommended for young children, and it may be risky for skittish adults or those with physical limitations.

Watercraft: Access is by canoe, kayak, or other boat.

Fees and Passes

Be aware that an increasing number of places are charging a use fee. In particular, the US Forest Service now requires a pass for many of its day-use sites. Purchase several day passes (or better yet, buy the annual pass), and keep them in your glove box to have them handy when they are required. You can purchase passes online at www.fs.usda.gov/main/r6/passes-permits. For non-federal lands, keep some small bills or a credit card handy in case you visit a place that charges a use fee.

Difficulty

Trails and bushwhacks are rated as easy, fairly easy, moderate, fairly hard, or hard. Ratings for individual hikes were determined primarily by considering trail length and overall steepness, as well as the condition of the trail surface and whether streams can be crossed via footbridges or must be forded by hopping rocks and wading. Unsigned or minimally signed trails are rated more difficult than those with clear signage.

Keep in mind these ratings are relative and will vary according to the abilities of each individual. If you are unsure of your physical condition, start with easier walks, then progress to more strenuous hikes. If you are not in good health, it would be wise to consult your doctor before embarking on trails that are not "easy" or "fairly easy."

Waterfall Magnitude

The one- to five-star scenic ratings described earlier were assigned in part based on waterfall magnitude. This numeric measure is calculated using four waterfall elements: height, width, discharge, and verticality. Greater importance is placed upon height versus width, with the final value modified by the latter two variables.

The ten greatest falls in magnitude known to occur within the Pacific Northwest are as follows:

1. Shoshone Falls, Idaho (120)
2. Rainy Lake Falls, Washington (112)
3. Comet Falls, Washington (106)
4. Fairy Falls (Mount Rainier), Washington (101)
5. Snoqualmie Falls, Washington (100)
6. Clear Creek Falls, Washington (99)
7. Watson Falls, Oregon (99)
8. Falls Creek Falls (Gifford Pinchot), Washington (99)
9. Sahalie Falls, Oregon (99)
10. Tie between Salt Creek Falls, Oregon and Spray Falls, Washington (98)

Each increase by a value of ten corresponds to a waterfall that is twice as large in magnitude. For example, Shoshone Falls in its full fury has four times the magnitude of Snoqualmie Falls. (A magnitude of 120 is twice that of 110, which is two times the magnitude of 100; therefore, a 120 magnitude is quadruple that of 100.) By way of comparison, the magnitudes of two of the most awesome waterfalls in the world, Niagara Falls in New York and Ontario and Yosemite Falls in California, are 130 and 123, respectively. So the best of the Pacific Northwest waterfalls rank favorably.

The magnitude values were calculated based upon the discharge conditions when field-truthed. If stream flow was other than moderate, the following codes are included: (t) trickle; (l) low flow; (h) heavy flow. Use the multiplication factors shown below to adjust the magnitude value if the viewed discharge of a waterfall varies from what is given in the book. With a substantial decrease in discharge, expect the scenic value to also decrease.

DISCHARGE GIVEN IN BOOK	VIEWED DISCHARGE			
	TRICKLE	LOW	MODERATE	HEAVY
Trickle	1.0	1.7	3.3	3.6
Low	0.6	1.0	2.0	2.2
Moderate	0.3	0.5	1.0	1.1
Heavy	0.2	0.4	0.9	1.0

Watershed Size, Precipitation, Elevation, and Seasonality

Many of the streams and rivers of Washington, Oregon, and Idaho vary in their water flow from one time period to the next. This variety, of course, can significantly affect the way they look; obviously waterfall lovers would prefer to visit them when they are flowing freely.

The volume of water present (the stream discharge) at a falls location is primarily determined by two factors: the size of the watershed and its long-term and short-term precipitation history. A watershed is defined as the entire area from which runoff can flow to a given location. Other factors being equal, the larger the watershed, the longer the periods of adequate discharge. Included with each falls description is watershed information with the following recommendations:

WATERSHED SIZE	WATERSHED AREA	RECOMMENDED TIME(S) TO VISIT
Very small	Less than 1 square mile	During a wet period
Small	1–4 square miles	During or soon after a wet period
Medium	4–16 square miles	Anytime except during or soon after a drought
Large	Greater than 16 square miles	Anytime except during a long drought

The preceding guidelines apply to most watersheds within the Northwest that average at least 20 inches of precipitation per year. In drier areas, the drainage basins must be substantially larger in order to sustain even modest flows.

Kent Creek Falls, The Panhandle, Idaho

If "(d)" follows the watershed category, it means a dam exists upstream from the falls. Glacial meltwaters are signified by "(g)." The designation "(s)" means the waterfall is directly fed by a spring. In each case, the discharge is more consistent, which means you have longer time spans to enjoy the beauty of the falls.

A question mark (?) indicates that the size of the watershed is a rough estimate. This situation occurs where springs or other sources of uncertain discharge feed most or all of the falls' water volume.

As a general guideline, cataracts at lower elevations are best visited from autumn through spring. Visits to waterfalls at higher elevations are usually limited to summer, because the area may be snowed in during the rest of the year. For more specific information, you should check with local officials about discharge and accessibility conditions before planning a trip.

Topographic Maps

The US Geological Survey (USGS) has published a series of large-scale topographic maps of the entire contiguous United States. Each 1:24,000 scale map (1 map inch equals 2000 feet on the ground) encompasses an area bounded within 7.5 minutes of longitude and 7.5 minutes of latitude, which corresponds to a little more than 49 square miles at the northern extreme of the Pacific Northwest, increasing to nearly 55.5 square miles at the southern end.

Accompanying each waterfall listed in this book is the name of the USGS 7.5-minute map on which it can be found. Since these maps are periodically revised, the version (in other words, year published) is also reported. If a cataract is not labeled on the USGS map, the annotation "(nl)" also appears. If it is not shown at all on the USGS map, the annotation "(ns)" appears.

Most university libraries and libraries in major cities throughout the United States have a complete collection of these maps and can also provide instructions for purchasing them through the USGS. They also are now available in digital format.

Latitude and Longitude

Coordinate values are listed with each entry for readers with a GPS unit. While the numbers provided are not of survey-level precision, they are sufficient for aiding navigation in conjunction with the maps provided (described below).

THE COMPUTER COMPANION

An online electronic supplement to this guidebook, entitled *The Computer Companion,* offers waterfall enthusiasts a wealth of information, plus provides additions and updates impractical or impossible to otherwise publish. It describes more than 1500 waterfalls in the Pacific Northwest. More than 700 digital color photographs are included, along with user-controlled pop-ups to topographic maps and satellite images documenting the location of every cataract.

The Companion also provides descriptions and directions for all of the one-star falls shown in the More Online listings in this book. When the term "EXPLORE!" accompanies a waterfall in the guidebook, it means that I have not yet visited it but that a government agency has documented it as accessible. *The Companion* hyperlinks these entries to the pertinent Forest Service or other agency web pages. Also found here are miscellaneous waterfalls, such as those that no longer exist and newly documented ones that missed the publication deadline for inclusion as full entries.

Waterfall listings can also be generated in *The Companion* alphabetically by name, chapter, USGS map, or county, with web links to each individual descent. The website is located at www.mymaps.com/nwfalls/toc.htm.

THE MAPS

To locate waterfalls, use each chapter's regional map, along with the more detailed section maps that appear with the written description for each individual waterfall. A state highway map or a GPS navigation system will also

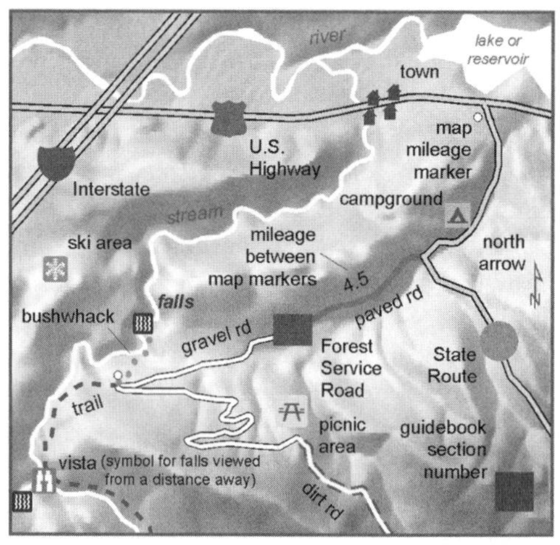

Map key

help you choose a route. A key to the map symbols is shown here and an overview map of the book's chapter regions is on page 11.

For the sake of consistency and to reduce map-reading problems, each map has north oriented upward, or toward the top of the page. Confirm the accuracy of your odometer, and remember that odometers may vary 0.1 mile or more. As a rough gauge of hiking times, it takes the average person 30 minutes to hike 1 mile over moderate terrain. To further assist readers, shaded relief has been included to help visualize the general terrain.

NEW ENTRIES

The quick reference chart reports the number of new entries in this fifth edition of the guidebook. Refer to the online *Computer Companion* version to find out in which edition of the hardcopy book each waterfall was first described.

A NOTE ABOUT SAFETY

Safety is an important concern in all outdoor activities. No guidebook can alert you to every hazard or anticipate the limitations of every reader. Therefore, the descriptions of roads, trails, routes, and natural features in this book are not representations that a particular place or excursion will be safe for your party. When you follow any of the routes described in this book, you assume responsibility for your own safety. Under normal conditions, such excursions require the usual attention to traffic, road and trail conditions, weather, terrain, the capabilities of your party, and other factors. Because many of the lands in this book are subject to development and/or change of ownership, conditions may have changed since this book was written that make your use of some of these routes unwise. Always check for current conditions, obey posted private property signs, and avoid confrontations with property owners or managers. Keeping informed on current conditions and exercising common sense are the keys to a safe, enjoyable outing.

Mountaineers Books

WASHINGTON

THE NORTH CASCADES

The Cascade Range extends from British Columbia through Washington and Oregon to Northern California. A progression of spectacular volcanic peaks marks the range from north to south, highlighted by Mount Baker, Mount Rainier, and Mount Adams in Washington; Mount Hood, the Three Sisters, and Mount McLoughlin in Oregon; and Mount Shasta in California. Since the Cascades encompass a large part of the Pacific Northwest and contain many waterfalls, the range has been divided into six chapters in this book.

The North Cascades extend from Interstate 90 to the Canadian border, dividing the Puget Sound area of Washington from the dry, eastern part of the state. This region features three large national forests, three wilderness areas, two national recreation areas, and North Cascades National Park. Of the 255 falls identified within the region, 111 are listed in this chapter.

Aside from its two major volcanoes, Mount Baker and Glacier Peak, most of the mountains of the North Cascades are older than those of the range's

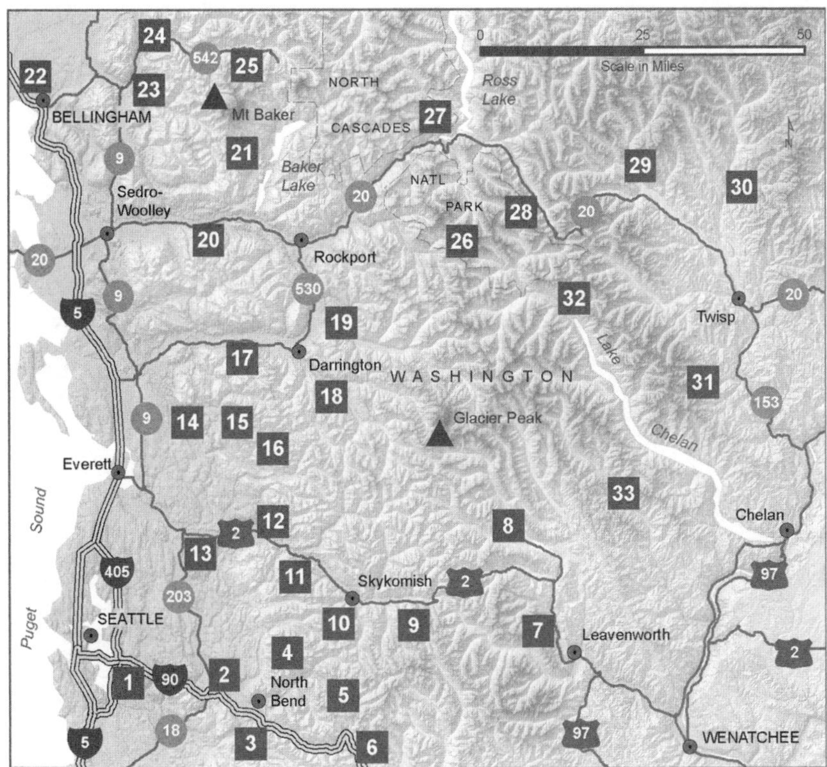

North Fork Falls

counterparts to the south. The North Cascades are a rugged and complex arrangement of various nonvolcanic materials, including large masses of granite. Other rock forms found in the area include gneiss and schist. These rock types vary from 50 million to 500 million years in age, but their arrangement in today's mountainous terrain is due to uplifting over the past 10 million years.

Intensive glaciation accounts for the region's pronounced relief. Four major periods of glacial activity occurred between 10,000 and 2 million years ago. The heads of glaciers eroded into the mountains, sharpening their peaks, and extended to lower elevations, deepening and widening valleys.

The abundance of waterfalls in the North Cascades is largely due to the glacial scouring of the range's bedrock surfaces. Many descents plummet from smaller glacial troughs, called hanging valleys, into deeper and wider troughs carved by much larger glaciers. Wallace Falls and Rainbow Falls (the one near Lake Chelan) are stunning examples. Others, such as Bridal Veil Falls, Gate Creek Falls, and Preston Falls, skip and bounce off rock walls into the troughs.

Sometimes cataracts are associated with a rounded depression previously eroded by the upper portion of a glacier. Water may pour into this cirque from ridge tops or tumble from its outlet into a trough. The falls of Horseshoe Basin and Twin Falls (at Twin Falls Lake) are examples.

Glaciers may erode unevenly when carving out their U-shaped troughs. The streams that presently occupy such valley floors are called misfit streams, and falls occur wherever there are sharp drops. Such descents are generally less dramatic than the types previously mentioned. Falls representative of this form include Sunset Falls and Teepee Falls. Snoqualmie Falls, the state's most famous waterfall, interestingly is not due to glaciation. It pours off of a ledge of andesite rock, an erosional remnant of an ancient volcano.

1 NEWCASTLE

Hiking the trails of Coal Creek Park and Cougar Mountain Regional Wildland Park makes you feel like you are a hundred miles away from Seattle. Developed and maintained by King County Parks, this is in reality an urban wilderness; physically fit runners often trek the backwoods trails. Due to the area's very small drainages, it is best to visit these falls during extended wet periods.

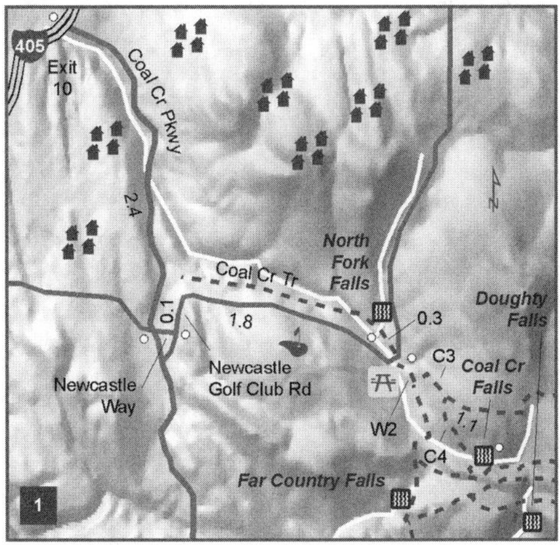

Access the area's Red Town trailheads by departing Interstate 405 at Coal Creek Parkway (Exit 10). Turn southeast toward Factoria. Follow the parkway from the first traffic light just east of the junction for 2.4 miles to a traffic light at Newcastle Way. Turn left here and drive 0.1 mile up the hill. At the four-way stop turn left on Newcastle Golf Club Road. Proceed 1.8 miles to the Cougar Mountain parking area on the right.

 NORTH FORK FALLS ★★

MAGNITUDE: 36
ELEVATION: 590 feet
WATERSHED: Very small
APPROACH: Trail (fairly easy)
LAT/LONG: 47.53716° N / 122.131903° W
USGS MAP: *Mercer Island* (2011 ns)

Water pours 20 to 25 feet into Coal Creek from its North Fork. Note the orange-brown staining of the bedrock behind the falls, most likely due to deposits left from historic mining activities upstream. From the parking area (described earlier), cross the road to access Coal Creek Trail. The route soon splits; you can take either fork as the paths merge back together in 0.3 mile near the falls.

 COAL CREEK FALLS ★★

MAGNITUDE: 38
ELEVATION: 940 feet
WATERSHED: Very small
APPROACH: Trail (moderate)
LAT/LONG: 47.525598° N / 122.116432° W
USGS MAP: *Issaquah* (2011 ns)

Coal Creek drops 20 to 30 feet in horsetail fashion before fanning another 8 to 12 feet over a bulge of bedrock. Its rating is lower if you are not visiting during a wet spell. From the parking area (described earlier), first pick up a detailed trail system map at the kiosk, as the trails can be a maze.

Embark upon Red Town Trail W2, go 0.1 mile, and turn left upon Cave Hole Trail C3. Hike another 0.1 mile, passing the junction to Red Town Creek Trail C2 on the left. Proceed an additional 0.4 mile, and bear right upon Coal Creek Falls Trail C4. After another 0.5 mile, you will encounter a log footbridge crossing the creek just below the base of the cataract.

MORE ONLINE:

Far Country Falls ★ USGS *Mercer Island* (2011 ns)
Doughty Falls ★ USGS *Issaquah* (2011 ns)
Weowna Falls (u) ★ USGS *Issaquah* (2011 ns)
Weowntoo Falls (u) ★ USGS *Issaquah* (2011 ns)

2 SNOQUALMIE

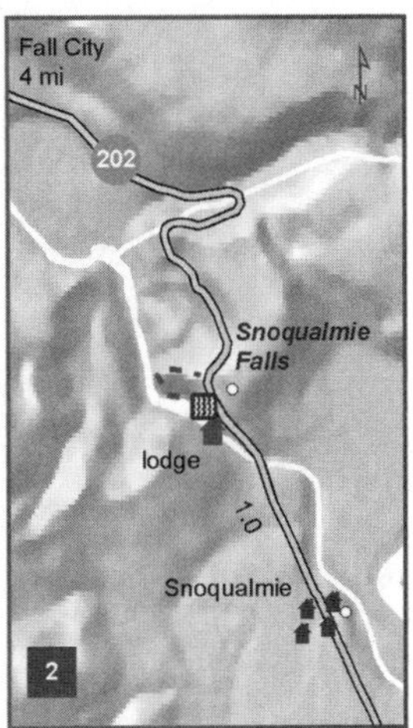

Hikers should not be surprised, particularly in developed areas, to see hydroelectric facilities in association with waterfalls. A great amount of force is required to turn turbines for generating kilowatts of electricity. Because water can serve as that force and its power is maximized where it is free-falling, falls sites can be desirable sources of energy. Water lines may be built into or beside the vertical escarpment and stream flow diverted to them. The scenic quality of the cataracts need not be lost, however, if enough water is allowed to continue its natural course. Such is the case, thankfully, for the following site.

SNOQUALMIE FALLS ★★★★★

MAGNITUDE: 100 (h)
ELEVATION: 390 feet
WATERSHED: Large (d)
APPROACH: Auto
LAT/LONG: 47.541752° N / 121.838169° W
USGS MAP: *Snoqualmie* (1993)

This 268-foot plunge is one of Washington's most visited attractions. Puget Sound Power and Light Company preserves the integrity of the falls while diverting enough of the Snoqualmie River to provide power for 16,000 homes.

This spectacle is located next to State Route 202, 1 mile northwest of Snoqualmie and 4 miles southeast of Fall City. Look for signs and parking areas. There are several vantage points of the cataract at the gorge rim adjacent to the lodge. Snoqualmie Falls River Trail, a steep 0.5-mile hike, which has been closed due to construction activities, is scheduled to reopen sometime in 2013. It offers views from the base of the gorge.

3 NORTH BEND

Although the Snoqualmie River is best known for its namesake falls, additional descents occur several miles upstream from the main attraction. The construction of Interstate 90 several decades ago made the cataracts practically inaccessible. In the 1990s, a new trail system reopened the area so that hikers could enjoy visiting the following waterfalls.

Twin Falls

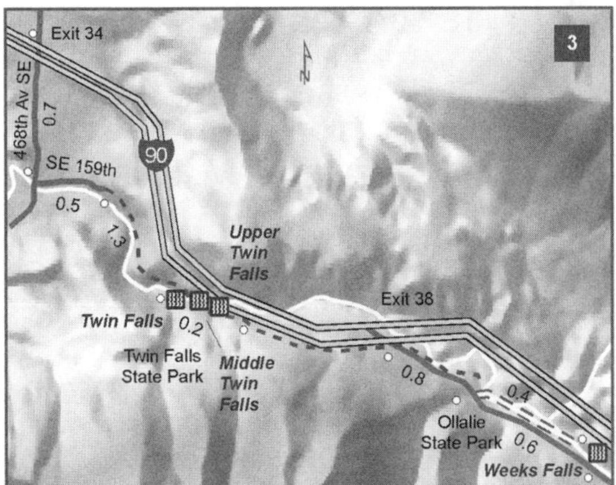

TWIN FALLS ★★★★

MAGNITUDE: 59
ELEVATION: 1020 feet
WATERSHED: Large (d)
APPROACH: Trail (moderate)
LAT/LONG: 47.444438° N / 121.694016° W
USGS MAP: *Chester Morse Lake* (1989)

The cliff-side viewing decks adjacent to this 135- to 150-foot plummet from the lip of a hanging valley offer an exhilarating experience. Also known as Upper Snoqualmie Falls, this waterfall, as well as the next two entries, is located within Twin Falls State Park, which is a day-use area.

Depart Interstate 90 at 468th Avenue Southeast (Exit 34). Proceed southward along this road for 0.7 mile. Turn left (east) at Southeast 159th Street, and drive another 0.5 mile to the parking area at the end of the street. From the signed trailhead, hike 0.8 mile to the first, moderately distant, view of the cataract. Continue another 0.5 mile up the hillside, bearing left at the signed "Old Growth Fir Tree." Eventually you will reach an unsigned spur, to the right, consisting of a set of wooden stairs. Proceed down the steps, ending at the observation decks and the falls.

MIDDLE TWIN FALLS (U) ★★

MAGNITUDE: 41
ELEVATION: 1080 feet
WATERSHED: Large (d)
APPROACH: Trail (moderate)
LAT/LONG: 47.444307° N / 121.69333° W
USGS MAP: *Chester Morse Lake* (1989 ns)

This pair of 10- to 15-foot punchbowls is located on the Snoqualmie River just upstream from Twin Falls (previously described). From the spur junction for Twin Falls, continue along the main trail for a moderately easy 0.1 mile to a wooden footbridge spanning the gorge. Looking upstream provides an excellent view of this falls.

UPPER TWIN FALLS (U) ★★

MAGNITUDE: 47
ELEVATION: 1090 feet
WATERSHED: Large (d)
APPROACH: Trail (fairly hard)
LAT/LONG: 47.444409° N / 121.692772° W
USGS MAP: *Chester Morse Lake* (1989 ns)

The Snoqualmie River plunges 20 to 30 feet before fanning out another 25 to 35 feet into a natural pool. From the footbridge below Middle Twin Falls (described earlier), hike another 0.1 mile up the steep trail to an open vista of this falls.

WEEKS FALLS ★★

MAGNITUDE: 37
ELEVATION: 1260 feet
WATERSHED: Large (d)
APPROACH: Auto
LAT/LONG: 47.432406° N / 121.646058° W
USGS MAP: *Chester Morse Lake* (1989 ns)

This series of cascades descends 30 to 40 feet along the South Fork Snoqualmie River. You can hike several additional miles beyond Twin Falls State Park (described earlier) to reach it, but the easiest access is by vehicle.

Depart Interstate 90 at the Forest Fire Training Center (Exit 38), and drive east for 0.8 mile to the entrance signed as Olallie State Park, South Fork Picnic Area. Continue 0.4 mile to an overlook of the falls. More cascades can be found by driving beyond the park entrance for 0.6 mile to a small hydroelectric facility. When leaving this area, eastbounders must first go west on I-90, then make a U-turn at Exit 34.

MORE ONLINE:
Crater Creek Falls (u) ★ USGS *Mount Si* (1989 ns)
Cedar Falls ★★★ USGS *North Bend* (1993 ns)

4 TAYLOR RIVER

For decades, access to this area of the North Bend Ranger District in Mount Baker-Snoqualmie National Forest was deplorable. Road improvements have at last been made, so even passenger cars can now readily make it up the Middle Fork Road without fear. This is definitely one place where funds from the Northwest Forest Pass fee system have been put to good use. You should drive a high-clearance vehicle, however, if you wish to make a side trip to Dingford Creek Falls.

MARTEN CREEK FALLS (U) ★★★

MAGNITUDE: 25
ELEVATION: 1800 feet
WATERSHED: Small
APPROACH: Trail (fairly hard)
LAT/LONG: 47.586383° N / 121.493451° W
USGS MAP: *Snoqualmie Lake* (1982 ns)

Depart Interstate 90 at 468th Avenue Southeast (Exit 34) and proceed northward. Go 0.4 mile, and then turn right (east) onto Middle Fork (Forest Service) Road 57. Regrettably, it's not signed until 2.5 miles farther. Continue an additional 9.1 miles, crossing the bridge over Taylor River. Stay upon Road 57 another 0.9 mile to the end of the road where you reach the trailhead for Taylor River Trail 1002. Embark upon the path. About 0.3 mile in, bear right along the river to stay on 1002 signed for Snoqualmie Lake. After another 2.2 miles of steady hiking, you meet the first major tributary.

The base of this 40- to 50-foot descent is barely visible from the trail, although the falls should certainly be audible. Walk 200 feet up the faint path next to the creek for a full view. The chemical action of hydrolysis has smoothed the granite streambed to such a degree that this place looks like it could be Bigfoot's waterslide! Its size makes it too risky for humans though.

OTTER FALLS ★★★★★

MAGNITUDE: 80 (l)
ELEVATION: 1900
WATERSHED: Small
APPROACH: Trail (hard)
LAT/LONG: 47.587628° N / 121.467273° W
USGS MAP: *Snoqualmie Lake* (1982)

If Marten Creek Falls (described earlier) is a slide for Bigfoot, then this 700- to 800-foot gargantuan must be Paul Bunyan's. Continue another mile along Taylor River Trail 1002, passing many side creeks. The one harboring the falls is actually a dry crossing because the stream has been diverted by a large

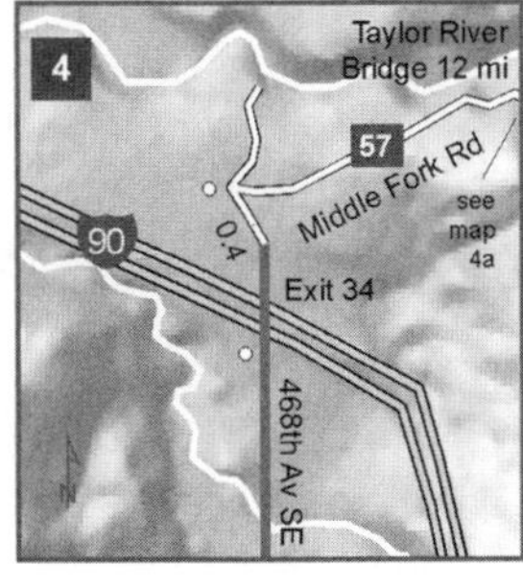

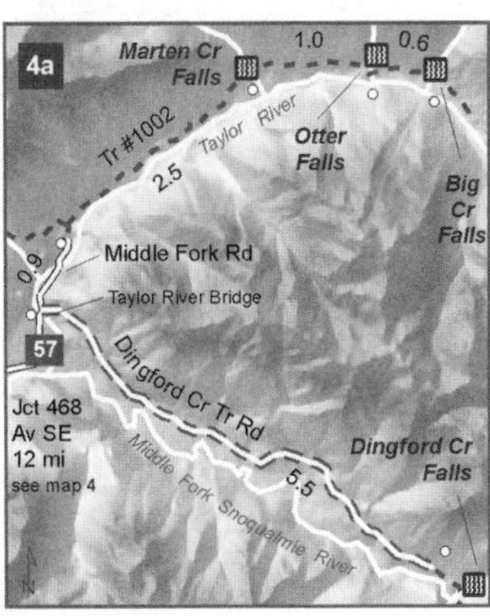

Otter Falls

5-foot-diameter drainage pipe, visible just below the trail. Proceed along the trail a few hundred feet farther to an unsigned side path to the left. Follow it into the woods where the path quickly splits. Take the one that goes straight up the small hill, veering slightly to the right, toward the sound of the falls. The top of the cataract will soon be visible.

In 0.1 mile you reach miniscule Lipsey Lake where you have full views of an awesome mountainside of water. It is best seen in late spring, as the creek usually dries up by the end of summer. Otter Falls is more than 1000 feet high, but "only" three-fourths of it can be seen from a safe vantage point.

BIG CREEK FALLS (U) ★★★

MAGNITUDE: 30
ELEVATION: 1800
WATERSHED: Small
APPROACH: Trail (hard)
LAT/LONG: 47.585587° N / 121.455536° W
USGS MAP: *Snoqualmie Lake* (1982 ns)

Although not as impressive as its two counterparts, this pretty cascade is worth the 0.6-mile hike beyond Otter Falls (described earlier). It is easy to find since the base of its 120- to 150-foot drop rushes down and under the only concrete footbridge along Taylor River Trail 1002. From here, it is 4.1 miles back to the trailhead.

DINGFORD CREEK FALLS ★★★

MAGNITUDE: 59
ELEVATION: 1520 feet
WATERSHED: Medium
APPROACH: High-clearance & trail (easy)
LAT/LONG: 47.51681° N / 121.450879° W
USGS MAP: *Snoqualmie Lake* (1982 ns)

Long ago, this is one of the first waterfalls I saw labeled on a small-scale national forest map that was absent from the corresponding large-scale topographic map. More than three decades later, I successfully made the rough trek to it. The upper visible tier veils 50 to 70 feet, while the lower counterpart descends an additional 25 to 35 feet before continuing downward beneath the bridge.

Just north of the bridge crossing Taylor River (described earlier), turn right off of Middle Fork Road 57 upon the forest road signed for Dingford Creek Trail. Crawl 5.5 bumpy miles to its end (by virtue of a gate) to a parking area. Walk a couple of hundred yards past the gate to a bridge at the base of the falls.

5 SNOQUALMIE PASS

This area's main campground and one of its waterfalls have the unfavorable distinction of lying between the lanes of Interstate 90! Actually it is not as bad as you may imagine, but the soft buzzing of the passing traffic does detract from the natural setting. Leave I-90 at Snoqualmie Pass Recreation Ski Area (Exit 52), and follow Denny Creek (Forest Service) Road 5800 for 2.7 miles to Forest Service Road 5830. Alternatively depart Exit 47, and drive 2 miles (0.2 mile past Denny Creek Camp) to FS Road 5830. All of the following falls are located within North Bend Ranger District, Mount Baker-Snoqualmie National Forest.

KEEKWULEE FALLS ★★

MAGNITUDE: 34 (l)
ELEVATION: 3330 feet
WATERSHED: Small
APPROACH: Trail (fairly hard)
LAT/LONG: 47.430846° N / 121.453004° W
USGS MAP: *Snoqualmie Pass* (1989)

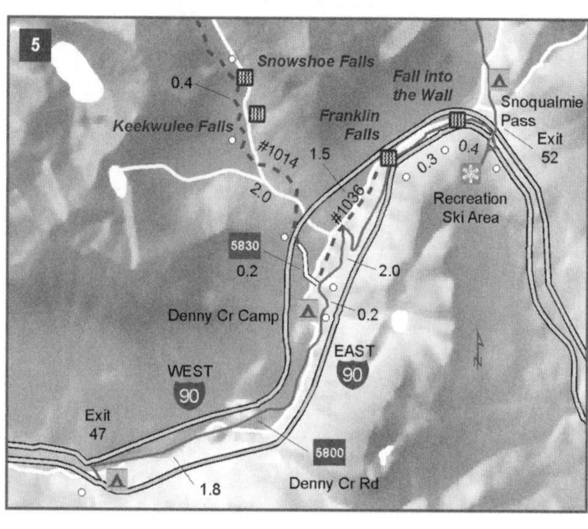

Water plunges 60 to 70 feet before tumbling another 15 feet along Denny Creek. *Keekwulee* is a Chinook word meaning "falling down." Take FS Road 5830 for 0.2 mile to its end at the trailhead to Denny Creek Trail 1014. The trail goes underneath the interstate and crosses Denny Creek twice, the second time at 1.5 miles. The trail ascends fairly steeply 0.5 mile farther to a full view of the cataract.

FRANKLIN FALLS ★★★

MAGNITUDE: 59
ELEVATION: 2600 feet
WATERSHED: Medium
APPROACH: Auto
LAT/LONG: 47.425039° N / 121.432469° W
USGS MAP: *Snoqualmie Pass* (1989)

South Fork Snoqualmie River plummets 70 feet into a small pool. Drive about 2 miles northeast of Denny Creek Camp along FS Road 5800 to the historic Snoqualmie Pass Wagon Road. This route, now a footpath, leads to the falls in less than 300 yards. Alternatively, you may take a moderately easy hike of about 1.5 miles along Franklin Falls Trail 1036 from Denny Creek Camp on FS Road 5830 (described earlier).

FALL INTO THE WALL (U) ★★

MAGNITUDE: 41
ELEVATION: 2780 feet
WATERSHED: Medium
APPROACH: Auto
LAT/LONG: 47.428407° N / 121.424637° W
USGS MAP: *Snoqualmie Pass* (1989 ns)

Keekwulee Falls

The South Fork Snoqualmie River pinches 20 to 25 feet into a cleft of bedrock. Drive 0.3 mile beyond the shorter path for Franklin Falls (described earlier) along FS Road 5800 to a small stone wall to your left overlooking the descent. When departing, the quickest access to I-90 is via Exit 52 in another 0.4 mile. The unofficial name of the falls was reportedly coined by kayakers.

MORE ONLINE:
Snowshoe Falls ★ USGS *Snoqualmie Pass* (1989)

6 STAMPEDE PASS

Although the next pair of falls is adjacent to private landholdings, both were accessible when last visited. Reach the area by departing Interstate 90 at Stampede Pass (Exit 62). Turn west and proceed on Lost Lake Road for 1.2 miles to a junction where the right fork is signed for Lost Lake.

6 ROARING CREEK FALLS (U) ★★★

MAGNITUDE: 64 (h)
ELEVATION: 2500 feet
WATERSHED: Medium
APPROACH: Trail (easy)
LAT/LONG: 47.328062° N / 121.371293° W
USGS MAP: *Stampede Pass* (1989 nl)

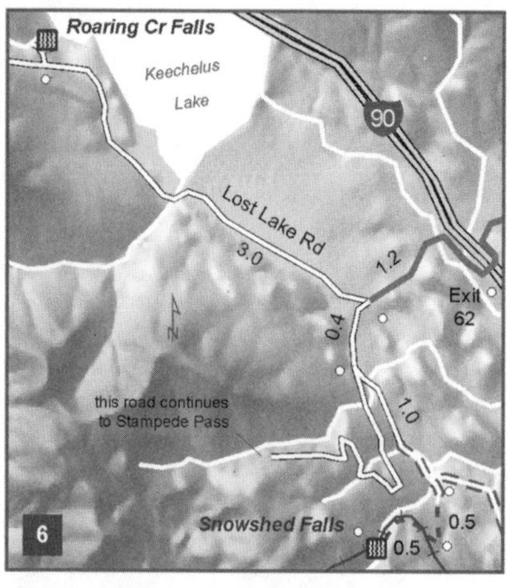

Roaring Creek lives up to its name as it plunges 55 to 70 feet into a small gorge before draining into Keechelus Lake. At the junction (described earlier), proceed toward Lost Lake, driving 3 miles, then turn right onto Roaring Creek Court. If the street is gated, find an unobstructed place to park and walk down the street a few hundred feet. Look to the right for a sign blocking a road, stating "No Motor Vehicles."

Turn here and walk 0.1 mile to its end. Turn left on a path into the woods, which almost immediately ends at the top of a 100-foot-tall rock outcrop. Here find an airy, unprotected vista of the falls. Be careful.

7 SNOWSHED FALLS ★★★★

MAGNITUDE: 53
ELEVATION: 2900 feet
WATERSHED: Small
APPROACH: Trail (fairly easy)
LAT/LONG: 47.278298° N / 121.323871° W
USGS MAP: *Stampede Pass* (1989)

Take a different kind of hike to a different kind of waterfall. Instead of taking the turn to Lost Lake at the junction (described earlier), continue straight for another 0.4 mile. Bear left on the "low road" at the next junction. As the road deteriorates, continue going straight, avoiding the many spurs. After another mile, park at a wide spot in the open area.

Start walking uphill along the road to the right. You will pass a gate preventing access to vehicles and then encounter a set of railroad tracks. The road parallels the tracks to its end in 1 mile at the base of the 90- to 100-foot falls. They are named for the snowshed that protects trains not only from snow during the winter but also from spray from the cataract. At this point, the rail tunnel heads beneath Stampede Pass, emerging 2 miles farther on the opposite side. For safety's sake, do not enter the tunnel.

7 LEAVENWORTH

Downtown Leavenworth is a place of Old World character, where seasonal activities such as the Mai Fest, Autumn Leaf Festival, and Christmas Lighting can be enjoyed. The traditional storefronts and the surrounding alpine setting are reminiscent of the German province of Bavaria.

1 DRURY FALLS ★★

MAGNITUDE: 51
APPROACH: Auto
ELEVATION: 4120 feet
LAT/LONG: 47.636753° N / 120.746596° W
WATERSHED: Small
USGS MAP: *Winton* (1989)

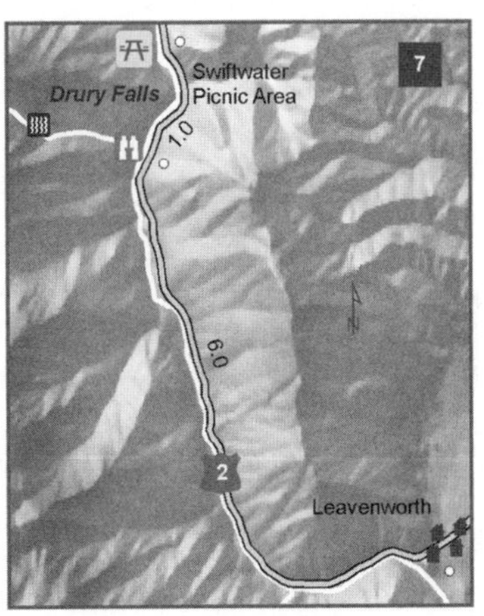

Fall Creek, located within Wenatchee River Ranger District, Okanogan-Wenatchee National Forest, drops more than 100 feet from the cliffs of Tumwater Canyon into the Wenatchee River. Only a moderately distant cross-river view of the cataract is possible, and the discharge decreases dramatically as summer wanes. Drive 6 miles north of Leavenworth, or 1 mile south of Swiftwater Picnic Area, along U.S. Highway 2 to an unsigned turnout.

MORE ONLINE:
Teanaway Falls ★ USGS *Mount Stuart* (1989 ns)

8 LAKE WENATCHEE

Lake Wenatchee is a popular vacation area for family camping, with several campsites on the eastern shore. Drive 14 miles northwest of Leavenworth along U.S. Highway 2 to State Route 207, then 10 miles north to the ranger station for Lake Wenatchee Ranger District, Okanogan-Wenatchee National Forest. All the area's falls are located upstream from Lake Wenatchee.

1 WHITE RIVER FALLS ★★★

MAGNITUDE: 53 (h)
ELEVATION: 2200 feet
WATERSHED: Large
APPROACH: Trail (fairly easy)
LAT/LONG: 47.952341° N / 120.940723° W
USGS MAP: *Mount David* (1989)

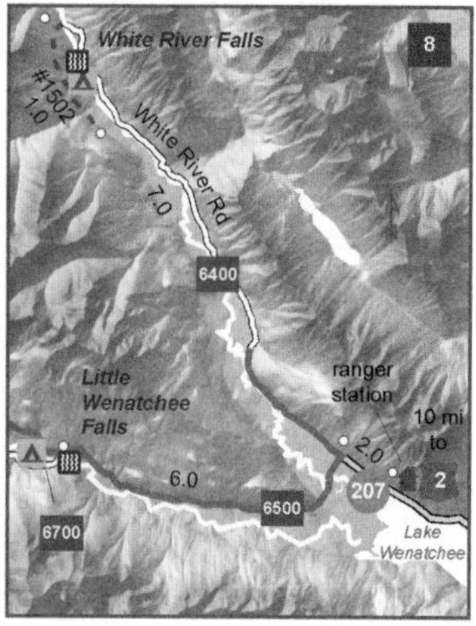

This forceful 60- to 100-foot cataract along the White River is situated next to a camp, but the best views require a modest hike. Drive to the end of White River (Forest Service) Road 6400 and park. Follow Indian Creek Trail 1502 across the White River, then go downstream. In 1 mile, a spur trail to the left leads to good views of the falls.

At White River Falls Campground, adults can also climb on chunks of bedrock for obstructed overviews of the descent. Be careful! This is definitely not a place for fooling around.

MORE ONLINE:

Little Wenatchee Falls (u) ★
USGS *Mount Howard* (1989 ns)

9 STEVENS PASS

Many waterfalls beckon from the roadside as you travel eastward along U.S. Highway 2 toward 4061-foot Stevens Pass.

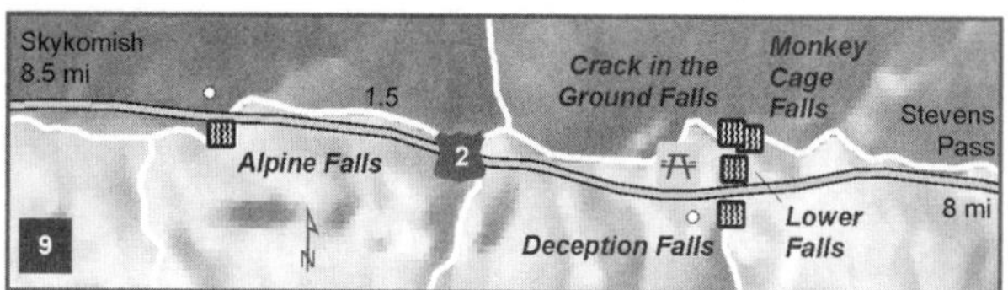

ALPINE FALLS ★★

MAGNITUDE: 17 (l)
ELEVATION: 1450 feet
WATERSHED: Large
APPROACH: Auto or bushwhack (fairly easy)
LAT/LONG: 47.716822° N / 121.226303° W
USGS MAP: *Scenic* (1982)

Situated on land owned by the state of Washington, the South Fork Skykomish River tumbles 30 to 50 feet downward. Drive along US 2 about 8.5 miles east of Skykomish or 1.5 miles west of Deception Falls (described later). Park at the unsigned turnout just past the bridge crossing the Tye River. A very short trail leads to the top of this entry. Determined bushwhackers can find better views by hiking down the slope to the river from the far end of the parking turnout.

Alpine Falls

 DECEPTION FALLS ★★

MAGNITUDE: 34 (h)
ELEVATION: 1850 feet
WATERSHED: Large
APPROACH: Trail (easy)
LAT/LONG: 47.714368° N / 121.194567° W
USGS MAP: *Scenic* (1982)

This entry has an upgraded rating because it now has a nice viewing deck. Take US 2 to Deception Falls Picnic Area, located 10 miles east of Skykomish and 8 miles west of Stevens Pass. Walk over to the east (right) side of the parking area. A paved walkway leads 0.1 mile over a footbridge, then under the highway to a vantage point of Deception Creek cascading 60 feet. This falls is also known as Upper Falls.

 LOWER FALLS ★★

MAGNITUDE: 26 (h)
ELEVATION: 1800 feet
WATERSHED: Large
APPROACH: Trail (easy)
LAT/LONG: 47.715292° N / 121.194589° W
USGS MAP: *Scenic* (1982 ns)

From the west side of the footbridge (described earlier), walk down the loop trail 100 or so feet, and look upstream to see Deception Creek tumbling 15 to 25 feet downward.

MONKEY CAGE FALLS (U) ★★

MAGNITUDE: 33 (h)
ELEVATION: 1740 feet
WATERSHED: Large
APPROACH: Trail (easy)
LAT/LONG: 47.716966° N / 121.194782° W
USGS MAP: *Scenic* (1982 ns)

There are several modest falls and rapids that challenge experienced kayakers along the upper reaches of Tye River. Among the pair easily accessible to terrestrials is this entry, which drops 10 to 15 feet within Deception Falls Picnic Area. From Lower Falls (previously described), follow the trail downstream. In 0.2 mile, you come to a short spur to your right, which quickly leads to a deck overlooking this cataract along the Tye.

CRACK IN THE GROUND FALLS (U) ★★

MAGNITUDE: 43 (h)
ELEVATION: 1720 feet
WATERSHED: Large
APPROACH: Trail (easy)
LAT/LONG: 47.717298° N / 121.19637° W
USGS MAP: *Scenic* (1982 ns)

The Tye River pours 15 to 20 feet into a fissure resulting in the stream taking a "hard right" along its course. Its rating is earned due to the unique character of the site. As explained on the interpretive sign at the falls, an abandoned channel indicates the river once flowed straight at this location. Among the explanations for its diversion include logjams, erosion through a softer rock layer, or weakness along a fault line.

Continue downstream from Monkey Cage Falls (described earlier) for a short distance along the looped nature trail. You will meet another short spur to the right, with a deckside view of The Crack. From here, the loop trail leads 0.3 mile back to the picnic area. The names of this and the previous descent were coined by kayakers.

10 ALPINE LAKES

"To cut or not to cut?" One criterion for designating an area as wilderness is that it is minimally impacted by humans. But what if an otherwise scenic viewpoint is obscured only by a couple of trees or some shrubs? Wearing my sightseer's hat, I would argue that if a trail is already impacting a location, let's enhance the wilderness experience by allowing the US Forest Service to perform some selective cutting. Putting on my safety hat, I would add that such minor alterations should reduce straying off the trail, reducing the risk of injury as well as lessening hikers' impact. Lastly, as I put on my geographer's hat, I seriously doubt minimal cutting would have any statistically valid impact on the environment.

Why this discourse? I've surveyed many waterfalls where the best vantage point is ever so slightly obscured. Several of them are not in wilderness areas

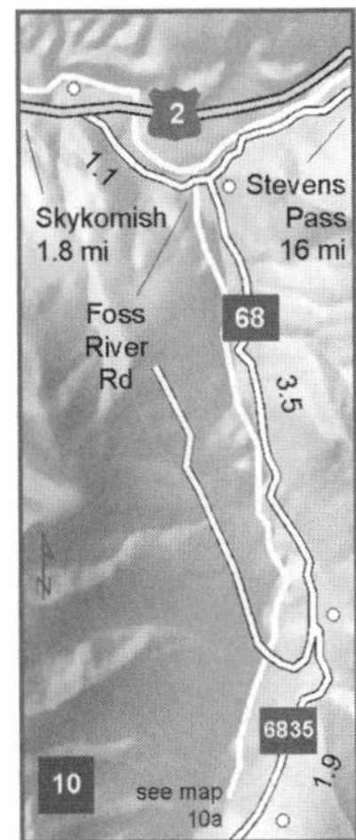

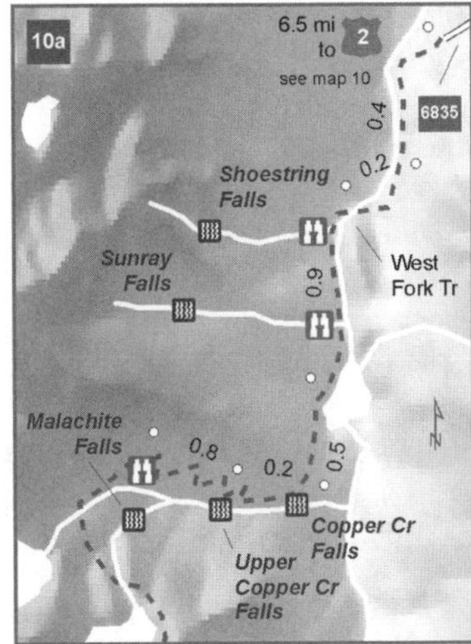

either. The following waterfall within the Alpine Lakes Wilderness serves as a classic example. It would otherwise possess a five-star rating and be one of the very best of the Northwest.

 MALACHITE FALLS ★★★★

MAGNITUDE: 80
ELEVATION: 3500 feet
WATERSHED: Small (g)
APPROACH: Trail (hard)
LAT/LONG: 47.611625° N / 121.329536° W
USGS MAP: *Big Snow Mtn.* (1965 ns)

Drive 1.8 miles east of Skykomish along U.S. Highway 2, or 16 miles west of Stevens Pass, and turn south upon Foss River Road (Forest Service Road 68). Bear right in 1.1 miles, and after another 3.5 miles turn left onto Forest Service Road 6835, signed for West Fork Camp. Proceed 1.9 miles to the trailhead at the road's end.

Embark upon West Fork Trail. After a moderately easy 0.4 mile, reach a clearing with a distant view of one of the higher tiers of Shoestring Falls (u) ★ USGS *Big Snow Mtn.* (1965 ns). Continue another 0.2 mile, and cross a series of log footbridges, the last one spanning the West Fork. About 0.1 mile farther, a distant view can be gained of Sunray Falls (u) ★ USGS *Big Snow Mtn.* (1965 ns), also descending from the cliffs to your right. Observant hikers can briefly see both of these falls in tandem just before the log crossings.

Proceed up the moderate slopes to the outlet of Trout Lake, another 0.8 mile. The route now ascends moderately steeply for 0.5 mile to Copper Creek. The top of Copper Creek Falls (u) ★ USGS *Big Snow Mtn.* (1965 ns) can be seen by taking a side path all the way to the water and looking downstream. Back on the trail, glimpses of Upper Copper Creek Falls (u) ★ USGS *Big Snow Mtn.* (1965 ns) will be gained 0.2 mile upstream.

The steep way now begins to switchback, time and again, progressively gaining better views of Malachite Falls, which roars 400 to 500 feet down a mountainside. Unfortunately, vegetation hinders a completely clear vantage point. The best trailside vista is around the sixth or seventh switchback in 1 mile from where Copper Creek is initially met. From the destination, it's 3 miles back to the trailhead.

MORE ONLINE:

See the four one-star waterfalls mentioned earlier.

11 INDEX

Although the following waterfalls are located near U.S. Highway 2 and have been labeled for decades as points of interest on many state highway maps, most people never see them because there are no signs.

BRIDAL VEIL FALLS ★★★

MAGNITUDE: 88
ELEVATION: 1800 feet
WATERSHED: Small
APPROACH: Trail (fairly hard) or auto
LAT/LONG: 47.791031° N / 121.567416° W
USGS MAP: *Index* (1989)

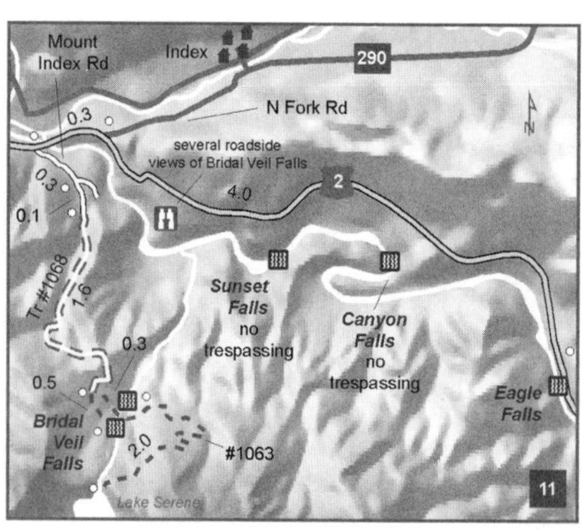

Water pours off Mount Index in four parts, each descending 100 to 200 feet along Bridal Veil Creek. The cataract is also visible from stretches of the main highway, appearing as silvery white threads. Located within Skykomish Ranger District, Mount Baker-Snoqualmie National Forest, it is usually reduced to a low flow by late summer.

For more intimate views of two of the tiers, depart US 2 on Mount Index Road, 0.3 mile past the turn for the hamlet of Index and immediately south of the bridge over the South Fork Skykomish River. After another 0.3 mile, bear right (south) where the road ends in 0.1 mile at a parking area.

Hike 1.6 miles along Lake Serene Trail 1068 to a reconstructed spur trail signed to the right for Bridal Veil Falls. Ascend 0.5 mile to admire one of the middle tiers from its base. Back at the trail junction, it's 0.3 mile to a footbridge crossing above the lower tier. If you wish to proceed to Lake Serene, you get to switchback 23 times over 2 miles before reaching the scenic destination.

MORE ONLINE:
Eagle Falls ★ USGS *Index* (1989)
Canyon Falls ★★★★ USGS *Index* (1989), currently "No Trespassing" signs posted
Sunset Falls ★★★ USGS *Index* (1989), currently "No Trespassing" signs posted

12 GOLD BAR

Wallace Falls State Park opened in 1977 to showcase and preserve one of the tallest single-drop cataracts in the Northwest. When first visited, the park promoted only its namesake. Now there are viewpoints to no less than six cataracts, with four of them officially named. Depart U.S. Highway 2 at Gold Bar and follow the signs for 2 miles to the state park.

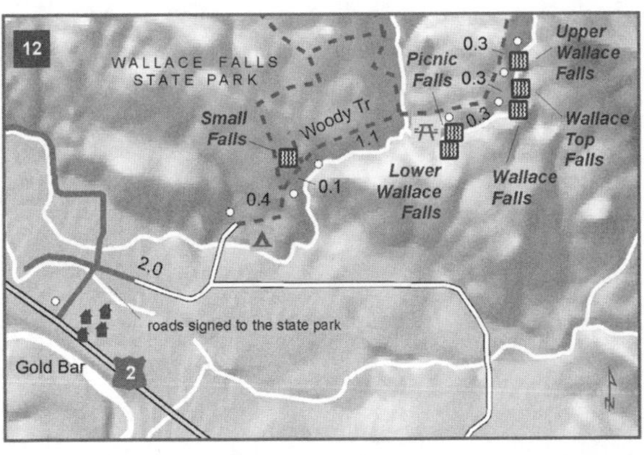

LOWER WALLACE FALLS ★★★

MAGNITUDE: 49
ELEVATION: 760 feet
WATERSHED: Medium
APPROACH: Trail (fairly hard)
LAT/LONG: 47.872188° N / 121.655822° W
USGS MAP: *Gold Bar* (1989 nl)

The Wallace River descends as a pair of 35- to 50-foot punchbowls. You can see them both from a single vantage point but can't photograph them together without a super-wide or fish-eye lens. Start hiking along Woody Trail, named after Frank Woody, a former state senator and lifelong outdoorsman.

After 0.4 mile, the trail diverges. Take the right fork. A short spur to Small Falls USGS *Gold Bar* (1989 ns) is encountered in 0.1 mile. The way then ascends moderately for 1.1 miles to a picnic area. Turn right and walk near the wooden guardrails to a viewpoint above a small gorge at the falls.

PICNIC FALLS (U) ★★

MAGNITUDE: 50
ELEVATION: 800 feet
WATERSHED: Medium
APPROACH: Trail (fairly hard)
LAT/LONG: 47.872389° N / 121.65492° W
USGS MAP: *Gold Bar* (1989 ns)

Wallace Falls

The Wallace River stairsteps a total of 50 to 60 feet. Although this one is probably considered to be a tier of Lower Wallace Falls (described earlier), I have described it separately because it is not visible with its counterpart directly downstream.

7 WALLACE FALLS ★★★★★

MAGNITUDE: 88
ELEVATION: 1300 feet
WATERSHED: Medium
APPROACH: Trail (fairly hard)
LAT/LONG: 47.87462° N / 121.646509° W
USGS MAP: *Gold Bar* (1989)

Whetting your appetite from the picnic site (mentioned earlier) is a distant view of Wallace River as it curtains 260 feet in great splendor into a small natural pool, surrounded by bedrock and coniferous forest. Hike 0.3 mile farther for an excellent, much closer vista. If you have made it this far, you may as well toughen up and experience more great scenery.

WALLACE TOP FALLS (U) ★★

MAGNITUDE: 43
ELEVATION: 1500 feet
WATERSHED: Medium
APPROACH: Trail (hard)
LAT/LONG: 47.875052° N / 121.646316° W
USGS MAP: *Wallace Lake* (1989 ns)

This tiered display, totaling 50 to 70 feet, is often mistaken for the Upper Falls, which occurs farther upstream. From the vista (described earlier), hike 0.3 mile up eight switchbacks to a pair of viewpoints. The first one is still of Wallace Falls, but it additionally offers a great view of the Skykomish Valley. The second vista not only reveals Wallace Top, but also showcases the Wallace River making a mad dash through a deep and narrow gorge all the way down beyond Lower Wallace Falls. Be very careful here!

UPPER WALLACE FALLS ★★★

MAGNITUDE: 69
ELEVATION: 1560 feet
WATERSHED: Medium
APPROACH: Trail (hard)
LAT/LONG: 47.875714° N / 121.645179° W
USGS MAP: *Wallace Lake* (1989 nl)

Signed as "Upper Falls," this double plunge first pours 25 to 35 feet down before plummeting another 80 to 100 feet. This last of the waterfalls along Wallace River is found by ascending another 0.3 mile beyond the previous entry. From this destination, it is 2.5 miles back to the parking area at the trailhead.

MORE ONLINE:

Small Falls (u) ★ mentioned earlier

13 MONROE

Several travel guides have in the past described a host of small waterfalls within the private timberlands southeast of Monroe. Invariably, public accessibility seems to wax and wane. Hopefully the following pair of entries can be reliably visited, as they occur along a road that leads to a deep woods residential area.

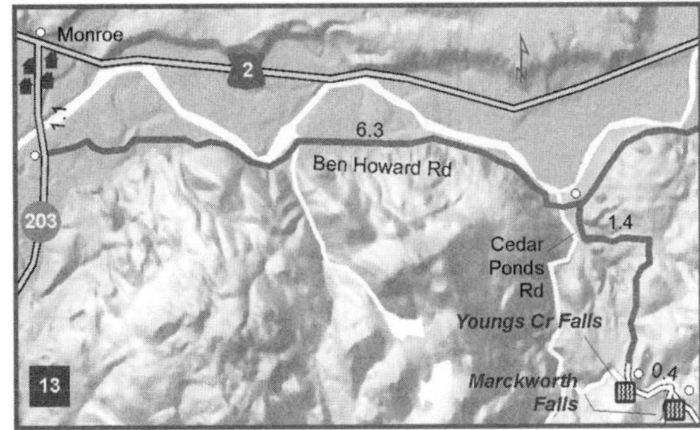

Youngs Creek Falls

YOUNGS CREEK FALLS (U) ★★

MAGNITUDE: 21
ELEVATION: 470 feet
WATERSHED: Medium
APPROACH: Bushwhack (easy)
LAT/LONG: 47.808371° N / 121.833212° W
USGS MAP: *Sultan* (2002 ns)

Natural potholes formed by running water frame this 30- to 40-foot drop into a narrow chasm of Youngs Creek. Depart State Route 203 at Ben Howard Road, located 1.1 miles south of the state route's junction with U.S. Highway 2 in Monroe. Proceed 6.3 miles eastward, then turn right upon Cedar Ponds Road. Drive 1.4 miles to a bridge crossing Youngs Creek. Park in the large unsigned parking area on the opposite side.

Walk back across the span, and find a faint path to your right. Ease down to the creekside, and walk under the bridge heading in the downstream direction. Reach the top of the falls in 100 feet.

MARCKWORTH FALLS (U) ★★

MAGNITUDE: 33
ELEVATION: 520 feet
WATERSHED: Medium
APPROACH: Auto
LAT/LONG: 47.808313° N / 121.824994° W
USGS MAP: *Sultan* (2002 ns)

This sibling of the previously described waterfall descends 20 to 30 feet, where Youngs Creek passes beneath the roadway. Drive 0.4 mile past the previous entry along Cedar Ponds Road to an unsigned turnout just before the next bridge spanning the stream.

MORE ONLINE:
McCauley Falls ★ USGS *Monroe* (1993)

14 GRANITE FALLS

The community of Granite Falls is named after these cascades, located north of town on the Mountain Loop Highway, which is an extension of State Route 92.

GRANITE FALLS ★★

MAGNITUDE: 27
ELEVATION: 300 feet
WATERSHED: Large
APPROACH: Auto
LAT/LONG: 48.102818° N / 121.953718° W
USGS MAP: *Granite Falls* (1989)

Water froths along the South Fork Stillaguamish River in a series of descents totaling 30 to 40 feet. A 580-foot fishway connects the upper and lower levels of the river via a 240-foot tunnel, allowing salmon to bypass the cascades and proceed upstream to spawn. Drive 1.4 miles north of town on the Mountain Loop Highway. Just before a bridge crossing the river, find a parking area and a short trail that leads to the falls.

MORE ONLINE:
Explorer Falls ★ USGS *Lake Chaplain* (1989 ns)

15 ROBE VALLEY

Small waterfalls abound in this area, where creeks flow from Mount Pilchuck into the South Fork Stillaguamish River. They all occur either on state land or within Darrington Ranger District, Mount Baker-Snoqualmie National Forest. Follow the Mountain Loop Highway 10 miles northeast from Granite Falls to the Verlot Ranger Station and townsite. After the main road crosses the South Fork Stillaguamish, 1.1 miles east of the ranger station, make two successive right turns, first on Pilchuck State Park Road 42, then onto Monte Cristo Grade Road (Forest Service Road 4201).

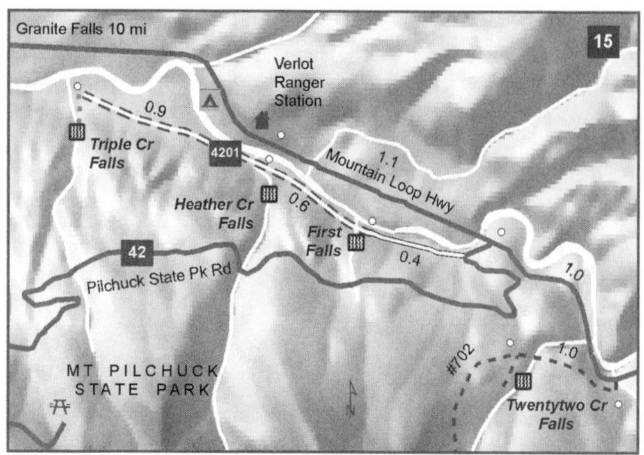

 TRIPLE CREEK FALLS (U) ★★

MAGNITUDE: 32
ELEVATION: 980 feet
WATERSHED: Very small
APPROACH: Trail (fairly easy)
LAT/LONG: 48.087469° N / 121.802742° W
USGS MAP: *Verlot* (1989 ns)

Upstream from this pretty 15- to 25-foot drop along Triple Creek is a 40-foot upper falls that can be reached by climbing (there is no trail) a few hundred feet. Drive along FS Road 4201, or begin hiking if the reportedly washed-out road is impassable. First Falls (u) ★ and Heather Creek Falls (u) ★, both in the area shown on USGS *Verlot* (1989 ns), will be encountered in 0.4 mile and 1 mile, respectively. Walk beyond the road's end after 1.9 miles along a well-worn path for a few hundred yards to the base of the lowest cataract along Triple Creek.

 TWENTYTWO CREEK FALLS (U) ★★

MAGNITUDE: 34
ELEVATION: 1400 feet
WATERSHED: Small
APPROACH: Trail (fairly hard)
LAT/LONG: 48.077563° N / 121.756737° W
USGS MAP: *Verlot* (1989 ns)

This series of three small falls is accessible from trails within Lake Twentytwo Research Natural Area. Drive along Mountain Loop Highway 2.1 miles past the Verlot Ranger Station to Twentytwo Creek Trailhead 702. The lowest falls is encountered after 0.5 mile of easy walking and another 0.5 mile of moderately strenuous hiking. A short distance farther, follow short spur trails to view the two other falls.

MORE ONLINE:

The one-star waterfalls mentioned earlier

Twentytwo Creek Falls

16 TWIN FALLS LAKE

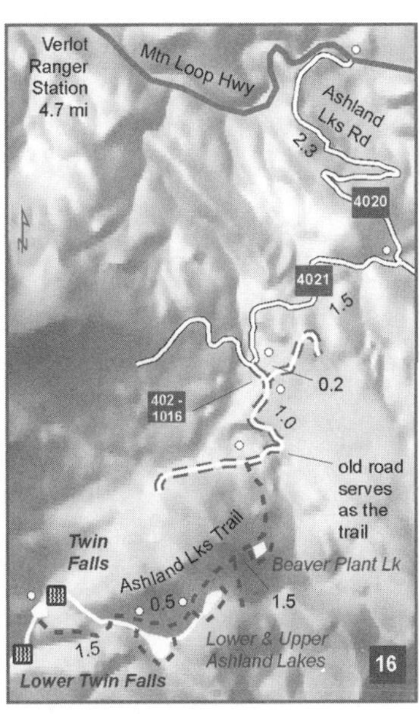

Spend the day hiking to an inspiring set of falls within which Wilson Creek pauses at minuscule Twin Falls Lake. Drive 4.7 miles east of the Verlot Ranger Station along the Mountain Loop Highway, and turn right onto Ashland Lakes Road (Forest Service Road 4020). In another 2.3 miles turn right (west) at the junction with Forest Service Road 4021. Drive to the next fork, in 1.5 miles, and turn left onto narrow Forest Service Road 402-1016. After another 0.2 mile reach the signed trailhead.

TWIN FALLS ★★★★

MAGNITUDE: 81 (h)
ELEVATION: 2300 feet
WATERSHED: Small
APPROACH: Trail (hard)
LAT/LONG: 48.029471° N / 121.740923° W
USGS MAP: *Mallardy Ridge* (1989)

Wilson Creek pounds 125 feet into Twin Falls Lake and then tumbles another 400 feet from the lake's outlet as Lower Twin Falls (u) ★ USGS *Mallardy Ridge* (1989 nl). Unfortunately, the only safe views of the lower falls are moderately distant and mostly obscured by the surrounding vegetation.

From the trailhead, begin a demanding, but rewarding journey along a path built by the state's Department of Natural Resources. The way begins in unassuming fashion, following an old dirt road for the first mile. When you reach a footpath signed for Ashland Lakes, turn left.

The way steepens a bit and after another mile, a spur goes left to Beaver Plant Lake. For the most direct way to the destination, stay to the right at this and all subsequent junctions. The trail becomes more difficult as wood planks, circular cedar cross-cuts, and granite blocks are provided to negotiate the marshy terrain over the next mile past Upper and Lower Ashland lakes. The route then steepens considerably along its last 1.5 miles to the falls. An interpretive sign at the lake provides a geologic history of the area.

17 BOULDER RIVER

The following entry occurs within Boulder River Wilderness, a part of Darrington Ranger District, Mount Baker-Snoqualmie National Forest. Access the area by taking State Route 530 to French Creek Road (Forest Service Road 2010), located 8 miles west of Darrington, or 8 miles east of Oso. Proceed south on FS Road 2010 for 4.5 miles, where the gravel road now reportedly ends for vehicular traffic. Look for the trailhead to your right.

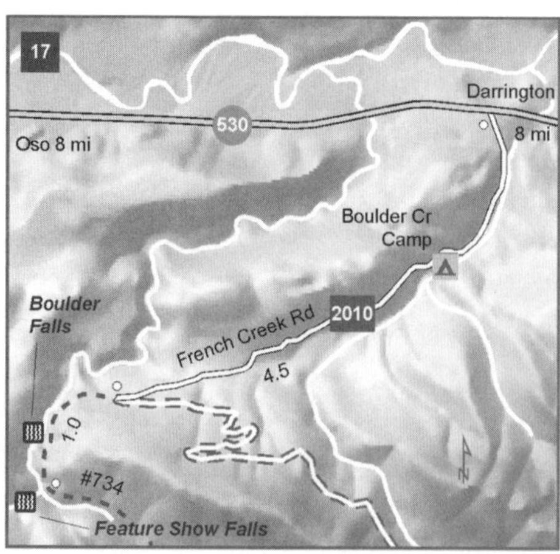

7 FEATURE SHOW FALLS ★★

MAGNITUDE: 23
ELEVATION: 1100 feet
WATERSHED: Very small
APPROACH: Trail (fairly easy)
LAT/LONG: 48.241775° N / 121.826925° W
USGS MAP: *Meadow Mtn.* (1989 nl)

Walk along Boulder River Trail 734 for 1 mile to a cross-river vista of Feature Show Falls, formed by an unnamed stream that curtains 80 feet over a cliff into Boulder Creek. With higher flows this entry appears as a fan; with lower flows it's segmented. Feature Show Falls was once erroneously thought to be Boulder Falls, which occurs on the main stream and was inaccessible when the area was last surveyed.

MORE ONLINE:

Ryan Falls ★ USGS *Stimson Hill* (2002 ns), currently on private property with "No Trespassing" signs

18 SAUK RIVER

1 NORTH FORK FALLS ★★★★

MAGNITUDE: 57 (h)
ELEVATION: 1480 feet
WATERSHED: Large
APPROACH: Trail (fairly easy)
LAT/LONG: 48.097408° N / 121.369555° W
USGS MAP: *Sloan Peak* (1982)

Water thunders 60 to 80 feet along the North Fork Sauk River. From Darrington, take Sauk River Road (Forest Service Road 20) south for 15.6 miles to

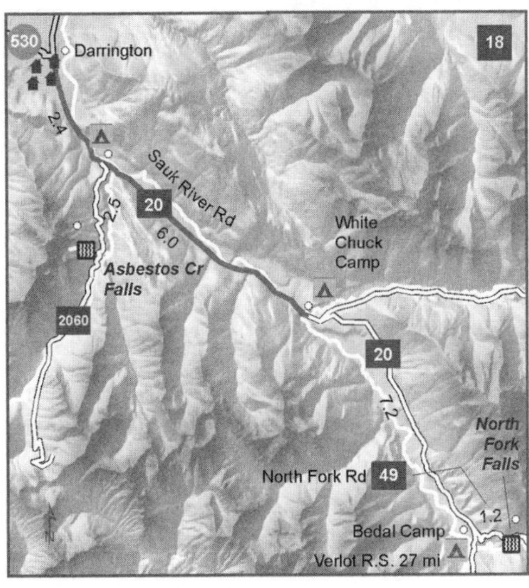

North Fork Road (Forest Service Road 49). Turn left and drive 1.2 miles to the sign for Trail 660. Hike 0.3 mile to an overlook above the falls, which is located within Darrington Ranger District, Mount Baker-Snoqualmie National Forest.

MORE ONLINE:

Asbestos Creek Falls (u) ★ USGS *Helena Ridge* (1989 ns)

19 SUIATTLE RIVER

The following four falls increase in stature as you progress up the drainage basin of the Suiattle River. Reach Suiattle River Road (Forest Service Road 26) via State Route 530 by driving 6.5 miles north of Darrington or 12 miles south of Rockport. Look for the turn 0.2 mile east of the highway's crossing of the Sauk River.

 TEEPEE FALLS ★★

MAGNITUDE: 34
ELEVATION: 1000 feet
WATERSHED: Medium
APPROACH: Auto
LAT/LONG: 48.343394° N / 121.439571° W
USGS MAP: *Prairie Mtn.* (1982)

Peer straight down from a bridge spanning the chasm of Big Creek into this series of 50- to 60-foot cascading waters. Proceed along FS Road 26 for 6.7 miles to reach this entry.

Teepee Falls

GIBSON FALLS ★★★

MAGNITUDE: 44
ELEVATION: 1600 feet
WATERSHED: Small
APPROACH: Trail & bushwhack (moderate)
LAT/LONG: 48.25502° N / 121.333377° W
USGS MAP: *Huckleberry Mtn.* (1982)

A narrow veil of water glistens 25 to 35 feet in a dimly lit recess of an unnamed stream, which is located within Darrington Ranger District, Mount Baker-Snoqualmie National Forest. Continue 3 miles past Teepee Falls (described earlier) along FS Road 26 and turn right onto Forest Service Road 25. Go 5 miles along this gravel route to a berm, which prevents any further driving.

Hike 1.4 miles to the stream crossing signed as Circle Creek, then continue another 0.1 mile to an unsigned turnout at another creek. Follow it upstream for 200 feet to the base of the falls.

MORE ONLINE:
Suiattle Falls (u) ★ USGS *Darrington* (1982 ns)
Huckleberry Falls (u) ★ USGS *Prairie Mtn.* (1982 ns)

20 SAUK VALLEY

Teenagers and nimble adults will enjoy Marietta Falls. Depart State Route 20 on Sauk Valley Road, located 1 mile west of Concrete. Proceed south, and then after crossing the Skagit River, bear right (west). Look for a creek crossing 8 miles from the state highway. Park at the unsigned area located immediately west of the bridge.

MARIETTA FALLS ★★★

MAGNITUDE: 53
ELEVATION: 400 feet
WATERSHED: Medium
APPROACH: Bushwhack (moderate)
LAT/LONG: 48.507401° N / 121.919279° W
USGS MAP: *Hamilton* (1989)

O'Toole Creek, also called Marietta Creek, tumbles a total of 100 to 125 feet with a plunge at the end of its final descent. This falls is probably on private property; don't trespass if signs label it as such. The 0.3-mile trail begins as a well-worn path. You ford the creek once or twice and climb over a small rock outcrop near the base of the falls.

21 MOUNT BAKER

Mount Baker is one of the dominant features of the North Cascades. This glacier-covered volcano rises thousands of feet above the surrounding mountains. Meltwaters from its northeast-facing glaciers feed numerous waterfalls, most of which plummet in rugged, inaccessible locations.

21 RAINBOW FALLS ★★★

MAGNITUDE: 70
ELEVATION: 1700 feet
WATERSHED: Medium (g)
APPROACH: Auto
LAT/LONG: 48.770765° N / 121.676958° W
USGS MAP: *Shuksan Arm* (1989)

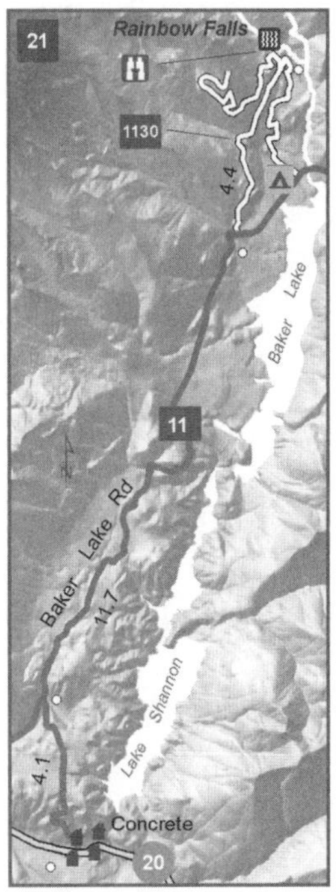

Rainbow Creek pours 150 feet into a gorge. Most of the cataract is visible from a moderately distant overlook across the canyon; the bottom portion is hidden by vegetation and the canyon escarpment. The waterfall occurs within Mount Baker Wilderness, in Mount Baker Ranger District, Mount Baker-Snoqualmie National Forest.

At Concrete, turn north off the North Cascades Highway (State Route 20), onto Baker Lake Road (Forest Service Road 11). (Eastbounders can take a shortcut to FS Road 11 by using the signed turnoff 6 miles west of Concrete.) After 15.8 or 18.5 miles, depending upon the route taken, turn left on Forest Service Road 1130. There are views of Mount Baker and Mount Shuksan before the turn. Follow FS Road 1130 for 4.4 miles to the signed parking lot for the falls. The viewpoint is only a few steps away.

22 BELLINGHAM

The following waterfalls provide a natural refuge from the urbanization of the Bellingham area. Depart Interstate 5 at Lakeway Drive (Exit 253). Proceed 1.5 miles eastward along Lakeway, then turn left onto Silver Beach Road at the sign marked for Whatcom Falls Park. Continue 0.6 mile to the parking area.

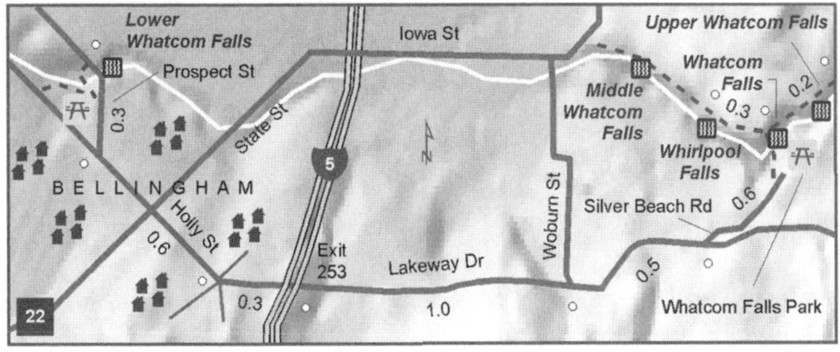

Lower Whatcom Falls

WHATCOM FALLS ★★★

MAGNITUDE: 58
ELEVATION: 260 feet
WATERSHED: Large
APPROACH: Auto
LAT/LONG: 48.751867° N / 122.429221° W
USGS MAP: *Bellingham North* (1994 nl)

One tier of the falls on Whatcom Creek pours 10 to 15 feet before the main display tumbles 25 to 30 feet over water-sculpted sandstone. Walk 50 feet from the parking area to the footbridge overlooking this descent.

UPPER WHATCOM FALLS ★★

MAGNITUDE: 45
ELEVATION: 290 feet
WATERSHED: Large
APPROACH: Trail (easy)
LAT/LONG: 48.753678° N / 122.427955° W
USGS MAP: *Bellingham North* (1994 ns)

This 35- to 45-foot display can be found 0.2 mile upstream from the footbridge (described earlier) along the trail nearly to the outlet for Lake Whatcom. You can also see a minor 3- to 5-foot block waterfall at the halfway point.

WHIRLPOOL FALLS ★★

MAGNITUDE: 29
ELEVATION: 200 feet
WATERSHED: Large
APPROACH: Trail (fairly easy)
LAT/LONG: 48.752617° N / 122.433598° W
USGS MAP: *Bellingham North* (1994 ns)

Whatcom Creek drops 8 to 12 feet in classic punchbowl fashion. From the footbridge (described earlier), turn left and follow the Lower Gorge Trail 0.3 mile to the descent and a short spur that offers a vista across the natural pool.

LOWER WHATCOM FALLS (U) ★★

MAGNITUDE: 37
ELEVATION: 20 feet
WATERSHED: Large
APPROACH: Auto
LAT/LONG: 48.755022° N / 122.481556° W
USGS MAP: *Bellingham North* (1994 ns)

Whatcom Creek makes one final drop of 10 to 15 feet before it enters Bellingham Bay. Views can be garnered either from the bridge over the falls or via trails leading to its base. This viewpoint is located downtown. From I-5 take Exit 253 for Lakeway Drive (mentioned earlier), proceed westward toward the city center for nearly 0.3 mile to a five-way intersection. Take the second turn to the right (you are still heading downtown) upon Holly Street. Proceed 0.6 mile and turn right on Prospect Street. Go 0.3 mile farther to where the street veers to the left. Cross the bridge and find a parking spot.

MORE ONLINE:
Middle Whatcom Falls, USGS *Bellingham North* (1994 ns) EXPLORE!

23 DEMING

The point of reference to drive to this next pair of cataracts is the eastern split of State Routes 9 and 542, located 1 mile southeast of the hamlet of Deming.

HARD SCRABBLE FALLS ★★★

MAGNITUDE: 60
ELEVATION: 500 feet
WATERSHED: Medium
APPROACH: Trail (moderate)
LAT/LONG: 48.759832° N / 122.229643° W
USGS MAP: *Deming* (1994)

Hard Scrabble Creek veils 40 to 60 feet over a bulge of rock before plunging a total of 55 to 70 feet in a double drop. It ranks higher during wet spells.

From the split (described earlier), drive southward on SR 9 for 2.1 miles, and turn right upon Potter Road. The paved surface ends in another 2.8 miles, with a wide spot in the road 0.3 mile farther on the right. Park here and find the unsigned trailhead by facing the sound of the creek, then

Racehorse Creek Falls

looking to your right. Although the path is only 0.3 mile, you need to be nimble for rock hopping, navigating through blowdown, and fording the small creek.

RACEHORSE CREEK FALLS (U) ★★★

MAGNITUDE: 62
ELEVATION: 400 feet
WATERSHED: Medium
APPROACH: Bushwhack (fairly easy)
LAT/LONG: 48.878935° N / 122.12523° W
USGS MAP: *Maple Falls* (1994 nl)

Racehorse Creek is aptly named as its waters accelerate 90 to 125 feet in a four-tiered display. From the split (described earlier), drive northeastward on SR 542 for 2.2 miles, and turn right upon Mosquito Lake Road. Proceed 1 mile, then turn left upon North Fork Road. Drive 4.1 miles farther, then turn right upon an unsigned gravel road. After 0.1 mile, park at the unsigned turnout on the right.

Find a faint trail across the road and follow its path, where it quickly peters out at a logjam. Proceed upstream amidst river boulders and more waterlogged timber. You have excellent views of the falls after 0.3 mile. Hardy souls may continue on to a large rock slab bisected by the stream at the base of the cataract.

24 MAPLE FALLS

MAPLE FALLS ★★

MAGNITUDE: 6
ELEVATION: 550 feet
WATERSHED: Medium
APPROACH: Trail (fairly easy)
LAT/LONG: 48.924749° N / 122.075169° W
USGS MAP: *Maple Falls* (1994 ns)

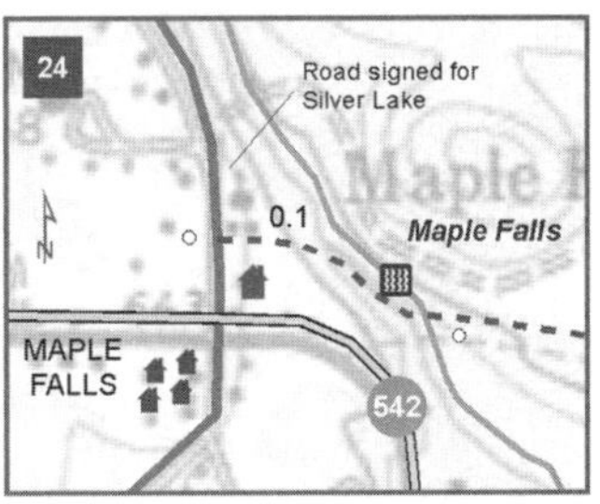

Yes, Virginia, there is a Maple Falls at Maple Falls—but only a modest one. Once in town, turn north onto a road signed for Silver Lake and find a place to park. Look for an unsigned trail behind the general store, and walk about 0.1 mile down to Maple Creek and its 10- to 15-foot set of cascades. A bit farther eastward the trail follows an old railroad grade.

25 NOOKSACK RIVER

As you near Washington's boundary with British Columbia, you can explore some wild and woolly cataracts.

NOOKSACK FALLS ★★★★

MAGNITUDE: 97 (h)
ELEVATION: 2600 feet
WATERSHED: Large (g)
APPROACH: Auto
LAT/LONG: 48.905274° N / 121.808901° W
USGS MAP: *Bearpaw Mtn.* (1989)

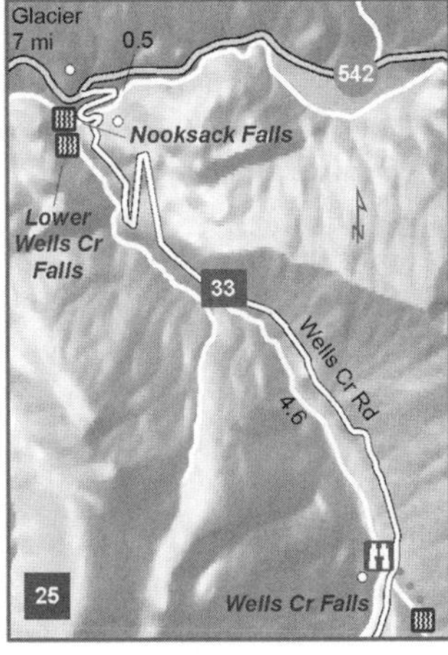

This 170-foot waterfall explodes over a sheer escarpment along the Nooksack River. The landowner, Puget Sound Power and Light, has reconstructed an observation platform, with a view of almost the entire cataract. Drive 34 miles east of Bellingham along State Route 542 to the hamlet of Glacier, and continue 7 miles east to Wells Creek Road (Forest Service Road 33). Turn right and drive 0.5 mile. If you cross the bridge over the river, turn around because you have passed the access to the parking area.

Nooksack Falls

WELLS CREEK FALLS (U) ★★

MAGNITUDE: 97 (h)
ELEVATION: 2600 feet
WATERSHED: Medium (g)
APPROACH: Bushwhack (moderate) or auto
LAT/LONG: 48.865019° N 121.763711° W
USGS MAP: *Mount Baker* (1989 nl)

The roadside view of this beautiful 80- to 100-foot plunge, located within Mount Baker Ranger District, Mount Baker-Snoqualmie National Forest, is somewhat distant and obscured. From Nooksack Falls (described earlier) continue 4.6 miles farther on Wells Creek Road (Forest Service Road 33) to an unsigned turnout, with a view of Mount Baker along the way. Better views of the falls require walking and scrambling along the creek, so plan on getting wet.

MORE ONLINE:

Lower Wells Creek Falls (u) H USGS *Bearpaw Mtn.* (1989 ns)

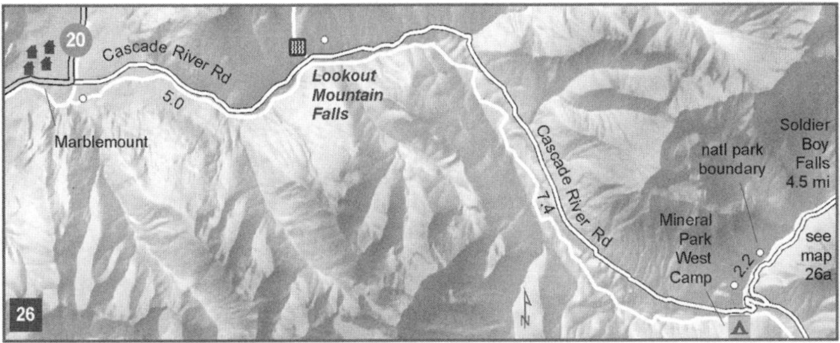

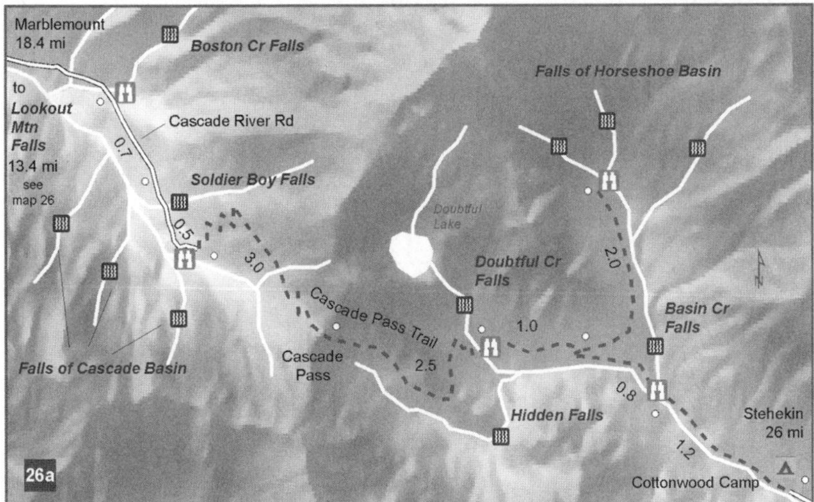

26 NORTH CASCADES NATIONAL PARK

While the majority of national parks within the continental United States have developed routes for motorized travel, North Cascades National Park remains overwhelmingly wilderness in character. The only mainland road that penetrates well into the park is the Cascade River Road. It begins in the town of Marblemount where State Route 20 bends northward and the highway junction is signed "Road to Trails for Cascade Pass and Stehekin." If you plan to backpack, obtain a permit from the Marblemount Wilderness Information Station before you turn here at the bridge crossing the Skagit River.

Speaking of Stehekin, hikers and backpackers often access the last four waterfalls in this section from that outpost. Take the Lake Chelan Boat Company's *Lady of the Lake* from Chelan (or splurge by flying one-way or round-trip on a seaplane) to Stehekin and the Stehekin River Road. A shuttle service transports hikers and backpackers to various campsites and trailheads along the road. Backpackers need to get a permit from the Golden West Visitors Center in Stehekin before getting on the bus. Go all the way to the end of the road at Cottonwood Camp. Refer to the Lake Chelan section (described later) for information about additional waterfalls in the Stehekin area.

LOOKOUT MOUNTAIN FALLS (U) ★★

MAGNITUDE: 36
ELEVATION: 800 feet
WATERSHED: Small
APPROACH: Auto
LAT/LONG: 48.531477° N / 121.336618° W
USGS MAP: *Big Devil Peak* (1989 ns)

On the way into North Cascades National Park, it's hard to miss this roadside cataract. Drive 5 miles down the Cascade River Road to a wide spot adjacent to this 25- to 35-foot drop along an unnamed stream. Also unofficially known as Mystery Falls, its rating decreases as summer progresses and its discharge shrinks.

SOLDIER BOY FALLS (U) ★★

MAGNITUDE: 41
ELEVATION: 2400 feet
WATERSHED: Small
APPROACH: Auto
LAT/LONG: 48.478434° N / 121.077173° W
USGS MAP: *Cascade Pass* (1974 ns)

For close-up views of Soldier Boy Creek veiling 20 to 30 feet down near the road, resume driving past Lookout Mountain Falls (described earlier), passing Mineral Park West Campground in 7.4 miles and reaching the signed entrance to North Cascades National Park in another 2.2 miles. Beyond this point the Cascade River Road usually opens in mid-June. Proceed 4.5 miles to an unsigned turnout to view this falls.

FALLS OF CASCADE BASIN (U) ★★★

MAGNITUDE: 61
ELEVATION: 4800 feet
WATERSHED: Small (g)
APPROACH: Auto
LAT/LONG: 48.47088° N / 121.076207° W
USGS MAP: *Cascade Pass* (1974 ns)

Unless there's a low overcast, a multitude of cascades and small falls can be seen descending down the sides of the glacial valley along the last several miles of the Cascade River Road. Only the most significant ones are described here. Drive to the end of the road, 0.5 mile beyond Soldier Boy Falls (described earlier). Look across the valley to your right for a moderately distant view of several cataracts streaming and plunging 200 to 400 feet upon the ruggedly sculpted terrain of Johannesburg Mountain, Cascade Peak, and The Triplets.

BOSTON CREEK FALLS (U) ★★★

MAGNITUDE: 68
ELEVATION: 4300 feet
WATERSHED: Small (g)
APPROACH: Auto
LAT/LONG: 48.492685° N / 121.075671° W
USGS MAP: *Cascade Pass* (1974 ns)

This moderately distant descent of 200 to 300 feet is most readily seen departing the area, hence its placement after the Falls of Cascade Basin (described earlier). From the road's end, drive 1.2 miles (heading back to Marblemount), and look way up the peaks on your side of the glacial valley. If you wish to linger, park at an unsigned turnout located a short distance farther at the crossing of Boston Creek.

HIDDEN FALLS (U) ★★★

MAGNITUDE: 61
ELEVATION: 4630 feet
WATERSHED: Small (g)
APPROACH: Backpack (fairly hard)
LAT/LONG: 48.460835° N / 121.03636° W
USGS MAP: *Cascade Pass* (1974 ns)

Ribbons of water descend steeply 260 to 300 feet from the meltwaters of Yawning Glacier. From the end of Cascade River Road (described earlier), embark upon Cascade Pass Trail. The route begins steeply as it ascends 3 miles to the pass. Proceed down the other side to the crossing of Doubtful Creek, 2.5 miles away. Enjoy cross-valley views of the cataract tumbling down an unnamed stream, with Pelton Peak providing a backdrop. Hikers from the opposite direction, marching westward from Cottonwood Camp (described earlier), will have a 3-mile journey to vantage points at the creek crossing.

DOUBTFUL CREEK FALLS (U) ★★

MAGNITUDE: 40
ELEVATION: 4470 feet
WATERSHED: Very small
APPROACH: Backpack (fairly hard)
LAT/LONG: 48.466328° N / 121.039622° W
USGS MAP: *Cascade Pass* (1974 ns)

The outlet of Doubtful Lake pours down a mountainside in a series of 20- to 50-foot cataracts. After admiring Hidden Falls from near the crossing of Doubtful Creek (described earlier), look upstream to see the upper tier of the waterfall directly above the ford, downstream to see the lower tier. Be careful when negotiating the ford.

FALLS OF HORSESHOE BASIN (U) ★★★★

MAGNITUDE: 63
ELEVATION: 6070 feet
WATERSHED: Very small (g)
APPROACH: Backpack (hard)
LAT/LONG: 48.485489° N / 121.020932° W
USGS MAP: *Cascade Pass* (1974 ns)

An entire series of waterfalls pours off the surrounding mountain ridges into Horseshoe Basin. Nineteen falls can be seen in a single view! The basin is a good example of a cirque, a bowl-shaped depression eroded by the upper portion of a former alpine glacier.

From Doubtful Creek (described earlier), hike 1 mile east to a fork in the trail. Westbounders will continue 0.8 mile past Basin Creek Falls (described later). Turn north and follow switchbacks steeply upward, meeting Basin Creek in 0.5 mile. The basin and falls are 1.5 miles farther. If there is a breeze, it may keep the black flies from biting you!

BASIN CREEK FALLS (U) ★★

Basin Creek Falls

MAGNITUDE: 82
ELEVATION: 3430 feet
WATERSHED: Small (g)
APPROACH: Backpack (fairly hard)
LAT/LONG: 48.466057° N / 121.017435° W
USGS MAP: *Cascade Pass* (1974 ns)

This 125- to 175-foot drop from Basin Creek would deserve a higher scenic rating, except only a distant view is possible. From the junction with the spur for Horseshoe Basin (described earlier), proceed eastward along Cascade Pass Trail. Hike 0.8 mile to the Basin Creek swinging bridge. The best vantage point of the cataract is 50 yards downstream from the footbridge. From here, it is 1.2 miles eastward to Cottonwood Camp, then another 26 miles to Stehekin via a shuttle bus.

27 ROSS LAKE

North Cascades National Park is bisected by Ross Lake National Recreation Area and its three reservoirs: Gorge Lake, Diablo Lake, and Ross Lake. Reach this rugged portion of Washington via the North Cascades Highway (State Route 20), which is normally open from June through October.

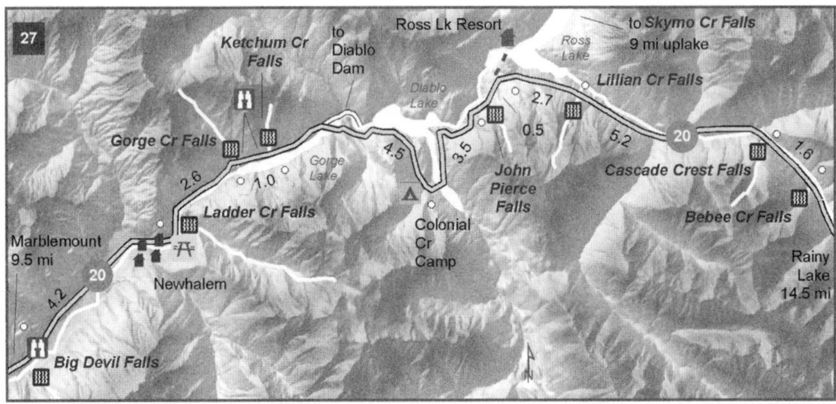

BIG DEVIL FALLS (U) ★★

MAGNITUDE: 78
ELEVATION: 900 feet
WATERSHED: Small
APPROACH: Auto
LAT/LONG: 48.626187° N / 121.320986° W
USGS MAP: *Big Devil Peak* (1989 ns)

This waterfall is tempting in that, despite the distant roadside view, you can tell it is of great stature. Drive along SR 20 to an unsigned turnout equivalent to mile marker 115.7, located 9.5 miles east of Marblemount and 4.2 miles west of the junction for the national park's visitors center in Newhalem. This 120- to 150-foot display deserves a higher rating, if only closer views were available.

LADDER CREEK FALLS ★★★

MAGNITUDE: 58
ELEVATION: 1410 feet
WATERSHED: Medium (g)
APPROACH: Trail (fairly easy)
LAT/LONG: 48.676326° N / 121.237087° W
USGS MAP: *Diablo Dam* (1963)

Ladder Creek drops four times, totaling 80 to 120 feet. Take SR 20 to the eastern side of Newhalem, and park near the Gorge Powerhouse. Walk across the footbridge spanning the Skagit River, and follow the trail through a landscaped rock garden, which contains many miniature cataracts. Viewing decks of the main display are 0.1 mile away. Years ago, Seattle City Light illuminated them at night.

GORGE CREEK FALLS ★★★

MAGNITUDE: 66
ELEVATION: 1660 feet
WATERSHED: Small
APPROACH: Auto
LAT/LONG: 48.702588° N / 121.21093° W
USGS MAP: *Diablo Dam* (1963 ns)

Early summer is the best time for waterfall hunting along the North Cascades Highway. The smaller streams have yet to dry up, and most of them harbor falls. This and the next half dozen entries all flow off escarpments adjacent to the highway. At Gorge Creek, water streams down 120 to 150 feet in three sections. Two smaller falls can also be seen adjacent to the featured attraction. From the Gorge Powerhouse (described earlier), take SR 20 east 2.6 miles to a parking area on the near (west) side of Gorge Creek Bridge. There are moderately distant views from the bridge walkway.

KETCHUM CREEK FALLS ★★

MAGNITUDE: 24 (l)
ELEVATION: 2280 feet
WATERSHED: Very small
APPROACH: Auto
LAT/LONG: 48.704755° N / 121.191489° W
USGS MAP: *Diablo Dam* (1963 ns)

This cataract descends 80 to 100 feet along Ketchum Creek. Drive 1 mile east from Gorge Creek Falls (described earlier). Park at the unsigned turnout on the far (east) side of the creek.

JOHN PIERCE FALLS ★★★

MAGNITUDE: 49
ELEVATION: 2200 feet
WATERSHED: Small
APPROACH: Auto
LAT/LONG: 48.718772° N / 121.069159° W
USGS MAP: *Ross Dam* (1971)

Water slides 40 to 50 feet toward Diablo Lake. Although the drainage extends 400 to 450 feet farther down, it is usually dry, its runoff absorbed by the rocky substrate. This falls is also known as Pierce Falls and Horsetail Falls. Drive east on SR 20 for 3.5 miles from Colonial Creek Camp, or west for 0.5 mile past the junction for Ross Dam, to an unsigned turnout on the northeast side of the highway.

SKYMO CREEK FALLS ★★

MAGNITUDE: 41
ELEVATION: 1700 feet
WATERSHED: Medium
APPROACH: Watercraft
LAT/LONG: 48.851543° N / 121.035835° W
USGS MAP: *Pumpkin Mtn.* (1969 ns)

Skymo Creek rushes 40 to 60 feet into Ross Lake about halfway up the reservoir. To reach Ross Dam and Ross Lake Resort, take a tugboat from Diablo Lake, or hike 1 mile along Ross Lake Trail signed at the North Cascades Highway (SR 20) about 0.5 mile east of John Pierce Falls (described earlier). Rent a boat at the resort. Unfortunately, there are reportedly no launching facilities for private craft. The cataract is located on the west shore of the lake across from aptly named Tenmile Island.

LILLIAN CREEK FALLS (U) ★★

MAGNITUDE: 50
ELEVATION: 2100 feet
WATERSHED: Small
APPROACH: Auto
LAT/LONG: 48.721533° N / 121.017918° W
USGS MAP: *Ross Dam* (1971 ns)

Each tier of this cataract is 20 to 25 feet high. It is located just off of the highway 2.7 miles east of SR 20's junction to Ross Lake Trail and Resort. Park at the wide unsigned turnout next to the stream on the mountain side of the highway.

Cascade Crest Falls

CASCADE CREST FALLS (U) ★★

MAGNITUDE: 38
ELEVATION: 2100 feet
WATERSHED: Small
APPROACH: Auto
LAT/LONG: 48.703651° N / 120.915736° W
USGS MAP: *Carter Mountain* (1973 ns)

This is another tiered falls, where an unnamed stream plunges 10 to 15 feet before cascading another 20 to 25 feet downward. Drive 5.2 miles southeast of Lillian Creek Falls (described earlier), 0.3 mile east of Canyon Creek Trailhead. Park at the unsigned turnout on the Granite Creek side of SR 20. Walk across the road to the tributary and a close-up view of its descent. (I named this falls after a nearby trail.) This and the next entry are located within Methow Valley Ranger District, Okanogan-Wenatchee National Forest.

BEBEE CREEK FALLS (U) ★★★

MAGNITUDE: 48 (h)
ELEVATION: 2200 feet
WATERSHED: Small
APPROACH: Auto
LAT/LONG: 48.687108° N / 120.890459° W
USGS MAP: *Carter Mountain* (1973 ns)

Water pours 45 to 60 feet into a tiny gorge at an unusual 110-degree angle. Find the "driveway" sort of turnout next to Bebee Creek, located 1.6 miles southeast of Cascade Crest Falls (described earlier), 0.2 mile northwest of where East Creek Trailhead is signed at SR 20. Also unofficially known as Emerald Pool Falls, it's located just south of mile marker 143.

28 RAINY PASS

Sure, I am biased toward waterfalls, but the exclusion of some scenic falls from maps and literature describing particular areas still confounds me. Such has been the case at Rainy Pass, home to one of the highest magnitude cataracts in the Pacific Northwest. Not until its understated mention in a recent edition of a national forest map did I know the falls even existed. It's always great to find out about more waterfalls!

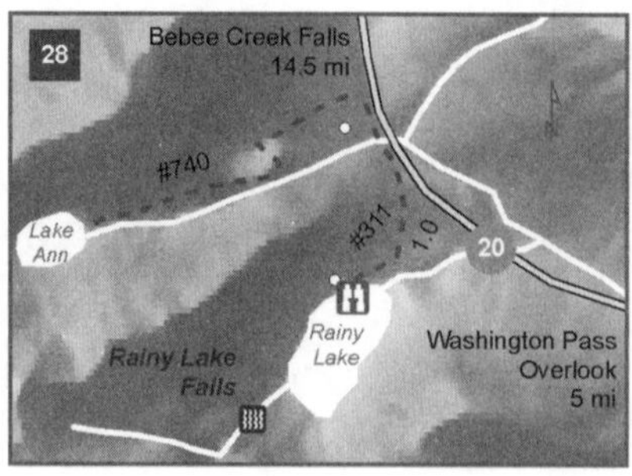

RAINY LAKE FALLS (U) ★★★★

MAGNITUDE: 112
ELEVATION: 5500 feet
WATERSHED: Very small (g)
APPROACH: Trail (fairly easy)
LAT/LONG: 48.497384° N / 120.744891° W
USGS MAP: *McAlester Mtn.* (1977 ns)

A pair of horsetails each drop 200 to 300 feet, where they can be seen being fed by the meltwaters of Lyall Glacier. Drive to the signed parking area for Rainy Lake, located 14.5 miles southeast of Bebee Creek Falls (described earlier) and 5 miles west of Washington Pass Overlook along State Route 20. There are actually two trails; take Trail 311, the one to the left, which proceeds southward (not Trail 740 to Lake Ann). The way is flat and paved to its end at Rainy Lake in 1 mile. This locale is a grandiose example of a cirque, a bowl-like depression carved into the mountains toward the upper end of a glacier.

Lyall Glacier is the remnant of what several thousands of years ago was a much more extensive glacier. Rainy Lake is geomorphically known as a tarn, a lake occupying a cirque. The vista at this place is truly awe-inspiring, though the cataract itself is a fair distance away. Those with an inflatable raft, or similar such watercraft, can paddle across the lake for a five-star vantage point. This site is located within Methow Valley Ranger District of Okanogan-Wenatchee National Forest.

29 METHOW VALLEY

The town of Mazama represents the eastern outpost for travel along the North Cascades Highway (State Route 20). For westbound travelers, it has the last facilities for 75 miles. The waterfalls listed below are situated in Methow Valley Ranger District of Okanogan-Wenatchee National Forest, as are the entries within the succeeding Winthrop and Foggy Dew Creek sections.

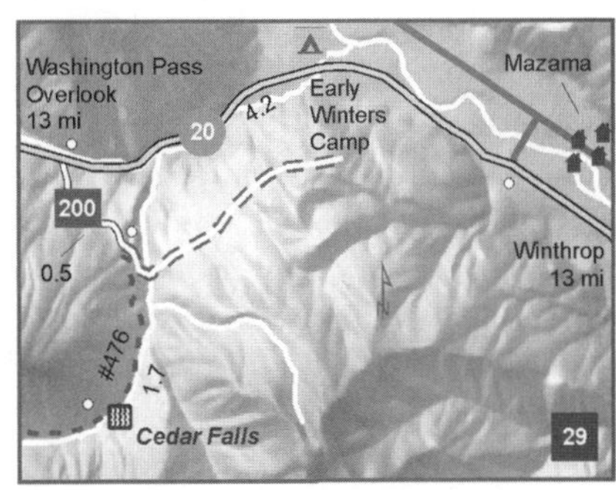

 CEDAR FALLS ★★★

MAGNITUDE: 39
ELEVATION: 3670 feet
WATERSHED: Medium
APPROACH: Trail (moderate)
LAT/LONG: 48.558532° N / 120.480468° W
USGS MAP: *Mazama* (1991)

Cedar Creek has cut deeply into granite bedrock to form this series of 20- to 30-foot cataracts. Drive 4.2 miles west of Mazama along SR 20, and turn left (south) on Sandy Butte–Cedar Creek Road (Forest Service Road 200). Follow this gravel route for 0.5 mile, and park near the marked Cedar Creek Trail 476, leading to the right. The trail ascends moderately for 1.7 miles before reaching the falls.

MORE ONLINE:

Gate Creek Falls (u) ★ USGS *McLeod Mtn.* (1991 nl)

30 WINTHROP

The town of Winthrop has certainly created a niche in Washington tourism. Here is one of the few places in the state that harkens of the Old West. Virtually the entire commercial district possesses a frontier-style facade that successfully eludes looking hokey. The place has the staples of a Northwest tourist town: shopping, eating, and to my delight, a brewpub. Not to mention waterfalls that led me here in the first place. All three falls occur up the watershed of the Chewuch River.

BOULDER CREEK FALLS (U) ★★

MAGNITUDE: 30
ELEVATION: 2300 feet
WATERSHED: Large
APPROACH: Bushwhack (fairly easy)
LAT/LONG: 48.579021° N / 120.156371° W
USGS MAP: *Lewis Butte* (1991 nl)

Tannic acids natural to the area create the rust-colored tint of Boulder Creek and the 10- to 15-foot drop of its segmented punchbowls. Drive a short distance west of Winthrop, turning north off State Route 20 onto Chewuch Road (Forest Service Road 51), located across from the Methow Valley Visitors Center. Go 5.6 miles and turn right onto an unsigned paved road. Proceed 0.2 mile and turn left at Forest Service Road 37. After another 1.8 miles, park along a wide spot in the road.

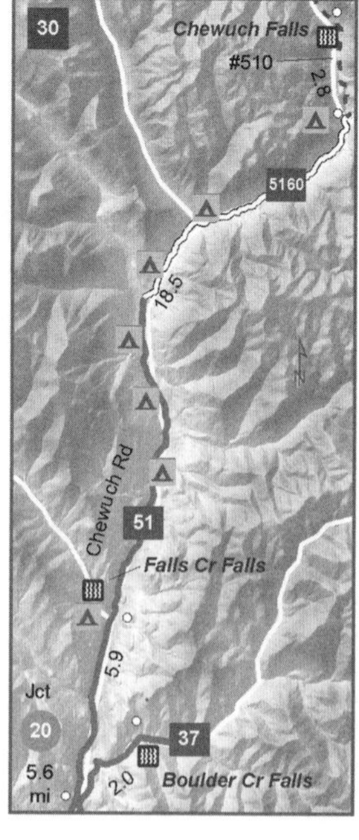

Listen for the falls. Once you gain a partial glimpse, you can climb less than 100 feet partway down the steep slope to a good view from some boulders. Only experienced bushwhackers should consider trying to go all the way into the canyon.

FALLS CREEK FALLS ★★★

MAGNITUDE: 57
ELEVATION: 2490 feet
WATERSHED: Large
APPROACH: Auto
LAT/LONG: 48.636823° N / 120.162422° W
USGS MAP: *Doe Mtn.* (1991)

Falls Creek pours over faulted (fractured) bedrock in a refreshing 35- to 50-foot drop. From the turn for Boulder Creek Falls (described earlier), continue northward another 5.9 miles along Chewuch Road (Forest Service Road 51) to Falls Creek Campground. An access trail along the south side of the creek leads quickly to the descent.

CHEWUCH FALLS ★★

MAGNITUDE: 35
ELEVATION: 4000 feet
WATERSHED: Large
APPROACH: Trail (fairly hard)
LAT/LONG: 48.858998° N / 120.025286° W
USGS MAP: *Coleman Peak* (2001)

Chewuch River descends 30 feet over granite benches. On some maps the falls and its surrounding features are spelled phonetically as "Chewack Falls." Follow Chewuch Road, labeled 5160 along its northern portion, to its end a short distance past Thirtymile Campground and park. Hike 2.8 miles along Thirtymile Trail 510 to this entry, located within the Pasayten Wilderness, which is part of Okanogan-Wenatchee National Forest.

31 FOGGY DEW CREEK

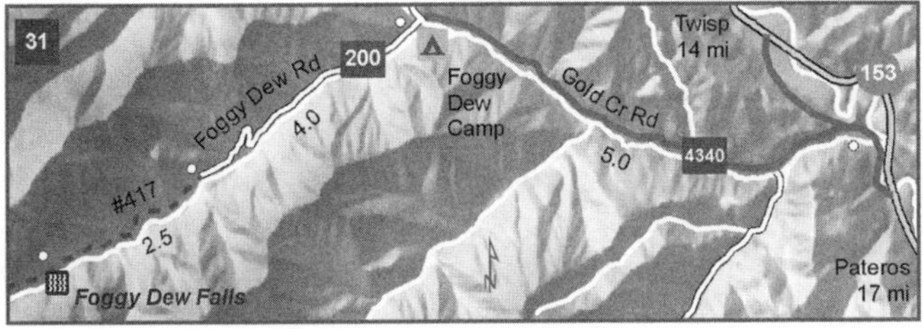

FOGGY DEW FALLS ★★

MAGNITUDE: 30
ELEVATION: 4410 feet
WATERSHED: Medium
APPROACH: Trail (moderate)
LAT/LONG: 48.169291° N / 120.278637° W
USGS MAP: *Martin Peak* (1969)

Foggy Dew Creek accelerates 100 feet through a narrow chute. Take State Route 153 to Gold Creek Road (Forest Service Road 4340), about halfway between the towns of Twisp and Pateros, and turn west. Go 5 miles and turn left (south) on Foggy Dew Road (Forest Service Road 200). The trailhead is 4 miles farther, at the end of the road. A 2.5-mile hike along Foggy Dew Trail 417 brings you to the falls.

32 LAKE CHELAN

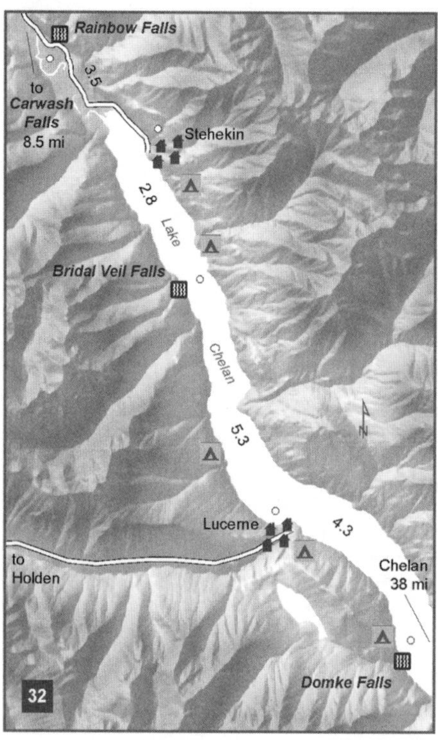

Lake Chelan is a classic example of a very large paternoster lake, one of a series of small lakes occupying depressions in a glacial valley—so-called after the chain's resemblance to the rosary beads used when reciting the Paternoster, or The Lord's Prayer. When glaciers carved out the Chelan Valley 10,000 to 12,000 years ago, they left behind an accumulation of rock debris known as a terminal moraine. The moraine acts as a natural dam for meltwater entering the valley from the adjacent snow-laden mountains. The lake is 51 miles long and attains a depth of more than 1500 feet. It is one of the largest alpine lakes in the contiguous United States.

Take the Lake Chelan Boat Company's *Lady of the Lake* from Chelan to Stehekin and the River Road. Visitors can also fly round-trip on a seaplane or take the boat one way and a plane the other. A shuttle service transports hikers and backpackers to various campsites and trailheads along the Stehekin River Road. Backpackers can obtain a permit from the Golden West Visitors Center in Stehekin. Adventurous souls are encouraged to go to the road's end and sleep under the stars at Cottonwood Camp. The eastern portal of the Cascade Pass Trail is located here, with several waterfalls beckoning. Refer to the North Cascades National Park section (described earlier) for further information.

Rainbow Falls

RAINBOW FALLS ★★★★★

MAGNITUDE: 92
ELEVATION: 1530 feet
WATERSHED: Medium
APPROACH: Watercraft & shuttle
LAT/LONG: 48.3437° / 120.699014° W
USGS MAP: *Stehekin* (1987)

Rainbow Creek makes a spectacular plunge—some 470 feet with a main plunge of 312 feet. This dramatic falls is situated within Lake Chelan National Recreation Area. Board Lake Chelan Boat Company's *Lady of the Lake,* or pilot your own craft from Chelan to the secluded village of Stehekin. Once in Stehekin, bus service is available to shuttle visitors 3.5 miles to the falls.

CARWASH FALLS ★★

MAGNITUDE: 24 (l)
ELEVATION: 1880 feet
WATERSHED: Small
APPROACH: Watercraft & shuttle
LAT/LONG: 48.399548° N / 120.852565° W
USGS MAP: *McGregor Mtn.* (1987 ns)

McGregor Creek descends 40 to 60 feet before splashing next to Stehekin River Road. If the tour bus gets wet 2 miles past High Bridge, you have obviously not missed this aptly named waterfall.

DOMKE FALLS ★★

MAGNITUDE: 33
ELEVATION: 1340 feet
WATERSHED: Medium
APPROACH: Watercraft
LAT/LONG: 48.1621° N / 120.543301° W
USGS MAP: *Lucerne* (1988)

Water rushes 30 to 50 feet into Lake Chelan from Domke Creek. The falls and the creek are named for the first settler in the vicinity and are located within Glacier Peak Wilderness, which is part of Chelan Ranger District, Okanogan-Wenatchee National Forest. The tour boat *Lady of the Lake* (described earlier) passes near the falls, located on the west side of the lake, on the return trip from Lucerne to Chelan.

MORE ONLINE:

Bridal Veil Falls ★ USGS *Stehekin* (1987)
Copper Falls, USGS *Holden* (1988 nl) EXPLORE!
Crown Point Falls, USGS *Suiattle Pass* (1988) EXPLORE!
Monkey Bear Falls, USGS *Pinnacle Mountain* (1988 ns) EXPLORE!
Ten Mile Falls, USGS *Holden* (1988 nl) EXPLORE!

33 ENTIAT VALLEY

Apple orchards are common along the fertile plain of the lower Entiat Valley. Farther upstream the valley becomes less gentle and the orchards give way to coniferous forest. The upper valley has three scenic though not overwhelming waterfalls. They are all a part of Entiat Ranger District, Okanogan-Wenatchee National Forest.

PRESTON FALLS ★★

MAGNITUDE: 22 (l)
ELEVATION: 2040 feet
WATERSHED: Medium
APPROACH: Auto
LAT/LONG: 47.882557° N / 120.431378° W
USGS MAP: *Brief* (1987)

Preston Creek slides 75 to 100 feet down the mountainside. Turn west off of Alternate U.S. Highway 97 onto Entiat River Road less than 1 mile south of the town of Entiat. Reach Ardenvoir in 8.5 miles and the falls 13.5 miles farther, approximately 1.2 miles past Entiat Valley Ski Area.

SILVER FALLS ★★★

MAGNITUDE: 47 (l)
ELEVATION: 2960 feet
WATERSHED: Medium
APPROACH: Auto or trail (moderate)
LAT/LONG: 47.961674° N / 120.532722° W
USGS MAP: *Silver Falls* (1987)

Silver Creek pours 100 to 140 feet from a cliff. The best shows are provided during wet conditions. From Preston Falls (described earlier), continue 9 miles along Entiat River Road, which becomes Okanogan-Wenatchee National Forest Road 51. There is a good, but moderately distant roadside view of the cataract from Silver Falls Service Station. For closer vantage points, ascend Silver Falls National Recreation Trail for 0.5 mile to the base of the falls. The trail is dedicated to J. Kenneth and Opal F. Blair, stewards of public lands in the 1950s and 1960s.

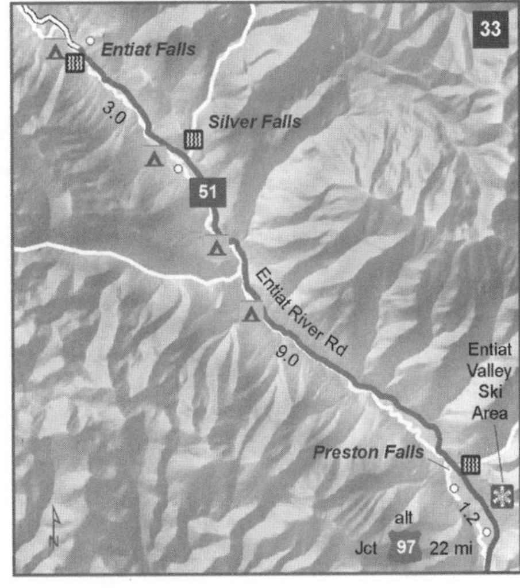

Silver Falls

❑ ENTIAT FALLS ★★

MAGNITUDE: 69 (h)
ELEVATION: 2780 feet
WATERSHED: Large
APPROACH: Auto
LAT/LONG: 47.985477° N / 120.576603° W
USGS MAP: *Silver Falls* (1987)

Entiat River breaks over a rock ledge and thunders 30 feet onto boulders below. *Entiat* is an American Indian word meaning "rapid water." Continue 3 miles past Silver Falls (described earlier) to the Entiat Falls viewpoint.

WASHINGTON

THE OLYMPICS AND VICINITY

The Olympic Peninsula is dominated by the mountains that rise 6000 to 8000 feet above its coastal margins. This abrupt relief causes moist air masses moving into the area to produce some of the highest annual precipitation in the continental United States. Normal figures reach 140 inches of rain on the Pacific Coast and 40 feet of snow in the high mountains. Most precipitation occurs from November to April.

Many small glaciers lie on the northern flanks of the highest mountains. Meltwater from the glaciers as well as from snowfields feeds the region's rivers and streams during the drier summer season. As a result, the larger watersheds throughout the Olympics drain liberally year-round. An abundance of water flowing over a mountainous landscape dissected by glaciation has created most of the 102 waterfalls that have been recognized throughout the peninsula. This chapter provides information for 45 of these falls.

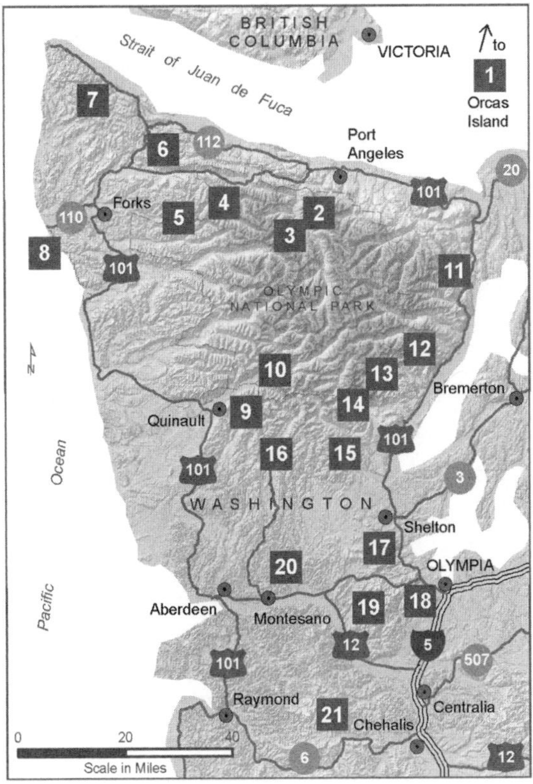

The Olympic Mountains are quite youthful geologically. The range was formed when two of the earth's large crustal plates collided and the contact zone was forced upward. The collision of these plates began about 70 million years ago and has continued to the present, so the mountain-building process is ongoing. During the four Ice Age episodes that occurred between 2 million and 10,000 years ago, alpine glaciers stretched to lower elevations than they do today and carved large U-shaped valleys. Major rivers presently rush along the base of these glacial troughs, sometimes descending over rocks that erode at unequal rates. More common are the falls created when tributary streams pour over the steep sides of glacial troughs on their way to the valley floors.

Gigantic continental glaciers played an important role in shaping Puget Sound and the Strait of Juan de Fuca. About 10,000 years ago the Laurentide Ice Sheet covered almost all of Canada and the northern tier of the eastern United States. A lobe of this massive glacial system extended into western Washington and gouged out large expanses of the Puget Lowland. As the glacier retreated, ocean water inundated the land area that had been eroded below sea level. Puget Sound and its surrounding bodies of water are the result of this inrush. Vashon, Bainbridge, Whidbey, and Camano Islands to the east and the San Juan Islands to the north represent remnants of the preglacial landscape that were not eroded away by the Puget Lobe of the ice sheet.

Coastal waterfalls are also distributed around the Olympic Peninsula. Along the northwestern portion of the coast, small streams tumble over marine cliffs carved by the wave action of the sea. Although most of these falls are visible only from watercraft, a few are accessible by trail.

1 ORCAS ISLAND

The San Juan Islands are one of the most beautiful archipelagos in the world. Orcas Island, the largest of the chain's 172 islands, has four miniature waterfalls. Board a Washington State ferry at Anacortes. After an enjoyable hour and a half churning across Puget Sound, get off at Orcas Landing. Follow Horseshoe Highway north for 12.8 miles, passing the hamlets of West Sound, Crow Valley, and Eastsound before arriving at Moran State Park. Drive 1.2 miles within the park to a fork in the road. Bear left, toward Mount Constitution, and continue 0.3 mile farther. Park at a turnout for the marked trailhead of the aptly named Cascade Creek Trail.

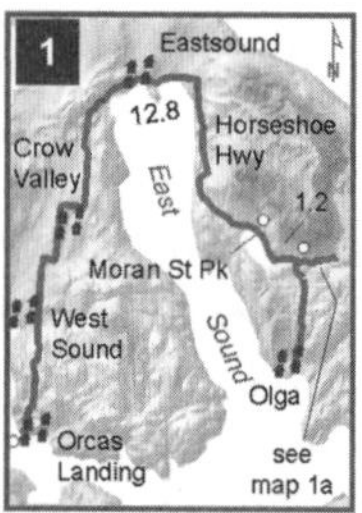

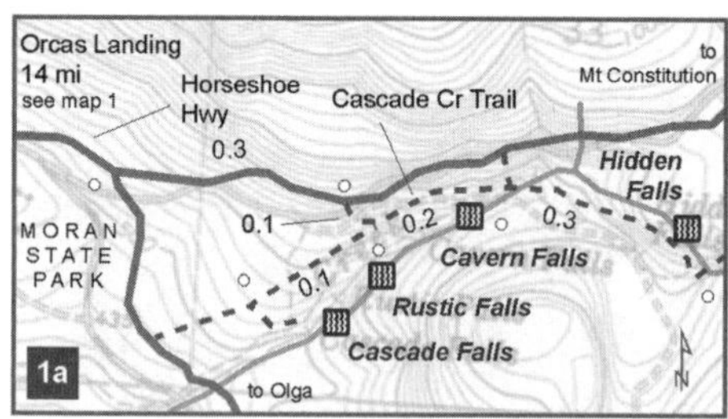

CASCADE FALLS ★★

MAGNITUDE: 38
ELEVATION: 620 feet
WATERSHED: Small
APPROACH: Trail (fairly easy)
LAT/LONG: 48.646323° N / 122.8324° W
USGS MAP: *Mount Constitution* (1994)

This is the largest of the four waterfalls on Orcas Island, spraying downward 40 to 50 feet. It is named after the creek and not its appearance, which is fan-shaped. Follow a short spur trail from the road to the small canyon of Cascade Creek, and walk downstream to the falls in 0.2 mile.

MORE ONLINE:
Rustic Falls ★ USGS *Mount Constitution* (1994)
Cavern Falls ★ USGS *Mount Constitution* (1994)
Hidden Falls ★ USGS *Mount Constitution* (1994)

2 ELWHA

Olympic National Park is best known for its lush rain forest valleys and snow-topped mountains, but its soothing cataracts also deserve attention. The waterfalls of seven of this chapter's sections are located within the park.

MADISON CREEK FALLS (U) ★★

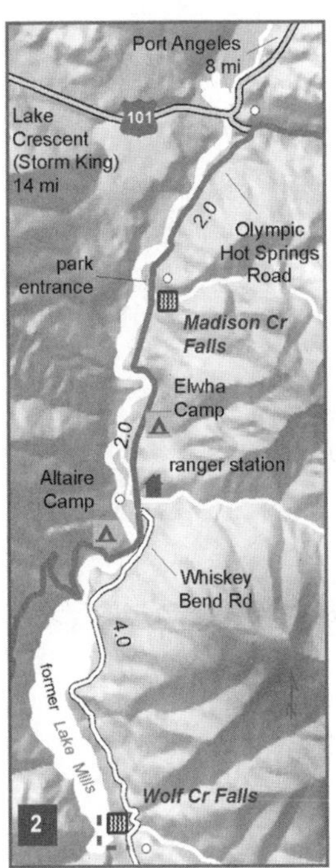

MAGNITUDE: 47
ELEVATION: 540 feet
WATERSHED: Small
APPROACH: Auto
LAT/LONG: 48.042054° N / 123.588375° W
USGS MAP: *Elwha* (1985 ns)

This unpublicized 40- to 50-foot descent is just off one of the main roads into the park. Take U.S. Highway 101 west from Port Angeles for 8 miles, and turn left onto Olympic Hot Springs Road. Drive 2 miles to the park boundary, and stop at the turnout on the left side of the road. A short walk into a wooded tract brings this entry into view.

WOLF CREEK FALLS (U) ★★★

MAGNITUDE: 41
ELEVATION: 850 feet
WATERSHED: Small
APPROACH: Trail (moderate)
LAT/LONG: 47.974022° N / 123.589255° W
USGS MAP: *Hurricane Hill* (2003 nl)

This is a double-tiered falls, but only the 30- to 40-foot lower section is clearly visible. The 50- to 70-foot upper portion is hidden by the shape of the gorge. Drive 2 miles beyond the park boundary on Olympic Hot Springs Road (described earlier); just past the ranger station turn left upon Whiskey Bend Road. After another 4 miles, park along the turnout for a trailhead that was blazed principally to reach former Lake Mills. The reservoir was drained from 2012 to 2013 with the removal of its dam. Follow the steep trail to its end in 0.4 mile. Walk around the ridge to the right to Wolf Creek. You can easily reach the base of the cataract by heading upstream less than 100 feet.

3 MOUNT CARRIE

To reach the trail system for the following falls, stay on Olympic Hot Springs Road 5.5 miles beyond the ranger station, 9.5 miles from U.S. Highway 101. Repair work has closed this park road; it may be reopened by 2014.

LOWER BOULDER CREEK FALLS ★★

MAGNITUDE: 48
ELEVATION: 2650 feet
WATERSHED: Small
APPROACH: Trail (fairly hard)
LAT/LONG: 47.967159° N / 123.71357° W
USGS MAP: *Mount Carrie* (1965 nl)

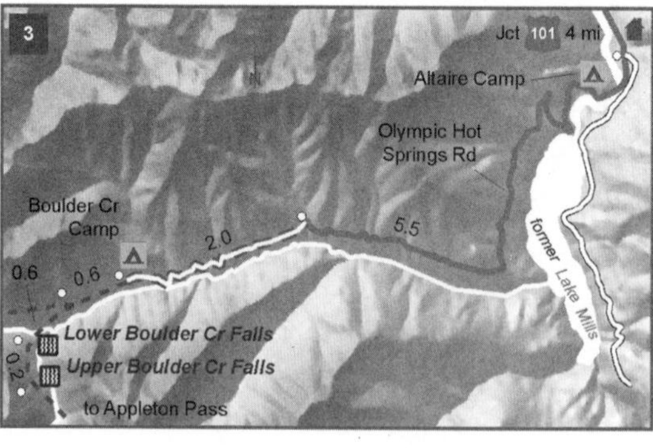

Water froths 25 to 35 feet downward into the upper reaches of Boulder Creek Gorge. Embark upon Boulder Creek Trail, whose first 2 miles consists of an old road. Pass by Boulder Creek Camp, whereby the route is now a bona fide trail. After 0.6 mile, bear left at the fork, heading toward Appleton Pass. The way ascends moderately over the next 0.6 mile before intersecting with a short spur path that quickly leads to the falls.

UPPER BOULDER CREEK FALLS ★★

MAGNITUDE: 56
ELEVATION: 3030 feet
WATERSHED: Small
APPROACH: Trail (fairly hard)
LAT/LONG: 47.966038° N / 123.713741° W
USGS MAP: *Mount Carrie* (1965 nl)

Boulder Creek tumbles 15 to 25 feet before taking a 75- to 100-foot plunge. A full view of the upper portion can be had at the end of the trail, but only the top of the main display is safely visible. Take the trail 0.2 mile beyond Lower Boulder Creek Falls (described earlier) to a second marked spur trail. This short path soon ends at a viewpoint between the tiers.

4 LAKE CRESCENT

Lake Crescent is in the northwestern corner of Olympic National Park's inland section as is one of the most scenic falls of the region. Drive along U.S. Highway 101, either 22 miles west from Port Angeles or 8 miles east from Fairholm, to Storm King Visitors Center and Ranger Station. The following entry is a short hike away.

Marymere Falls

 MARYMERE FALLS ★★★★

MAGNITUDE: 62
ELEVATION: 1030 feet
WATERSHED: Small

APPROACH: Trail (fairly easy)
LAT/LONG: 48.049489° N / 123.789015° W
USGS MAP: *Lake Crescent* (1985)

Falls Creek plunges and horsetails 90 feet over a rock wall. At the Storm King Visitors Center, embark upon Falls Nature Trail, which leads to the cataract in 0.8 mile. Take a self-guided tour or accompany a scheduled group.

5 SOLEDUCK

For years, many of the names in this valley have been given as "Soleduck," an English variant of the American Indian phrase *Sol Duc,* meaning "magic waters." The Geographic Names Information System, a database maintained by the US Geological Survey, now uses the original spelling for the names of natural features but has retained the variant for cultural places.

SOL DUC FALLS ★★★

MAGNITUDE: 58
ELEVATION: 2190 feet
WATERSHED: Medium

APPROACH: Trail (moderate)
LAT/LONG: 47.951324° N / 123.820064° W
USGS MAP: *Bogachiel Peak* (1950)

The waters of the Sol Duc River rush 40 to 60 feet downward at a right angle to create this falls, which is also spelled Soleduck Falls (u). Drive west from Fairholm for 1.8 miles on U.S. Highway 101 to Soleduck Road, which leads to Sol Duc Hot Springs in 12 miles. The road ends at Soleduck Trailhead 1.5 miles farther. Hike 1 mile beyond the trailhead, then turn right (south) at the first junction. The falls can be seen from the footbridge crossing the river.

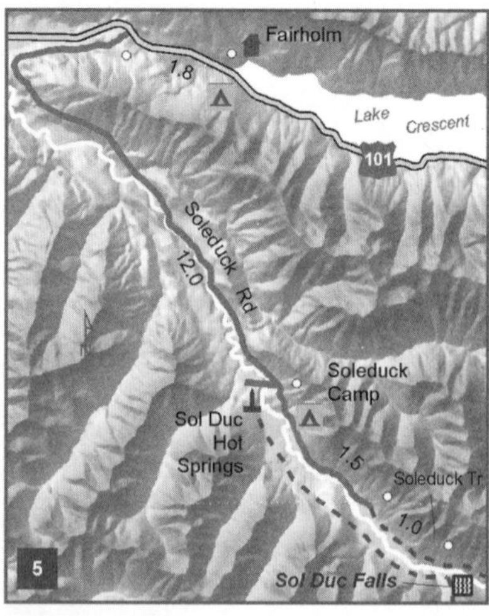

6 BEAVER CREEK

The waterfalls in this and the next section are located outside Olympic National Park, but they were accessible to the public when last field-truthed. Don't trespass if signage indicates the situation has changed.

BEAVER FALLS ★★★

MAGNITUDE: 34 (l)
ELEVATION: 600 feet
WATERSHED: Medium
APPROACH: Bushwhack (moderate)
LAT/LONG: 48.094137° N / 124.266684° W
USGS MAP: *Lake Pleasant* (2000)

Beaver Creek tumbles 30 to 40 feet in three sections across an 80-foot-wide rock escarpment. Turn off U.S. Highway 101 at Sappho upon State Route 113, whose junction is 12 miles north of Forks and 17 miles west of Fairholm. Head north 2 miles to an unsigned turnout 0.1 mile past the bridge over Beaver Creek. A short, unimproved path leads to the cataract.

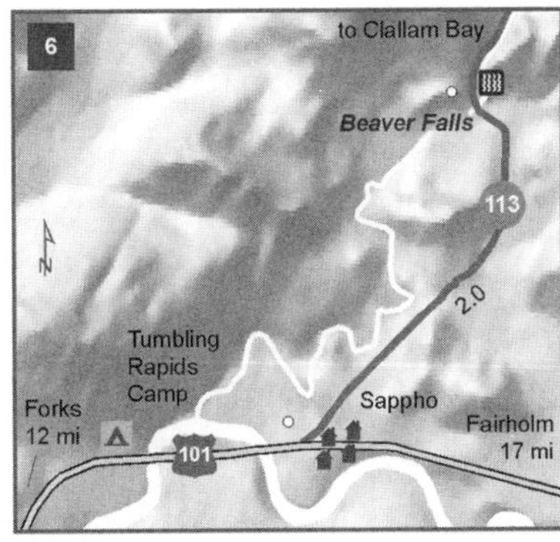

7 CLALLAM BAY

Passing motorists probably miss the following cataracts as they admire the Clallam Bay portion of the Strait of Juan de Fuca, the passage connecting Puget Sound with the Pacific Ocean.

HOKO FALLS ★★

MAGNITUDE: 28 (h)
ELEVATION: 210 feet
WATERSHED: Large
APPROACH: Bushwhack (fairly easy)
LAT/LONG: 48.200212° N / 124.431436° W
USGS MAP: *Hoko Falls* (1984)

The normally calm waters of the Hoko River rush about 10 feet at a narrow reach where erosion-resistant rock constricts the stream. Follow State Route 112 to the seaside village of Clallam Bay. Continue on SR 112 for 4.1 miles, then turn left (south) toward Ozette

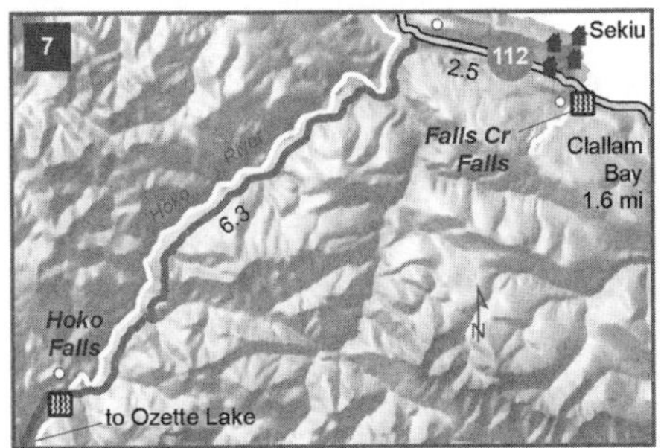

Lake. Proceed 6.3 miles to a bridge over the Hoko River, parking on the far side. Angler's paths lead down to a view near the base of the falls.

MORE ONLINE:

Falls Creek Falls (u) ★ USGS *Clallam Bay* (1984 nl)
Beach Creek Falls (u) ★ USGS *Cape Flattery* (1984 nl)
Titacoclos Falls ★ USGS *Cape Flattery* (1984)
Flattery Creek Falls (u) ★ USGS *Cape Flattery* (1984 nl)

8 OLYMPIC COAST

For safe access to the following waterfall, hikers or backpackers must be aware of tide conditions. Some of the beaches are inundated by the Pacific at high tide. You can obtain appropriate information for coastal hiking, such as tide tables, at the Mora or Kalaloch ranger stations of Olympic National Park.

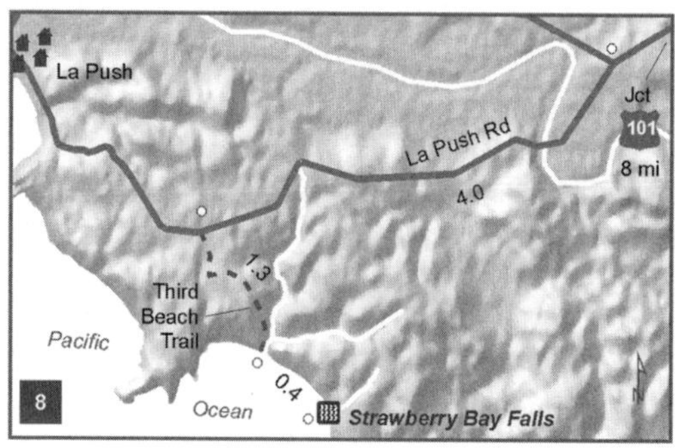

1 STRAWBERRY BAY FALLS (U) ★★

MAGNITUDE: 29 (l)
ELEVATION: 80 feet
WATERSHED: Very small
APPROACH: Trail (fairly hard)
LAT/LONG: 47.872882° N / 124.577477° W
USGS MAP: *Toleak Point* (1982 nl)

An unnamed creek pours 100 to 120 feet into the surf. Five miles north of Forks turn left off U.S. Highway 101, heading toward La Push and the Pacific Coast. After 8 miles, turn left (south), staying on La Push Road, and continue 4 miles to Third Beach Trailhead. Hike 1.3 miles to the ocean, then head 0.4 mile southeast to the nearest beachside view of the falls. Closer vantage points are possible from wave-cut rocks, but for safety's sake walk on the rocks only when the tide is receding.

9 QUINAULT

The waterfalls listed here are all situated within the Pacific Ranger District of Olympic National Forest. Depart U.S. Highway 101 upon South Shore Road, heading eastward for Lake Quinault. Drive 2.3 miles to Quinault Ranger Station.

GATTON CREEK FALLS ★★

MAGNITUDE: 25
ELEVATION: 400 feet
WATERSHED: Small
APPROACH: Trail (fairly easy)
LAT/LONG: 47.467532° N / 123.831351° W
USGS MAP: *Lake Quinault East* (1990 ns)

Gatton Creek stairsteps irregularly 40 to 50 feet within the temperate rain forest of the windward Olympic Mountains. Proceed eastward along South Shore Road for 0.5 mile beyond Quinault Ranger Station (mentioned earlier), and turn right upon Wrights Canyon Road. Continue for 0.4 mile to an unsigned turnout where Gatton Creek Trail crosses the road.

Embark upon the westward portion of the trail, to your right. After walking 0.3 mile, cross a footbridge spanning the stream. From the bridge you can see the tops of several larger tiers, but unfortunately I could not find an access route when I scouted the area. Walk just beyond the footbridge to view two of the smaller tiers. There are more small tiers farther downstream.

MERRIMAN FALLS ★★★

MAGNITUDE: 46
ELEVATION: 220 feet
WATERSHED: Very small
APPROACH: Auto
LAT/LONG: 47.500348° N / 123.784401° W
USGS MAP: *Finley Creek* (1990 nl)

Merriman Creek showers 40 to 50 feet over an escarpment where a road skirts past its base. Its rating decreases during dry spells. Drive eastward 4.3 miles

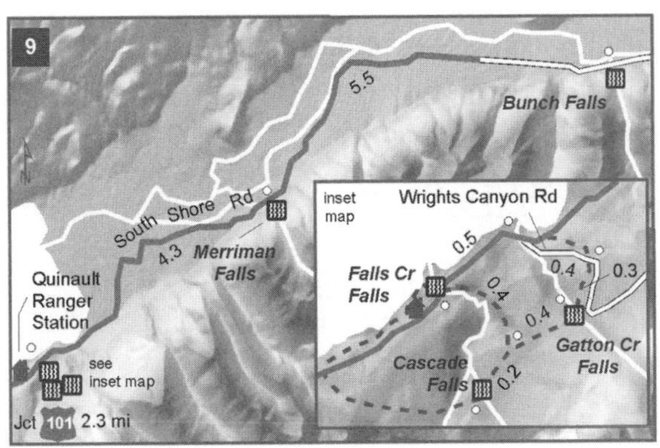

Merriman Falls

past Quinault Ranger Station, 3.7 miles beyond Gatton Creek (described earlier) along South Shore Road. Park along the unsigned turnout that offers a roadside view of the cataract.

BUNCH FALLS ★★

MAGNITUDE: 31
ELEVATION: 400 feet
WATERSHED: Small
APPROACH: Auto
LAT/LONG: 47.528884° N / 123.695953° W
USGS MAP: *Bunch Lake* (1990 ns)

The Quinault and Graves Creek entrance to Olympic National Park welcomes you with water tumbling from Bunch Canyon as a 40- to 60-foot cataract. Drive 5.5

miles eastward past Merriman Falls (described earlier) along South Shore Road. Look for the falls next to the sign marking the boundary of the national park.

MORE ONLINE:

Cascade Falls ★ USGS *Lake Quinault East* (1990 ns)

Falls Creek Falls ★ USGS *Lake Quinault East* (1990 ns)

10 ENCHANTED VALLEY

This entry is for all the waterfall enthusiasts who also like to backpack. Marvel at the Enchanted Valley, located in the southern part of Olympic National Park. The most popular trailhead for accessing the valley, Graves Creek, is 23 miles east of Quinault, off U.S. Highway 101, near the ranger station.

VALLEY OF 10,000 WATERFALLS (U) ★★★★

MAGNITUDE: incalculable
ELEVATION: 3400 to 4200 feet
WATERSHED: Small (g)
APPROACH: Backpack (fairly hard)
LAT/LONG: 47.675752° N / 123.394773° W
USGS MAP: *Chimney Peak* (1990 nl and ns)

Many visitors and longtime residents of the Olympic Peninsula prefer the name Valley of 10,000 Waterfalls to the more common Enchanted Valley. Although the number of falls may be exaggerated in the name, you would be hard-pressed to keep track of the scores of waterfalls you can see during a single day's journey in this valley. Practically every tributary encountered along Enchanted Valley Trail breaks into a waterfall as it enters the glacially carved valley of the Quinault River. Varied vegetation completes the serene scenery of the gorge.

Secure a backcountry permit at the Graves Creek or Dosewallips ranger stations. Most of the falls are within 0.3 mile of the Enchanted Valley Ranger Station, which is 13 miles from the trailhead and is open during the summer if you need information or assistance.

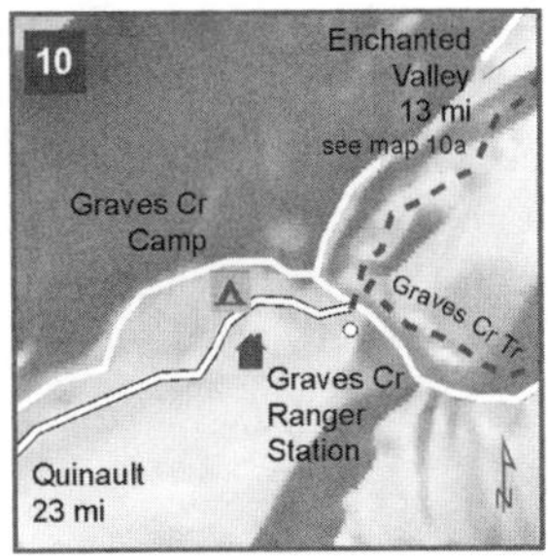

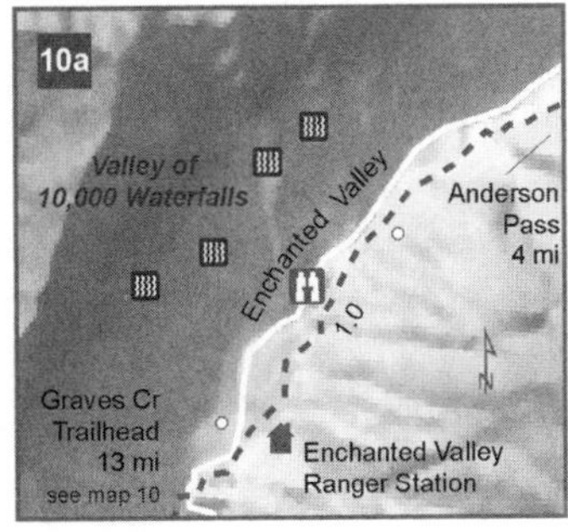

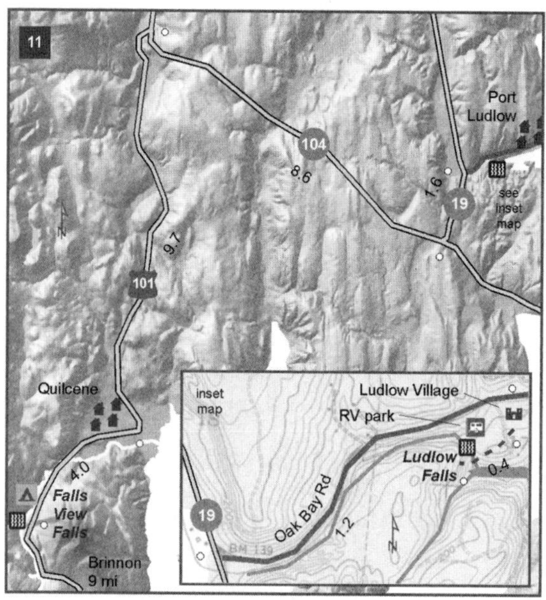

11 QUILCENE

LUDLOW FALLS ★★

MAGNITUDE: 16 (l)
ELEVATION: 80 feet
WATERSHED: Medium
APPROACH: Trail (fairly easy)
LAT/LONG: 47.917511° N / 122.708074° W
USGS MAP: *Port Ludlow* (1973 ns)

Ludlow Creek tumbles twice a total of 10 to 20 feet within a privately owned nature area open to the public. Drive 1.6 miles along State Route 19 beyond its junction with State Route 104, and turn right upon Oak Bay Road. Proceed 1.2 miles to the public parking lot at the small shopping area named Ludlow Village. Find a large trail board on the west side of the lot, which shows a system of six trails. Embark on the Ludlow Falls Interpretive Trail, which starts on the road leading to an RV park.

Walk 0.2 mile down to the RV loop road, following the signs to the trailhead. Take the right turn, then another 0.2 mile to a vista, which has an interpretive sign about the falls. More cascades can also be seen immediately downstream. The trail loops 0.3 mile more and then returns to the RV park.

FALLS VIEW FALLS (U) ★★

MAGNITUDE: 26 (l)
ELEVATION: 280 feet
WATERSHED: Very small
APPROACH: Auto
LAT/LONG: 47.79128° N / 122.929517° W
USGS MAP: *Mount Walker* (1995 ns)

An unnamed creek drops 80 to 120 feet into the Big Quilcene River. The flow is greatest during the wet season from autumn to spring. It may disappear entirely during droughts. The cataract is also known as Campground Falls.

Turn off U.S. Highway 101 at Falls View Camp, 4 miles south of Quilcene and 9 miles north of Brinnon. A short trail at the south end of the campground leads to a fenced vista high above the canyon floor. This falls is located within Hood Canal Ranger District of Olympic National Forest in the vicinity of Quilcene Ranger Station.

12 DOSEWALLIPS

Kudos to a local resident for pointing out the first of the following three falls. Although it is likely situated on private land this otherwise obscure yet entertaining spectacle was accessible when last visited. It is currently listed as a recreation opportunity in material authored by Olympic National Forest.

ROCKY BROOK FALLS (U) ★★★★

MAGNITUDE: 71
ELEVATION: 500 feet
WATERSHED: Medium
APPROACH: Auto
LAT/LONG: 47.72072° N / 122.941705° W
USGS MAP: *Brinnon* (1999 ns)

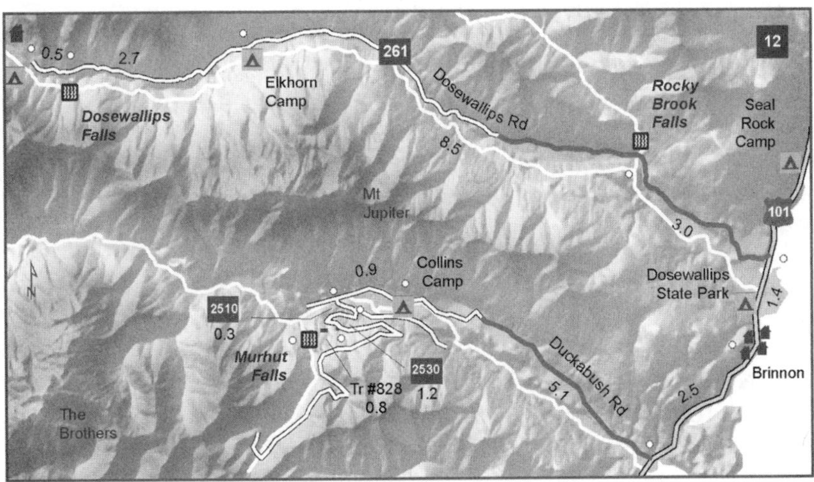

Rocky Brook Falls

Water thunders 100 to 125 feet over a massive scarp. If you also plan on taking a day trip to Dosewallips Falls (described next), save this one for last. Drive 1.4 miles north of Brinnon on U.S. Highway 101, then turn left (west) onto Dosewallips Road (Forest Service Road 261), signed "Dosewallips Recreation Area." Proceed west for 3 miles, and park at the unsigned turnout on the west side of the bridge crossing Rocky Brook. A well-worn trail quickly leads to the base of the falls.

DOSEWALLIPS FALLS ★★★

MAGNITUDE: 53
ELEVATION: 1400 feet
WATERSHED: Large
APPROACH: Auto
LAT/LONG: 47.732397° N / 123.1539° W
USGS MAP: *The Brothers* (1985 nl)

Water pours 100 to 125 feet over and around boulders along the Dosewallips River. This scenic cascade is located within Olympic National Park. Continue driving 11.2 miles westward past Rocky Brook Bridge (described earlier) along Dosewallips Road (Forest Service Road 261). A signed turnout will be seen near the base of the cataract, 0.7 mile beyond the park boundary.

MURHUT FALLS ★★★★

MAGNITUDE: 58
ELEVATION: 1160 feet
WATERSHED: Small
APPROACH: Trail (moderate)
LAT/LONG: 47.673054° N / 123.050538° W
USGS MAP: *Mt. Jupiter* (1985 ns)

A trail within the Hood Canal Ranger District of Olympic National Forest was constructed just a few years ago to enable access to this double-drop descent totaling 95 to 125 feet along Murhut Creek. Depart U.S. Highway 101 south of Brinnon in 2.5 miles to Duckabush Road. It should be signed for Duckabush Recreation Area.

The pavement ends in 3.7 miles, and 1.4 miles farther you pass Collins Camp. Proceed another 0.9 mile, and bear left upon Forest Service Road 2510; then turn right 0.3 mile farther on Forest Service Road 2530. The parking area for the trailhead is 1.2 miles beyond. Embark upon Murhut Falls Trail 828. You reach a vista of the falls at the trail's end in 0.8 mile.

13 JEFFERSON PEAK

Adults should enjoy this pair of cataracts near Jefferson Peak within Hood Canal Ranger District of Olympic National Forest. Thin paths discourage families from bringing the kids. Depart U.S. Highway 101 upon Hamma Hamma Road, whose junction is located 8 miles south of Duckabush and 3.2 miles south of Triton Cove State Park.

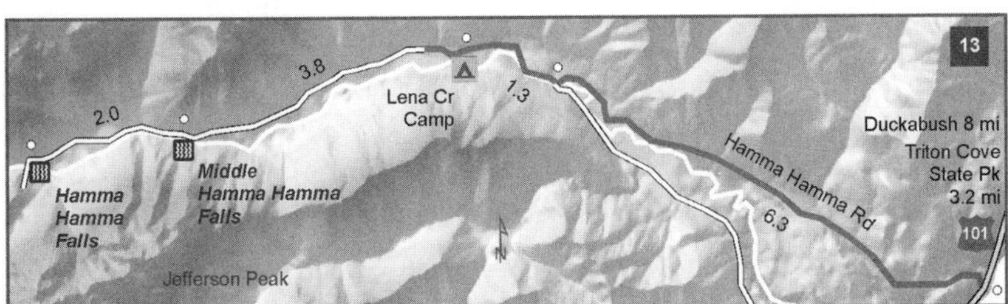

MIDDLE HAMMA HAMMA FALLS (U) ★★

MAGNITUDE: 31
ELEVATION: 1380 feet
WATERSHED: Medium
APPROACH: Bushwhack (fairly easy)
LAT/LONG: 47.581853° N / 123.223294° W
USGS MAP: *Mt. Washington* (1985 nl)

Water gurgles 40 to 50 feet over and around boulders choking the Hamma Hamma River. Proceed 6.3 miles along Hamma Hamma Road, then turn right

Hamma Hamma Falls

(staying on the paved road), toward Lena Creek Camp. Pass the campground 1.3 miles beyond. Continue for another 3.8 miles, finding an unsigned turnout on the streamside. Park here. Follow a faint path next to the large roadside boulder for a couple of hundred feet to moss-covered rocks overlooking the descent. This fairly easy bushwhack is not recommended for young children.

 HAMMA HAMMA FALLS ★★★★

MAGNITUDE: 60
ELEVATION: 1780 feet
WATERSHED: Medium
APPROACH: Bushwhack (moderate)
LAT/LONG: 47.575499° N / 123.26063° W
USGS MAP: *Mt. Skokomish* (1990 nl)

The Hamma Hamma River drops 25 to 35 feet before roaring 55 to 75 feet into a tight gorge at the entrance to Mount Skokomish Wilderness of Olympic National Forest. A high-span bridge completes the scene, framed by dense forest.

Drive 2 miles past the middle falls (described earlier) to a large unsigned turnout just before the bridge crossing the river. Look for a faint path about two-thirds of the way down the guardrail. A cairn (small stack of rocks) signified its location when I last visited it. Make your way for a couple of hundred feet to an airy vista on an outcrop. The terrain is steep here, so be careful. Until a safer trail is constructed, do not bring children here or visit if you are not nimble. Motorists and hikers can, however, also gain a heart-pounding view of the gorge and nearby peaks from the high bridge.

14 LAKE CUSHMAN

CUSHMAN FALLS ★★

MAGNITUDE: 44
ELEVATION: 850 feet
WATERSHED: Small
APPROACH: Auto
LAT/LONG: 47.496046° N / 123.256618° W
USGS MAP: *Lightning Peak* (1990 nl)

An unnamed creek slides 25 to 35 feet, nearly spraying onto the road. This falls is located on a strip of private property adjacent to Olympic National Park. Depart U.S. Highway 101 at the hamlet of Hoodsport; the turnoff is signed "Olympic National

Cushman Falls

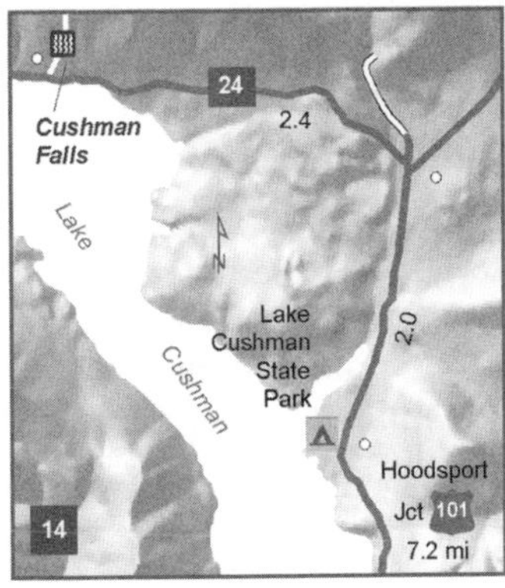

Park—Staircase Area." You reach Lake Cushman State Park in 7.2 miles. In another 2 miles turn left onto Forest Service Road 24 toward the Staircase Area, and then reach the waterfall in another 2.4 miles.

15 SKOKOMISH VALLEY

1 VINCENT CREEK FALLS (U) ★★

MAGNITUDE: 30 (l)
ELEVATION: 460 feet
WATERSHED: Small
APPROACH: Auto
LAT/LONG: 47.367977° N / 123.281616° W
USGS MAP: *Vance Creek* (1990 nl)

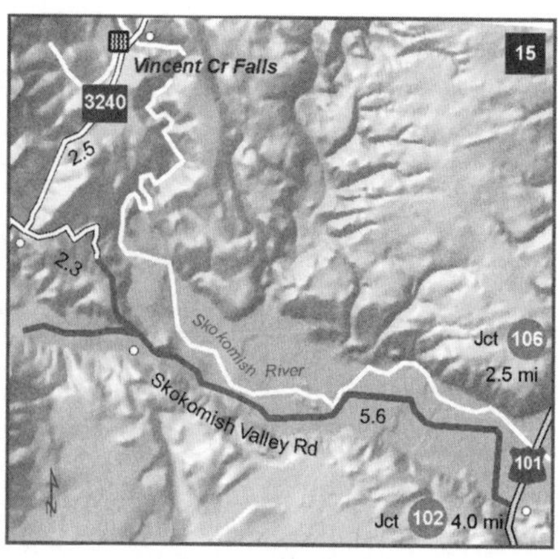

Vincent Creek veils 80 to 100 feet into South Fork Skokomish River. It's an exhilarating experience, as the vantage point is from a bridge spanning hundreds of feet above the floor of the gorge. This falls occurs within the Hood Canal Ranger District of Olympic National Forest.

Depart U.S. Highway 101 upon Skokomish Valley Road, whose turn is located 2.5 miles south of the junction of US 101 and State Route 106, as well as 4 miles north of the junction of US 101 and State Route 102. After 5.6 miles, bear right at the fork, then turn right in another 2.3 miles upon Forest Service Road 3240. Go 2.5 miles more, and park on the far side of High Steel Bridge. Walk a short ways upon the span to gain a cross-canyon view of the cataract.

16 WYNOOCHEE LAKE

The south-central portion of Olympic National Forest's Hood Canal Ranger District, being remote from travelers' facilities, is one of the lesser-frequented areas of the Olympic Peninsula. The most reliable access to the following cataracts is from the south. Depart U.S. Highway 12 at Devonshire Road, 1.5 miles west of Montesano. After 0.1 mile, turn left (north) on Wynoochee Road (Forest Service Road 22), and drive 34 miles to its junction with Forest Service Road 23 near Wynoochee Dam.

Spoon Creek Falls

WYNOOCHEE FALLS ★★

MAGNITUDE: 44
ELEVATION: 1010 feet
WATERSHED: Medium
APPROACH: Auto
LAT/LONG: 47.471414° N / 123.526091° W
USGS MAP: *Wynoochee Lake* (1995 nl)

This pretty double punchbowl tumbles 25 to 35 feet along the Wynoochee River. At Wynoochee Dam turn north onto Forest Service Road 2270. In 7 miles pass Noname

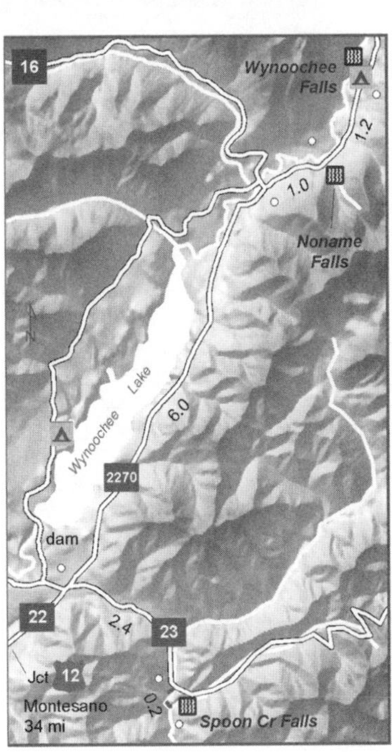

Falls (u) USGS *Wynoochee Lake* (1995 ns). Proceed 1.2 miles farther, and turn left into an old national forest campground. Proceed to the north end of the camp, and then walk along any of the several footpaths, all of which lead to the falls in 50 to 100 yards.

SPOON CREEK FALLS ★★★

MAGNITUDE: 53
ELEVATION: 1990 feet
WATERSHED: Small
APPROACH: Trail & bushwhack (fairly easy)
LAT/LONG: 47.353564° N / 123.564758° W
USGS MAP: *Grisdale* (1990 nl)

Water veils 50 to 60 feet in a serene setting. From the road intersection for Wynoochee Dam (described earlier), turn right (eastward, in the opposite direction from the dam) upon Forest Service Road 23. Proceed 2.4 miles to just beyond the bridge crossing of Satsop River. Park here and find the trailhead to the right.

Hike down the path 0.2 mile to its end at the base of the creek, then rock hop 100 feet upstream around the bend to the base of the falls. The water may be too high in springtime; if it is, the only view will be an obscured one just off-trail near the road.

MORE ONLINE:

Noname Falls (u) ★ mentioned earlier

17 KAMILCHE

KENNEDY FALLS ★★

MAGNITUDE: 38
ELEVATION: 240 feet
WATERSHED: Medium
APPROACH: Trail (moderate)
LAT/LONG: 47.077413° N / 123.126871° W
USGS MAP: *Kamilche Valley* (1981)

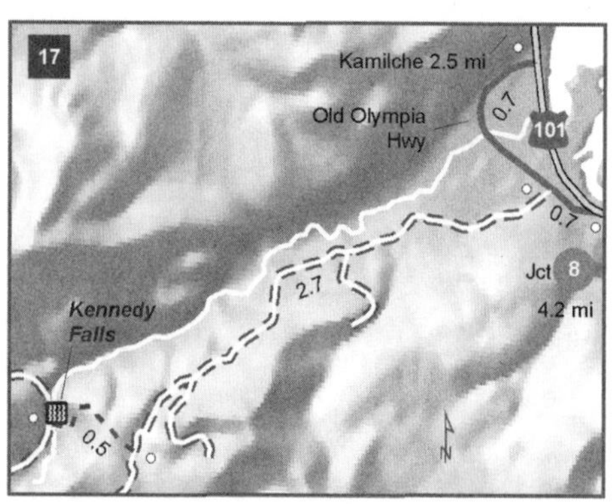

Kennedy Creek drops to an emerald-tinted gorge in two major tiers. The upper portion of this small but pleasant waterfall tumbles about 10 feet into a pool. A short distance downstream, the creek pours 20 to 30 feet into the narrow gorge.

Turn off U.S. Highway 101 onto Old Olympia Highway 2.5 miles south of the exit for

Kamilche and State Route 108 and 4.2 miles northwest of the junction of US 101 and State Route 8. Drive 0.7 mile to the dirt road south of Kennedy Creek. Turn west and stay on the main route for 2.7 miles, bearing right (toward the creek) at all major forks.

Park along the side of the road at its junction with an unsigned jeep trail, and hike for 0.5 mile to the creek. The best views of the falls are from the north side of the valley. Walk a short distance upstream to a fairly easy ford above the upper descent, and then progress downstream to a clear, unguarded vista. This site is most likely on private land, so proceed only if access continues to be allowed.

MORE ONLINE:

Goldsborough Creek Falls (u) ★ USGS *Shelton* (1981 nl)

18 OLYMPIA

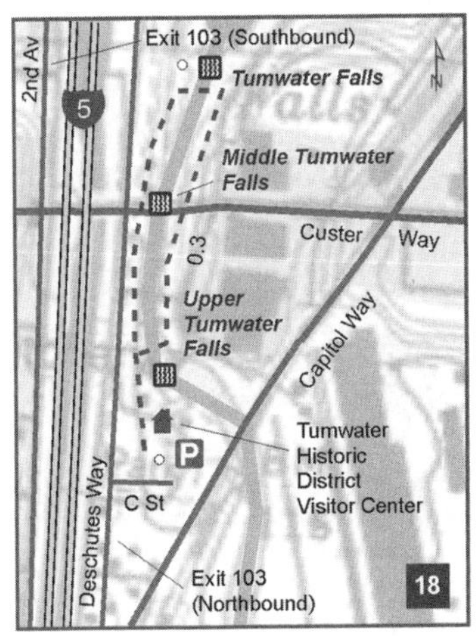

Once the grounds of the now-defunct Olympia Brewing Company, Tumwater Falls Park remains open (to everyone's delight) to public visitation courtesy of the Olympia Tumwater Foundation. The park is a part of the Tumwater Historic District, which additionally is dedicated to preserving the built environment adjacent to three waterfalls along the Deschutes River. You will find many interpretive signs throughout the district.

Depart Interstate 5 at Exit 103, signed as 2nd Avenue for southbounders and Deschutes Way for those traveling north. Drive to C Street, and turn east toward the river to this site's parking area. *Deschutes* is French for "of the falls."

UPPER TUMWATER FALLS ★★

MAGNITUDE: 55
ELEVATION: 90 feet
WATERSHED: Large (d)
APPROACH: Auto
LAT/LONG: 47.014906° N / 122.904484° W
USGS MAP: *Tumwater* (1997 nl)

From the parking lot, walk past the visitors center to the river and its initial 10- to 20-foot drop. A sawmill and shingle factory occupied the west side during the mid- to late 1800s. Along the opposite side, the headgates for a water flume are still visible.

TUMWATER FALLS ★★★

MAGNITUDE: 41
ELEVATION: 60 feet
WATERSHED: Large (d)
APPROACH: Trail (easy)
LAT/LONG: 47.018066° N / 122.904183° W
USGS MAP: *Tumwater* (1997 nl)

This 40-foot waterfall is known for its likeness on the labels of the Olympia brands of beer, now produced out-of-state since the onsite brewery's closure in 2003. First called Puget Sound Falls by European settlers in 1829, it was renamed Shutes River Falls in 1841. In 1845 Michael Troutman Simmons led a party of American settlers to the vicinity. He coined the name "Tumwater" based on a Chinook word for running water *tumtum* because the sound was like that of a throbbing heart.

From the parking lot, walk downstream 0.3 mile to a vista overlooking the falls. A footbridge crosses above the descent. Along the way you pass Middle Tumwater Falls USGS *Tumwater* (1997 ns). A trail along the opposite side of the river offers a loop route back to your vehicle.

MORE ONLINE:

Middle Tumwater Falls ★ mentioned earlier

Olympia Falls (u) ★★ USGS *Tumwater* (1997 ns), artificial water source has been cut off and so it no longer exists

19 PORTER

PORTER FALLS ★★

MAGNITUDE: 32
ELEVATION: 400 feet
WATERSHED: Medium
APPROACH: Trail (fairly easy)
LAT/LONG: 46.977543° N / 123.267784° W
USGS MAP: *Malone* (1993 nl)

This largest in a series of small cataracts along West Fork Porter Creek drops 10 to 15 feet just above the stream's confluence with North Fork Porter Creek. It is located within Capitol State Forest. Leave U.S. Highway 12 at the hamlet of Porter on unsigned Porter Creek Road. Drive 2.7 miles, where the road turns into a gravel surface. Continue another 0.5 mile to the Porter Creek entrance to the state forest. Stay on this road, now called B-Line, for another 0.6 mile to a generic trail sign immediately before the entrance to Porter Creek Camp.

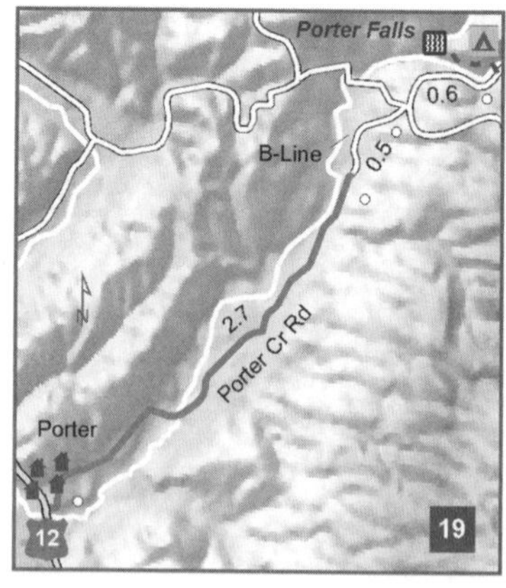

Park here, where an interpretive sign describes the logging railroad that played a large role in the history of the area. The 0.5-mile trail parallels the North Fork for 0.3 mile before ending at the falls along the West Fork.

MORE ONLINE:
Mima Falls ★ USGS *Littlerock* (1993)

20 MONTESANO

SYLVIA CREEK FALLS (U) ★★

MAGNITUDE: 32
ELEVATION: 400 feet
WATERSHED: Medium
APPROACH: Trail (easy)
LAT/LONG: 46.996206° N / 123.598956° W
USGS MAP: *Malone* (1993 nl)

Sylvia Creek Falls

Although not advertised in literature for Lake Sylvia State Park, this pretty 35- to 45-foot drop from the lake is worthy of mention. Depart U.S. Highway 12 through the town of Montesano, following the signs 2 miles to the state park entrance. Turn left, crossing the bridge, reaching a parking lot at the road's end 0.2 mile farther.

Start hiking down the trail, crossing the dam to the left. Then turn right, heading up the small hill in the downstream direction. You will have partially obscured views just beyond interpretive post #15, 0.2 mile from your starting point.

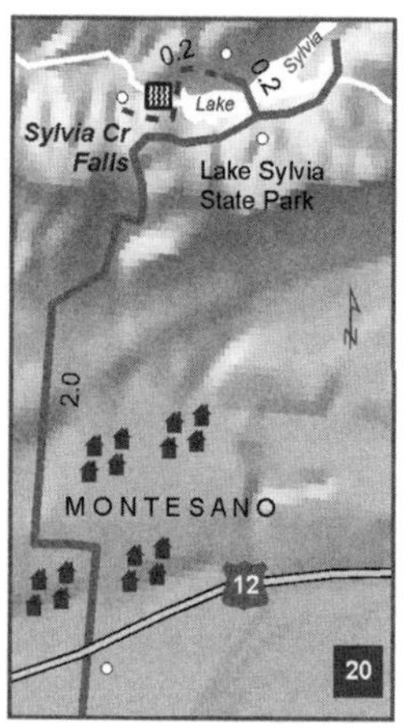

21 RAINBOW FALLS STATE PARK

The following entry just might hold the title of being the smallest waterfall with a state park named after it. More noteworthy is that its scenic value is best at *lower* stream flows, which exposes bulbous bedrock pinching the river.

1 RAINBOW FALLS ★★

MAGNITUDE: 24 (h)
ELEVATION: 400 feet
WATERSHED: Large
APPROACH: Auto
LAT/LONG: 46.630563° N / 123.231906° W
USGS MAP: *Rainbow Falls* (1994)

A large pool at the base of this about 10-foot interruption along the Chehalis River serves as a popular swimming hole during the summer. A signed wayside for the small waterfall occurs along State Route 6, about 3 miles east of Doty and 12 miles west of Adna. A bridge once spanned the river here to access the park's camping and day-use areas, but it has since been removed.

If you also wish to visit the park proper, drive either 2.3 miles west of the wayside to River Road or 0.9 mile east to Chandler Road to eventually gain entrance to the recreational facilities.

WASHINGTON

MOUNT RAINIER REGION

The region within and surrounding Mount Rainier National Park is among the most scenic in North America. While the mountain itself, called *Takhoma* by the Yakama Indians, is the centerpiece of the area, many other attractions await discovery. Of the 179 waterfalls known to occur within the area, 84 are mentioned in this chapter.

This is a land of fire and ice. The oldest rocks in the area predate Mount Rainier itself. Between 30 million and 60 million years ago, the region was part of a large, low-lying coastal zone scattered with terrestrial and subterranean volcanoes, which deposited thick accumulations of lava over a wide area. Between 10 million and 30 million years later, continued volcanic activity forced molten material, or magma, toward the surface of the earth. Most of this magma cooled before it could pour from the volcanoes' vents as lava. It solidified to become bedrock, which was later thrust to the surface by internal earth forces or exposed by erosion.

Because of this complex history, the landscape along the periphery of Mount Rainier comprises many different types of rocks that streams erode at unequal rates. Silver Falls occurs where the Ohanapecosh River intersects resistant vertical layers of basalt before continuing its course along relatively weak volcanic breccia, which was formed when lava intermingled with sandstone and siltstone. At Lower Stevens Falls, magma was injected into an older rock complex, and the resulting bedrock proved to be more resistant than the neighboring material.

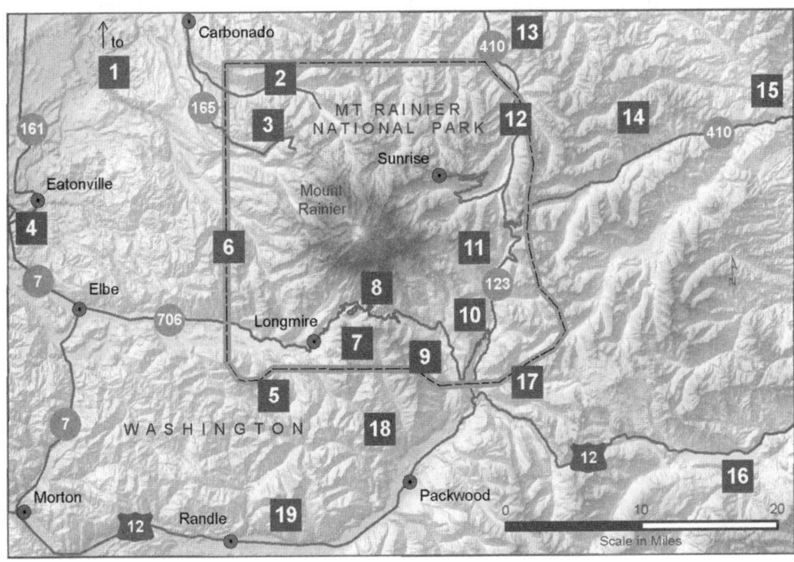

Mount Rainier formed some 1 million to 5 million years ago and is composed of interlayered andesitic lava and volcanic ash from repeated eruptions. One large lava flow blocks the northward course of Maple Creek, diverting the stream eastward. Coincidentally, a vertical break in the local topography, called a fault, is positioned along the redefined route of the stream. Maple Falls (currently inaccessible) plummets down this fault.

The abundance of waterfalls in the region is due not only to the processes described above but also to the large-scale landscape modifications achieved by glaciers. A total of 27 named glaciers surround Mount Rainier today; 10,000 years ago these awesome phenomena, the earth's greatest erosive agents, extended to much lower elevations.

A topographic feature called a step is common to the higher valleys of this area. It occurs where an alpine glacier gouges its valley floor unevenly. Clear Creek Falls and Sylvia Falls lie along breaks that were probably formed in this manner. Waterfalls that drop from hanging valleys are also common around Mount Rainier. These hanging valleys formed when small tributary glaciers could not erode their valleys as deeply as the large, main glaciers could. Therefore, the floor of a smaller glacial valley is high above that of a main glacial valley where the two meet. Comet Falls and Spray Falls are dramatic examples of this type.

1 SUMNER

You barely need to leave the Tacoma metropolitan area, heading toward Mount Rainier, to encounter a quite scenic waterfall. No signs announce its existence, so follow these directions carefully. Depart State Route 162 at the hamlet of McMillin, turning eastward upon 128th Street East. Drive 1.8 miles, then turn right upon Rhodes Lake Road. Stay on this road for another 1.5 miles to your destination near a sharp bend in the road. When I last visited this falls, the large parking area was inexplicably closed; you may need to find a wide spot elsewhere to safely park.

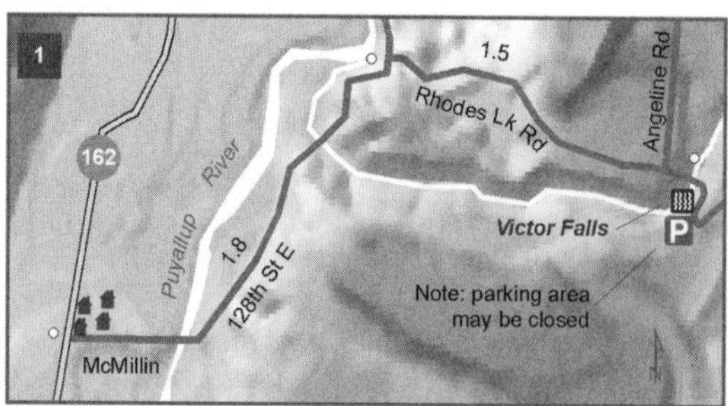

Victor Falls

VICTOR FALLS ★★★

MAGNITUDE: 53
ELEVATION: 320 feet
WATERSHED: Medium
APPROACH: Trail (easy)
LAT/LONG: 47.149232° N / 122.186092° W
USGS MAP: *Sumner* (1993)

Fennel Creek drops 50 to 60 feet into the Puyallup River Valley. Find the trailhead along the right side of the gorge rim. Be very careful while looking for it, as vehicles zoom around the bend with little regard for pedestrians. Follow the path a quick 0.1 mile to full views. Stay on the path, as there are no guardrails. It would be wise to leave the children home for this one.

MORE ONLINE:

Resort Falls ★★ USGS *Cumberland* (1993 ns)

2 CARBON RIVER

Few travelers to Mount Rainier National Park have visited its northwestern corner, favoring better-known places such as Sunrise and Paradise. It is now even less frequently visited, since the park's Carbon River Road has been closed, perhaps permanently, due to major damage caused in 2006 by significant flooding. Known by local residents as "Our Own Little Corner of the Mountain," it's even more so now. If you decide to backpack, you need to apply for a permit from the Longmire Wilderness Information Center.

Drive to the city of Buckley on State Route 410, then go south along State Route 165 through the historic mining towns of Wilkeson and Carbonado. As shown on the chapter map, the highway forks about 3 miles south of Carbonado. Bear left and follow the highway along the Carbon River for another 9 miles to the park entrance. Visitors are allowed to bicycle on the road, but bikes are not permitted on the trails.

 RANGER FALLS★★★★

MAGNITUDE: 70
ELEVATION: 2800 feet
WATERSHED: Small
APPROACH: Road & trail (fairly hard)
LAT/LONG: 46.983803° N / 121.854753° W
USGS MAP: *Mowich Lake* (1971)

This entry tumbles a total of 100 to 125 feet along Ranger Creek. The form is eye-catching because the lower portion splits into twin falls. From the park

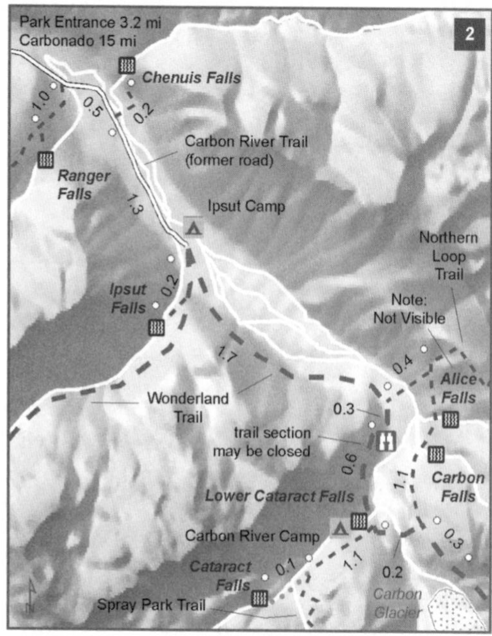

entrance, hike or bike 3.2 miles along Carbon River Trail to Green Lake Trailhead. The trail ascends moderately 1 mile to a marked spur leading to the falls.

CHENUIS FALLS ★★

MAGNITUDE: 17 (l)
ELEVATION: 2180 feet
WATERSHED: Medium
APPROACH: Road & trail (fairly hard)
LAT/LONG: 46.992981° N / 121.842458° W
USGS MAP: *Mowich Lake* (1971)

Water slides 70 to 100 feet across rock layers along Chenuis Creek. Continue 0.5 mile past Green Lake Trailhead (described earlier) to a parking turnout adjacent to the Carbon River. The falls is only 0.2 mile away. A log bridge provides access across the river.

IPSUT FALLS ★★★

MAGNITUDE: 38
ELEVATION: 2600 feet
WATERSHED: Small
APPROACH: Road & trail (fairly hard)
LAT/LONG: 46.970436° N / 121.832137° W
USGS MAP: *Mowich Lake* (1971)

This double falls along Ipsut Creek totals 40 to 60 feet. Hike or bike 1.3 miles beyond the trailhead for Chenuis Falls (described earlier), just beyond Ipsut Camp to the end of the old park road. Embark upon this spur path, which soon meets at a T-junction with the Wonderland Trail. Bear right (south) and walk a short distance to a signed spur trail leading 0.2 mile to the falls.

CARBON FALLS (U) ★★

MAGNITUDE: 50
ELEVATION: 3300 feet
WATERSHED: Very small
APPROACH: Road & trail or backpack (hard)
LAT/LONG: 46.956715° N / 121.789651° W
USGS MAP: *Mowich Lake* (1971 nl)

The only view of this tributary creek tumbling toward the Carbon River is from across the valley. The waterfall is best viewed when it is overcast or during the afternoon. Its rating decreases during the low-water periods of late summer. From Ipsut Camp (described earlier), hike 1.7 miles along Carbon River on the Wonderland Trail to a junction with Northern Loop Trail. Soon after passing the junction, you leave the forested area and in 0.3 mile catch sight of the slopes across the river. The waterfall should come into view from a distance: first the lower falls and then the upper portion. Alice Falls, USGS *Mowich Lake* (1971), is located along the next tributary north of this entry. Since the surrounding vegetation masks it from view, it has no scenic rating.

Note: Due to 2006 flooding, the Wonderland Trail was rerouted using a portion of Northern Loop Trail. If this remains the case, you will need to bushwhack the last 0.3 mile along the former route to the cross-valley vista.

CATARACT FALLS ★★★

MAGNITUDE: 63
ELEVATION: 4020 feet
WATERSHED: Small
APPROACH: Backpack & bushwhack (hard)
LAT/LONG: 46.94206° N / 121.812127° W
USGS MAP: *Mowich Lake* (1971)

Cataract Creek drops a total of 50 to 75 feet. If the National Park Service has reopened the Wonderland Trail across from Carbon Falls (described previously), hike 0.6 mile more to Lower Cataract Falls (u) USGS *Mowich Lake* (1971 ns). Otherwise it is a 1.7-mile detour, as shown on the accompanying map. From this point, embark up Spray Park Trail for 1.1 miles. Just as the way switchbacks up next to a tributary, backtrack a bit to find a path to bushwhack upon. In 1988, a large blowdown of trees blocked ready access to the descent, and the 0.1-mile spur path was abandoned. Before heading 8.8 miles back to the park entrance, take the worthy side trip to nearby Carbon Glacier, whose toe extends to the lowest elevation of any glacier in the contiguous United States.

MORE ONLINE:

Lower Cataract Falls (u) ★, mentioned earlier

3 MOWICH LAKE

While the road along the Carbon River is closed (described previously), fortunately the gravel extension of State Route 165 remains open to vehicles. Three miles beyond Carbonado, turn right at the junction, as shown on the regional map at the beginning of this chapter. The route provides imposing views of Mount Rainier; it reaches the boundary of Mount Rainier National Park in another 11 miles and ends 6 miles farther at Mowich Lake.

SPRAY FALLS ★★★★★

MAGNITUDE: 98
ELEVATION: 5100 feet
WATERSHED: Small (g)
APPROACH: Trail (moderate)
LAT/LONG: 46.915566° N / 121.842018° W
USGS MAP: *Mowich Lake* (1971)

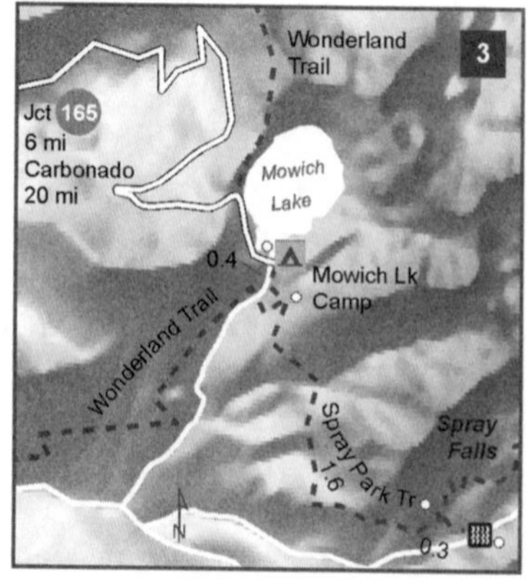

This enormous display descends 300 to 350 feet along Spray Creek and is 50 to 80 feet wide. It is fed mostly from meltwaters of snowfields in Spray Park. Reach the falls by taking a substantial

Spray Falls

but not overly difficult hike of 2.3 miles. Embark upon the Wonderland Trail at the southeast end of Mowich Lake, and proceed for 0.4 mile. Turn left onto Spray Park Trail, and follow it for 1.6 miles. Finally, turn right at Spray Falls Trail. You will be rewarded with an exciting view of the spectacle 0.3 mile farther.

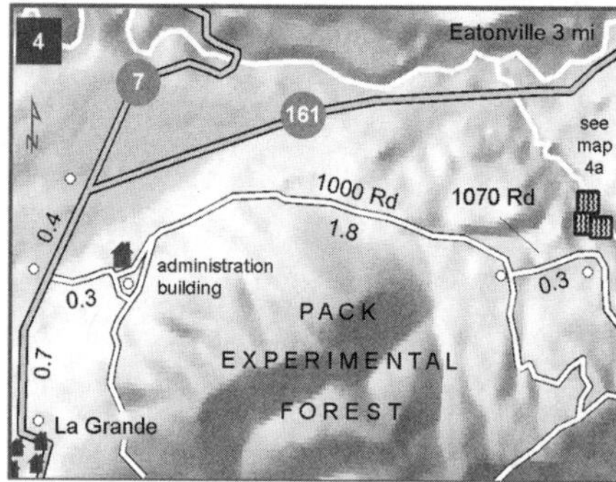

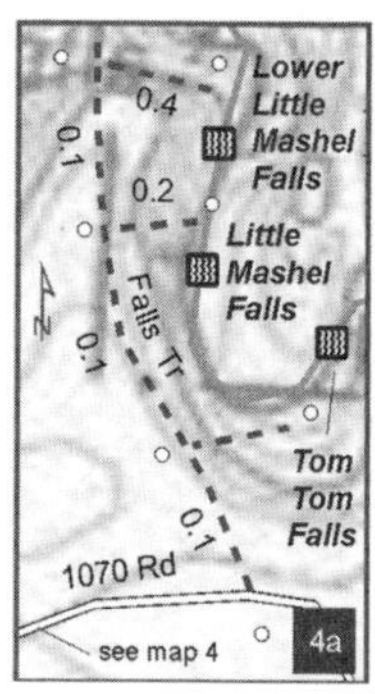

4 EATONVILLE

Nimble folks once accessed the falls of this area from the east—not any longer, not unless they want their car to be towed. Now you must drive into Charles Lathrop Pack Experimental Forest, and hike a substantial extra distance. Owned by the University of Washington's College of Forest Resources, the forest is dedicated to research in sustainable forestry and allows the public hiking privileges.

Drive into the forest entrance, located along State Route 7 about 0.4 mile south of the highway's junction with State Route 161 or 0.7 mile north of the hamlet of La Grande. Proceed 0.3 mile to the parking lot at the forest's administration building. Park here.

TOM TOM FALLS ★★

MAGNITUDE: 28
ELEVATION: 1080 feet
WATERSHED: Large
APPROACH: Trail (moderate)
LAT/LONG: 46.847557° N / 122.272802° W
USGS MAP: *Eatonville* (1990 ns)

The Little Mashel River slides steeply 25 to 30 feet over a rock escarpment. From the administration building, start walking along the northern section of 1000 Road, which visitors are not allowed to drive on. Hike 1.8 miles, staying on the main route until you reach 1070 Road to your left. From here, it's 0.3 mile to the start of Falls Trail on the left. Proceed about 0.1 mile to where the way drops down toward the river. Look for side paths, which quickly lead you upstream to the base of the cataract, which is situated just off of forest property.

LITTLE MASHEL FALLS ★★★

MAGNITUDE: 48
ELEVATION: 1040 feet
WATERSHED: Large
APPROACH: Trail (hard)
LAT/LONG: 46.848159° N / 122.273103° W
USGS MAP: *Eatonville* (1990)

From the base of Tom Tom Falls (described earlier), return to Falls Trail and head north. After 0.1 mile, you will encounter a spur path that should be marked with a blue blaze. Follow it steeply down for 0.2 mile to an excellent vista of a narrow fan descending 50 to 70 feet.

LOWER LITTLE MASHEL FALLS (U) ★★

MAGNITUDE: 59
ELEVATION: 980 feet
WATERSHED: Large
APPROACH: Trail (hard)
LAT/LONG: 46.849318° N / 122.272995° W
USGS MAP: *Eatonville* (1990 ns)

The Little Mashel River splits, and time and again it plunges and curtains 20 to 40 feet in four strands. From the main trail at the junction for Little Mashel Falls (described earlier), continue in the downstream direction for another 0.1 mile, turning once again at a blue-blazed spur and following these blazes 0.4 mile moderately steeply down to a partially obstructed vantage point. From here, it is 0.7 mile back to 1070 Road.

MORE ONLINE:
Deschutes Falls ★★ USGS *Bald Hill* (1990)
Upper Deschutes Falls (u) ★★ USGS *Bald Hill* (1990 ns)

5 BIG CREEK

Located southeast of Mount Rainier National Park, this drainage area reportedly harbors several waterfalls. Thus far, however, Cora Falls and its lower counterpart are the only ones found to be readily accessible.

7 CORA FALLS (U) ★★

MAGNITUDE: 43 (l)
ELEVATION: 3640 feet
WATERSHED: Very small
APPROACH: Trail (moderate)
LAT/LONG: 46.691665° N / 121.888131° W
USGS MAP: *Sawtooth Ridge* (1989 ns)

Depart State Route 706 onto Kernahan Road (Forest Service Road 52), whose junction is located 2.4 miles east of Ashford. Proceed 4.7 miles, then turn right on High Rock Lookout Road (Forest Service Road 84). Take this route 4.2 miles, and turn right onto Big Creek Road (Forest Service Road 8420). Continue 1.6 miles to the trailhead on the left side of the road. From here, it's a moderately steep 0.3-mile hike to the creek crossing at the 60- to 80-foot veil of water from the outlet of Cora Lake, the headwaters of Big Creek.

MORE ONLINE:
Lower Cora Falls (u) ★ USGS *Sawtooth Ridge* (1989 ns)

Denman Falls

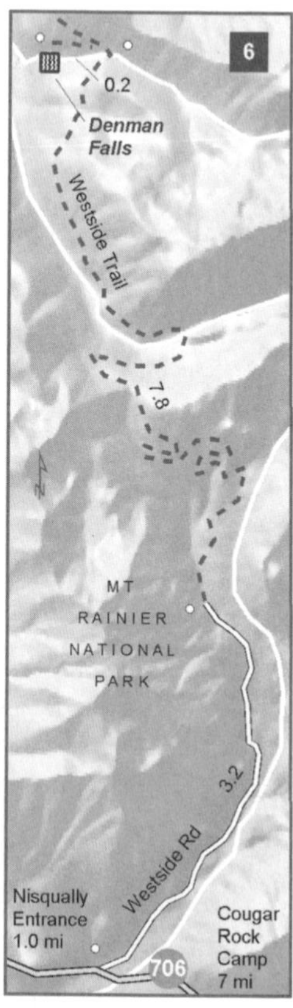

6 WESTSIDE ROAD

For the past three decades, most visitors have been turned back from exploring much of the southwestern corner of Mount Rainier National Park because the Westside Road repeatedly washed out. The National Park Service finally said "enough" and closed most of the route to vehicular traffic. By hiking and mountain biking I finally recently documented the following waterfall.

DENMAN FALLS ★★★

MAGNITUDE: 68
ELEVATION: 3520 feet
WATERSHED: Medium
APPROACH: Trail (hard)
LAT/LONG: 46.835698° N / 121.907979° W
USGS MAP: *Mount Wow* (1971)

St. Andrews Creek free-falls 122 feet in solitude. Drive north on Westside Road, located 1 mile from the park's western Nisqually entrance along State Route 706. Go 3.2 miles to the road's end. Trek 7.8 miles up and down the Westside Trail (the former road) to a path on the left, signed for Denman Falls Trail. Walk 0.2 mile to an airy vista looking from above and into the falls.

7 NISQUALLY RIVER

The south-central part of Mount Rainier National Park has a wealth of waterfalls. The area is bounded on the west by Cougar Rock Camp and on the east by the entrance to the Paradise area.

CARTER FALLS ★★★

MAGNITUDE: 61
ELEVATION: 3650 feet
WATERSHED: Medium (g)
APPROACH: Trail (fairly easy)
LAT/LONG: 46.764969° N / 121.76892° W
USGS MAP: *Mt. Rainier West* (1971)

This 50- to 80-foot entry is named for Harry Carter, who built much of the early Paradise Trail. Drive along State Route 706 to Cougar Rock Camp, located 8 miles east of the Nisqually entrance to the park. Embark eastward on the Wonderland Trail, which you can access just across the highway from the camp entrance. A sign directs you toward the falls, but you must first cross the Nisqually River on one of two footbridges. Hike 1.3 miles up the trail to the falls.

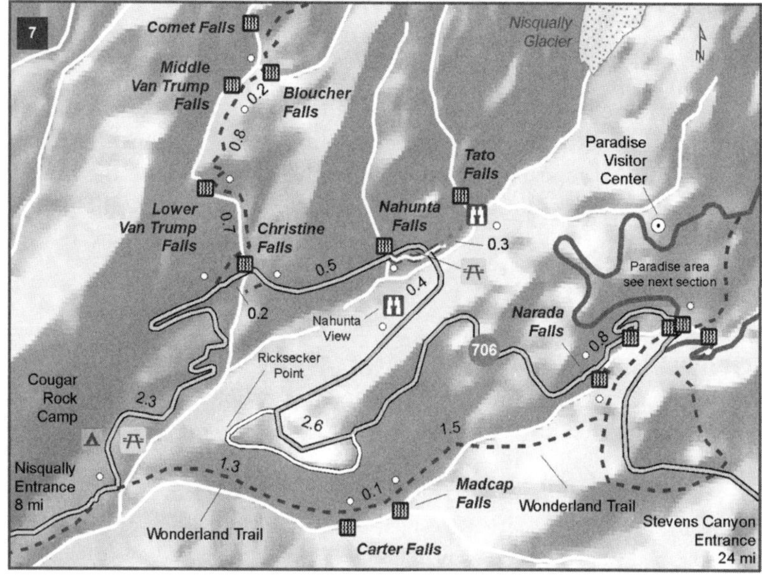

 MADCAP FALLS ★★

MAGNITUDE: 22
ELEVATION: 3800 feet
WATERSHED: Medium (g)
APPROACH: Trail (fairly easy)
LAT/LONG: 46.76616° N / 121.764027° W
USGS MAP: *Mt. Rainier West* (1971)

The Paradise River tumbles 20 to 30 feet. The USGS topographic map shows this feature about 0.2 mile farther upstream, but I could not find anything resembling falls in that location when I field-truthed this entry. Rather, continue a short distance past Carter Falls (described earlier) to an unsigned spur trail. Take it 0.1 mile to views of this cascade, a total of 1.4 miles from the trailhead.

 NARADA FALLS ★★★★

MAGNITUDE: 91
ELEVATION: 4400 feet
WATERSHED: Small (g)
APPROACH: Auto or trail (fairly easy)
LAT/LONG: 46.775022° N / 121.746067° W
USGS MAP: *Mt. Rainier West* (1971)

This popular tourist attraction veils 168 feet along bedrock before plunging another 73 feet to its base. A branch of the Theosophical Society of Tacoma named the falls after their guru, Narada, in 1893. Drive to the signed parking area located along State Route 706 about 0.8 mile west of the entrance to the Paradise area. Alternatively, continue hiking 1.5 miles eastward along the Wonderland Trail beyond Madcap Falls (described earlier).

Narada Falls

MIDDLE VAN TRUMP FALLS (U) ★★

MAGNITUDE: 61 (h)
ELEVATION: 4520 feet
WATERSHED: Small (g)
APPROACH: Trail (fairly hard)
LAT/LONG: 46.792051° N / 121.78173° W
USGS MAP: *Mt. Rainier West* (1971 nl)

Van Trump Creek possesses several series of falls. Four major descents are described in this and the next two summaries. This particular waterfall drops 40 to 50 feet and is easily seen from a few feet off the trail. Drive 2.3 miles east of Cougar Rock Camp to the signed Comet Falls Trailhead. The trail is steep but safe, ascending 1400 feet in 1.6 miles. It is usually free of snow after mid-July. You can hear the roar of Lower Van Trump Falls (u) USGS *Mt. Rainier West* (1971 nl) after the first 0.7 mile. The shape of the canyon hides it from view so it has no scenic rating. You encounter the Middle Falls after an additional 0.8 mile.

BLOUCHER FALLS ★★★

MAGNITUDE: 54 (h)
ELEVATION: 4600 feet
WATERSHED: Small (g)
APPROACH: Trail (fairly hard)
LAT/LONG: 46.792977° N / 121.778189° W
USGS MAP: *Mt. Rainier West* (1971 nl)

Van Trump Creek crashes 60 to 90 feet in tiered fashion. Do not give up at Middle Van Trump Falls (described earlier). This double drop is only 0.2 mile farther, and you are fewer than 100 yards away from the best of them all. I informally named this feature Van Trump Falls in earlier editions of this guidebook, but Bloucher is its official name.

COMET FALLS ★★★★★

MAGNITUDE: 106 (h)
ELEVATION: 5100 feet
WATERSHED: Small (g)
APPROACH: Trail (fairly hard)
LAT/LONG: 46.796091° N / 121.780228° W
USGS MAP: *Mt. Rainier West* (1971)

This spectacular 320-foot plunge is a classic example of a waterfall descending from a hanging valley, an escarpment that occurs where a tributary glacier did not erode as deeply as its larger relative. The viewpoint for this descent is just beyond Bloucher Falls (described earlier), 1.7 miles from the trailhead. If you haven't had enough aerobic exercise by now, Comet Falls Trail continues steeply for another mile toward the top of the cataract.

CHRISTINE FALLS ★★★

MAGNITUDE: 57
ELEVATION: 3680 feet
WATERSHED: Small (g)
APPROACH: Auto
LAT/LONG: 46.781017° N / 121.779734° W
USGS MAP: *Mt. Rainier West* (1971)

The stone masonry of the highway bridge picturesquely frames this 40- to 60-foot drop along the lower reaches of Van Trump Creek. Drive along State Route 706 eastward past Comet Falls Trailhead for 0.2 mile to the turnout on the east side of the bridge. Stairs lead quickly down to a view of this entry.

TATO FALLS ★★

MAGNITUDE: 45
ELEVATION: 4280 feet
WATERSHED: Small (g)
APPROACH: Bushwhack (fairly easy)
LAT/LONG: 46.785925° N / 121.759736° W
USGS MAP: *Mt. Rainier West* (1971)

Only a moderately distant view is available of this 40- to 60-foot display as it drops along an unnamed tributary of the Nisqually River. Park at an old gravel spur road 0.5 mile east of Van Trump Creek Bridge on State Route 706. Walk along the gravel spur 0.3 mile to its end. Look up the valley and to the left for the falls. Surrounding vegetation obscures closer views. Although Nahunta Falls USGS *Mt. Rainier West* (1971) is nearby, you need to drive 0.4 mile to the opposite side of the glacial trough to see it, albeit from a distance.

MORE ONLINE:

Nahunta Falls ★, mentioned earlier.
Pearl Falls ★ USGS *Mt. Rainier West* (1971)
Kautz Creek Falls (u) ★ USGS *Mt. Rainier West* (1971 nl)
Tatoosh Falls (u) ★ USGS *Mt. Rainier West* (1971 ns)

8 PARADISE

At 5800 feet of elevation, Paradise is the highest point to which you can drive on Mount Rainier's southern face. Travel 15 miles east from the park's Nisqually entrance or 24 miles west from the Stevens Canyon entrance along the park's extension of State Route 706. The contemporary-looking visitors center and the traditionally rustic Paradise Inn are located about 2 miles off the main road and are accessible via the Paradise Loop Road.

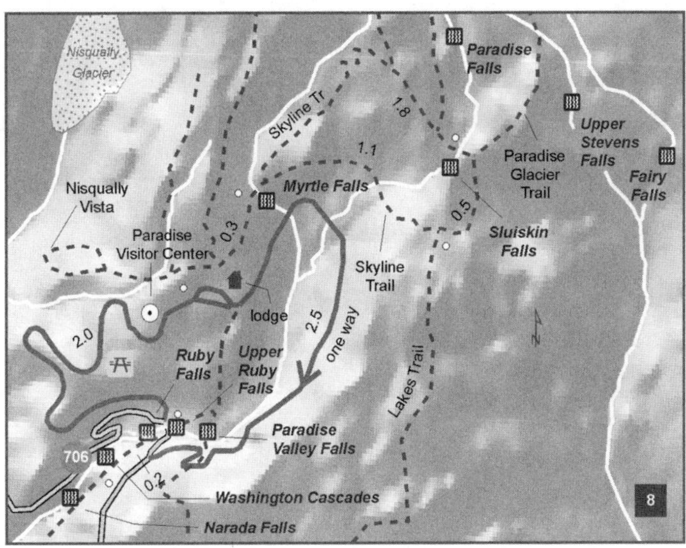

☐ RUBY FALLS ★★

MAGNITUDE: 48 (h)
ELEVATION: 4780 feet
WATERSHED: Small (g)
APPROACH: Trail (easy) or auto
LAT/LONG: 46.778446° N / 121.739566° W
USGS MAP: *Mt. Rainier East* (1971 ns)

Before departing the main highway, park at the unsigned turnout at the road junction to Paradise, and admire several modest descents along the Paradise

Paradise Valley Falls

River. The first is this entry. Walk a couple of hundred feet along the downstream trail for the best view.

WASHINGTON CASCADES ★★

MAGNITUDE: 33
ELEVATION: 4600 feet
WATERSHED: Small (g)
APPROACH: Trail (fairly easy)
LAT/LONG: 46.777931° N / 121.742505° W
USGS MAP: *Mt. Rainier East* (1971 ns)

Capture an idyllic view of five small falls along the Paradise River interspersed with rapids. What each 10- to 15-foot tier lacks in stature, collectively the 60- to

70-foot sum is greater than the individual parts. From Ruby Falls (described earlier) walk downstream 0.2 mile along Narada Falls Trail. Each tier comes into view individually, culminating in a trailside vista of them all when the route bends to the right.

MYRTLE FALLS ★★★

MAGNITUDE: 34 (l)
ELEVATION: 5560 feet
WATERSHED: Small (g)
APPROACH: Trail (easy)
LAT/LONG: 46.791331° N / 121.732442° W
USGS MAP: *Mt. Rainier East* (1971 ns)

This entry provides one of the signature views of Mount Rainier, as Edith Creek tumbles 60 to 80 feet in the foreground. Find the Skyline Trail, which begins next to Paradise Inn. Walk an easy 0.3 mile to a stairway, descending to the overlook for a superb vista.

SLUISKIN FALLS ★★★

MAGNITUDE: 40 (l)
ELEVATION: 5920 feet
WATERSHED: Small (g)
APPROACH: Trail & bushwhack (moderate) or auto
LAT/LONG: 46.793418° N / 121.716992° W
USGS MAP: *Mt. Rainier East* (1971)

A distant view of this 300-foot slide along the Paradise River is available from the 360-degree observation floor of the visitors center. For a closer vantage point, go just past Myrtle Falls (described earlier), and take the southern loop of the Skyline Trail to its junction with Lakes Trail, 1.4 miles from the trailhead. Bear left at the trail junction. Proceed another 0.5 mile, passing in succession the Paradise Glacier Trailhead, the Stevens-Van Trump historic monument, and a footbridge crossing the Paradise River.

Proceed a few hundred yards farther to a view of the top portion of the falls. Short side spurs from the trail provide full views. Children and nervous adults should stay on the main trail, since the spurs end abruptly at cliffs. Either return the way you came, or continue on for 2.1 miles to complete the northern portion of the loop. The falls was named for an American Indian guide who aided Hazard Stevens and P. B. Van Trump in the first recorded climb of Mount Rainier in 1870.

MORE ONLINE:
Upper Ruby Falls (u) ★ USGS *Mt. Rainier East* (1971 ns)
Paradise Valley Falls (u) ★ USGS *Mt. Rainier East* (1971 ns)
Paradise Falls (u) ★ USGS *Mt. Rainier East* (1971 nl)

9 STEVENS CANYON

It is no exaggeration to say that the National Park Service's eastward extension of State Route 706 is one of the most scenic roads ever engineered. The Stevens Canyon stretch is not as convoluted as other sections of the route, but its construction was just as daring an undertaking. The view across the canyon from the Wonderland Trail confirms that judgment. The fine line of the highway can be seen cut into the side of Stevens Ridge more than 400 feet above the canyon floor.

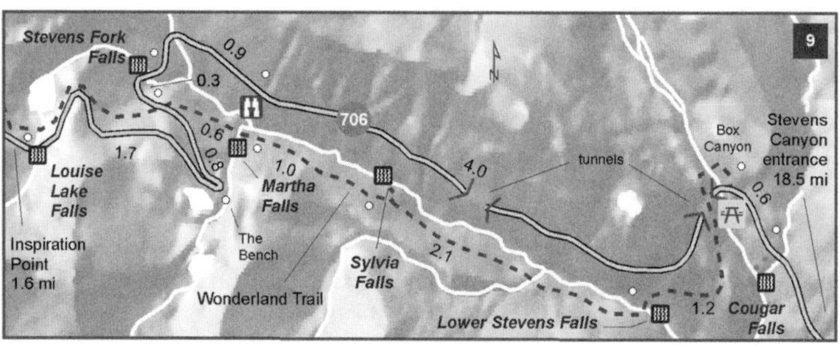

 LOUISE LAKE FALLS (U) ★★

MAGNITUDE: 33
ELEVATION: 4800 feet
WATERSHED: Very small
APPROACH: Auto
LAT/LONG: 46.765748° N / 121.718162° W
USGS MAP: *Mt. Rainier East* (1971 ns)

One fork of the headwaters feeding Louise Lake rushes a total of 20 to 30 feet downward before descending below the roadway. Drive to unsigned turnouts on either side of the bridge located 1.6 miles east of Inspiration Point (2.8 miles west of Stevens Fork Falls, described later). After viewing the cataract, gander over the downstream side of the bridge. You will see the top of a third tier as the unnamed drainage takes a plunge on its way to the lake. How many waterfalls are in this basin? Every time I visit, I find another unmapped one.

STEVENS FORK FALLS (U) ★★

MAGNITUDE: 36
ELEVATION: 4030 feet
WATERSHED: Very small
APPROACH: Auto
LAT/LONG: 46.775874° N / 121.7031° W
USGS MAP: *Mt. Rainier East* (1971 ns)

Here is another roadside cataract, this one of an unnamed tributary pouring 20 to 25 feet on its way to Stevens Creek. Drive to an unsigned turnout 2.8 miles east of Louise Lake Falls (described earlier) and 0.9 mile west of the viewpoint for Martha Falls (described later).

MARTHA FALLS ★★★★

MAGNITUDE: 80
ELEVATION: 3680 feet
WATERSHED: Small
APPROACH: Auto or trail (fairly easy)
LAT/LONG: 46.767086° N / 121.694022° W
USGS MAP: *Mt. Rainier East* (1971)

Water spills 125 to 150 feet along Unicorn Creek. It can be viewed at a moderate distance from the highway or close up from the trailside. Sightseers in cars can drive along SR 706 to the Martha Falls wayside, located 0.9 mile east of Stevens Fork Falls (described earlier) and 4 miles west of Box Canyon. Hikers can access the Wonderland Trail where it intersects the highway 0.8 mile north of The Bench or 0.3 mile south of Stevens Fork Falls. Embark upon the trailhead on the east side of the road, where the path winds moderately down 0.6 mile to a footbridge overlooking the falls.

SYLVIA FALLS ★★★

MAGNITUDE: 38 (l)
ELEVATION: 3080 feet
WATERSHED: Medium (g)
APPROACH: Trail (moderate)
LAT/LONG: 46.764984° N / 121.676277° W
USGS MAP: *Mt. Rainier East* (1971)

Stevens Creek tumbles 80 to 100 feet over a rock step within Stevens Canyon. Continue along the Wonderland Trail past Martha Falls (described earlier) for an additional mile. Look for an unsigned, but well-worn, spur trail that quickly leads to a view of the descent.

LOWER STEVENS FALLS (U) ★★

MAGNITUDE: 23
ELEVATION: 2580 feet
WATERSHED: Medium (g)
APPROACH: Trail (moderate)
LAT/LONG: 46.754665° N / 121.641515° W
USGS MAP: *Mt. Rainier East* (1971 nl)

Water cascades 30 to 40 feet over granite bedrock along Stevens Creek. Hike 1.2 miles south from Box Canyon on the Wonderland Trail, or continue 2.1 miles past Sylvia Falls (described earlier) for a total of 3.7 miles from the westward trailhead, to the footbridge above the falls.

COUGAR FALLS ★★★

MAGNITUDE: 65
ELEVATION: 2800 feet
WATERSHED: Medium
APPROACH: Bushwhack (moderate)
LAT/LONG: 46.759795° N / 121.628641° W
USGS MAP: *Mt. Rainier East* (1971)

This impressive 100- to 125-foot plunge shoots through a tight gorge. The hike to it is not recommended for children. Drive southeast from Box Canyon along SR 706 for 0.6 mile to the unsigned turnout immediately northwest of the Nickel Creek Bridge. Walk down the primitive trail to direct views of the falls in 0.1 mile. Stay away from the bare rock surfaces near the creek. There are no guardrails along the precipitous rim, which slopes sharply into the steep canyon!

MORE ONLINE:

Fairy Falls ★ USGS *Mt. Rainier East* (1971)

Upper Stevens Falls (u) ★ USGS *Mt. Rainier East* (1971 nl)

10 UPPER OHANAPECOSH

This popular area near the southeast entrance of Mount Rainier National Park boasts hot springs and a stand of forest giants in addition to waterfalls. Walk a short distance from Ohanapecosh Camp to the natural setting of the hot springs. Feel dwarfed by the Grove of the Patriarchs between the Stevens Canyon entrance and Olallie Creek.

1 SILVER FALLS ★★★

MAGNITUDE: 55 (h)
ELEVATION: 2000 feet
WATERSHED: Large
APPROACH: Trail (easy)
LAT/LONG: 46.752268° N / 121.559611° W
USGS MAP: *Chinook Pass* (1987)

Rushing water thunders 30 to 40 feet into a pool. Limit your views to those available from the trail and designated vantage points. While the falls do not look dangerous, the tumultuous river has claimed the lives of many who failed to heed the posted warnings.

From the Stevens Canyon entrance drive 0.3 mile south along State Route 123 to the East Side Trailhead on the right (west) side of the road. A short trail leads down to the bottom of the gorge and the falls along the Ohanapecosh River. A pair of trails from Ohanapecosh Camp also provides a leisurely 1-mile stroll to the falls. There are three smaller descents immediately upstream and one downstream from the main falls.

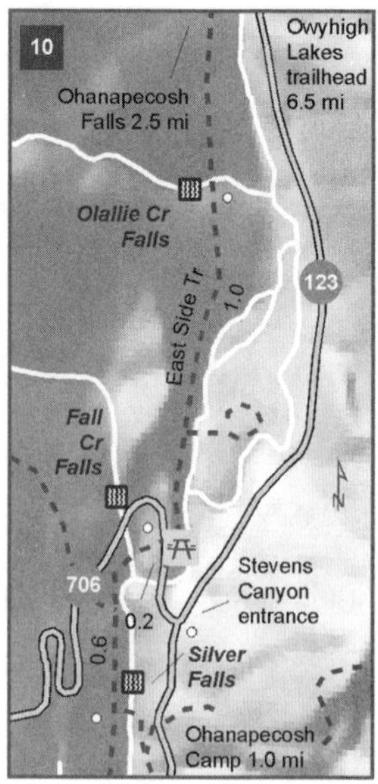

FALL CREEK FALLS (U) ★★

MAGNITUDE: 24 (l)
ELEVATION: 2280 feet
WATERSHED: Very small
APPROACH: Auto
LAT/LONG: 46.759825° N / 121.560663° W
USGS MAP: *Chinook Pass* (1987 ns)

Fall Creek drops 30 to 50 feet, nearly spraying onto the highway before flowing beneath it. It deserves a lower rating during the low-water periods of late summer. You can glimpse this entry from the car from State Route 706 just 0.2 mile from the Stevens Canyon entrance. If you wish to linger, stop at the parking area 0.1 mile past the entrance and walk up the road.

MORE ONLINE:
Olallie Creek Falls (u) ★ USGS *Chinook Pass* (1987 nl)

11 CHINOOK CREEK

This pleasant collection of waterfalls lies along a sparsely used but easily accessible trail system within Mount Rainier National Park. Drive to the Owyhigh Lakes Trailhead next to State Route 123, located 6.5 miles north of the Stevens Canyon entrance and 5 miles south of Cayuse Pass. Alternatively, hikers can continue north past Olallie Creek (refer to the previous section) along the East Side Trail.

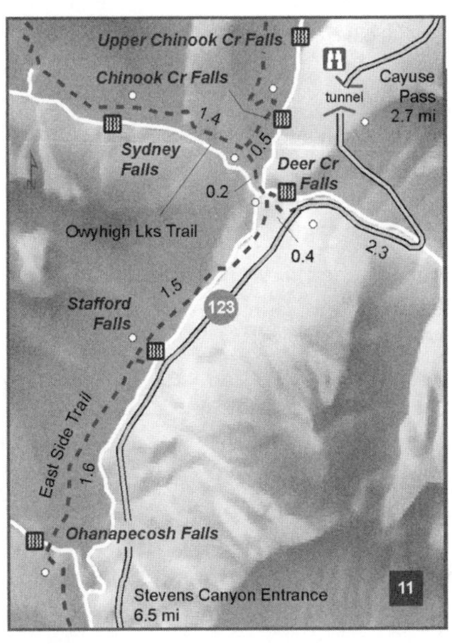

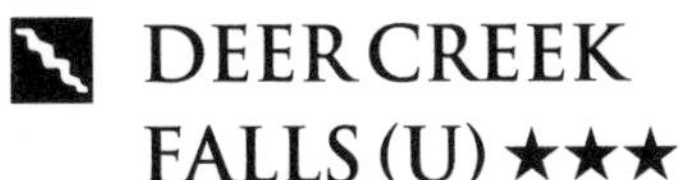

DEER CREEK FALLS (U) ★★★

MAGNITUDE: 45
ELEVATION: 3000 feet
WATERSHED: Medium
APPROACH: Trail (fairly easy)
LAT/LONG: 46.83434° N / 121.536622° W
USGS MAP: *Chinook Pass* (1987 nl)

Deer Creek cascades steeply 60 to 80 feet on the way to its confluence with Chinook Creek. Wind down Owyhigh Lakes Trail, reaching Deer Creek in 0.2 mile. Look back upstream into the small gorge to see the falls.

CHINOOK CREEK FALLS (U) ★★

MAGNITUDE: 54
ELEVATION: 3120 feet
WATERSHED: Medium
APPROACH: Trail (moderate)
LAT/LONG: 46.84118° N / 121.537566° W
USGS MAP: *Chinook Pass* (1987 nl)

This series of steep cascades totaling 75 to 100 feet descends from Chinook Creek. Views of it are partially obstructed by trees in the foreground. From Deer Creek Falls (described earlier), continue hiking a short distance farther to the East Side Trail. Turn right at the junction and proceed 0.2 mile, passing the junction with Owyhigh Lakes Trail. Go 0.5 mile farther, where the falls are visible just before the trail switchbacks uphill.

SYDNEY FALLS ★★★★

MAGNITUDE: 65
ELEVATION: 3520 feet
WATERSHED: Small
APPROACH: Trail & bushwhack (fairly hard)
LAT/LONG: 46.8403° N / 121.559045° W
USGS MAP: *Chinook Pass* (1987 nl)

Kotsuck Creek zigzags 125 to 150 feet over a bulbous escarpment. The best views, however, require a short bushwhack not recommended for children. From its junction with the East Side Trail (described earlier), ascend moderately along Owyhigh Lakes Trail. You reach an uninspiring view at the top of the falls in 1.4 miles. For a better vista, retrace your steps down the trail, then carefully make your way through the woods to the canyon rim facing the falls. I unofficially called it Kotsuck Creek Falls in prior editions of this guidebook.

STAFFORD FALLS ★★★

MAGNITUDE: 48
ELEVATION: 2700 feet
WATERSHED: Large
APPROACH: Trail (fairly easy)
LAT/LONG: 46.820422° N / 121.551921° W
USGS MAP: *Chinook Pass* (1987)

Water plummets 30 to 40 feet into a large pool along Chinook Creek. Follow the East Side Trail south from its junction with the Deer Creek access (described earlier). An easy 1.5 miles later, an unsigned but well-worn spur trail quickly leads to this pretty descent.

OHANAPECOSH FALLS (U) ★★★★

MAGNITUDE: 56
ELEVATION: 2400 feet
WATERSHED: Medium (g)
APPROACH: Trail (moderate)
LAT/LONG: 46.804518° N / 121.56486° W
USGS MAP: *Chinook Pass* (1987 nl)

This tiered punchbowl waterfall drops 50 to 75 feet along the grayish waters of the Ohanapecosh River. The color of the water is due to ground-up rock

Pass Falls

called glacial flour being carried by this glacier-fed stream. Continue south past Stafford Falls (described earlier) for 1.6 miles to the point where the East Side Trail crosses the Ohanapecosh River, a total of 3.5 miles from SR 123, or 2.5 miles north of Olallie Creek Falls (see the *Computer Companion*). The best view is just south of the footbridge, a few feet off the trail.

MORE ONLINE:

Upper Chinook Creek Falls (u) ★ USGS *Chinook Pass* (1987 ns)

12 CAYUSE PASS

PASS FALLS (U) ★★

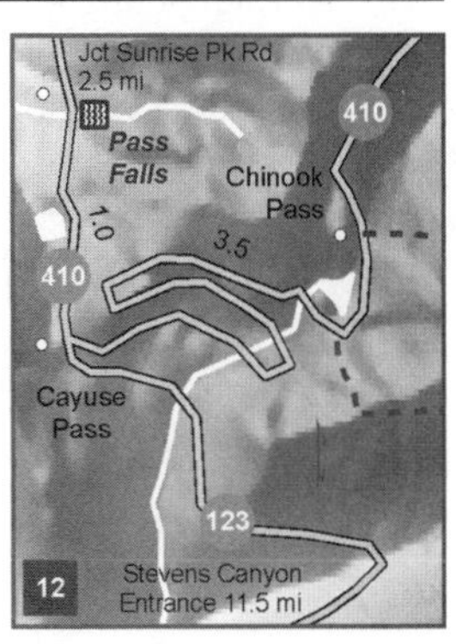

MAGNITUDE: 25
ELEVATION: 4460 feet
WATERSHED: Very small
APPROACH: Auto
LAT/LONG: 46.879152° N / 121.538789° W
USGS MAP: *White River Park* (1971 ns)

This is one of the best of the multitude of seasonal roadside waterfalls in the national park. Drive 1 mile north of Cayuse Pass, and park along an unsigned turnout on the west side of the road. This triple-tiered drop totaling 30 to 50 feet is easy for southbounders to miss; it's safest to simply continue to Cayuse Pass and backtrack.

MORE ONLINE:
Dewey Lake Falls (u) ★ USGS *Cougar Lake* (2000 ns)

13 CAMP SHEPPARD

Camp Sheppard is a Boy Scouts of America site, but visitors are welcome to use the trail system. In fact, the Boy Scouts blazed the pathways for that purpose. The entrance to the camp is along State Route 410, 10.9 miles south of Greenwater and 5 miles north of Mount Rainier National Park.

SKOOKUM FALLS ★★

MAGNITUDE: 32 (l)
ELEVATION: 2920 feet
WATERSHED: Very small
APPROACH: Auto
LAT/LONG: 47.050389° N / 121.576613° W
USGS MAP: *Sun Top* (1986 nl)

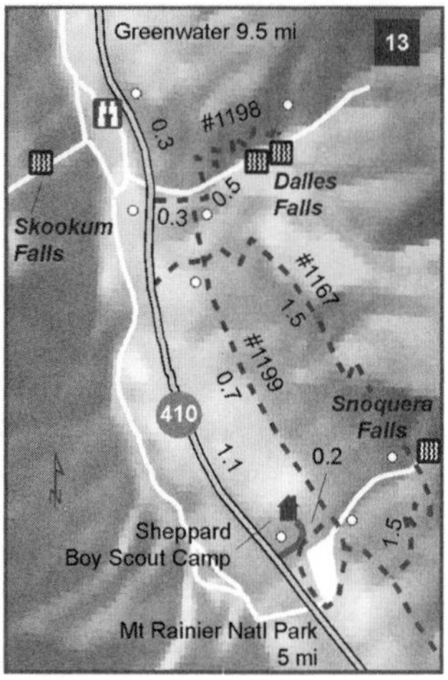

Skookum Creek can be seen from a moderate distance as silvery threads descending 150 to 200 feet in two primary tiers. This falls is located within White River Ranger District of Mount Baker-Snoqualmie National Forest. Drive 1.4 miles north of Camp Sheppard Boy Scout camp along SR 410 to an unsigned turnout. From this point enjoy a cross-valley view of the cataract.

MORE ONLINE:
Snoquera Falls ★ USGS *Sun Top* (1986 nl)
Dalles Falls ★ USGS *Sun Top* (1986 ns)
Doe Falls, USGS *Sun Top* (1986 ns) EXPLORE!

14 RAINIER VALLEY

For an excellent example of a glacial trough shaped by the enormous erosive powers of an alpine glacier, look down from Chinook Pass and admire the characteristic steep-sided, U-shaped form of Rainier Valley. The glacier has long since disappeared, with the Rainier Fork and American River now flowing along the valley floor. The pass was also formed by glacial activity and is what is known geomorphically as a "col," a notch eroded in a ridge by glaciers flowing from either side. The following pair of waterfalls are located within wilderness areas of Naches Ranger District, Okanogan-Wenatchee National Forest.

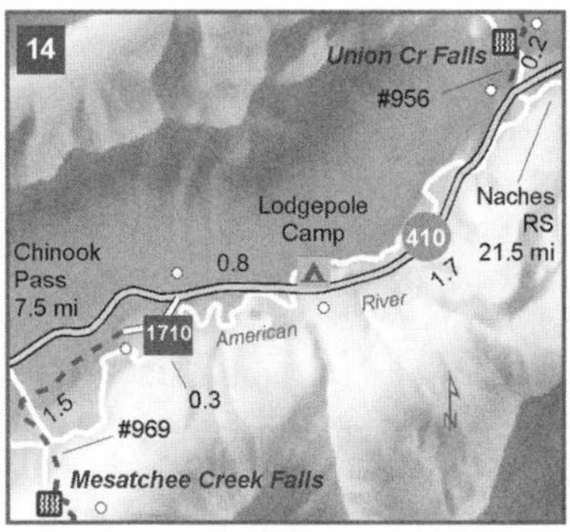

7 MESATCHEE CREEK FALLS ★★★

MAGNITUDE: 72
ELEVATION: 3840 feet
WATERSHED: Small

APPROACH: Trail (fairly hard)
LAT/LONG: 46.89421° N / 121.414608° W
USGS MAP: *Norse Peak* (2000 nl)

Mesatchee Creek Falls

Water shimmers 100 feet along Mesatchee Creek, which is located within William O. Douglas Wilderness. Drive 7.5 miles east from Chinook Pass on State Route 410, and turn south on Forest Service Road 1710. Drive 0.3 mile to the end of this gravel route to the trailhead for Mesatchee Creek Trail 969. After crossing Morse Creek and the American River, the trail steepens considerably and reaches an open vista of the descent after 1.5 miles.

7 UNION CREEK FALLS ★★★

MAGNITUDE: 64
ELEVATION: 3520 feet
WATERSHED: Medium
APPROACH: Trail (fairly easy)
LAT/LONG: 46.936525° N / 121.360921° W
USGS MAP: *Goose Prairie* (2000)

This picturesque 40- to 60-foot drop along Union Creek is located within Norse Peak Wilderness. Turn into the parking and picnic area at Union Creek Trail 956, located 10 miles east of Chinook Pass. Follow the trail about 0.2 mile to a well-traveled but unmarked spur that quickly leads to the cataract.

MORE ONLINE:
Copper Creek Falls (u) ★ USGS *Bumping Lake* (2000 ns)
Lower Deep Creek Falls (u) ★★ USGS *Bumping Lake* (2000 ns)
Lower Bumping River Falls (u) ★★★ USGS *Cougar Lake* (2000 ns)
Bumping River Falls (u) ★★ USGS *Cougar Lake* (2000 nl)

15 NACHES

The following three waterfalls are situated within the rain shadow of the Cascades in ponderosa pine and Douglas-fir forests within Naches Ranger District, Okanogan-Wenatchee National Forest, and thus are best visited during a wet spell. The point of departure for all three is the junction of State Route 410 and Little Naches Road (Forest Service Road 19), located 23.5 miles east of Chinook Pass and 38 miles northwest of Yakima.

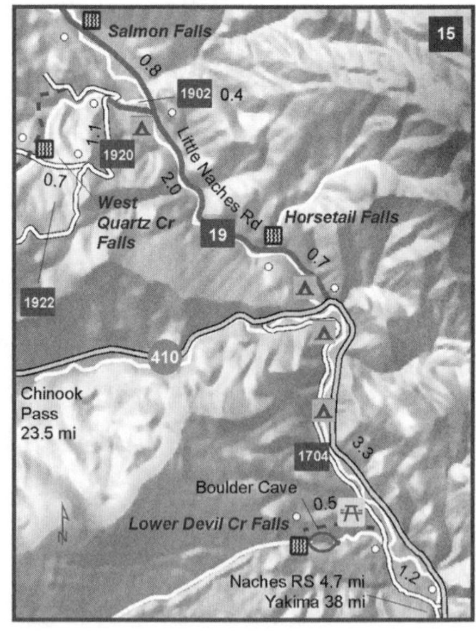

WEST QUARTZ CREEK FALLS ★★

MAGNITUDE: 35 (l)
ELEVATION: 3160 feet
WATERSHED: Very small
APPROACH: Trail (fairly easy)
LAT/LONG: 47.006572° N / 121.156118° W
USGS MAP: *Mount Clifty* (1989 ns)

Low-volume West Quartz Creek plummets 150 to 175 feet into a canyon. Drive about 2.7 miles north along Little Naches Road (Forest Service Road 19), and turn left onto Forest Service Road 1902, proceeding 0.4 mile to gravel Forest Service Road 1920. Turn left again and drive 1.1 miles, then bear right onto Forest Service Road 1922 and go 0.7 mile to the creek crossing. Walk down the trail 0.1 mile to trailside views back into the falls. Be careful at the unfenced canyon rim, which drops a sheer 200 feet.

SALMON FALLS ★★

MAGNITUDE: 23
ELEVATION: 2770 feet
WATERSHED: Large
APPROACH: Auto
LAT/LONG: 47.025314° N / 121.149917° W
USGS MAP: *Mount Clifty* (1989 ns)

Drive to Salmon Falls Interpretive Site to see this modest 10- to 15-foot drop along Little Naches River. From the junction of Forest Service Roads 19 and 1902 (described earlier), continue northward along the former for 0.8 mile to the parking area. You may get to see fish negotiating the descent or its adjacent natural-looking fish ladder.

LOWER DEVIL CREEK FALLS (U) ★★

MAGNITUDE: 16 (l)
ELEVATION: 2720 feet
WATERSHED: Medium
APPROACH: Trail (fairly easy)
LAT/LONG: 46.95781° N / 121.096487° W
USGS MAP: *Cliffdell* (2000 nl)

By itself, this 20- to 30-foot falls would deserve a lower rating, but this area's unique geology is not to be missed. The cataract is viewed from within a recess shaped like an amphitheater. Immediately downstream is Boulder Cave, which was formed when a landslide blocked the course of Devil Creek and the stream eventually eroded a tunnel through the debris. Bring a flashlight to explore the cavern.

Drive south on SR 410 for 3.3 miles beyond the junction with Little Naches Road (Forest Service Road 19). Depart the main road here, turning right to cross the bridge over the Naches River, and then turn right again, heading north on Naches River Road (Forest Service Road 1704). Park in 1.2 miles at Boulder

Cave Picnic Area. Hike an easy 0.5 mile along the canyon rim, then drop down to the base of the descent.

MORE ONLINE:

Horsetail Falls ★ USGS *Cliffdell* (2000)

16 RIMROCK LAKE

The Rimrock Lake area possesses several waterfalls near or next to roadways. All are located within Naches Ranger District, Okanogan-Wenatchee National Forest. The small hamlet of Rimrock, located below the spillway for the reservoir of Rimrock Lake, is the primary reference point for the beginning of this chapter section. The community is located 38 miles west of Yakima and 15 miles east of White Pass along U.S. Highway 12.

☐ SOUTH FORK FALLS ★★★

MAGNITUDE: 66
ELEVATION: 3840 feet
WATERSHED: Large
APPROACH: Trail (moderate)
LAT/LONG: 46.521564° N / 121.263208° W
USGS MAP: *Pinegrass Ridge* (2000 nl)

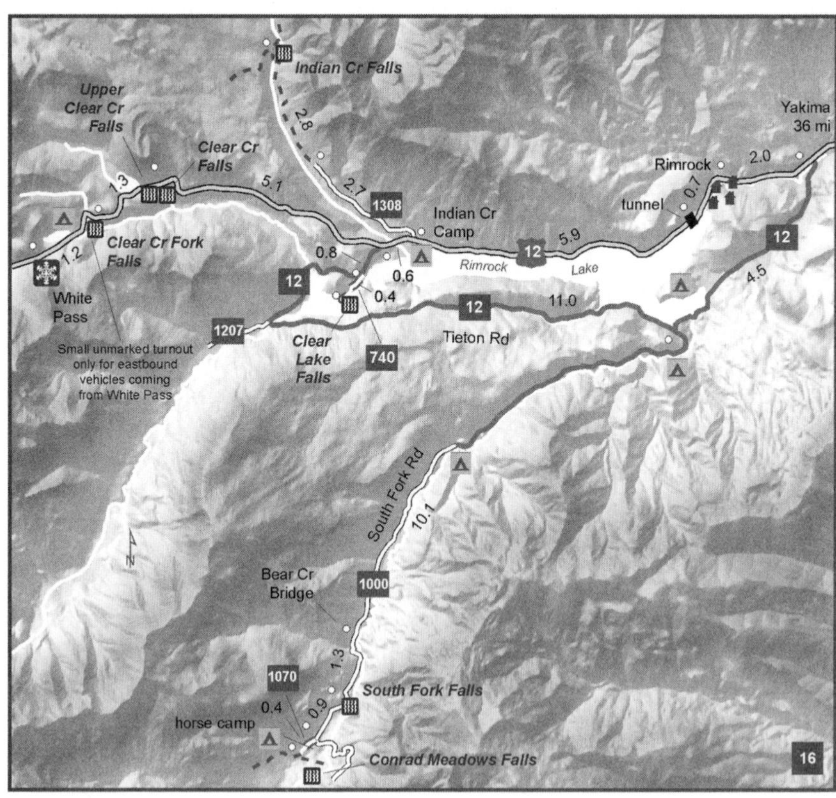

A misty vista makes this modest 30- to 40-foot curtain along the South Fork Tieton River an unforgettable experience. Drive 2 miles east of Rimrock, then turn right (south) on Tieton Road (Forest Service Road 12). After 4.5 miles, turn left (south) on South Fork Road (Forest Service Road 1000). Continue for 11.4 miles (1.3 miles past the bridge over Bear Creek) to an unsigned turnout and a moderately steep trail that leads to the river in 0.2 mile.

CONRAD MEADOWS FALLS (U) ★★

MAGNITUDE: 32
ELEVATION: 3880 feet
WATERSHED: Large
APPROACH: Trail (fairly easy)
LAT/LONG: 46.505911° N / 121.2784° W
USGS MAP: *Pinegrass Ridge* (2000 ns)

South Fork Tieton River bends in a tight gorge before descending 15 to 25 feet. From South Fork Falls (described earlier), continue 0.9 mile southward and bear right upon Forest Service Road 1070. Continue 0.4 mile to the entrance for a horse camp and park your vehicle. Start walking straight up the road, passing the latrines and an interpretive sign. Walk uphill, and after 0.1 mile turn upon a path to your left. (To the right is a gate signed Trail 1120.) Follow the path in the downstream direction, passing the top of the descent to a vista in another 0.1 mile.

CLEAR LAKE FALLS ★★

MAGNITUDE: 33
ELEVATION: 2960 feet
WATERSHED: Large
APPROACH: Auto
LAT/LONG: 46.628454° N / 121.269629° W
USGS MAP: *Spiral Butte* (1988 ns)

Water tumbles 40 to 60 feet at the outlet from Clear Lake and flows toward Rimrock Lake. Proceed 7.2 miles west of Rimrock, and turn right (south) off US 12 onto Tieton Road (Forest Service Road 12). Drive 0.8 mile to Clear Lake Road (Forest Service Road 740) and turn left. The pair of cascades is 0.4 mile away and is divided by a bridge spanning the drainage.

INDIAN CREEK FALLS ★★

MAGNITUDE: 72 (l)
ELEVATION: 4320 feet
WATERSHED: Small
APPROACH: Trail & bushwhack (hard)
LAT/LONG: 46.695654° N / 121.301188° W
USGS MAP: *Spiral Butte* (1988 nl)

Take a strenuous 2.8-mile trek into William O. Douglas Wilderness to this tantalizing 135- to 160-foot waterfall. Depart U.S. Highway 12 upon Indian Creek Road (Forest Service Road 1308), located just west of Indian Creek Camp, as shown on the map. Drive 2.7 miles to the end of the road. Start hiking along Indian Creek Trail 1106 steadily and surely up the valley for 2.3 miles. The way then switchbacks down to a stream ford and then steeply back up the opposite side over the next 0.4 mile.

Reach a clearing to the right in the next 0.1 mile where you will need to depart the trail a few yards to see Indian Creek cascading downward 35 to 40 feet before taking a 100- to 120-foot free fall. Carefully follow the unguarded rim of the small canyon to see more of the main display from above. This falls would deserve a higher rating if a full view were possible.

UPPER CLEAR CREEK FALLS (U) ★★★★

MAGNITUDE: 74
ELEVATION: 4000 feet
WATERSHED: Medium
APPROACH: Auto
LAT/LONG: 46.656035° N / 121.351506° W
USGS MAP: *Spiral Butte* (1988 nl)

Every waterfall collector should see this unusual configuration. One side of the 60- to 80-foot falls horsetails, while the other side veils downward into a pool adjacent to the main portion of the creek. Drive 12.3 miles west of Rimrock or 2.5 miles east of White Pass along US 12 to the signed Clear Creek Falls parking area. Take the short trail to the right (west) a few yards past the parking area to the fenced vista high above the falls.

CLEAR CREEK FALLS ★★★★★

MAGNITUDE: 99
ELEVATION: 3800 feet
WATERSHED: Medium
APPROACH: Auto
LAT/LONG: 46.656139° N / 121.349897° W
USGS MAP: *Spiral Butte* (1988)

Enjoy a grand canyon-rim view of this spectacular 300-foot plunge along Clear Creek. From the Clear Creek Falls parking area take the short trail to the left to the fenced viewpoint.

CLEAR CREEK FORK FALLS (U) ★★★

MAGNITUDE: 57
ELEVATION: 4120 feet
WATERSHED: Small
APPROACH: Bushwhack (fairly easy)
LAT/LONG: 46.648406° N / 121.375474° W
USGS MAP: *Spiral Butte* (1988 nl)

Otherworldly should be your first impression when you arrive at this surreal scene of an unnamed tributary of South Fork Clear Creek. It plummets 70 to 90 feet in the midst of columnar basalt, treacherous talus slopes of volcanic ash and gravel, shrubs, wildflowers, and coniferous forest. Its rating drops as summer wanes.

From the parking area for Upper Clear Creek Falls (described earlier), drive 2.5 miles westward to White Pass. Perform a U-turn, backtrack 1.2 miles, and park at the small unsigned turnout on the right side (south) of the road as

Clear Creek Falls

you cannot park on the north side. Walk through the woods toward the sound of the water. A marvelous open rimtop vista across the gorge is afforded in a couple hundred feet. Use caution.

17 LOWER OHANAPECOSH

Vacationers tend to zip past the northeast portion of Packwood Ranger District, Gifford Pinchot National Forest, on their way to Mount Rainier during the summer and to White Pass during the winter. Slow down. Better yet, stop and explore. The fine scenery includes, of course, waterfalls.

LAVA CREEK FALLS ★★★

MAGNITUDE: 86
ELEVATION: 2600 feet
WATERSHED: Medium
APPROACH: Auto
LAT/LONG: 46.667743° N / 121.508576° W
USGS MAP: *Ohanapecosh Hot Springs* (1989 nl)

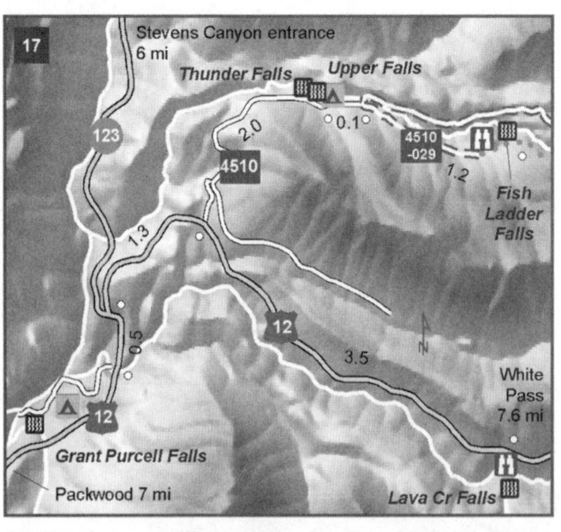

These braids of water rushing 200 to 250 feet down the facing canyon wall are hard to see on a sunny day. Drive along U.S. Highway 12 to an obscurely marked turnout 7.6 miles west of White Pass or 4.8 miles east of the junction with State Route 123. A viewpoint overlooks the Clear Fork Cowlitz River Canyon.

Lava Creek Falls

UPPER FALLS (U) ★★

MAGNITUDE: 35
ELEVATION: 2180 feet
WATERSHED: Medium
APPROACH: Auto
LAT/LONG: 46.710236° N / 121.539197° W
USGS MAP: *Ohanapecosh Hot Springs* (1989 ns)

Rushing water skips 25 to 35 feet across slabs of bedrock on Summit Creek. From U.S. Highway 12, 1.3 miles east of the junction with State Route 123, turn north on Summit Creek Road (Forest Service Road 4510). Drive 2 miles farther, and park at the unmarked turnout on the north side of the road. Follow the well-worn trail about 40 yards to these cascades.

THUNDER FALLS ★★★

MAGNITUDE: 72
ELEVATION: 2120 feet
WATERSHED: Medium
APPROACH: Trail & bushwhack (moderate)
LAT/LONG: 46.710185° N / 121.53983° W
USGS MAP: *Ohanapecosh Hot Springs* (1989 ns)

Close-up views of this 80-foot cataract spreading outward along Summit Creek are possible. From Upper Falls (described earlier) continue along the path in the downstream direction. The way becomes thin and steep toward the end, so it is recommended only for nimble hikers.

FISH LADDER FALLS ★★★

MAGNITUDE: 48
ELEVATION: 2760 feet
WATERSHED: Medium
APPROACH: Bushwhack (fairly hard)
LAT/LONG: 46.707368° N / 121.512224° W
USGS MAP: *Ohanapecosh Hot Springs* (1989)

Peer from a canyon-rim vantage point to enjoy this pristine 60-foot drop roaring along Summit Creek. Drive 0.1 mile past the trailhead for Thunder Falls (described earlier), and bear right on dirt Forest Service Road 4510-029. When I last visited it, most of the 1.2-mile route was overgrown with shrubs. Park at a dry ravine near the end of the road.

Walk up the route a short distance, bear right at a junction, and continue 0.1 mile to the top of a small knoll at a fire pit. Bushwhack another 0.1 mile through a clear-cut to an open vista hundreds of feet above the falls at an unguarded cliff. You may need to walk along the wooded canyon rim in one direction or the other to find the unmarked viewpoint.

MORE ONLINE:
Grant Purcell Falls ★ USGS *Ohanapecosh Hot Springs* (1989)

18 JOHNSON CREEK

RAINBOW FALLS ★★

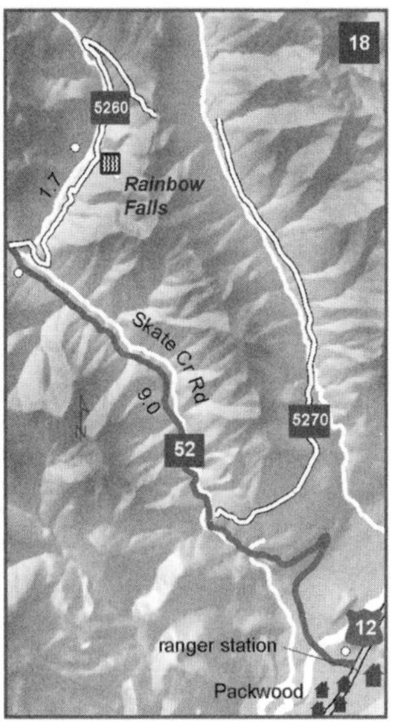

MAGNITUDE: 21 (t)
ELEVATION: 2900 feet
WATERSHED: Very small
APPROACH: Bushwhack (moderate) **USGS**
LAT/LONG: 46.691356° N / 121.752851° W
MAP: *Wahpenayo Peak* (1989 nl)

This 100-foot drop from an unnamed tributary of Johnson Creek is reduced to a trickle in late summer. It is located in Packwood Ranger District, Gifford Pinchot National Forest. Leave U.S. Highway 12 at Skate Creek Road (Forest Service Road 52), across from the Packwood Ranger Station.

In 9 miles, just after FS Road 52 crosses Skate Creek for the second time, turn right (northeast) onto Dixon Mountain Road (Forest Service Road 5260). Drive 1.7 miles farther and park along the road. Scramble 100 yards up the small draw to the base of the falls.

19 SILVERBROOK

HOPKINS CREEK FALLS (U) ★★

MAGNITUDE: 24 (l)
ELEVATION: 1600 feet
WATERSHED: Small
APPROACH: Trail (easy)
LAT/LONG: 46.537666° N / 121.84028° W
USGS MAP: *Purcell Mtn.* (1994 nl)

Water tumbles 50 to 75 feet in a narrow spot along Hopkins Creek, which is likely located on and accessible via private property; don't trespass if it is signed as such. Turn off U.S. Highway 12 onto Silverbrook Road, 5.5 miles east of Randle or 11.4 miles west of Packwood. Park at the wide spot to your immediate left. Find the unmarked trailhead just past the first driveway on the right. The well-worn path leads easily and quickly to the base of the cataract.

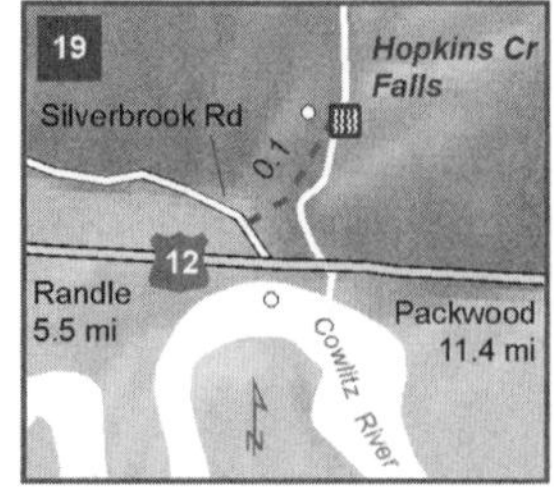

Covell Creek Falls
(Gifford Pinchot Country, Washington)

Shellburg Falls
(The Middle Cascades, Oregon)

Previous page: *Cave Falls (The Snake River Plain, Idaho)*

Dry Falls (The Inland Empire, Washington)

Palouse Falls (The Inland Empire, Washington)

South Fork Falls (Mount Rainier Region, Washington)

Opposite: *Wy'East Falls (The Columbia Gorge, Oregon)*

Husum Falls (The Columbia Gorge, Washington)

Q'emlin Falls (The Panhandle, Idaho)

Quartz Creek Falls (Gifford Pinchot Country, Washington)

Opposite: *Upper Clear Creek Falls (Mount Rainier Region, Washington)*

Elowah Falls (The Columbia Gorge, Oregon)

Yasko Falls
(The South Cascades, Oregon)

Rock Creek Falls (The Inland Empire, Washington)

Beaver Creek Falls (Southern Coast Range, Oregon)

Shoshone Falls (The Snake River Plain, Idaho)

Opposite: *Outlet Falls (Gifford Pinchot Country, Washington)*

Snoqualmie Falls (The North Cascades, Washington)

Pillar Falls (The Snake River Plain, Idaho)

Ludlow Falls (Olympics and Vicinity, Washington)

Rainy Lake and Falls (The North Cascades, Washington)

Dagger Falls (Central Wilderness Areas, Idaho)

Drift Creek Falls, (The Northern Coast Range, Oregon)

Next page: *Moyie Falls (The Panhandle, Idaho)*

WASHINGTON

GIFFORD PINCHOT COUNTRY

Gifford Pinchot National Forest is named after the pioneer of professional forestry in the United States. Pinchot was the first chief of the US Forest Service, from 1898 to 1910, serving under Presidents McKinley, Roosevelt, and Taft. During his tenure, the entire forest service system and administrative structure were developed. Pinchot's leadership in the conservation movement of this period was important to developing a policy of preserving and managing public lands.

There are 134 waterfalls known to occur within this region; 92 are referred to in this chapter. In addition, long ago Wayne Parsons, with the US Forest Service, informed me that he had inventoried more than 150 falls within Gifford Pinchot National Forest. (I wish I knew what happened to that list!) More falls have been discovered as time has marched on. Some have been made accessible, although a few jaw-dropping ones are limited to the domain of *extreme* bushwhackers.

The waterfalls of this region are the result of many different combinations of geologic forces, including volcanism, mountain-building, and glaciation. For more information, see the introduction to the chapter on Mount Rainier.

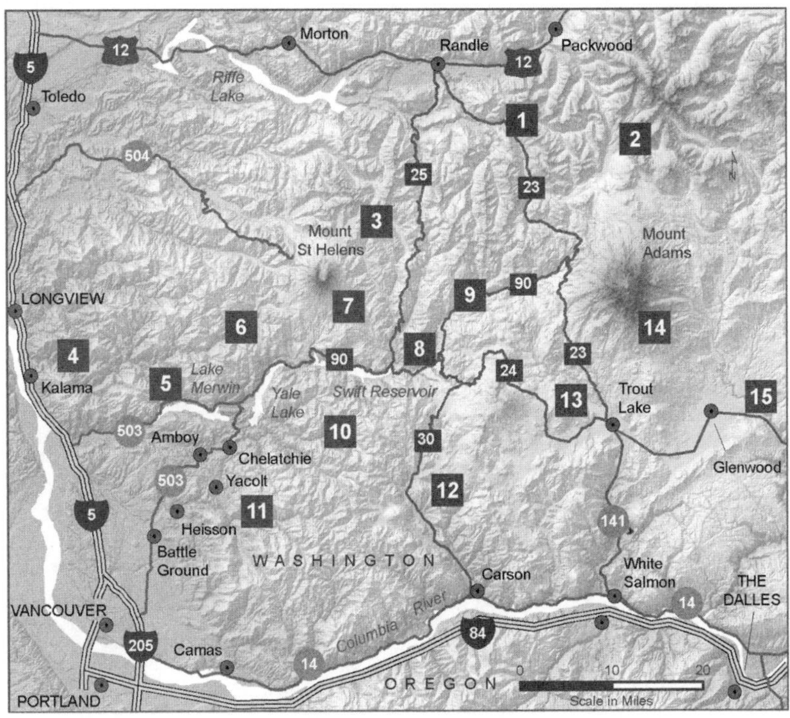

With the establishment of Mount St. Helens National Volcanic Monument following the volcano's catastrophic eruption on May 18, 1980, the administrative areas of the national forest were subsequently reconfigured. The other units are the Mount St. Helens National Volcanic Monument Administrative Area, Cowlitz Valley Ranger District, and Mount Adams Ranger District. All of these units offer a host of recreational opportunities, including, of course, a wealth of waterfalls.

1 NORTH FORK CISPUS RIVER

A multitude of falls occur along the tributaries of this drainage basin, with most of their flows decreasing to a trickle as summer progresses. All are located within Cowlitz Valley Ranger District.

BRIDAL FALLS (U) ★★

MAGNITUDE: 41
ELEVATION: 2040 feet
WATERSHED: Very small
APPROACH: Trail & bushwhack (fairly hard)
LAT/LONG: 46.423264° N / 121.849539° W
USGS MAP: *Tower Rock* (1994 ns)

This entry and the following pair of cataracts are all accessible via trails in the vicinity of the Cispus Learning Center, a facility whose mission is to support

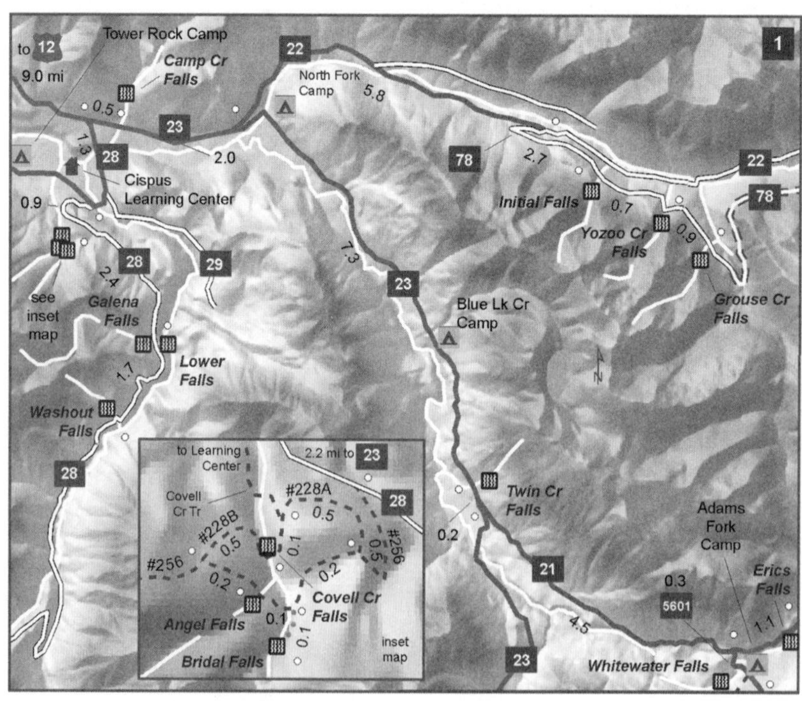

outdoor education and leadership training for young people. Learning opportunities are not only available to students but to adult groups as well. Perhaps you will encounter some of these folks during your hike.

Turn south off U.S. Highway 12 onto Randle–Lewis River Road (Forest Service Road 25) about 1.3 miles west of Randle Ranger Station; after 1 mile, turn left (east) on Cispus Road (Forest Service Road 23). Continue an additional 8 miles eastward along this route, then turn right onto Pinto Road (Forest Service Road 28), signed for the Cispus Learning Center and Tower Rock. Continue for 1.3 miles and bear left, staying on FS Road 28. From here, it is 0.9 mile to parking on the left for Burley Mountain Trail 256, whose trailhead is across the road.

The trail ascends steeply for 0.5 mile where it reaches a junction. For a loop trip to progressively better waterfalls, stay straight instead of bearing right. The route levels off then moderately descends to a stream in 0.2 mile. Gain a view of Bridal Falls by bushwhacking 0.1 mile up the unnamed creek. My nephew, Corey Gillum, discovered this falls, while we were exploring the area. I've named the 25- to 35-foot spray after its appearance.

ANGEL FALLS ★★★

MAGNITUDE: 30 (l)
ELEVATION: 2150 feet
WATERSHED: Very small
APPROACH: Trail (fairly hard)
LAT/LONG: 46.424004° N / 121.85205° W
USGS MAP: *Tower Rock* (1994 ns)

Water gracefully tumbles 120 to 150 feet down a mountainside. From the creek crossing for Bridal Falls (described above) continue 0.1 mile farther along the trail to the base of the cataract. It deserves a higher rating during wet periods and a lower one in dry spells.

COVELL CREEK FALLS ★★★

MAGNITUDE: 54
ELEVATION: 1800 feet
WATERSHED: Small
APPROACH: Trail (fairly hard)
LAT/LONG: 46.426134° N / 121.851084° W
USGS MAP: *Tower Rock* (1994 nl)

This falls, a 50- to 70-foot plunge also known as Curtain Falls, is the highlight of the hike. From Angel Falls (described earlier), proceed steeply up for 0.2 mile to the junction of Burley Mountain Trail 256 and Angel Falls Loop Trail 228B. Turn right and descend steeply down the path, reaching the cataract in 0.5 mile. Note the numerous hillside exposures of grayish deposits of volcanic ash.

Return to the parking area by continuing past the falls where Trail 228B ends in a short 0.1 mile. From here take the route to the right (the left turn goes to the Cispus Learning Center). This is Covell Creek Falls Trail 228A, which follows a hillside pitted with numerous rock shelters along the way. You meet Trail 256 once again in another 0.5 mile, completing the loop. Turn

Camp Creek Falls

left, and descend 0.5 mile back to the parking area. The overall journey to all three waterfalls is a 2.8-mile aerobic adventure. Note: The Forest Service uses a variant spelling of "Covel."

GALENA FALLS (U) ★★★

MAGNITUDE: 53
ELEVATION: 2000 feet
WATERSHED: Small
APPROACH: Bushwhack (fairly easy)
LAT/LONG: 46.404151° N / 121.823532° W
USGS MAP: *Tower Rock* (1994 nl)

Kudos to waterfall adventurer Bryan Swan for finding this entry and its smaller counterparts. Drive Pinto Road (Forest Service Road 28) southeastward 2.4 miles past the junction with Burley Mountain Trail 256 (described earlier). Park at the unmarked turnout along the left side of the road at signed Galena Creek. From here, it's a quick bushwhack up the creek to the base of this 70- to 85-foot gem.

CAMP CREEK FALLS ★★

MAGNITUDE: 48
ELEVATION: 1700 feet
WATERSHED: Medium
APPROACH: Trail (fairly easy)
LAT/LONG: 46.451767° N / 121.831204° W
USGS MAP: *Keel Mtn.* (1984 nl)

Camp Creek Falls Trail 260 goes 0.2 mile up to its namesake. The signed trailhead is located along Cispus Road (Forest Service Road 23), about 0.5 mile eastward from the junction with Forest Service Road 28. See nice side views of the stream glistening 30 feet down.

YOZOO CREEK FALLS ★★

MAGNITUDE: 18 (l)
ELEVATION: 3000 feet
WATERSHED: Very small
APPROACH: Auto
LAT/LONG: 46.429957° N / 121.667717° W
USGS MAP: *Blue Lake* (1994 ns)

Here, a roadside vantage point offers water veiling 25 to 40 feet from Yozoo Creek. Beyond the trailhead for Camp Creek Falls (described earlier), continue driving eastward along Cispus Road (Forest Service Road 23) for 2 miles to its junction with North Fork Cispus Road (Forest Service Road 22). Bear left onto FS Road 22 and proceed 5.8 miles, then turn right on Timonium Road (Forest Service Road 78) and, after another 3.4 miles, the falls will appear.

TWIN CREEK FALLS (U) ★★

MAGNITUDE: 20
ELEVATION: 2000 feet
WATERSHED: Very small
APPROACH: Auto
LAT/LONG: 46.374527° N / 121.726318° W
USGS MAP: *East Canyon Ridge* (1994 ns)

Twin Creek plunges 10 to 15 feet before sliding another 15 to 20 feet downward. This falls rating decreases as summer progresses. From the junction of Forest Service Road 23 and Forest Service Road 22 (described earlier), turn right, staying on FS Road 23. Drive 7.3 miles to an unsigned turnout about 0.2 mile before the road's junction with Forest Service Road 21. A view from the base of the cataract is only steps away.

WHITEWATER FALLS (U) ★★

MAGNITUDE: 28
ELEVATION: 2500 feet
WATERSHED: Large
APPROACH: Trail (easy)
LAT/LONG: 46.336229° N / 121.646796° W
USGS MAP: *East Canyon Ridge* (1994 ns)

While a 10- to 15-foot waterfall may not sound intimidating, this frothing torrent along the Cispus River demands respect. The raging waters are treacherous, so take special care next to the unguarded vantage points. From Twin Creek Falls (described earlier), continue 0.2 mile along Forest Service Road 23, then bear left upon Forest Service Road 21. Proceed 4.5 miles and turn right upon Forest Service Road 5601. Pass Adams Fork Camp, crossing a bridge over the Cispus River 0.3 mile beyond the last turn. Park here and follow the trail downstream a quick 0.1 mile to the falls.

ERICS FALLS (U) ★★★

MAGNITUDE: 50 (h)
ELEVATION: 2700 feet
WATERSHED: Large
APPROACH: Trail (fairly easy)
LAT/LONG: 46.345177° N / 121.627441° W
USGS MAP: *East Canyon Ridge* (1994 ns)

Water thunders 20 to 30 feet over a rock ledge. The unofficial name of the falls is in memory of a teenager who died here in the Cispus River. Drive 1.1 miles past Forest Service Road 5601 along Forest Service Road 21, and park at the unsigned turnout on the right. A few feet from the trailhead a preserved stump serves as a memorial to the drowning victim. It's only 0.1 mile down to the river where there is a second memorial at the base of a tree at the natural vista overlooking the falls.

MORE ONLINE:

Lower Galena Falls (u) ★ USGS *Tower Rock* (1994 ns)
Washout Falls (u) ★ USGS *Tower Rock* (1994 ns)
Initial Falls (u) ★ USGS *Blue Lake* (1994 ns)
Grouse Creek Falls (u) ★ USGS *Blue Lake* (1994 ns)
Echo Falls (u) ★ USGS *Vanson Peak* (1998 ns)
Cowlitz Falls ★ USGS *Cowlitz Falls* (1994), drowned by the Lake Scanewa reservoir

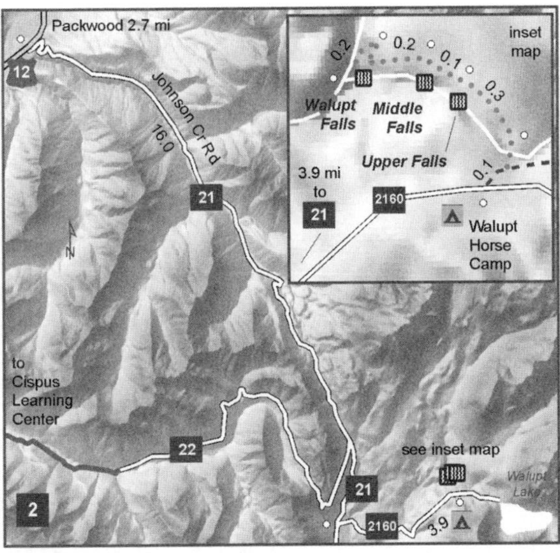

2 WALUPT LAKE

When I first read extreme kayaker Tom O'Keefe's description of and saw his photograph of Walupt Creek Falls, I knew I had to try to reach it. My first attempt several years ago failed, but fellow falls enthusiast Brian Swan has since found a successful and not overly difficult access route. As a bonus, you pass two additional cataracts en route to this little-known crown jewel of Goat Rocks Wilderness within Cowlitz Valley Ranger District.

Drive 2.7 miles southwest of Packwood along U.S. Highway 12, and turn south upon Johnson Creek Road (Forest Service Road 21). Proceed 16 miles along this route, then turn left upon Forest Service Road 2160. Drive 3.9 miles. A couple of hundred yards beyond the entrance to Walupt Horse Camp, park on the right. This excursion is recommended for experienced bushwhackers only.

☐ UPPER WALUPT CREEK FALLS (U) ★★

MAGNITUDE: 37
ELEVATION: 3700 feet
WATERSHED: Medium
APPROACH: Bushwhack (moderate)
LAT/LONG: 46.430549° N / 121.492687° W
USGS MAP: *Walupt Lake* (1970 ns)

Find an unmarked path across the road. Follow it a couple of hundred feet, then veer left along a side path to the stream. Find one of many logs that enable you to tightrope over the two channels of the creek. Get above the stream channel, and follow it downstream. There is no established path, but the sparse understory lets you maintain a steady pace.

Walupt Creek Falls

After 0.3 mile the creek begins dropping down into a gorge. Stay above the rim. Soon thereafter you come to a vista, with a couple of trees partially obscuring the 20- to 30-foot steeply sliding falls.

MIDDLE WALUPT CREEK FALLS (U) ★★★

MAGNITUDE: 60
ELEVATION: 3650 feet
WATERSHED: Medium
APPROACH: Bushwhack (moderate)
LAT/LONG: 46.430904° N / 121.494833° W
USGS MAP: *Walupt Lake* (1970 ns)

From Upper Walupt Creek Falls (described earlier), continue 0.1 mile along the gorge rim to partially obscured views of the stream pouring 30 to 40 feet downward.

WALUPT CREEK FALLS (U) ★★★★★

MAGNITUDE: 95
ELEVATION: 1790 feet
WATERSHED: Medium
APPROACH: Bushwhack (fairly hard)
LAT/LONG: 46.431539° N / 121.499382° W
USGS MAP: *Walupt Lake* (1970 ns)

Once you witness this behemoth dropping a total of 175 to 225 feet, fanning out 200 to 250 feet from the mouth of Walupt Creek, you know it's been worth the effort. Continue along the gorge rim for 0.2 mile beyond Middle Walupt Creek Falls (described earlier) to a vista above the falls. While the viewpoint is superb, only about half of the display is visible at this juncture. For better views from below, find the thin path that begins to the right, then winds 0.2 mile steeply down to the confluence of Walupt Creek and Cispus River. The setting is nearly indescribable; like a dream in a fantasy landscape.

3 NORTH ST. HELENS

The following cataracts are all within Mount St. Helens National Volcanic Monument or its administrative area of Gifford Pinchot National Forest, with the first one inside the blast zone of the May 18, 1980, eruption.

HARMONY FALLS ★★

MAGNITUDE: 15 (l)
ELEVATION: 3480 feet
WATERSHED: Very small
APPROACH: Trail (fairly hard)
LAT/LONG: 46.281683° N / 122.115646° W
USGS MAP: *Spirit Lake East* (1994)

The predecessor of this waterfall, which fell 50 feet into Spirit Lake, has been drowned. As the volcano erupted, debris deposits dammed the outlet of the lake, which subsequently caused the water level to rise. The current 40- to 60-foot descent, occurring above the lake level along the same unnamed stream, has inherited the name. The landscape at the falls will continue to change as its watershed matures along with successional changes in the accompanying vegetative cover. While here, observe the extremely hazardous logjam on this part of the lake. When the volcano erupted laterally, the lake's waters surged into a multitude of gas-blasted trees, sweeping them into the lake upon the return flow of the tidal-like wave.

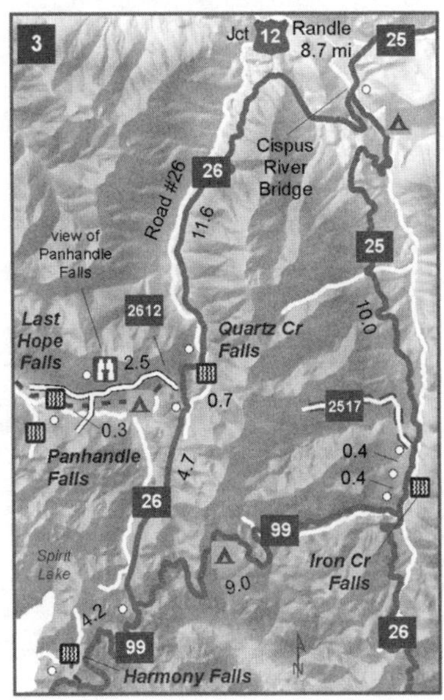

Turn south off U.S. Highway 12 about 1.3 miles west of the Cowlitz Valley Ranger Station onto Randle–Lewis River Road (Forest Service Road 25). Follow FS Road 25 for 8.7 miles, crossing the Cispus River Bridge. From here, proceed 10.8 miles to Spirit Lake–Iron Creek Road (Forest Service Road 99), then turn right (west). In a little less than 5 miles you enter the national volcanic monument, and 4 miles farther pass the route's junction with Forest Service Road 26.

Continue 4.2 miles more, and park at Harmony Viewpoint. The current cataract is located adjacent to the end of Harmony Trail 224, a moderately steep hike of 1 strenuous mile. You can also drive to the trailhead via FS Road 26, as shown on the map.

1 IRON CREEK FALLS ★★★

MAGNITUDE: 48
ELEVATION: 2740 feet
WATERSHED: Medium
APPROACH: Trail (fairly easy)
LAT/LONG: 46.327458° N / 121.971901° W
USGS MAP: *French Butte* (1994 ns)

Iron Creek hurtles 25 to 35 feet into a small pool within the Cowlitz Valley Ranger District. Look for a signed turnout along the east side of Randle–Lewis River Road (Forest Service Road 25, described earlier), located 0.4 mile past the junction with Big Creek Road (Forest Service Road 2517) and 0.4 mile before Spirit Lake–Iron Creek Road (Forest Service Road 99).

Iron Creek Falls

LAST HOPE FALLS ★★★

MAGNITUDE: 49
ELEVATION: 2760 feet
WATERSHED: Medium
APPROACH: Trail (fairly easy)
LAT/LONG: 46.351323° N / 122.114187° W
USGS MAP: *Spirit Lake East* (1994 ns)

Water pours 35 to 45 feet downward along Green River. From the junction of Forest Service Roads 99 and 26 (described earlier), head north along the latter route. After 4.7 miles, turn left upon Forest Service Road 2612, signed for Green River Trail and Horse Camp. Proceed 2.5 miles, then bear left at the fork.

Park at the trail crossing in another 0.1 mile, then start hiking along the trail section to your right (west). There is a bench overlooking this descent, which morphs into a full-fledged block-type during wet conditions, in 0.3 mile.

QUARTZ CREEK FALLS (U) ★★

MAGNITUDE: 48
ELEVATION: 2900 feet
WATERSHED: Small
APPROACH: Bushwhack (fairly easy)
LAT/LONG: 46.36129° N / 122.055114° W
USGS MAP: *Spirit Lake East* (1994 ns)

Quartz Creek drops four times a total of 55 to 75 feet before passing beneath Forest Service Road 26. From the junction of Forest Service Roads 2612 and 26 (described earlier), continue north along the latter route. In 0.7 mile, park in a wide spot along the left side of the road.

Walk a short distance farther to the bridge crossing, and descend a short distance to the stream (the hardest part of the bushwhack). There is a great view of the lower pair a couple of hundred feet away. To see the upper pair a few hundred feet farther, follow the right side of the creek, and then climb a small promontory to a natural vista.

MORE ONLINE:

Panhandle Falls (u) ★, formerly called Last Hope Falls, USGS *Spirit Lake East* (1994 ns)
Paradise Falls (u) ★★ USGS *Smith Creek Butte* (2000)
Pinto Falls (u) ★★ USGS *French Butte* (1994 ns)
Falls of Abraham (u) ★ USGS *Mount St. Helens* (1998 ns)
Lower Loowit Falls (u) ★ USGS *Mount St. Helens* (1998 ns)
Step Falls (u) and Lower Step Falls (u) ★ both USGS *Mount St. Helens* (1998 nl)
Loowit Falls ★★★ USGS *Mount St. Helens* (1998 nl)
East Smith Falls (u), USGS *Smith Creek Butte* (2000 nl) EXPLORE!
West Smith Falls (u), USGS *Smith Creek Butte* (2000 nl) EXPLORE!
Benham Creek Falls (u) ★★ USGS *Greenhorn Buttes* (1994 ns), currently buried by landslides

4 KALAMA RIVER ROAD

MARIETTA FALLS ★★

MAGNITUDE: 30 (l)
ELEVATION: 60 feet
WATERSHED: Small
APPROACH: Auto or watercraft
LAT/LONG: 46.042316° N / 122.787185° W
USGS MAP: *Kalama* (1990)

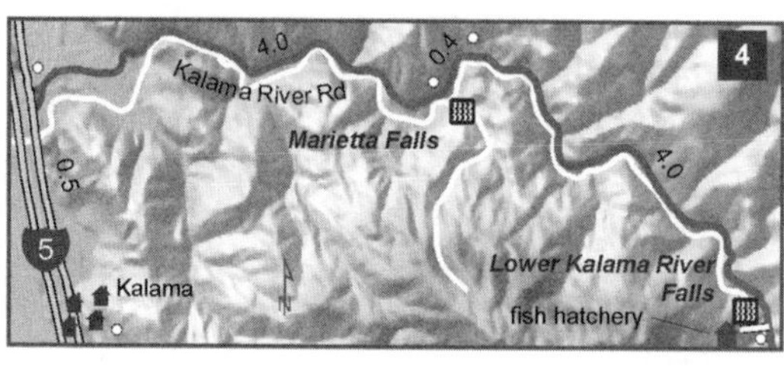

Marietta Creek tumbles 75 to 100 feet into the Kalama River. Depart Interstate 5 onto Kalama River Road, located 0.5 mile north of the town of Kalama. Drive 4 miles east to a vantage point across the river from the falls. Unfortunately, the only safe roadside view is from the car window, as there are no parking turnouts. For better views, you will need to either hike down the road or bring an inner tube or canoe and float down the main river. Start walking or launch your craft from access points 0.4 mile upstream from the falls. This entry is located outside of the national forest.

MORE ONLINE:

Lower Kalama River Falls ★ USGS *Woolford Creek* (1993)

5 LAKE MERWIN

Lake Merwin is the first of three reservoirs along the Lewis River. The other two are Yale Lake and Swift Reservoir. The valley sides are steep, with three waterfalls accessible in the area. All are outside the national forest. Turn off Interstate 5 at Woodland, and drive east on State Route 503.

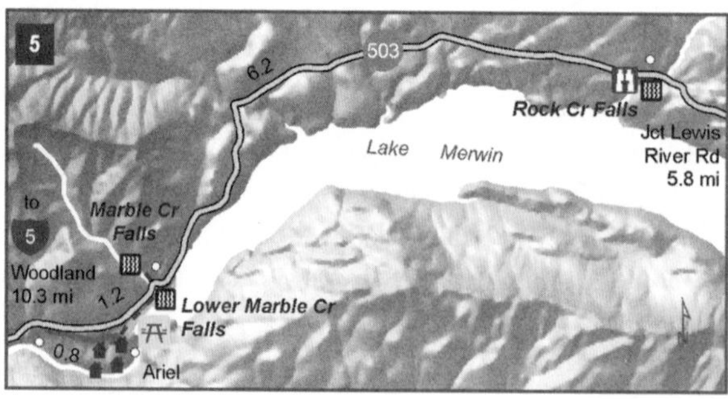

MARBLE CREEK FALLS (U) ★★

MAGNITUDE: 37
ELEVATION: 540 feet
WATERSHED: Small
APPROACH: Trail & bushwhack (fairly easy)
LAT/LONG: 45.965407° N / 122.55864° W
USGS MAP: *Ariel* (1994 nl)

Marble Creek descends 40 to 60 feet in an undeveloped area. Take SR 503 east 11.5 miles past Woodland, 1.2 miles beyond the junction signed for Merwin Dam, to Marble Creek. Park at the turnout on the east side of the culvert. Walk upstream through the lush meadow, then along a short footpath through a wooded tract.

LOWER MARBLE CREEK FALLS (U) ★★

MAGNITUDE: 44
ELEVATION: 270 feet
WATERSHED: Small
APPROACH: Trail (fairly easy) or watercraft
LAT/LONG: 45.963409° N / 122.554713° W
USGS MAP: *Ariel* (1994 nl)

Marble Creek pours 25 to 35 feet into Lake Merwin. A wooden deck offers a moderately distant view that is partly obscured when the surrounding vegetation is in leaf. Boaters have a clearer view.

From the turnout for Marble Creek Falls (described earlier), backtrack westward 1.2 miles along SR 503 to Merwin Village Road, signed for Merwin Dam. Drive 0.8 mile to the picnic area at the end of the road. Park and head up along the lake until you reach the signed Marble Creek Trailhead. Maintained by Pacific Power and Light, the 0.4-mile route ends near the cataract.

ROCK CREEK FALLS ★★

MAGNITUDE: 72 (h)
ELEVATION: 480 feet
WATERSHED: Medium
APPROACH: Auto
LAT/LONG: 45.993709° N/ 122.461286° W
USGS MAP: *Amboy* (1993 nl)

Peer down into a rugged gorge to see this 75- to 100-foot cataract as well as the creek making a 180-degree bend around a rock outcrop near the falls. Drive SR 503 east 17.7 miles past Woodland (6.2 miles past Marble Creek Falls, described earlier), and park at the large unsigned turnout on the west side of the new Rock Creek Bridge. Look across the gorge from the fenced vista framed by trees for a moderately distant yet nice view of the waterfall.

6 KALAMA FALLS

1 KALAMA FALLS ★★

MAGNITUDE: 57
ELEVATION: 1300 feet
WATERSHED: Large
APPROACH: Trail (fairly easy or moderate)
LAT/LONG: 46.1104° N / 122.358611° W
USGS MAP: *Cougar* (2000)

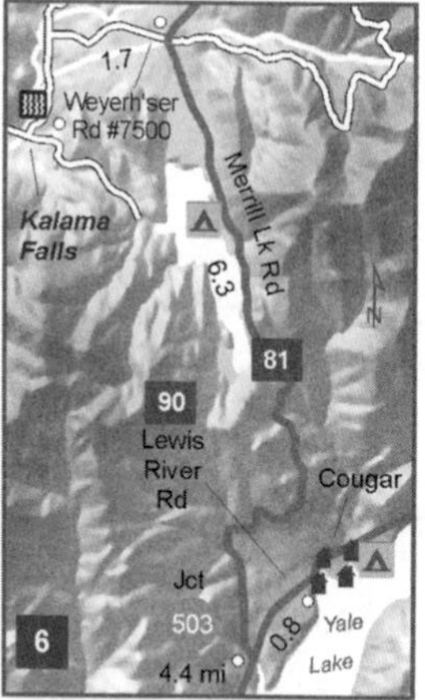

The falls and the trail to it are owned by Weyerhaeuser Company, which invites the public to visit. At the northeastern extreme of State Route 503 (shown on the chapter map), turn east on Lewis River Road (Forest Service Road 90), and go 4.4 miles to Merrill Lake Road (Forest Service Road 81). Drive north 6.3 miles, then turn left (west) on Kalama River Road (Weyerhauser Road, 7500). Continue 1.7 miles farther, and park at any available turnout. A short trail leads down to the Kalama River and then upstream to the base of the falls. If FS Road 7500 is gated, park without blocking the gate and hike that last 1.7 miles.

7 SOUTH ST. HELENS

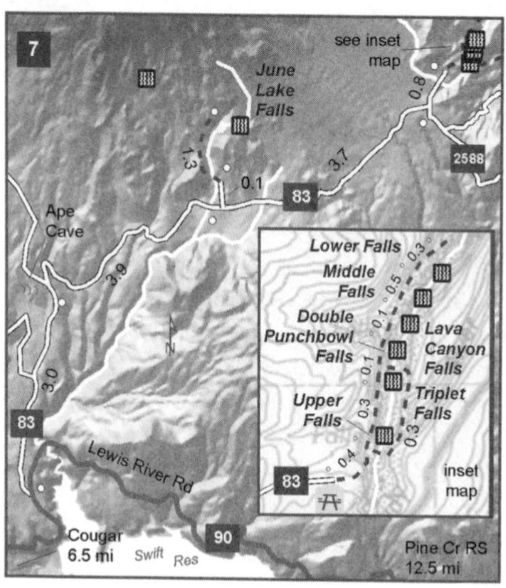

Understandably, most accounts of the 1980 eruption of Mount St. Helens have focused upon its destructive consequences. Less well known is the fact that the volcano also contributed to the creation of some new geographic features. Lava Canyon, for instance, was sculpted when glacial meltwaters and mudflows set forth by the eruption scoured away weaker volcanic deposits that covered a 1900-year-old lava flow. As a result the bottom of the gorge consists of several erosional remnants of andesite that waterfalls now plunge over. All of the following entries occur within Mount St. Helens National Volcanic Monument.

June Lake Falls

JUNE LAKE FALLS (U) ★★★

MAGNITUDE: 61
ELEVATION: 3200 feet
WATERSHED: Very small
APPROACH: Trail (moderate)
LAT/LONG: 46.15235° N / 122.157574° W
USGS MAP: *Mount St. Helens* (1998 ns)

After several failed attempts to find the trail to June Lake, I finally found it in 2003, as the trail is now signed. Drive 6.5 miles eastward past the community of Cougar along Lewis River Road (Forest Service Road 90, described in the previous section). Turn left (north) on Forest Service Road 83, and continue 6.9 miles to the turnoff marked for June Lake. Proceed 0.1 mile to the parking area.

Hike 1.3 miles to see an unnamed stream pouring 60 to 80 feet into a tiny idyllic lake. Close-up views can be gained with an inflatable raft or other such portable watercraft. This descent survived the volcanic eruption because of its location on the opposite side of the lateral blast, and it was not in the path of a lahar (a moving mass of volcanic debris and water) caused by rapid glacial melting.

UPPER LAVA CANYON FALLS (U) ★★

MAGNITUDE: 50 (h)
ELEVATION: 2450 feet
WATERSHED: Medium (g)
APPROACH: Trail (fairly easy)
LAT/LONG: 46.166752° N / 122.08464° W
USGS MAP: *Smith Creek Butte* (2000 nl)

While June Lake Falls (described earlier) is an appropriate place for quiet reflection, the journey into Lava Canyon will get your heart pounding as the Muddy River roars through the gorge. Drive 4.5 miles eastward past the junction for June Lake along Forest Service Road 83 to the parking and interpretive area.

Six major waterfalls occur within Lava Canyon. Access to the first two is appropriate for children, but the hiking conditions for the latter four are too precarious even for skittish adults. The trail begins on paved and wooden surfaces, providing a pleasant 0.4-mile walk to this particular entry, which was named Lava Canyon Falls in a previous edition of this guidebook. Protected viewpoints are provided for this 60- to 80-foot plummet.

TRIPLET FALLS (U) ★★★

MAGNITUDE: 47 (h)
ELEVATION: 2380 feet
WATERSHED: Medium (g)
APPROACH: Trail (fairly easy)
LAT/LONG: 46.168654° N / 122.083138° W
USGS MAP: *Smith Creek Butte* (2000 ns)

The Muddy River tumbles 50 to 70 feet over three steps of resistant rhyolite. From Upper Lava Canyon Falls (described earlier), the trail roughens but is still moderately easy to hike. Proceed down either side of the canyon 0.3 mile farther for full views from the excitement of a swinging footbridge.

DOUBLE PUNCHBOWL FALLS (U) ★★

MAGNITUDE: 40 (h)
ELEVATION: 2280 feet
WATERSHED: Medium (g)
APPROACH: Trail (fairly hard)
LAT/LONG: 46.169189° N / 122.082901° W
USGS MAP: *Smith Creek Butte* (2000 ns)

Continuing downstream from the footbridge (described above), the path steepens and becomes much narrower. Don't go farther if you are wary of heights or have someone immature with you. Within 0.1 mile, you have a good trailside view of Muddy River dropping a total of 25 to 35 feet.

LAVA CANYON FALLS (U) ★★★★

MAGNITUDE: 81 (h)
ELEVATION: 2120 feet
WATERSHED: Medium (g)
APPROACH: Trail (hard)
LAT/LONG: 46.170169° N / 122.082773° W
USGS MAP: *Smith Creek Butte* (2000 nl)

When hiking, sometimes it's good to have some fear. It makes you more cautious. And caution cannot be overstated when visiting this entry. The trail is very narrow, moderately steep, very crumbly, and situated along the side of a cliff. Continue past Double Punchbowl Falls (described earlier) for another 0.1 mile to an exhilarating trailside vantage point of Muddy River plunging 110 to 135 feet downward in a double drop.

MIDDLE LAVA CANYON FALLS (U) ★★★

MAGNITUDE: 66 (h)
ELEVATION: 2080 feet
WATERSHED: Medium (g)
APPROACH: Trail (hard)
LAT/LONG: 46.172636° N / 122.082172° W
USGS MAP: *Smith Creek Butte* (2000 nl)

Muddy River plunges and cascades a total of 70 to 100 feet. Continue carefully beyond Lava Canyon Falls (described earlier) another 0.5 mile. The best views are from a small promontory adjacent to the trail. This waterfall has an ancestor, as the pre-eruption topographic map shows a cataract at the same location.

LOWER LAVA CANYON FALLS (U) ★★

MAGNITUDE: 70 (h)
ELEVATION: 2050 feet
WATERSHED: Medium (g)
APPROACH: Trail (hard)
LAT/LONG: 46.173216° N / 122.081593° W
USGS MAP: *Smith Creek Butte* (2000 nl)

This waterfall deserves a higher rating, but views of it descending a total of 120 to 145 feet are obstructed. Proceed carefully beyond Middle Lava Canyon Falls (described earlier) for 0.3 mile. The best vantage point is after crossing a side creek and descending a steel ladder. Look for a 20- to 25-foot-tall chunk of volcanic rock next to you; perhaps someday a ladder will be attached to it, enabling a clear view of this tiered entry. From here, you can see the small side creek pouring 80 to 100 feet into the gorge.

From this location, it is 1.7 miles back to the trailhead, although some adventurers may wish to first go 0.2 mile farther and climb very steeply up a sentinel called The Ship, a 100-foot-tall volcanic erosional remnant.

MORE ONLINE:
Chocolate Falls, USGS *Mount St. Helens* (1998 ns) EXPLORE!

8 EAGLE CLIFF

Upstream from Swift Reservoir are the following five waterfalls that pour from tributaries descending into Lewis River. All occur within Mount St. Helens National Volcanic Monument Administrative Area.

CURLY CREEK FALLS ★★★★

MAGNITUDE: 66 (h)
ELEVATION: 1120 feet
WATERSHED: Medium
APPROACH: Trail (easy)
LAT/LONG: 46.05898° N / 121.973092° W
USGS MAP: *Burnt Peak* (1998)

Despite its modest size, the natural arch that has been formed between the tiers of its 50- to 75-foot drop puts Curly Creek Falls on everyone's must-see

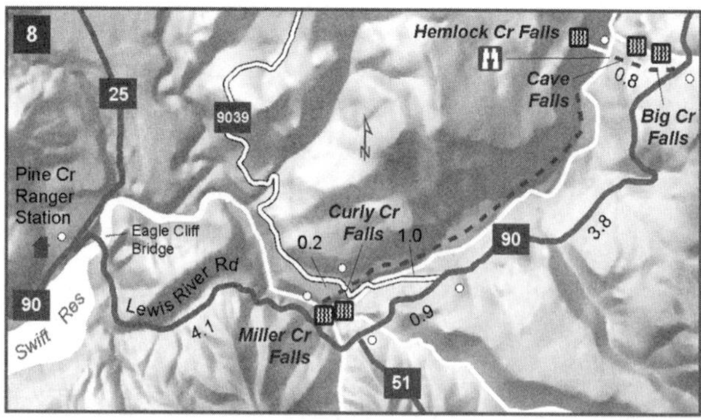

list. Look closely; stream erosion is in the process of constructing a second arch from the bedrock. At the northeastern extreme of State Route 503, turn east on Lewis River Road (Forest Service Road 90). Follow Lewis River Road for 5 miles past the Eagle Cliff Bridge (19 miles east of Cougar). Turn left (west) on Forest Service Road 9039, and drive about 1 mile to a parking area on the near side of the Lewis River. Walk across the bridge, and follow Curly Creek Falls Trail 31-A downstream for 0.1 mile to a view of the falls from across the river.

MILLER CREEK FALLS ★★

MAGNITUDE: 52
ELEVATION: 1120 feet
WATERSHED: Small
APPROACH: Trail (easy)
LAT/LONG: 46.057819° N / 121.975559° W
USGS MAP: *Burnt Peak* (1998 nl)

Miller Creek pours 40 to 60 feet into the Lewis River. Continue 0.1 mile beyond Curly Creek Falls (described earlier). Find the cataract on the opposite side of the river from the trail.

BIG CREEK FALLS ★★★★

MAGNITUDE: 76 (h)
ELEVATION: 1600 feet
WATERSHED: Medium
APPROACH: Trail (easy)
LAT/LONG: 46.094778° N / 121.909534° W
USGS MAP: *Burnt Peak* (1998)

The view from the rim of this natural gorge is breathtaking as Big Creek plummets 125 feet into an obscured pool. Drive 3.8 miles beyond Forest Service Road 9039 (described earlier) along Lewis River Road, a total of 8.8 miles east from Eagle Cliff Bridge. From the signed parking area, walk 0.1 mile down the trail to a vista from a wooden observation deck.

HEMLOCK CREEK FALLS ★★

MAGNITUDE: 32 (l)
ELEVATION: 1700 feet
WATERSHED: Very small
APPROACH: Trail (fairly easy)
LAT/LONG: 46.096519° N / 121.927795° W
USGS MAP: *Burnt Peak* (1998 nl)

Here is a moderately distant, cross-canyon view of water plummeting 90 to 120 feet down the side of Lewis River Canyon. This falls deserves a lesser rating during its very low flow of summer. Hike past Big Creek Falls (described earlier) for 0.5 mile to a fenced vantage point along the gorge of Big Creek, where unfortunately you have a dismal view of Cave Falls USGS *Burnt Peak* (1998 nl) sliding down 80 to 100 feet. From here it is 0.2 mile farther to the end of the trail at an overlook of the canyon and the descent of Hemlock Creek.

MORE ONLINE:
Cave Falls ★, mentioned earlier
Upper Curly Creek Falls ★ USGS *Burnt Peak* (1998 ns)
Rush Creek Falls ★★★★ USGS *Burnt Peak* (1998 ns), road closure

9 LEWIS RIVER

The scenic quality of the following falls within Mount St. Helens National Volcanic Monument Administrative Area tends to decrease as you proceed upstream. The following entries are listed from most scenic to least scenic, opposite of the order in which most visitors reach them. Drive northeastward to the upper reaches of Lewis River Road (FS Road 90), then visit the cataracts as you retrace the route downstream.

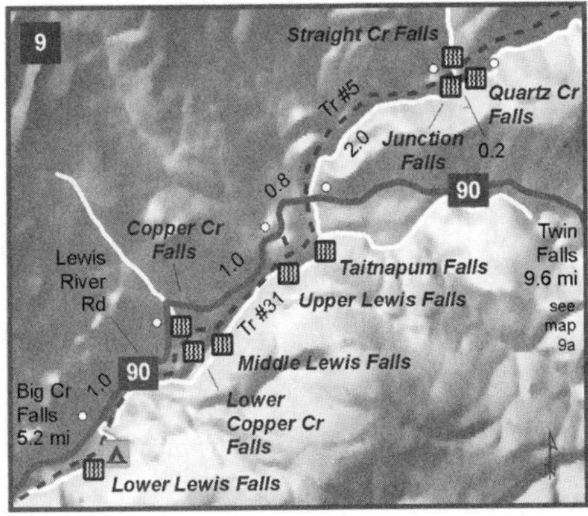

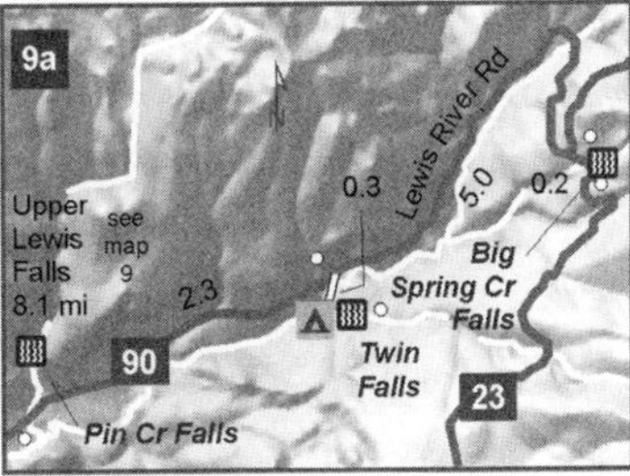

BIG SPRING CREEK FALLS (U) ★★

MAGNITUDE: 23
ELEVATION: 3580 feet
WATERSHED: Very small (s)
APPROACH: Auto
LAT/LONG: 46.231811° N / 121.625022° W
USGS MAP: *Mount Adams West* (2000 ns)

Once while I was driving to another destination, what should appear? This photogenic triple-tier dropping a total of 25 to 35 feet along a spring-fed stream. Drive to the eastern end of Forest Service Road 90, located 31.4 miles beyond Eagle Cliff Bridge (described in the previous section). Turn right (south) onto Forest Service Road 23 for 0.2 miles to an unsigned turnout at the cataract.

TWIN FALLS ★★

MAGNITUDE: 64
ELEVATION: 2660 feet
WATERSHED: Small
APPROACH: Auto
LAT/LONG: 46.214783° N / 121.668516° W
USGS MAP: *Steamboat Mtn.* (2000)

Twin Falls Creek is named for the successive 15- to 20-foot punchbowls that occur above its confluence with the Lewis River. From the east end of Lewis River Road (described earlier), backtrack westward for 5 miles to an unsigned access road on the left (south). Proceed 0.3 mile to its end at the now-decommissioned Twin Falls Camp. The view of the falls is from across Lewis River.

PIN CREEK FALLS (U) ★★★

MAGNITUDE: 64
ELEVATION: 2420 feet
WATERSHED: Medium
APPROACH: Bushwhack (moderate)
LAT/LONG: 46.205606° N / 121.712333° W
USGS MAP: *Steamboat Mtn.* (2000 ns)

Wade 0.2 mile up Pin Creek in ankle- to knee-deep water to this photogenic 30- to 40-foot entry. From the access road to Twin Falls (described earlier), drive in the downstream direction of Lewis River Road (Forest Service Road 90) for 2.3 miles to the Pin Creek Bridge, and find a wide spot to park. The hardest part of the trek is getting down to the creekbed from the span; try scrambling down the embankment from the left side looking upstream.

STRAIGHT CREEK FALLS ★★

MAGNITUDE: 30
ELEVATION: 1980 feet
WATERSHED: Medium
APPROACH: Trail (fairly hard)
LAT/LONG: 46.198129° N / 121.828424° W
USGS MAP: *Quartz Creek Butte* (2011 ns)

This pleasant series of cascades along Straight Creek totals 30 to 60 feet. The highlight when I surveyed this entry was the appearance of several elk along the trail. Drive along Lewis River Road (Forest Service Road 90) to the parking area for Quartz Creek Trail 5, located 16.8 miles northeast of Eagle Cliff Bridge and 7.3 miles southwest of the Pin Creek Bridge (described earlier). Hike a somewhat strenuous 2 miles to Straight Creek. Walk across the logs over the stream, then pick your own path upstream to a viewpoint.

☐ QUARTZ CREEK FALLS (U) ★★★

MAGNITUDE: 53
ELEVATION: 1940 feet
WATERSHED: Large
APPROACH: Trail & bushwhack (fairly hard)
LAT/LONG: 46.195946° N / 121.825055° W
USGS MAP: *Quartz Creek Butte* (2011 ns)

Quartz Creek pours 20 to 25 feet in a secluded setting near an informal campsite, complete with a nice swimming hole below its base. After crossing Straight Creek (described earlier), turn right and go through the campsite. Head a hundred feet or so downstream to see the top of Junction Falls (u) ★, USGS *Quartz Creek Butte* (2011 ns), whose tantalizing drop from both Straight Creek and Quartz Creek is blocked from view by cliffs serving as sentinels on both flanks. From here, walk in the upstream direction along Quartz Creek for a short 0.1 mile. Just after passing a minor 2-foot waterfall, enter the creek and make your way another quick 0.1 mile to this destination.

☐ TAITNAPUM FALLS ★★★

MAGNITUDE: 63
ELEVATION: 1720 feet
WATERSHED: Large
APPROACH: Trail (fairly easy)
LAT/LONG: 46.177955° N / 121.846449° W
USGS MAP: *Quartz Creek Butte* (2011 ns)

The least well-known waterfall on the Lewis River not only has the best name but also rivals the others in beauty. Find the spur path for Lewis River Trail 31 located across the road from the trailhead for Quartz Creek (described above). Walk down to the river, then proceed downstream for a total of 0.3 mile to a signed airy vista that lets you look down to this 80- to 100-foot-wide display dropping 20 to 25 feet. This falls is also known by the variant spelling *Taidnapam*.

☐ UPPER LEWIS FALLS ★★★

MAGNITUDE: 65
ELEVATION: 1620 feet
WATERSHED: Large
APPROACH: Trail (moderate)
LAT/LONG: 46.175578° N / 121.85265° W
USGS MAP: *Quartz Creek Butte* (2011)

In this area the Lewis River thunders 35 feet over a massive slab of bedrock. This waterfall and those described in the next four entries are all interconnected by the Lewis River trail system. For access, find the Upper Falls spur trail next to Lewis River Road as indicated by a sign 0.8 mile southwest of Quartz Creek

Copper Creek Falls

Trail 5 (described earlier). The path is moderately steep but only 0.3 mile long. At its end are the falls and the junction with Lewis River Trail.

COPPER CREEK FALLS ★★

MAGNITUDE: 44
ELEVATION: 1680 feet
WATERSHED: Very small
APPROACH: Trail (fairly easy)
LAT/LONG: 46.168386° N / 121.866469° W
USGS MAP: *Quartz Creek Butte* (2011 nl)

This sharp 40- to 60-foot drop along Copper Creek can be viewed by descending beneath a footbridge. Drive 1 mile southwest of Upper Falls Trail (described earlier) along Lewis River Road to the parking area for an unnamed trail that leads down to the Lewis River. After walking along the path for several hundred yards, look back toward the footbridge framing the cataract.

☐ MIDDLE LEWIS FALLS ★★

MAGNITUDE: 56
ELEVATION: 1560 feet
WATERSHED: Large
APPROACH: Trail (moderate)
LAT/LONG: 46.167093° N / 121.863314° W
USGS MAP: *Quartz Creek Butte* (2011)

This 30-foot descent along the Lewis River is the least inspiring of the river's four falls. Take the trail to Copper Creek Falls (described earlier). Continue another 0.5 mile to Lewis River Trail 31 and views of this cataract.

☐ LOWER COPPER CREEK FALLS (U) ★★

MAGNITUDE: 29
ELEVATION: 1600 feet
WATERSHED: Very small
APPROACH: Trail (moderate)
LAT/LONG: 46.166707° N / 121.864967° W
USGS MAP: *Quartz Creek Butte* (2011 ns)

Copper Creek slides steeply into the Lewis River. A footbridge along Lewis River Trail passes over this 20- to 30-foot drop. Walk a short distance downstream from Middle Lewis Falls (described earlier) to this entry.

☐ LOWER LEWIS FALLS ★★★★

MAGNITUDE: 67
ELEVATION: 1480 feet
WATERSHED: Large
APPROACH: Auto
LAT/LONG: 46.154624° N / 121.879579° W
USGS MAP: *Spencer Butte* (1998)

Water crashes 35 feet over a broad expanse of the Lewis River in an especially scenic block form. Drive along Lewis River Road (Forest Service Road 90) to Lewis River Campground, located 1 mile south of Copper Creek (14 miles northwest of Eagle Cliff Bridge) and 5.2 miles north of Big Creek Falls. Park in the southeast part of the campground. A short trail leads to good vistas overlooking the falls.

10 CHELATCHIE

All of the following waterfalls occur along Siouxon Creek and its tributaries. Enjoy an entire day hiking to eight delightful cataracts, all located in Mount St. Helens National Volcanic Monument Administrative Area. Depart State Route 503 at the hamlet of Chelatchie, turning east onto Northeast Healy Road. Drive 9.2 miles, passing the nearly perfectly symmetrical cinder cone of Tum

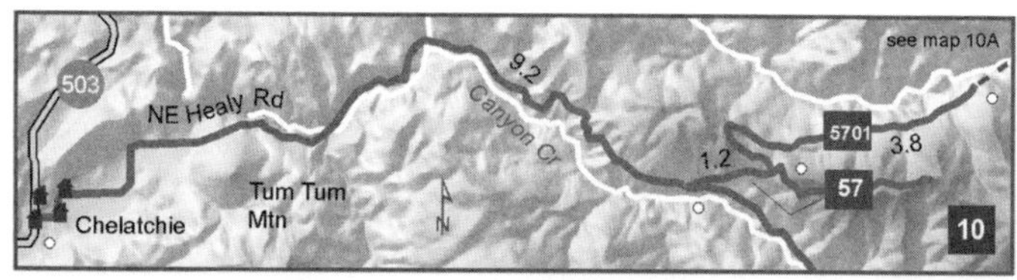

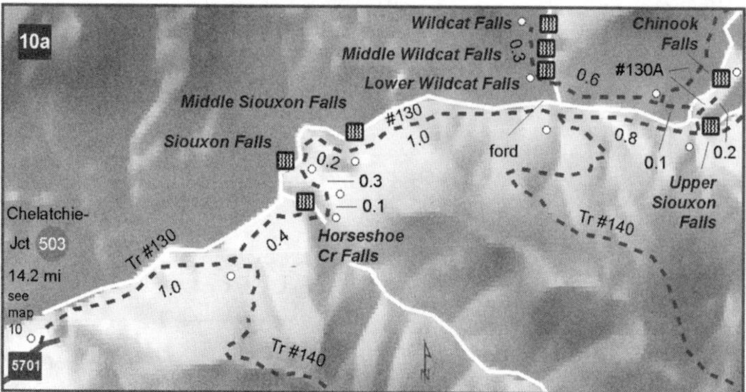

Tum Mountain before paralleling the gorge of Canyon Creek. Turn left onto Forest Service Road 57, motoring 1.2 miles up the ridge. Take another left onto Forest Service Road 5701, which descends the other side, and then continue along Siouxon Creek to the parking area near the road's end 3.8 miles farther.

HORSESHOE CREEK FALLS ★★

MAGNITUDE: 46
ELEVATION: 1350 feet
WATERSHED: Small
APPROACH: Trail (moderate)
LAT/LONG: 45.955779° N / 122.153782° W
USGS MAP: *Siouxon Peak* (2000 ns)

The first cataract encountered along Siouxon Trail 130 is this nice double horsetail totaling 35 to 50 feet. Follow the trail for 1.4 miles, crossing a footbridge over the falls. Continue another 0.1 mile to a signed spur to your left, which ends at a good vantage point in another 0.1 mile.

SIOUXON FALLS ★★

MAGNITUDE: 23 (h)
ELEVATION: 1250 feet
WATERSHED: Large
APPROACH: Trail (moderate)
LAT/LONG: 45.957823° N / 122.153674° W
USGS MAP: *Siouxon Peak* (2000 ns)

A trailside bench enables hikers to rest their feet while admiring this classic 20- to 30-foot punchbowl falls. Continue past the spur junction for Horseshoe Creek Falls (described earlier) for 0.3 mile to this entry. Incidentally, numerous unmapped cascades and small falls occur along Siouxon Creek. Only the larger, accessible ones are listed here.

MIDDLE SIOUXON FALLS (U) ★★

MAGNITUDE: 26 (h)
ELEVATION: 1280 feet
WATERSHED: Large
APPROACH: Trail (moderate)
LAT/LONG: 45.959463° N / 122.148245° W
USGS MAP: *Siouxon Peak* (2000 ns)

Continue along Siouxon Trail 130 for 0.2 mile beyond Siouxon Falls (described earlier), where the trail meets up with this 10- to 15-foot drop along Siouxon Creek.

UPPER SIOUXON FALLS (U) ★★

MAGNITUDE: 37
ELEVATION: 1460 feet
WATERSHED: Medium
APPROACH: Trail (fairly hard)
LAT/LONG: 45.960075° N / 122.116338° W
USGS MAP: *Bare Mtn.* (2000 ns)

Continue past Middle Siouxon Falls (described earlier) for 1.8 miles where a footbridge crosses the stream. Look upstream to see the 15- to 20-foot drop over rock slabs. Closer views are available farther up Trail 130. Although this is the last of the accessible waterfalls on this section of Siouxon Creek, don't turn back yet. The tallest of the falls beckon from tributaries pouring into the valley from the north.

CHINOOK FALLS ★★★

MAGNITUDE: 59
ELEVATION: 1560 feet
WATERSHED: Medium
APPROACH: Trail (fairly hard)
LAT/LONG: 45.963088° N / 122.11505° W
USGS MAP: *Bare Mtn.* (2000 nl)

Chinook Creek veils 50 feet down a rock wall into a pool below. Proceed across the footbridge (described earlier) up Chinook Trail 130A for 0.2 mile to the base of the falls.

WILDCAT FALLS ★★★★

MAGNITUDE: 66
ELEVATION: 1750 feet
WATERSHED: Small
APPROACH: Trail (hard)
LAT/LONG: 45.966071° N / 122.130607° W
USGS MAP: *Siouxon Peak* (2000 nl)

It's always nice when the last waterfall on a long hike is the best one. Such is the case with this 100- to 120-foot beauty set in a serene setting. However, lack of signage makes it challenging to find. Ford Chinook Creek (described earlier) immediately below the 2-foot block-shaped falls that just precedes Chinook Creek Falls. Pick up the trail here.

After 0.1 mile is a junction; continue straight on the unnamed path instead of switchbacking up Chinook Trail 130A. Proceed an easy 0.6 mile and ford Wildcat Creek. Rejoin the path, which very quickly ends at unsigned Wildcat Trail. The route climbs steeply; you have partial views of Lower Wildcat Falls (u) ★ and Middle Wildcat Falls (u) ★, both USGS *Siouxon Peak* (2000 ns), along the way. Reach a superb vista 0.3 mile up this trail.

From here, it is 5.1 miles back to the parking area. However, you can shorten your hike 1.6 miles by taking a shortcut, but only if Siouxon Creek isn't too swift to ford when you visit.

MORE ONLINE:

The one-star waterfalls mentioned earlier

11 EAST FORK LEWIS RIVER

Six small waterfalls tumble within the drainage basin of East Fork Lewis River. Access the area from either the hamlet of Heisson or of Yacolt, both located off of State Route 503 a few miles south of Amboy and east of Battle Ground.

☐ LUCIA FALLS ★★

MAGNITUDE: 44 (h)
ELEVATION: 400 feet
WATERSHED: Large
APPROACH: Trail (easy)
LAT/LONG: 45.839515° N / 122.446657° W
USGS MAP: *Yacolt* (1990)

The park surrounding this 15- to 25-foot waterfall was once privately owned but thankfully has since been turned over to the public. Drive 2.4 miles east of the junction for Heisson along Lucia Falls Road, and turn into Lucia Falls County Park. The cataract is located 0.1 mile upstream from the parking lot. Simply follow the sound of the falls.

Lucia Falls

YACOLT FALLS (U) ★★

MAGNITUDE: 37
ELEVATION: 550 feet
WATERSHED: Large
APPROACH: Trail (easy)
LAT/LONG: 45.833947° N / 122.385632° W
USGS MAP: *Yacolt* (1990 ns)

The confluence of Yacolt Creek and Big Tree Creek descends 20 to 25 feet within Moulton Falls County Park. Interestingly, this unofficially named cataract is more scenic than the waterfall for which the park is named. Drive 3.5 miles east of Lucia Falls County Park (described earlier), 0.3 mile beyond the parking area for Moulton Falls. Park in the wide spots across from the junction where Lucia Falls Road meets Sunset Falls Road. Walk down to the picnic area, then continue 0.1 mile across a footbridge to a developed vista.

SUNSET FALLS ★★

MAGNITUDE: 60 (h)
ELEVATION: 980 feet
WATERSHED: Large
APPROACH: Auto
LAT/LONG: 45.819279° N / 122.248109° W
USGS MAP: *Gumboot Mtn.* (2000 nl)

East Fork Lewis River splashes 20 feet within Wind River Ranger District. From Lucia Falls, follow Lucia Falls Road east for 3.5 miles to its end, and turn right (southeast) onto Sunset Falls Road, which rises 100 to 200 feet above the

East Fork. Drive 7.6 miles farther to Sunset Picnic Area. Walk a short distance upstream to the descent.

BIG TREE CREEK FALLS (U) ★★★

MAGNITUDE: 56
ELEVATION: 980 feet
WATERSHED: Medium
APPROACH: Trail (easy)
LAT/LONG: 45.880289° N / 122.347716° W
USGS MAP: *Dole* (2000 nl)

The horsetail half of this unique waterfall so forcefully strikes part of the escarpment that it causes the water to plunge the rest of the way down. From the hamlet of Yacolt, specifically at the intersection of Railroad Avenue and Yacolt Road, proceed eastward on the latter road for 0.6 mile, where it becomes Falls Road. Here it makes a sweeping bend to the right. Continue an additional 1.6 miles, and park at an unsigned turnout, but don't block the gate.

Walk down the gravel road for a flat 0.1 mile to an unmarked path to the right, just before the bridge crossing the falls. Go down the path a short distance to a nice unguarded vista above and views into the cataract, which is located on property owned by the Weyerhaeuser Company.

MORE ONLINE:
Moulton Falls ★ USGS *Yacolt* (1990)
Horseshoe Falls ★ USGS *Dole* (2000)
Hidden Falls, USGS *Dole* (2000 nl) EXPLORE!

12 WIND RIVER ROAD

Three of the most impressive waterfalls of the region reside in the drainage basin of the Wind River. All are located within the Mount Adams Ranger District of Gifford Pinchot National Forest.

PANTHER CREEK FALLS ★★★★

MAGNITUDE: 74
ELEVATION: 1790 feet
WATERSHED: Medium
APPROACH: Trail (easy)
LAT/LONG: 45.868464° N / 121.824728° W
USGS MAP: *Big Huckleberry Mtn.* (1994 ns)

This 50- to 75-foot waterfall is unique because it is actually two waterfalls dropping side by side from Panther Creek and Big Creek. From State Route 14 turn north onto Wind River Road (Forest Service Road 30). Pass Carson in 1 mile, and after another 5.8 miles turn right (east) on Old State Road. Almost immediately, take a left (north) onto Panther Creek Road (Forest Service Road 65). Drive 7.4 miles up this road, and find a safe place to park near its junction with Forest Service Road 6511. Find the Forest Service trail that quickly leads to a viewing platform overlooking the cataract.

Panther Creek Falls

FALLS CREEK FALLS ★★★★★

MAGNITUDE: 99 (h)
ELEVATION: 2200 feet
WATERSHED: Large

APPROACH: Trail (moderate)
LAT/LONG: 45.909947° N / 121.913735° W
USGS MAP: *Termination Point* (2000)

This fantastic triple-tiered waterfall totals 250 feet and is too outstanding for such a generic name. Several vantage points are afforded toward the end of the trail, although the shape of the cataract is such that all three tiers cannot be viewed together.

Drive north on Wind River Road (Forest Service Road 30), and continue 9.5 miles past Panther Creek Road (Forest Service Road 65, described earlier) to Forest Service Road 3062-057. Turn right and proceed 2.3 miles to Lower Falls Creek Trail 152A. The trail crosses Falls Creek in 0.8 mile. A half mile beyond is a steeply sloping cascade—ford it carefully when it's high—after which the upper and middle portions of the falls soon come into view. The trail ends in front of the middle and lower falls 0.2 mile farther.

PUFF FALLS ★★★

MAGNITUDE: 65
ELEVATION: 1560 feet
WATERSHED: Medium

APPROACH: Bushwhack (fairly hard)
LAT/LONG: 45.930763° N / 121.972057° W
USGS MAP: *Termination Point* (2000 ns)

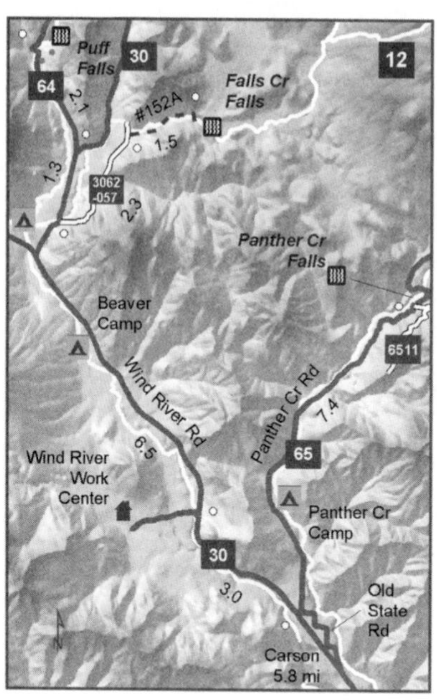

Dry Creek leaps 120 feet into a pool, which makes a good secluded swimming hole if you can bear the chilly water. Proceed 1.3 miles past Forest Service Road 3062-057 (described earlier) along Wind River Road (Forest Service Road 30) to Dry Creek Road (Forest Service Road 64). Turn left onto FS Road 64, and proceed 2.1 miles to the point where the road crosses the creek. Proceeding upstream to the falls, also known as Dry Creek Falls, is not overly difficult, but the 0.8-mile route along the faint path and sometimes through the stream is slow going and requires perseverance.

13 TROUT LAKE

The point of departure for these attractive waterfalls is the small town of Trout Lake. The first entry occurs in the community, while the other two are located within the Mount Adams Ranger District of Gifford Pinchot National Forest.

TROUT LAKE CREEK FALLS (U) ★★

MAGNITUDE: 16
ELEVATION: 1900 feet
WATERSHED: Large

APPROACH: Auto
LAT/LONG: 45.998777° N / 121.529556° W
USGS MAP: *Guler Mtn.* (1983 ns)

Trout Lake Creek tumbles about 10 feet in a serene setting, and it's proof that (lack of) size isn't always the judge of the aesthetics of a waterfall. Drive north at the crossroads in the hamlet of Trout Lake, where the streets were not signed when I last visited. Find an appropriate place to park just after the road meets the stream in 0.1 mile. Refrain from leaving the road, as the descent most likely occurs on private property.

LITTLE GOOSE CREEK FALLS ★★★

MAGNITUDE: 80
ELEVATION: 3000 feet
WATERSHED: Medium

APPROACH: Bushwhack (easy)
LAT/LONG: 46.059069° N / 121.669482° W
USGS MAP: *Sleeping Beauty* (2000 ns)

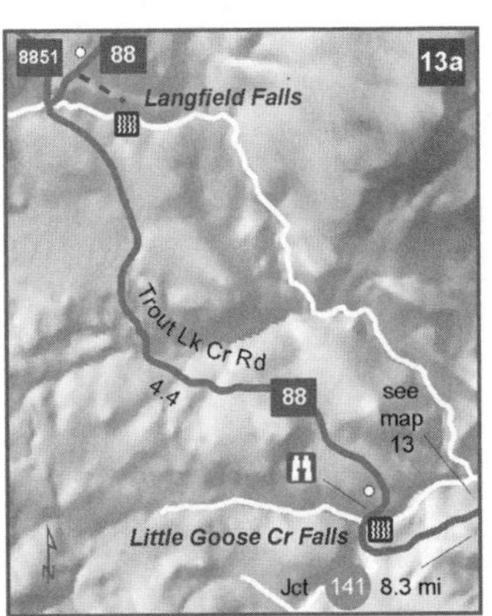

Peer into a canyon, looking down on this 75- to 100-foot triplet descending from Little Goose Creek. Be careful at the rim; there is no fence, and the sheer cliffs are dangerously abrupt! Drive west of town along State Route 141 for 1.5 miles, then turn right (north) on Trout Lake Creek Road (Forest Service Road 88). After 8.3 more miles, park on the far (northwest) side of the gorge where the paved road leaves the creek. Although there is no trail, viewpoints at the canyon rim are easily and quickly reached. This falls is located within the Mount Adams Ranger District.

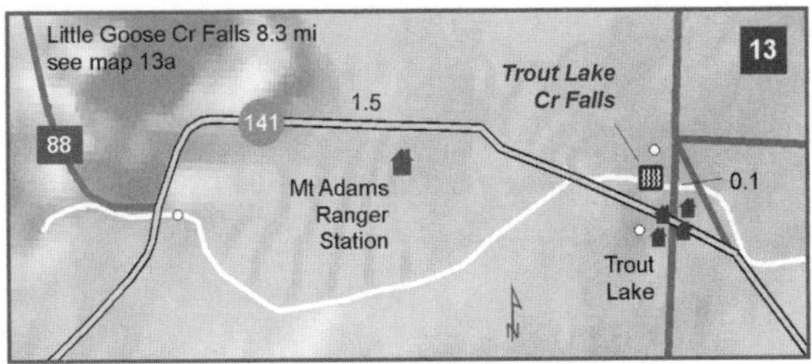

LANGFIELD FALLS ★★★★

MAGNITUDE: 86
ELEVATION: 3400 feet
WATERSHED: Medium
APPROACH: Trail (fairly easy)
LAT/LONG: 46.098349° N / 121.719264° W
USGS MAP: *Sleeping Beauty* (2000)

Mosquito Creek veils 110 feet, deep within the forest. The waterfall is named after a retired ranger who is credited with its discovery. Drive along Trout Lake Creek Road (Forest Service Road 88) for 4.4 miles past Little Goose Creek Falls (described earlier) to a marked turnout for Langfield Falls. A short trail leads to a viewpoint in front of the descent, which is in the Mount Adams Ranger District.

MORE ONLINE:

Tillicum Creek Falls (u) ★★ USGS *Quartz Creek Butte* (1998 ns)

14 MOUNT ADAMS

These high-country waterfalls are all accessible from the Yakama Indian Reservation, adjacent to Mount Adams Wilderness, which is managed by Gifford Pinchot National Forest. The best visiting period is from late summer to early autumn. The roads are rough and slow but usually navigable by passenger vehicles. Proceed north from Trout Lake along Forest Service Road 23 for 1.3 miles, then bear right onto Forest Service Road 80. Bear right again after 0.6 mile, this time onto Forest Service Road 82. When I last visited this area, the road turned to gravel after 2.7 miles at its junction with Forest Service Road 8225. Stay on FS Road 82 for another 5.8 miles and enter the reservation. Turn left (north) upon Mount Adams Road (Forest Service Road 8290).

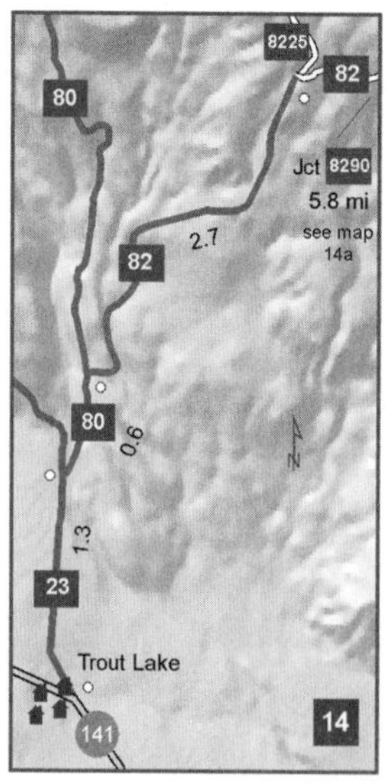

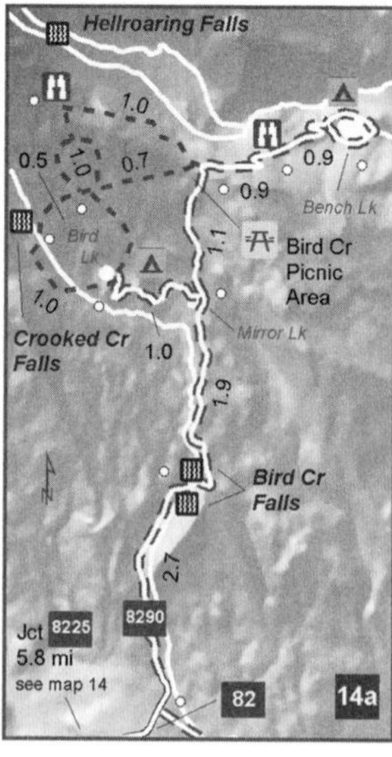

BIRD CREEK FALLS ★★

MAGNITUDE: 16 (h)
ELEVATION: 4800 feet
WATERSHED: Small (g)
APPROACH: Auto
LAT/LONG: 46.117332° N / 121.4245° W
USGS MAP: *King Mtn.* (2000 ns)

Spy a series of 5- to 10-foot cascades and punchbowls adjacent to both sides of the road on the way to Mount Adams. From the junction of Forest Service Roads 82 and 8290, proceed 2.7 miles north along FS Road 8290 to an unmarked turnout at the creek.

CROOKED CREEK FALLS ★★★

MAGNITUDE: 50
ELEVATION: 6100 feet
WATERSHED: Small (g)
APPROACH: Trail (moderate)
LAT/LONG: 46.146968° N / 121.454433° W
USGS MAP: *Mount Adams East* (2000)

Water pours 35 to 50 feet from a small cliff, then cascades steeply along the stream course. Lots of flowering plants and miniature waterfalls make the 1-mile hike absolutely charming. Proceed northward past Bird Creek Falls (described earlier) along Forest Service Road 8290 for 1.9 miles. Turn left at Mirror Lake, and drive 1 mile to Bird Lake and the trailhead at the end of this access road.

HELLROARING FALLS ★★

MAGNITUDE: 68
ELEVATION: 6800 feet
WATERSHED: Small (g)
APPROACH: Auto or trail (fairly hard)
LAT/LONG: 46.169619° N / 121.451965° W
USGS MAP: *Mount Adams East* (2000 nl)

Distant views of several 100- to 150-foot cataracts are dwarfed by the specter of Mount Adams in the background. A roadside vista is afforded from Hellroaring Falls Overlook, which is located 2.0 miles beyond Mirror Lake. A closer, yet still-distant view is available from Hellroaring Viewpoint, a moderately strenuous 1-mile hike. The shortest trail to the viewpoint starts at Bird Creek Picnic Area. Reach the picnic site by backtracking along FS Road 8290 for 0.9 mile from the overlook.

15 GLENWOOD

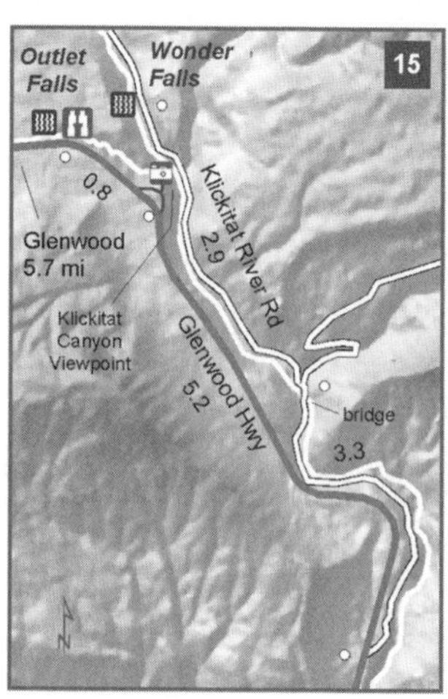

The hamlet of Glenwood serves as the point of departure for the following pair of obscure, yet remarkable waterfalls. From BZ Corner, located past White Salmon on State Route 141, drive northeast for 20 miles on BZ Corner–Glenwood Road. Alternatively you can drive 17 miles east of Trout Lake along Trout Lake–Glenwood Road, which becomes Main Street upon entering the town.

OUTLET FALLS

★★★★★

MAGNITUDE: 74
ELEVATION: 1600 feet
WATERSHED: Medium
APPROACH: Auto
LAT/LONG: 46.017652° N / 121.173734° W
USGS MAP: *Outlet Falls* (1970)

Outlet Creek roars toward Klickitat Canyon in an exciting 120- to 150-foot plummet. The gorge-rim vista into the cataract and its large natural amphitheater is unguarded, making it very dangerous to the unwary. From Glenwood at the corner of Ash and Main streets, proceed eastward on Main (which becomes Glenwood Highway), for 5.7 miles to a small unsigned turnout to the left. The vantage point is only a few steps away. For additional orientation in case you drive too far, 0.8 mile beyond is an obscure sign to the left (north) marking Klickitat Canyon Viewpoint.

WONDER FALLS ★★★

MAGNITUDE: 53
ELEVATION: 1600 feet
WATERSHED: Very small (s)
APPROACH: Auto
LAT/LONG: 46.018054° N / 121.157555° W
USGS MAP: *Outlet Falls* (1970 ns)

An unnamed spring gushes from the side of a canyon, pouring 35 to 45 feet into the Klickitat River. I learned about this new entry after outfitters from Husum informed me of its existence while I was field-truthing other waterfalls. From Outlet Falls (described earlier), drive eastward and then south a total of 6 miles to unsigned Klickitat River Road on the left. Descend 3.3 miles into Klickitat Canyon, then turn left just after the bridge crossing. You have cross-river views after another 2.9 miles. Be sure to pull over to the side of the road as far as is practical, as log trucks may come barreling down the thruway.

WASHINGTON

THE INLAND EMPIRE

The eastern half of the state of Washington is known locally as the Inland Empire. The name was popularized in the late 1800s, when the region ceased to be part of the frontier. Since then it has grown into a substantial producer of agricultural products, timber, minerals, and hydroelectric power. Railroads played a vital role in developing the Inland Empire and establishing Spokane as its center of commerce. The region's rail passenger service is still known as "The Empire Builder."

There are 59 falls recognized within this region; 33 of them are described on the following pages. Waterfalls are distributed throughout the Inland Empire, being found in the Selkirk Mountains, Okanogan Highlands, and the Channeled Scablands.

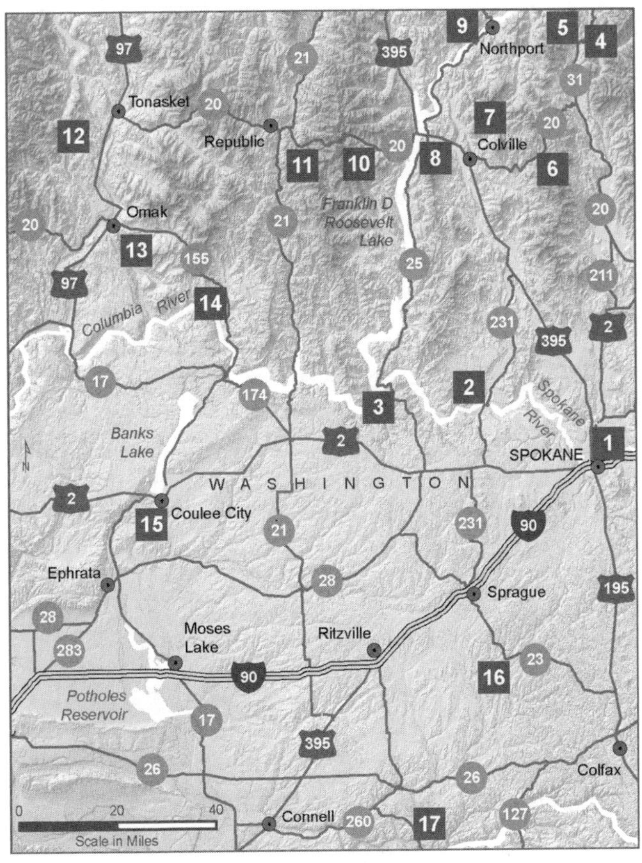

The Selkirks are composed of old sedimentary rocks that range from 80 million to 500 million years old. Recent folding and faulting, 1 million to 3 million years ago, was followed by glaciation, giving the range its present appearance.

The Okanogan Highlands, a complex metamorphic mixture of schists and gneisses, were formed and uplifted 50 million to 75 million years ago. Glaciation and stream erosion have sharpened the peaks and valleys. Most of the falls in this mountainous terrain formed where rivers flow over rocks of variable erodibility, creating escarpments wherever an outcrop of resistant bedrock eroded more slowly than weaker rocks downstream.

The Channeled Scablands, west and southwest of Spokane, are a uniquely eroded province of the Columbia Plateau where waterfall development has paralleled scabland formation. Toward the end of the last Ice Age, 10,000 to 14,000 years ago, glacial Lake Missoula occupied an area in western Montana roughly half the size of Lake Michigan. This glacial lake was created when a natural ice dam blocked the valley's drainage at Clark Fork in northern Idaho. The ice dam broke repeatedly, each time liberating staggering volumes of water, which spread across the Columbia Plateau and portions of the Palouse Hills. These events, called the Spokane Floods, scoured the landscape and created waterfalls that drop from the rims of the Columbia and Snake river canyons. Most have since dried up, but some were so powerful that their plunge pools remain, such as at Dry Falls.

The Palouse River originally flowed into the Columbia River, but the Spokane Floods caused it to divert its course into a fracture in the basaltic bedrock near the present site of Washtucna. The new river course flowed south and eventually plunged into the Snake River. The waterfall has since eroded its way 7.5 miles upstream, creating a canyon 400 to 800 feet deep from the Snake River to the present location of Palouse Falls.

1 SPOKANE

A renaissance occurred decades ago in downtown Spokane when the city hosted Expo 74, an international fair. The resulting national image boost has had a lasting effect. The former fair site is now Riverfront Park. It includes gardens, exhibits, an impressive opera house, and several falls along the Spokane River.

SPOKANE FALLS ★★★★

MAGNITUDE: 82 (h)
ELEVATION: 1780 feet
WATERSHED: Large (d)
APPROACH: Auto
LAT/LONG: 47.661096° N / 117.425892° W
USGS MAP: *Spokane NW* (1986)

Take an exciting gondola ride above these falls, where the Spokane River absolutely roars 60 to 100 feet downward as white water foams. After Niagara, it is the largest urban waterfall in the United States. Turn off Interstate 90 at the exit for U.S. Highway 2, U.S. Highway 395, and Division Street. Turn north at the end of the ramp, and drive eight blocks north to Spokane Falls Boulevard. Turn left and proceed six blocks westward to the entrance for Riverfront Park.

Canada Island Falls

When the park's aerial tramway is not operating, there is another good vista of the falls from the Monroe Street Bridge, two blocks west of the park.

UPPER FALLS ★★★

MAGNITUDE: 60 (h)
ELEVATION: 1840 feet
WATERSHED: Large (d)
APPROACH: Trail (easy)
LAT/LONG: 47.663004° N / 117.422738° W
USGS MAP: *Spokane NW* (1986 nl)

Gain a sprayside view of a wide pair of 15- to 30-foot cataracts by strolling 0.1 mile over to the walkway bridges, crossing above them where Canada Island splits the Spokane River. You can see them both at once by walking a half block west of the park to the Post Street Bridge.

CANADA ISLAND FALLS (U) ★★

MAGNITUDE: 49 (h)
ELEVATION: 1850 feet
WATERSHED: Large (d)
APPROACH: Trail (easy)
LAT/LONG: 47.664174° N / 117.420291° W
USGS MAP: *Spokane NW* (1986 ns)

Water tumbles about 10 feet downward over a 200- to 250-foot breadth of the Middle Channel of the Spokane River. Once you are between the walkway bridges of Upper Falls (described earlier), follow the path eastward for 0.1 mile along Canada Island to a larger pedestrian bridge, named the Centennial Trail. Turn left here, and continue a short distance farther to Inspiration Point on your right.

MORE ONLINE:

Diversion Dam Falls (u) ★ USGS *Spokane NW* (1986 ns)

2 SPOKANE INDIAN RESERVATION

Do not bring your rod and reel to the following waterfalls. The Spokane Indian Reservation, like most American Indian lands, prohibits public fishing in its streams.

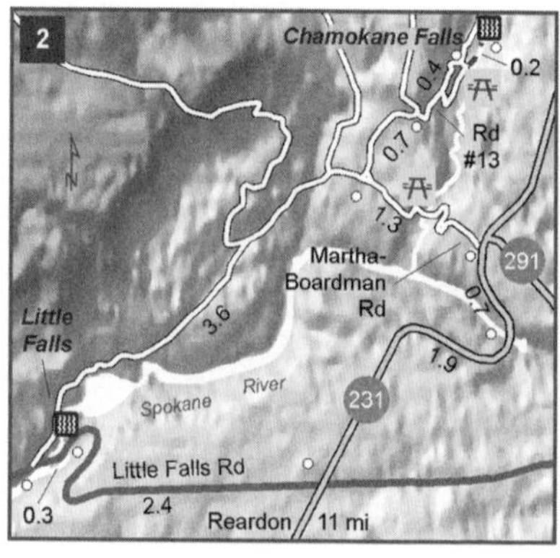

 CHAMOKANE FALLS ★★

MAGNITUDE: 35
ELEVATION: 1500 feet
WATERSHED: Large
APPROACH: Trail (fairly easy)
LAT/LONG: 47.865005° N / 117.85732° W
USGS MAP: *Long Lake* (1973)

Water tumbles 25 to 35 feet along Chamokane Creek near some picnic tables. From the junction of State Route 291 and State Route 231, drive less than 0.1 mile south to Martha-Boardman Road. Proceed along this often dusty road for 1.3 miles, then bear right and travel another 0.7 mile. Bear right again upon Road 13. Proceed 0.4 mile to an obscure road junction. Park along a wide spot here, and walk 0.1 mile down a dirt road and then 0.1 mile up a path to the falls.

 LITTLE FALLS ★★★

MAGNITUDE: 51 (h)
ELEVATION: 1400 feet
WATERSHED: Large (d)
APPROACH: Auto
LAT/LONG: 47.830415° N / 117.917358° W
USGS MAP: *Little Falls* (1973 ns)

The Spokane River pours from V-shaped Little Falls Dam and then cascades downward 20 to 30 feet over a jumble of boulders. From the junction of State Routes 291 and 231, take the latter route 2.6 miles, then turn right (west) upon the access road signed for Little Falls. Drive 2.4 miles to an unsigned turnout on the near (east) side of the river. There are good views adjacent to the bridge.

3 LAKE ROOSEVELT

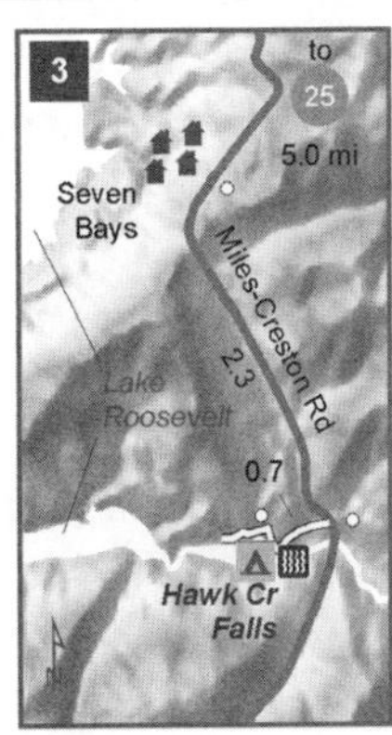

The following entry is the most readily accessible of several waterfalls that pour from tributary streams into Franklin D. Roosevelt Lake (commonly called Lake Roosevelt), a 151-mile impoundment of the Columbia River by Grand Coulee Dam, the largest hydroelectric producer in the United States. The portion of the reservoir described in this section is a part of Lake Roosevelt National Recreation Area.

 HAWK CREEK FALLS ★★

MAGNITUDE: 46
ELEVATION: 1320 feet
WATERSHED: Large
APPROACH: Auto or watercraft
LAT/LONG: 47.813768° N / 118.323348° W
USGS MAP: *Olsen Canyon* (1985 nl)

This nice 35- to 50-foot drop next to Hawk Creek Campground is sheltered in a narrow crevice. Depart State Route 25 at Miles-Creston Road, signed for Fort

Hawk Creek Falls

Spokane Visitors Center and Seven Bays. Proceed 7.3 miles to an access road for the lake, and turn right, reaching the camp and falls in 0.7 mile. Boaters may also gain a view by proceeding to the mouth of Hawk Creek.

MORE ONLINE:

Quillisascut Creek Falls (u) ★ USGS *Rice* (1992 nl)

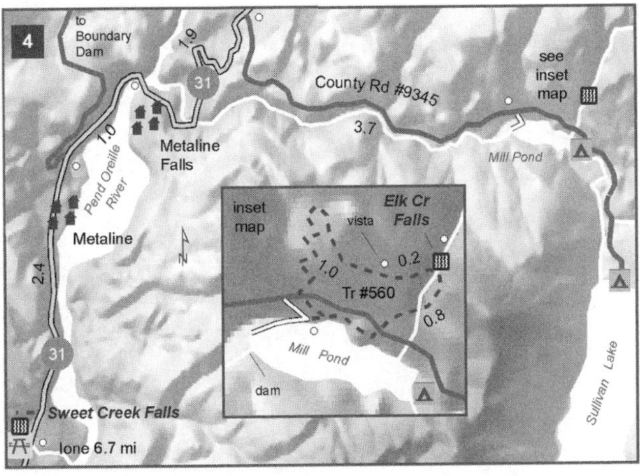

4 METALINE

Head on up to Washington's far northeastern corner to visit the descents in this section and the next one. The following two falls are new entries near the town of Metaline, as trails to both were constructed and advertised since the last edition of this guidebook was published.

SWEET CREEK FALLS ★★★

MAGNITUDE: 47
ELEVATION: 2120 feet
WATERSHED: Medium
APPROACH: Trail (easy)
LAT/LONG: 48.823784° N / 117.399907° W
USGS MAP: *Metaline* (1992 ns)

Sweet Creek drops three times, totaling 50 to 65 feet, all in horsetail fashion. A small kiosk at the parking area describes the settlement history of the area. Drive 6.7 miles north of the town of Ione along State Route 31. Turn left at the sign for the rest area and its parking. From here, it's only 0.1 mile up the trail to a stone masonry overlook.

ELK CREEK FALLS ★★

MAGNITUDE: 38
ELEVATION: 2960 feet
WATERSHED: Small
APPROACH: Trail (fairly hard)
LAT/LONG: 48.86053° N / 117.290494° W
USGS MAP: *Metaline Falls* (1992 ns)

Elk Creek plunges 10 to 15 feet, fans out another 10 to 15 feet, and then cascades yet another 10 to 15 feet. This falls is located within Colville National Forest. Drive 1.9 miles northbound beyond the bridge crossing Pend Oreille River at Metaline Falls. Turn right upon County Road 9345,

Peewee Falls

signed for Mill Pond Historic Site, and proceed 3.7 miles to the parking area above Mill Pond.

Embark upon Elk Creek Trail 560, which soon crosses the road before steeply ascending. You have great vistas of the valley in 1.0 mile. Reach a creek crossing at the falls in another 0.2 mile. From here, it's 0.8 mile via the loop trail back to the parking area.

5 BOUNDARY DAM

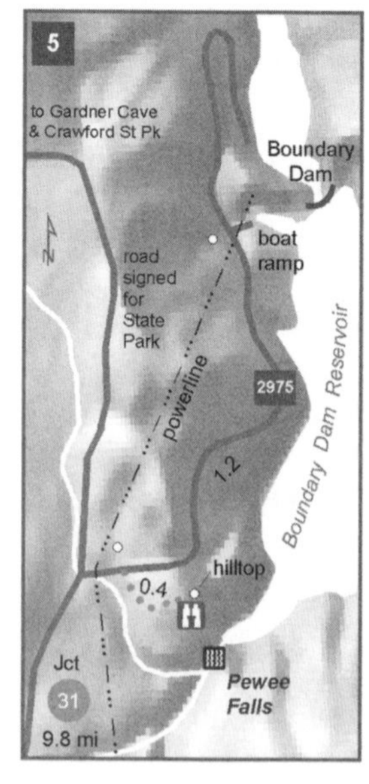

The following descent is one of the largest in eastern Washington, but it's accessible only by watercraft or bushwhacking. If you do not want to use either of these methods, you can still enjoy attractions such as Boundary Dam and Gardner Cave.

PEWEE FALLS ★★★★

MAGNITUDE: 78
ELEVATION: 2270 feet
WATERSHED: Medium
APPROACH: Bushwhack (fairly hard) or watercraft
LAT/LONG: 48.970915° N / 117.35506° W
USGS MAP: *Boundary Dam* (1986)

Pewee Creek ribbons 150 to 200 feet down a vertical rock wall into Boundary Dam Reservoir. Talk about your misleading names! This starkly beautiful waterfall was originally named Periwee Falls in 1895 by a French-Canadian hunter and prospector, but the name was later shortened.

Turn northward off State Route 31 onto Crawford Park Road (Forest Service Road 2975), which is located about 1 mile southwest of the town of Metaline Falls. Drive 11 miles to a boat launch site just below Boundary Dam. Boaters can follow the shoreline southward along the west shore of the lake approximately 1.5 miles to the falls.

Bushwhackers can gain a hilltop vista of the cataract as follows: Backtrack 1.2 miles by car from the boat ramp to an unsigned parking spot just west of the powerlines. Walk back up the road a short distance in order to avoid a marsh, then turn left, following the powerlines into the woods. After a few hundred yards, bear left (east) and progress 0.4 mile toward the top of a small knob. *Warning:* Do not attempt to get close to the waterfall, its stream, or the lake. The slopes in this area are dangerously unstable.

6 PARK RAPIDS

Formerly located on private land in an area historically known as Park Rapids, the following waterfall is now a part of day-use Crystal Falls State Park.

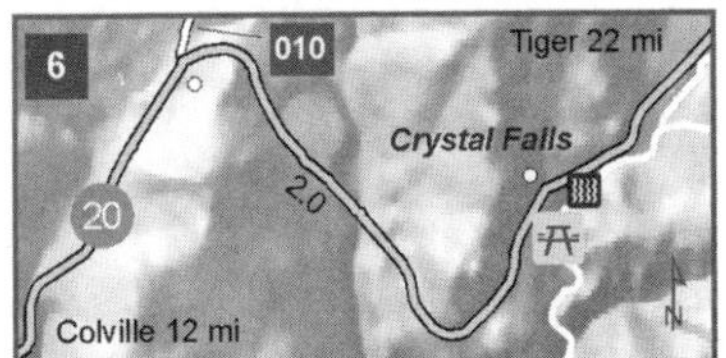

CRYSTAL FALLS ★★★

MAGNITUDE: 75 (h)
ELEVATION: 2780 feet
WATERSHED: Large
APPROACH: Auto
LAT/LONG: 48.512177° N / 117.656787° W
USGS MAP: *Park Rapids* (1992)

The Little Pend Oreille River shoots 60 to 80 feet in tiered fashion. Look for a marked turnout along State Route 20 approximately 14 miles east of Colville and 22 miles southwest of the ghost town of Tiger.

7 COLVILLE

The small city of Colville developed from old Fort Colville, a US Army outpost from 1859 to 1882. The following falls are nearby.

MARBLE CREEK FALLS (U) ★★

MAGNITUDE: 41
ELEVATION: 3120 feet
WATERSHED: Small
APPROACH: Auto
LAT/LONG: 48.679125° N / 117.759205° W
USGS MAP: *Gillette Mountain* (1992 nl)

Marble Creek descends 25 to 35 feet and is located within Colville National Forest. Drive 1.2 miles east of Colville along State Route 20, and turn left (north) on signed County Road 700. After 2 miles, bear right onto Alladin Road and proceed 11 miles. Look for obscurely marked Forest Service Road 200 to the left (west). Park along this primitive route, which quickly deteriorates into a well-worn path that leads in a short distance to the falls.

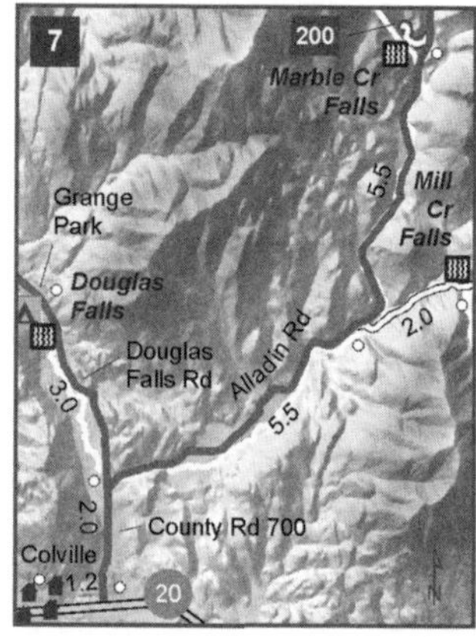

 DOUGLAS FALLS ★★★

MAGNITUDE: 71
ELEVATION: 1800 feet
WATERSHED: Large
APPROACH: Auto
LAT/LONG: 48.613683° N / 117.89928° W
USGS MAP: *Colville* (1992)

Mill Creek veils downward 60 feet within historic Douglas Falls Grange Park (Washington State Department of Natural Resources). In 1855, R. H. Douglas harnessed the cataract for a gristmill, which he later converted into a sawmill. Failing to negotiate a lumber contract with Fort Colville, Douglas abandoned the project, but not his entrepreneurship. He turned his talents to the production of distilled spirits!

From the junction of County Road 700 and Alladin Road (described earlier), bear left onto Douglas Falls Road. It is 3 additional miles to the entrance of the park. The falls can be seen from a sheltered viewpoint adjacent to the picnic and playground areas.

MORE ONLINE:
Mill Creek Falls (u) ★ USGS *Park Rapids* (1992 nl)

8 KETTLE FALLS

Kettle Falls is now only the name of a town. A cascade used to tumble nearby along the Columbia River, but the river's once mighty waters have been pacified by the Grand Coulee Dam, which created Lake Roosevelt. However, the following waterfall still exists in the vicinity.

Douglas Falls

❑ UPPER MEYERS FALLS (U) ★★

MAGNITUDE: 31
ELEVATION: 1510 feet
WATERSHED: Large (d)

APPROACH: Auto
LAT/LONG: 48.594031° N / 118.060471° W
USGS MAP: *Kettle Falls* (1969 ns)

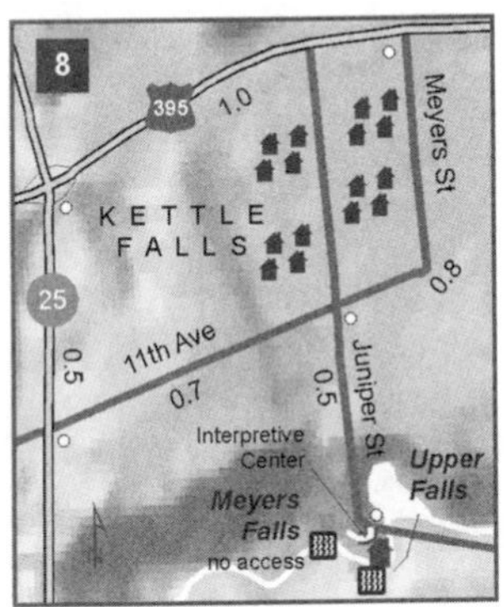

Colville River drops 15 to 20 feet into a small rock basin. This area has recently been developed as Meyers Falls Interpretive Center, describing its industrial history. Water power has been generated here since 1826, making it the oldest continuously operating facility west of the Mississippi.

Turn off U.S. Highway 395 upon Meyers Street, driving southward through the town of Kettle Falls. The way becomes 11th Avenue where it sweeps to the west. After 0.8 mile, turn left upon Juniper Street. Enter the park in

Sheep Creek Falls

another 0.5 mile; be alert, as the entrance sneaks up on you. The descent is just steps away. Among the features in the park are some funky concrete "loveseats."

MORE ONLINE:

Meyers Falls ★★★ USGS *Kettle Falls* (1969), no public access

9 NORTHPORT

When I last visited this area, the landowner who operates a small hydroelectric facility allowed visitation to the following waterfall. Help keep this interesting physical and cultural site open to the public by not trespassing on the equipment and by not littering.

SHEEP CREEK FALLS ★★★★

MAGNITUDE: 63 (h)
ELEVATION: 1600 feet
WATERSHED: Large
APPROACH: Trail (moderate)
LAT/LONG: 48.948401° N / 117.794717° W
USGS MAP: *Northport* (1982)

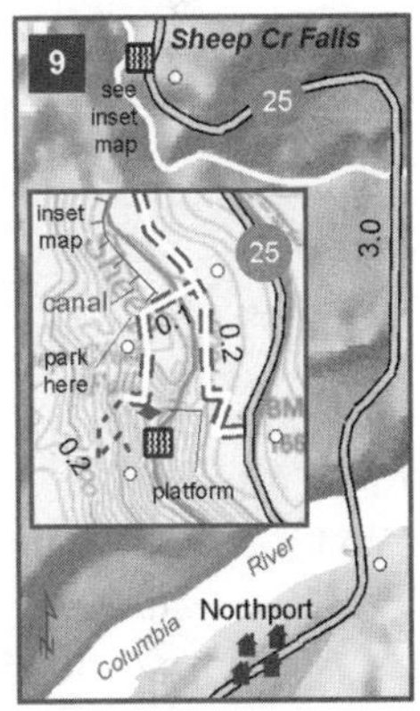

Sheep Creek drops 125 to 150 feet over a sharp escarpment. Drive 3 miles beyond Northport along State Route 25. Note your odometer reading when you first begin to cross the Columbia River proceeding northward. Depart the highway upon the unsigned dirt road to your left. Immediately proceed to the right, going down the road for 0.2 mile, then turn left and cross the bridge over Sheep Creek. Park in a safe spot in the open area, where you can see a canal.

Walk a short distance along the road to your left where you quickly arrive atop a small gorge. You will see a wooden tram platform to your left. Don't go there; admire it from a distance. Turn right, away from the creek, where a trail switchbacks 0.2 mile down to the base of the falls next to a small hydroelectric plant at the bottom of the tram.

MORE ONLINE:

Upper Falls ★★ USGS *Northport* (1982), current public access uncertain

10 SHERMAN CREEK

Both of these waterfalls are located within Colville National Forest.

UPPER SHERMAN CREEK FALLS ★★

MAGNITUDE: 26
ELEVATION: 3800 feet
WATERSHED: Medium

APPROACH: Auto
LAT/LONG: 48.624464° N / 118.419329° W
USGS MAP: *Sherman Peak* (1992 nl)

Sherman Creek drops 15 to 25 feet next to the highway. Take State Route 20 eastward for 5 miles beyond Sherman Pass to an unsigned turnout preceding the falls. Walk along the highway for a short distance to a vantage point of the cataract.

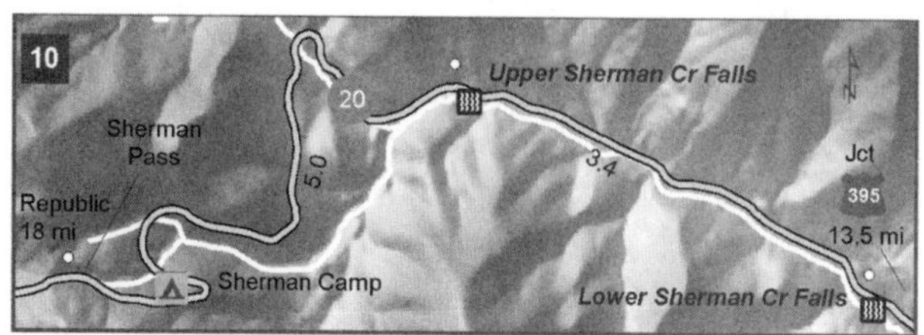

LOWER SHERMAN CREEK FALLS ★★

MAGNITUDE: 42
ELEVATION: 3090 feet
WATERSHED: Large

APPROACH: Auto or bushwhack (moderate)
LAT/LONG: 48.60317° N / 118.359569° W
USGS MAP: *So. Huckleberry Mountain* (1992 nl)

Water drops 35 to 50 feet along Sherman Creek; this entry requires a short, steep bushwhack for the best views. Continue eastward past Upper Sherman Creek Falls (described earlier) for 3.4 miles to another unsigned turnout. A moderately distant vista is available from the road. Close-up vantage points require a scramble down the slope to the creek.

11 REPUBLIC

NINE MILE FALLS ★★

MAGNITUDE: 38
ELEVATION: 3300 feet
WATERSHED: Small

APPROACH: Trail (fairly easy)
LAT/LONG: 48.546324° N / 118.638068° W
USGS MAP: *Bear Mountain* (1992 ns)

Water stairsteps steeply for 40 to 50 feet along Ninemile Creek within the Republic Ranger District of Colville National Forest. This falls deserves a lower rating during dry spells. Turn south off of State Route 20 upon Hall Creek Road, whose junction is located 6.9 miles east of Republic or 9.8 miles west of Sherman Pass. Drive 5.2 miles, then bear right upon Forest Service Road 2053. Proceed 2.7 miles to a T junction. Park here.

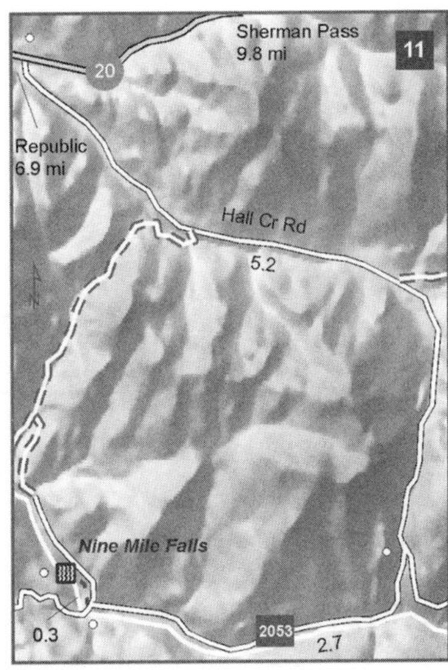

Walk about 50 feet down the road to your left, and find the trailhead on your right. Hike 0.3 mile down this path, which switchbacks a bit along its second half, ending at a wooden-fenced vista of the cataract. Note: The US Forest Service uses two words for the waterfall name ("Nine Mile"), while the US Geological Survey combines it ("Ninemile") for the name of the stream.

12 CONCONULLY

Conconully is a small resort town 22 miles northwest of Omak in north-central Washington. The following waterfall is located in the vicinity within Methow Valley Ranger District of Okanogan-Wenatchee National Forest.

SALMON FALLS ★★

MAGNITUDE: 38
ELEVATION: 3130 feet
WATERSHED: Large
APPROACH: Trail & bushwhack (moderate)
LAT/LONG: 48.554449° N / 119.846586° W
USGS MAP: *Conconully West* (2001)

West Fork Salmon Creek drops 300 feet over a 0.2-mile length of the stream. Starting at the hamlet of Conconully, drive west on Forest Service Road 2017,

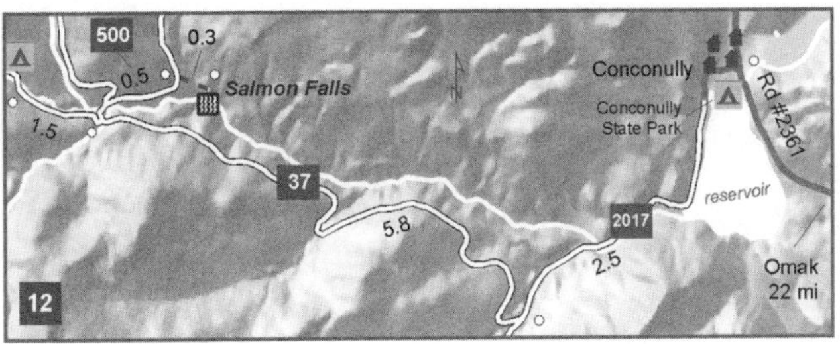

Mission Falls

which becomes Forest Service Road 37 after 2.5 miles. Proceed another 5.8 miles, then bear right onto Forest Service Road 500. Go another 0.5 mile to a jeep trail on the right. Park here. Walk down this dirt road for 0.3 mile to several paths leading to the various descents. Be careful! The ground tends to be somewhat steep and crumbly.

13 ST. MARY'S

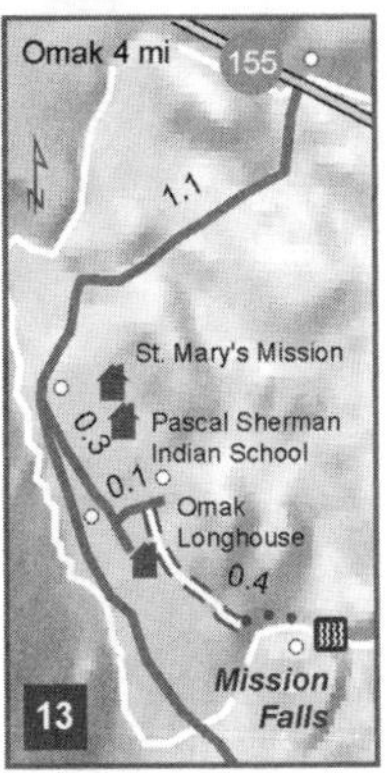

Near the town of Omak, the past education of American Indians intersects with the present. Drive 4 miles east of town, turning right (south) off of State Route 155 at the sign for Omak Lake and St. Mary's Mission. Drive 1.1 miles and bear left at the fork, up the paved road signed for historic St. Mary's Mission. It was founded in 1886 by Jesuit Father Etienne de Rouge to minister to the bands of the Colville Federation. The present Catholic church was built in 1910 and remains active today. Next to it is the modern Pascal Sherman Indian School, the only boarding school for American Indians in Washington. It is managed by the Colville Confederated Tribes.

MISSION FALLS ★★

MAGNITUDE: 38
ELEVATION: 1500 feet
WATERSHED: Large

APPROACH: Bushwhack (fairly easy)
LAT/LONG: 48.369929° N / 119.438353° W
USGS MAP: *Omak Lake* (1980)

Omak Creek descends in a series within a small canyon. From the second sign for St. Mary's Mission, proceed 0.3 mile, passing the church and school. Just beyond, turn left at the Omak Longhouse sign. Find the first dirt road to the right (south) in 0.1 mile, and take it to its end in 0.4 mile. It's a moderately easy rock hop of a couple hundred feet to vantage points of the drops totaling 20 to 30 feet within the gorge.

14 NESPELEM

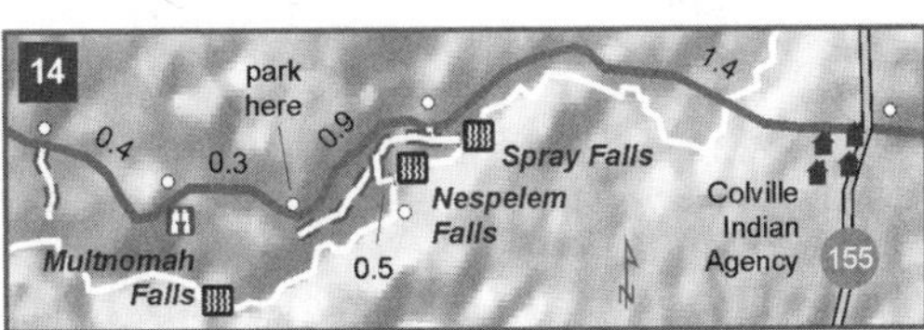

Over the years, I have taken many waterfall expeditions. None of them happened to pass through this part of Colville Indian Reservation until I found a trio

Spray Falls

of waterfalls along the Nespelem River in 2003 that is certainly worth a visit. Drive along State Route 155 to the north end of Colville Indian Agency. Turn west onto an unmarked road; there may be a sign pointing in that direction advertising the Nespelem Junior Rodeo.

SPRAY FALLS ★★

MAGNITUDE: 42
ELEVATION: 1600 feet
WATERSHED: Large
APPROACH: Trail (easy)
LAT/LONG: 48.133438° N / 119.003814° W
USGS MAP: *Armstrong Creek* (1989)

The Nespelem River rushes 15 to 20 feet into a large plunge pool. From the junction with SR 155, drive down the road 1.4 miles, and find a dirt road on the left. Turn here and park. From here, the route splits two ways. Walk up the route to the left for 0.1 mile where a beaten path leads to full side views of the descent.

NESPELEM FALLS (U) ★★★

MAGNITUDE: 53
ELEVATION: 1540 feet
WATERSHED: Large
APPROACH: Trail (fairly easy)
LAT/LONG: 48.132908° N / 119.006325° W
USGS MAP: *Armstrong Creek* (1989 nl)

It is ironic that the most scenic falls along the Nespelem River is the one that is not officially named. From the dirt road (described earlier), walk down the route to the right. Follow it 0.5 mile to an overlook directly into water tumbling 50 to 70 feet. Rock outcrops mask parts of the cataract.

 MULTNOMAH FALLS ★★

MAGNITUDE: 50
ELEVATION: 1140 feet
WATERSHED: Large
APPROACH: Auto
LAT/LONG: 48.12685° N / 119.019628° W
USGS MAP: *Armstrong Creek* (1989)

Who knew there was more than one Multnomah Falls? While many orders of magnitude smaller than its more famous namesake in Oregon, it nevertheless possesses scenic value. Continue along the paved road from the turnout (described earlier) for 0.9 mile to another unsigned turnout on the left. Park here and walk down the road an additional 0.3 mile to a moderately distant view of ribbons of water dropping 40 to 60 feet before cascading onward.

15 COULEE CITY

One of the engineering feats of the modern world was the construction of Grand Coulee Dam. One of the engineering feats of planet Earth is just to the south at Dry Falls.

 DRY FALLS ★★★★

MAGNITUDE: 10,000 years ago: 174;
today: 0
ELEVATION: 1510 feet
APPROACH: Auto
LAT/LONG: 47.607502° N / 119.350871° W
USGS MAP: *Coulee City* (1965)

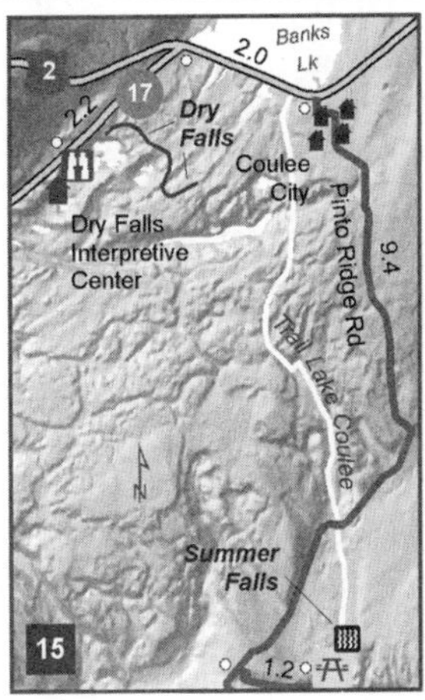

At one time the largest waterfall ever known plunged 400 feet over cliffs in five sweeping horseshoes totaling 3.5 miles in width! The discharge was 40 times mightier than Niagara Falls. Follow U.S. Highway 2 west from Coulee City, and turn south on State Route 17. Stop at the scenic turnout, viewpoint, and interpretive site 2.2 miles farther.

 SUMMER FALLS ★★

MAGNITUDE: 34 (l)
ELEVATION: 1490 feet
WATERSHED: Large (d)
APPROACH: Auto
LAT/LONG: 47.502744° N / 119.294201° W
USGS MAP: *Coulee City* (1965)

This entry is once again accessible to the public, as the Bureau of Reclamation (US Department of the Interior) has reopened the area previously administered by Washington State Parks. Drive 9.4 miles south of Coulee City along Pinto Ridge Road. Turn left (east) at the access road to the park. A picnic area and the waterfall are located in 1.2 miles at the route's end. During the irrigation season of summer, water is diverted from Banks Lake through Trail Lake Coulee in part to generate hydroelectric power. Some of the flow is allowed to descend over a 70- to 100-foot natural escarpment into Billy Clapp Lake.

16 ROCK CREEK COULEE

ROCK CREEK FALLS ★★

MAGNITUDE: 50
ELEVATION: 1700 feet
WATERSHED: Large
APPROACH: Trail (fairly easy)
LAT/LONG: 47.109006° N / 117.765996° W
USGS MAP: *Texas Lake* (1964)

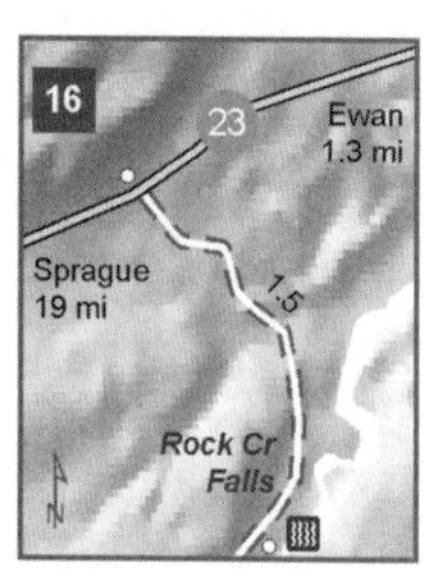

This cooling 10- to 15-foot sheet of water in a sagebrush setting along Rock Creek is located on private property. Fortunately, as the posted signs indicate, you can ask the adjacent landowner for permission to hike to it. From Ewan, drive west along State Route 23 for about 1.3 miles. Find a dusty back road to the left (south). Walk along this route for 1.5 miles to the stream and the falls.

17 PALOUSE CANYON

Who would think a powerful waterfall could exist in a semiarid sagebrush setting? Where does the water come from? In this case, it's due to a river whose waters originate in a more humid environment. Geomorphologists call these features exotic streams, and they are not all that uncommon within the Pacific Northwest's drier environments.

PALOUSE FALLS ★★★★★

MAGNITUDE: 86
ELEVATION: 770 feet
WATERSHED: Large
APPROACH: Auto
LAT/LONG: 46.663406° N / 118.223924° W
USGS MAP: *Palouse Falls* (2011)

The Palouse River hurtles 185 feet into Lower Palouse Canyon in a thundering display. The Wilkes Expedition of 1841 called this descent Aputapat Falls. In 1875 W. P. Breeding erected a flour mill at the falls, envisioning a vibrant Palouse City at the site, but it never came to be.

Palouse Falls

From Washtucna follow State Route 260 south to State Route 261, turn left, and drive 9 miles southeast to the marked access road to Palouse Falls State Park. You can also reach the park entrance from the south by turning west onto SR 261 from U.S. Highway 12 about 15 miles north of Dayton. The picnic area and falls are 2.3 miles from the entrance.

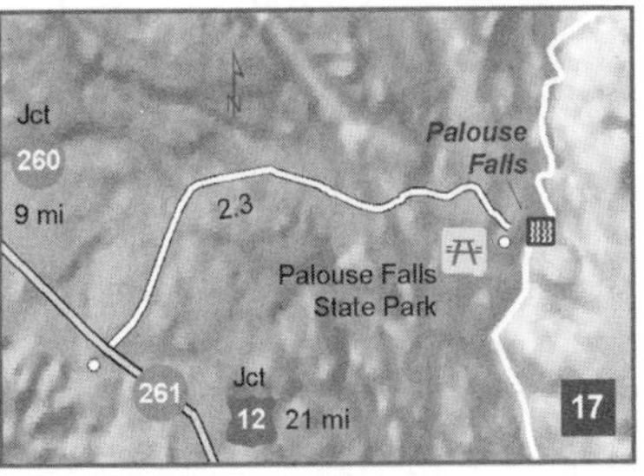

MORE ONLINE:

Little Palouse Falls ★★★ USGS *Palouse Falls* (2011), no public access
Upper Palouse Falls (u) ★ USGS *Palouse Falls* (2011 nl), no public access

OREGON & WASHINGTON

THE COLUMBIA GORGE

The Columbia Gorge is a haven for waterfall lovers. Although it is the smallest of the fourteen regions in this book, it has the greatest density of waterfalls. There are 122 recognized falls in this area of 1700 square miles; descriptions of 74 are given in this chapter. The others cannot be viewed either because no trails lead to them or because they are in watersheds in which travel is restricted.

The majority of the falls along the Oregon side of the Gorge were formed by the same geological events that shaped the region. Two major lava flows, which covered much of the Pacific Northwest, impacted this area, one more than 30 million years ago and the other about 15 million years ago.

As the layers of lava cooled, they mainly formed a type of rock called basalt. The Cascade Range was formed when this bedrock material was uplifted by internal earth forces. Because basalt is relatively resistant to erosion by running water, the rise of the Cascades diverted the course of most rivers. But the Columbia River was powerful enough to erode through the rising bedrock to shape the Columbia Gorge. The small streams that flow into the Columbia from the adjacent upland cannot effectively erode the basalt, so their courses are interrupted by the sharp, vertical breaks of the Gorge, resulting in spectacular waterfalls.

Because landslides have modified the steepness of relief on the Washington side, these great waterfalls are limited to the south side of the Gorge, with those on the Washington side being smaller and fewer in number than those in Oregon. Sections 1 through 12 of this chapter cover the Oregon side of the Gorge; sections 13 through 18, the Washington side.

A federal law that went into effect in 1986 designated most of this region, more than 225,000 acres, as the Columbia River Gorge National Scenic Area (NSA). The first of its kind, this national scenic area legislation was the result of two primary concerns: first, to protect and provide for the enhancement of the scenic, cultural, recreational, and natural resources of the area and, second, to protect and support the economy of the Gorge by encouraging growth in

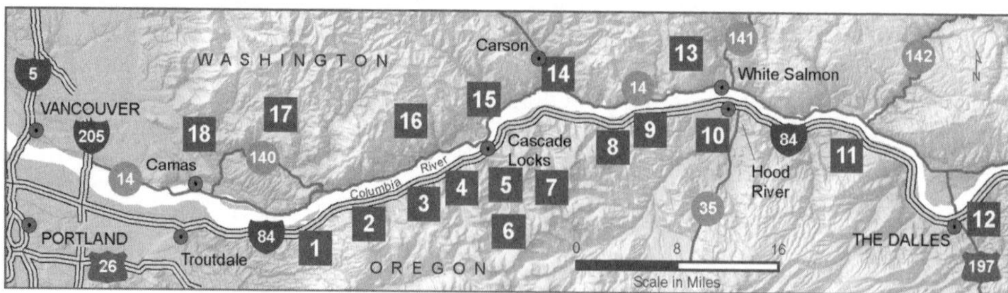

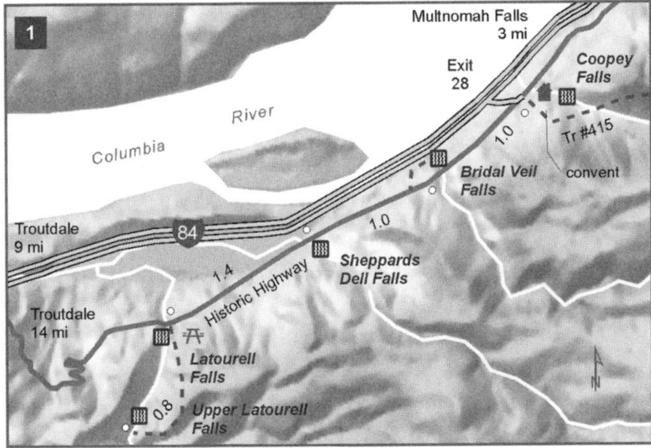

existing urban areas and by allowing future economic development outside these areas where it is compatible with Gorge resources.

1 BRIDAL VEIL

The Historic Columbia River Highway is accessible from Interstate 84 for eastbounders at Troutdale (Exit 17), Lewis and Clark State Park (Exit 18), Corbett (Exit 22), or Bridal Veil (Exit 28). Westbounders can access the area at Dodson (Exit 35) or Warrendale (Exit 37).

LATOURELL FALLS ★★★★★

MAGNITUDE: 83
ELEVATION: 400 feet
WATERSHED: Small

APPROACH: Auto
LAT/LONG: 45.536844° N / 122.218152° W
USGS MAP: *Bridal Veil* (1994)

This 249-foot waterfall along Latourell Creek is within Guy W. Talbot State Park, the land for which was donated to the state of Oregon in 1929 by Mr. and Mrs. Guy W. Talbot. The waterfall was named in August 1887, after Joseph Latourell, a prominent local settler. From Exit 28 on I-84 drive 3.4 miles west on the Historic Columbia River Highway to the day-use park. It is a very short walk from the picnic area to the viewpoint.

UPPER LATOURELL FALLS ★★★

MAGNITUDE: 65
ELEVATION: 680 feet
WATERSHED: Small

APPROACH: Trail (moderate)
LAT/LONG: 45.530396° N / 122.221113° W
USGS MAP: *Bridal Veil* (1994)

It is possible to walk behind this 75- to 100-foot cataract on Latourell Creek. Continue along the upper trail past the top of Latourell Falls (described earlier) for 0.8 mile to the upper falls.

SHEPPARDS DELL FALLS (U) ★★

MAGNITUDE: 30 (l)
ELEVATION: 200 feet
WATERSHED: Small
APPROACH: Auto
LAT/LONG: 45.546388° N / 122.197681° W
USGS MAP: *Bridal Veil* (1994 nl)

A roadside view of a pair of falls is available by looking upstream from the bridge crossing at Shepperds Dell State Park. The lower tier is of the horsetail form and drops 40 to 60 feet. The 35- to 50-foot plunge of the upper portion is not as clearly visible. The day-use park is located 1.4 miles east of Latourell Falls (described earlier) or 2 miles west of Exit 28 on the Historic Columbia River Highway. Note: Gorge NSA publications use the above spelling for the falls, while the US Geological Survey and Oregon State Parks use "Shepperds" for the dell and park.

BRIDAL VEIL FALLS ★★★

MAGNITUDE: 59
ELEVATION: 200 feet
WATERSHED: Small
APPROACH: Trail (moderate)
LAT/LONG: 45.554322° N / 122.180214° W
USGS MAP: *Bridal Veil* (1994)

Bridal Veil Creek drops abruptly twice, the upper portion falling 60 to 100 feet and the lower portion falling 40 to 60 feet. Along the trail to the falls, you can look across the Columbia River to distant views of some seasonal cataracts descending from the Washington side of the Gorge. Drive to a parking area located about 2.4 miles east of Latourell Falls (described earlier), or 1 mile

Bridal Veil Falls

west of Exit 28 on the Historic Columbia River Highway. A trail winds 0.1 mile down to the base of the cataract.

COOPEY FALLS ★★

MAGNITUDE: 59
ELEVATION: 360 feet
WATERSHED: Small
APPROACH: Auto
LAT/LONG: 45.562284° N / 122.164572° W
USGS MAP: *Bridal Veil* (1994)

This waterfall drops 150 to 175 feet along Coopey Creek, which is named for Charles Coopey, who once owned the adjacent land. It is located on the Historic Columbia River Highway just east of Exit 28. A convent owned by the Franciscan Sisters of the Eucharist at the base of the falls serves meals to the public and invites guests to stroll up to the falls. Partial views can also be gained above the descent by hiking 0.6 mile up nearby Angels Rest Trail 415.

2 MULTNOMAH FALLS

Multnomah Falls is the most famous waterfall in Oregon. In the same vicinity are several other falls that are worth a visit; all can be accessed from the Historic Columbia River Highway or from the rest area at Exit 31 on Interstate 84.

WAHKEENA FALLS ★★★★

MAGNITUDE: 59
ELEVATION: 560 feet
WATERSHED: Small
APPROACH: Auto
LAT/LONG: 45.572665° N / 122.126635° W
USGS MAP: *Bridal Veil* (1994)

Wahkeena Creek glistens 242 feet down the mountainside. It was once known as Gordan Falls and was renamed by the Mazamas outdoor recreation association in 1915. *Wahkeena* is a Yakama Indian word meaning "most beautiful."

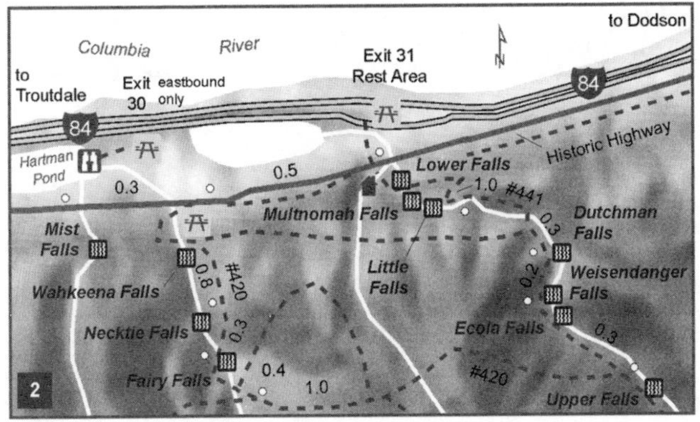

Multnomah Falls

To view the falls, drive to the signed Wahkeena Picnic Area 0.5 mile west of Multnomah Falls Lodge on the Historic Columbia River Highway.

7 NECKTIE FALLS ★★

MAGNITUDE: 49
ELEVATION: 800 feet
WATERSHED: Small

APPROACH: Trail (fairly hard)
LAT/LONG: 45.571193° N / 122.125798° W
USGS MAP: *Multnomah Falls* (1994 ns)

This aptly named cataract veils 30 to 50 feet along Wahkeena Creek. Embark upon the moderately steep Wahkeena Trail 420 from Wahkeena Picnic Area (described earlier). After 0.8 mile, a spur trail quickly leads to the falls.

FAIRY FALLS ★★★

MAGNITUDE: 45
ELEVATION: 1000 feet
WATERSHED: Small
APPROACH: Trail (fairly hard)
LAT/LONG: 45.569916° N / 122.124682° W
USGS MAP: *Multnomah Falls* (1994 ns)

Wahkeena Creek tumbles 20 to 30 feet in pleasant fashion. Continue 0.3 mile past the spur path for Necktie Falls (described earlier) to the point where Wahkeena Trail 420 crosses in front of the base of this cataract.

MULTNOMAH FALLS ★★★★★

MAGNITUDE: 93
ELEVATION: 620 feet
WATERSHED: Medium
APPROACH: Auto
LAT/LONG: 45.575879° N / 122.115455° W
USGS MAP: *Multnomah Falls* (1994 nl)

Descending a total of 620 feet, Multnomah Falls is the tallest waterfall in the United States easily accessible year-round. The main portion plunges 542 feet off a sheer cliff, while below a stone masonry footbridge erected by Simon Benson in 1914 Lower Multnomah Falls ★★, USGS *Multnomah Falls* (1994 ns), drops 69 feet.

One of most popular tourist attractions in Oregon, the falls is accessible from either the Historic Columbia River Highway or I-84 via a rest area (Exit 31) built expressly for visiting here. Adjacent to the cataract is Multnomah Falls Lodge. Constructed in 1925, it now houses a visitors center, restaurant, and gift shop.

The falls occur due to Multnomah Creek flowing over the basalt cliffs of the Columbia Gorge, as the Columbia River managed to maintain its course during the rise of the Cascade Range millions of years ago. Nature alters the appearance of Multnomah Falls, sometimes slowly, sometimes abruptly. On September 4, 1995, a 400-ton slab of rock fell 225 feet into the upper pool. Twenty persons sustained minor injuries from flying, gravel-sized rock chips from a 100-foot-high splash that soaked the footbridge and beyond.

American Indian folklore has a different account of the origin of Multnomah Falls; below is excerpted from a plaque at the waterfall:

> Many years ago, a terrible sickness came over the village of the Multnomah people and many died. An old medicine man of the tribe told the Chief that a pure and innocent maiden must go to a high cliff above the Big River and throw herself on the rocks below and the sickness would leave at once. The Chief did not want to ask any maiden to make the sacrifice. But when his daughter saw the sickness on the face of her lover, she went to the high cliff and threw herself on the rocks below. The sickness went away. As a token of the maiden's welcome,

the Great Spirit took water, silvery white, and streamed it over the cliff, breaking it into a floating mist.

DUTCHMAN FALLS (U) ★★

MAGNITUDE: 37
ELEVATION: 840 feet
WATERSHED: Small
APPROACH: Trail (fairly hard)
LAT/LONG: 45.574121° N / 122.107494° W
USGS MAP: *Multnomah Falls* (1994 ns)

In this series of three falls along Multnomah Creek, the lower and upper falls drop 10 to 15 feet while the middle section tumbles 15 to 20 feet. Embark upon Larch Mountain Trail 441, which begins to the left of Multnomah Falls Lodge (described earlier). The steep trail offers a variety of views of Multnomah Falls in its 1-mile journey to a short spur path, which ends at a viewpoint at the top of the cataract. Look upstream to see the 10- to 15-foot descent of Little Multnomah Falls (u) ★ USGS *Multnomah Falls* (1994 ns). Continue along the main trail, where you will encounter the trio comprising Dutchman Falls over the next 0.2 to 0.3 mile.

WEISENDANGER FALLS ★★★

MAGNITUDE: 62
ELEVATION: 960 feet
WATERSHED: Small
APPROACH: Trail (fairly hard)
LAT/LONG: 45.572619° N / 122.107838° W
USGS MAP: Multnomah Falls (1994 ns)

Multnomah Creek plunges 50 to 75 feet next to Larch Mountain Trail 441. Continue along the route for 0.2 mile past Dutchman Falls (described earlier), a total of 1.6 miles from the trailhead. Just beyond, only the top of Ecola Falls ★ USGS *Multnomah Falls* (1994 ns) can be seen.

MIST FALLS ★★

MAGNITUDE: 29 (l)
ELEVATION: 700 feet
WATERSHED: Small
APPROACH: Auto
LAT/LONG: 45.573851° N / 122.131591° W
USGS MAP: *Bridal Veil* (1994)

Water spirals hundreds of feet down tiny Mist Creek. Depart I-84 at Benson State Park (Exit 30), available to eastbound traffic only. Walk down from the near end of the parking lot along the short paved path signed for Hartman Pond. Gaze up at the moderately distant cliffs; the cataract is normally reduced to a trickle during the summer. Only fleeting views are available from the Historic Columbia River Highway.

MORE ONLINE:
The waterfalls mentioned earlier
Upper Multnomah Falls (u) ★ USGS *Multnomah Falls* (1994 ns)

Lower Oneonta Falls

3 ONEONTA GORGE

The cool, moist north-facing slopes and sheltered drainages of the Oregon side of the Columbia Gorge provide an environment for lush, diverse vegetation. This setting is best experienced at Oneonta Gorge Botanical Area, 2 miles east of Multnomah Falls along the Historic Columbia River Highway. (See the Bridal Veil section of this chapter for information about accessing the Historic Highway.)

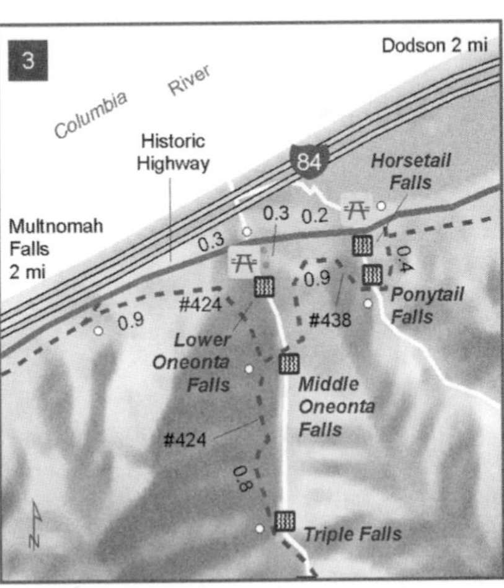

LOWER ONEONTA FALLS (U) ★★★

MAGNITUDE: 49
ELEVATION: 220 feet
WATERSHED: Medium
APPROACH: Bushwhack (fairly hard)
LAT/LONG: 45.587608° N / 122.074085° W
USGS MAP: *Multnomah Falls* (1994 ns)

Water plummets 50 to 70 feet into the narrow emerald-green Oneonta Gorge. Pick your way up Oneonta Creek from the signed entrance of the botanical area. When the water is high, you will need to briefly wade or swim along the 0.3-mile journey.

MIDDLE ONEONTA FALLS (U) ★★

MAGNITUDE: 63
ELEVATION: 240 feet
WATERSHED: Medium
APPROACH: Trail (fairly hard)
LAT/LONG: 45.58516° N / 122.072819° W
USGS MAP: *Multnomah Falls* (1994 ns)

Water slides steeply 60 to 75 feet along Oneonta Creek. Hike up moderately strenuous Oneonta Trail 424 for 0.9 mile to its junction with Horsetail Falls Trail 438. Follow Trail 438 for a few hundred yards to the footbridge overlooking the falls. In previous editions, this entry was thought to be Oneonta Falls USGS *Multnomah Falls* (1994), which in actuality occurs off-trail farther upstream.

TRIPLE FALLS ★★★★★

MAGNITUDE: 71
ELEVATION: 560 feet
WATERSHED: Small
APPROACH: Trail (fairly hard)
LAT/LONG: 45.578492° N / 122.072433° W
USGS MAP: *Multnomah Falls* (1994)

This is a jewel of waterfalls, as three rivulets of Oneonta Creek plunge 100 to 135 feet. The trail provides an aerial view high above the cataract. Walk along Oneonta Trail 424 for 1.7 miles from the trailhead (0.8 mile past the junction with Horsetail Falls Trail 438) to Triple Falls.

HORSETAIL FALLS ★★★★

MAGNITUDE: 82 (h)
ELEVATION: 240 feet
WATERSHED: Small
APPROACH: Auto
LAT/LONG: 45.58941° N / 122.068549° W
USGS MAP: *Multnomah Falls* (1994)

Horsetail Creek sprays 176 feet next to the Historic Columbia River Highway in a classic example of its namesake form. Drive to the signed turnout 2.5 miles east of Multnomah Falls Lodge (described earlier). An interpretive sign here informs readers about the different shapes of waterfalls. It is based upon the form classification that I first devised.

PONYTAIL FALLS ★★★

MAGNITUDE: 76 (h)
ELEVATION: 240 feet
WATERSHED: Small
APPROACH: Trail (moderate)
LAT/LONG: 45.588554° N / 122.068248° W
USGS MAP: *Multnomah Falls* (1994 ns)

Horsetail Creek shoots 100 to 125 feet over a bulbous escarpment. The trail goes behind the base of the falls. It is also known as Upper Horsetail Falls. Hike 0.4 mile from the Historic Highway along Horsetail Falls Trail 438, which starts at Horsetail Falls (described earlier).

4 YEON STATE PARK

John B. Yeon State Park is a day-use area located next to the east end of the Historic Columbia River Highway, just before the juction with Interstate 84 at Exit 37.

ELOWAH FALLS ★★★★★

MAGNITUDE: 83
ELEVATION: 400 feet
WATERSHED: Small
APPROACH: Trail (fairly easy)
LAT/LONG: 45.611794° N / 121.994606° W
USGS MAP: *Tanner Butte* (1994)

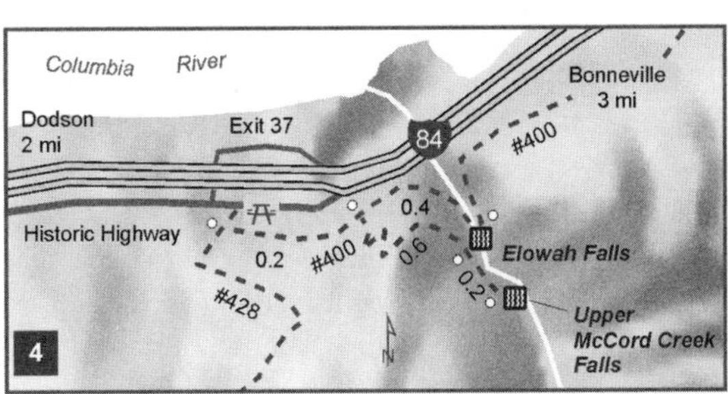

McCord Creek plummets 289 feet within John B. Yeon State Park. A committee of the Mazamas, an outdoor recreation association, named the falls in 1915. Begin on Gorge Trail 400, turning left at the first trail junction. A second junction occurs 0.2 mile from the parking area. For an aerial view of the falls, turn right on Elowah Falls Trail and take this moderately steep route 0.6 mile. To reach the base of the falls, stay on Trail 400 for 0.4 mile.

UPPER MCCORD CREEK FALLS ★★★

MAGNITUDE: 39 (l)
ELEVATION: 480 feet
WATERSHED: Small
APPROACH: Trail (fairly hard)
LAT/LONG: 45.611269° N / 121.994284° W
USGS MAP: *Tanner Butte* (1994 nl)

McCord Creek tumbles 100 to 125 feet. Continue 0.2 mile past the upper viewpoint of Elowah Falls (described earlier) to the end of Elowah Falls Trail.

5 TANNER CREEK

Turn off Interstate 84 at Bonneville Dam (Exit 40), and proceed south several hundred yards to the parking area for the Columbia Gorge NSA's Wahclella Falls Trail 436, which starts out as a dirt road. Note: Gorge Trail 400 does not pass the following waterfalls.

 MUNRA FALLS (U) ★★

MAGNITUDE: 27 (l)
ELEVATION: 80 feet
WATERSHED: Very small
APPROACH: Trail (easy)
LAT/LONG: 45.626472° N / 121.95302° W
USGS MAP: *Bonneville Dam* (1994 ns)

An unnamed creek drops 35 to 50 feet into Tanner Creek. I have named the falls after nearby Munra Point. Walk 0.2 mile from the trailhead where the dirt road turns into a footpath.

 WAHCLELLA FALLS ★★★★

MAGNITUDE: 75 (h)
ELEVATION: 420 feet
WATERSHED: Medium
APPROACH: Trail (easy)
LAT/LONG: 45.617663° N / 121.951283° W
USGS MAP: *Tanner Butte* (1994 nl)

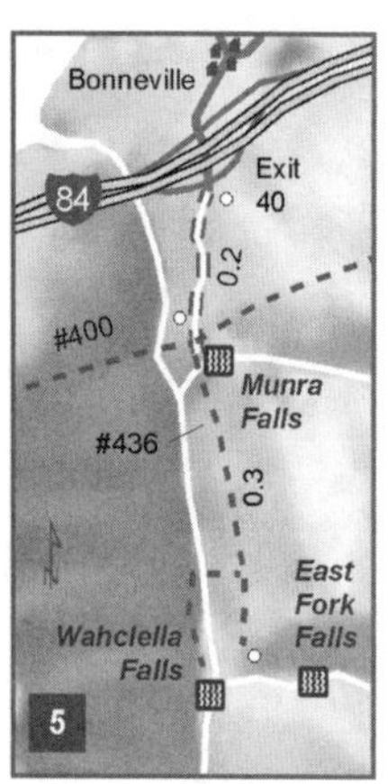

The upper portion of this thunderous waterfall plunges 15 to 25 feet before veiling downward 50 to 70 feet into a pool. It is also known as Tanner Falls. Wahclella is the name of a nearby American Indian locality and was given to the falls in 1915 by a committee of the Mazamas, an outdoor recreation association. Proceed 0.3 mile beyond Munra Falls (described earlier) to the end of Trail 436 near the descent. A spur path, not recommended for youngsters, quickly leads to more dramatic views.

MORE ONLINE:
East Fork Falls (u) ★ USGS *Tanner Butte* (1994 nl)

Wahclella Falls

6 EAGLE CREEK

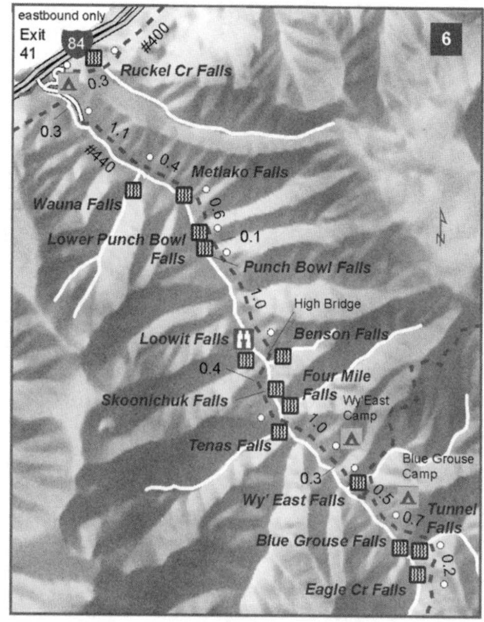

The most spectacular hike in the Columbia Gorge NSA is along Eagle Creek Trail 440. You will encounter a dozen waterfalls as you take this moderately ascending 1400-foot route over the 6 miles of beautiful, narrow Eagle Creek Gorge. Be sure to issue yourself a free backcountry permit at the self check-in when you reach mile 5. *Warning:* The trail passes along exposed cliffs; children should either be carefully supervised or left with a babysitter.

Eastbound travelers can access the trailhead by turning off Interstate 84 at Eagle Creek Park (Exit 41). Westbounders will have to make a U-turn at Bonneville Dam (Exit 40) to reach Exit 41. When departing, make a similar turn at Cascade Locks (Exit 44) to get back on the westbound freeway.

WAUNA FALLS (U) ★★

MAGNITUDE: 22
ELEVATION: 480 feet
WATERSHED: Very small
APPROACH: Trail (moderate)
LAT/LONG: 45.628393° N / 121.908603° W
USGS MAP: *Bonneville Dam* (1994 nl)

This minor cataract is the first of the dozen falls along Eagle Creek Trail 440. I named it after nearby Wauna Point. Look across the gorge at this descent along the first major tributary to Eagle Creek. It is located about 1.1 miles from the trailhead.

METLAKO FALLS ★★★★

MAGNITUDE: 73 (h)
ELEVATION: 240 feet
WATERSHED: Large
APPROACH: Trail (moderate)
LAT/LONG: 45.628198° N / 121.898947° W
USGS MAP: *Bonneville Dam* (1994)

This is the highest cataract on Eagle Creek, dropping 100 to 150 feet. It was named in 1915 by a committee of the Mazamas, an outdoor recreation association, for the legendary American Indian goddess of salmon. Continue 0.4

mile beyond Wauna Falls (described earlier) to the signed vista for a partially obscured view of this entry.

LOWER PUNCH BOWL FALLS ★★★

MAGNITUDE: 19
ELEVATION: 340 feet
WATERSHED: Large
APPROACH: Trail (moderate)
LAT/LONG: 45.62275° N / 121.895364° W
USGS MAP: *Tanner Butte* (1994 ns)

Despite possessing only a modest 10- to 15-foot drop, this exquisite punchbowl and its upper counterpart (described next) have been made famous by photographers worldwide. Hike 0.6 mile beyond Metlako Falls (described earlier), 2.1 miles from the trailhead of Eagle Creek Trail 440. Take the signed spur that quickly leads streamside in front of the descent.

PUNCH BOWL FALLS ★★★★

MAGNITUDE: 48 (h)
ELEVATION: 360 feet
WATERSHED: Large
APPROACH: Trail (moderate)
LAT/LONG: 45.621535° N / 121.894527° W
USGS MAP: *Tanner Butte (1994)*

This falls is the larger of the pair of punchbowls, as Eagle Creek pours 20 to 40 feet into a large amphitheater. Continue along Eagle Creek Trail 440 for 0.1 mile beyond the spur to Lower Punch Bowl Falls (described earlier). The trailside view is high above the descent.

LOOWIT FALLS ★★

MAGNITUDE: 21 (l)
ELEVATION: 720 feet
WATERSHED: Small
APPROACH: Trail (moderate)
LAT/LONG: 45.608222° N / 121.885343° W
USGS MAP: *Tanner Butte* (1994)

Gain a cross-canyon view of the 50- to 60-foot drop of Loowit Creek into Eagle Creek Gorge. Hike 1 mile past Punch Bowl Falls (described earlier) to the next viewpoint for this entry, a total of 3.2 miles from the Eagle Creek Trailhead. If you have reached the crossing of Eagle Creek at High Bridge, you have gone too far and will need to backtrack a short distance.

SKOONICHUK FALLS ★★

MAGNITUDE: 61
ELEVATION: 640 feet
WATERSHED: Large
APPROACH: Trail (moderate)
LAT/LONG: 45.604424° N / 121.880258° W
USGS MAP: *Tanner Butte* (1994 nl)

Eagle Creek drops a total of 50 to 70 feet as a pair of punchbowls. Lack of unobstructed views prevents a higher scenic rating. Proceed 0.4 mile past High

Bridge along Eagle Creek Trail 440 (described earlier). Besides trailside views, a very short spur trail goes to the top of the cataract.

WY'EAST FALLS (U) ★★

MAGNITUDE: 30 (l)
ELEVATION: 1120 feet
WATERSHED: Very small
APPROACH: Trail & bushwhack (fairly hard)
LAT/LONG: 45.592683° N / 121.864336° W
USGS MAP: *Wahtum Lake* (1994 nl)

A small unnamed tributary drips 90 to 110 feet, a short distance off Eagle Creek Trail 440. I named it after the nearby campsite. Walk along Eagle Creek Trail for 1 mile beyond Skoonichuk Falls (described earlier) to Wy'East Camp. Proceed another 0.3 mile to a stream crossing and a mostly obscured view of the cataract. A fairly easy 0.1-mile bushwhack up the drainage leads to an open vantage point.

TUNNEL FALLS ★★★★★

MAGNITUDE: 67
ELEVATION: 1200 feet
WATERSHED: Medium
APPROACH: Trail or backpack (fairly hard)
LAT/LONG: 45.58483° N / 121.852298° W
USGS MAP: *Wahtum Lake* (1994)

This exciting cataract is named for the passageway blasted though the bedrock behind its 100-foot plummet. The scenery is further accentuated by the fact that Eagle Creek Trail 440 is cut into the gorge wall, halfway up the falls! This unmistakable feature is located 0.7 mile past Blue Grouse Camp, nearly 6 worthwhile miles from Eagle Creek Trailhead.

Tunnel Falls

EAGLE CREEK FALLS (U) ★★★

MAGNITUDE: 37
ELEVATION: 1160 feet
WATERSHED: Medium
APPROACH: Trail or backpack (fairly hard)
LAT/LONG: 45.582112° N / 121.85217° W
USGS MAP: *Wahtum Lake* (1994 nl)

View a cornucopia of waterfall shapes as Eagle Creek descends in four distinct forms: punchbowl, cascade, plunge, and horsetail. Follow Eagle Creek Trail 440 for 0.2 mile past Tunnel Falls (described earlier). Bathing rocks and a small punchbowl waterfall are located a short distance farther upstream.

MORE ONLINE:
Ruckel Creek Falls (u) ★ USGS *Bonneville Dam* (1994 ns)
Benson Falls (u) ★ USGS *Tanner Butte* (1994 nl)
Tenas Falls (u) ★ USGS *Tanner Butte* (1994 ns)
Four Mile Falls (u) ★ USGS *Tanner Butte* (1994 nl)
Blue Grouse Falls (u) ★ USGS *Wahtum Lake* (1994 nl)

7 CASCADE LOCKS

The following waterfalls are accessible via Pacific Crest National Scenic Trail 2000. From Interstate 84 at Cascade Locks, eastbounders take the ramp at Exit 44 and drive 0.3 mile. Once passing under Bridge of the Gods, turn right to the trailhead parking on the right. Westbounders depart I-84 at Exit 45 and proceed along Cascade Locks Highway for 1.5 miles; turn left and then right into the same parking area. All of the following cataracts are located within the Columbia Gorge NSA.

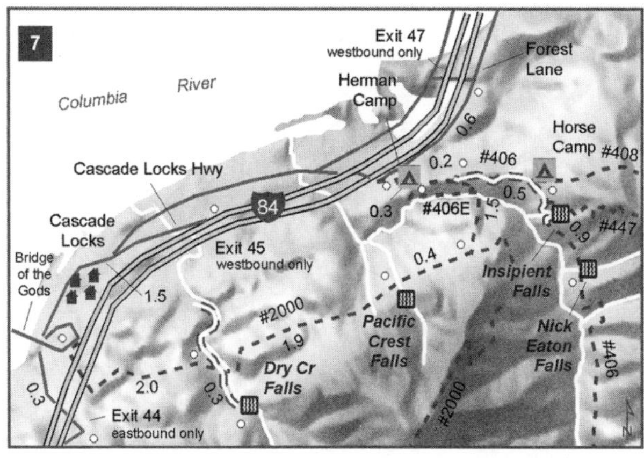

Dry Creek Falls

DRY CREEK FALLS (U) ★★★

MAGNITUDE: 49
ELEVATION: 1400 feet
WATERSHED: Small
APPROACH: Trail (fairly easy)
LAT/LONG: 45.657031° N / 121.866589° W
USGS MAP: *Carson* (1994 nl)

Dry Creek plunges 50 to 70 feet. The drainage is a part of the watershed for the city of Cascade Locks. Obey the signs posted near the falls. From Bridge of the Gods, hike 2 miles along Pacific Crest Trail 2000 to Dry Creek. For those departing from the Work Center or Herman Camp, take the appropriate spur trail to Trail 2000 and hike 2.3 miles westward to Dry Creek. Once you reach the drainage, follow a dirt road 0.3 mile upstream to the base of the descent.

NICK EATON FALLS (U) ★★★

MAGNITUDE: 59
ELEVATION: 900 feet
WATERSHED: Very small
APPROACH: Trail (fairly hard)
LAT/LONG: 45.671952° N / 121.820197° W
USGS MAP: *Carson* (1994 nl)

An 80- to 100-foot ribbon of Falls Creek splashes just a few feet from a trail. The easiest access to this specific entry is from Herman Camp. Westbounders depart

I-84 at Herman Creek (Exit 47). Eastbound traffic will need to use Wyeth (Exit 51) as a U-turn. Once off the interstate ramp, cross under the freeway and turn right (west) along the frontage road, named Forest Lane. Proceed 0.6 mile and turn left for Herman Camp (signs may also be seen for the Columbia Gorge Work Center). Go up the road, which quickly leads to the camp and trailhead on the west end. Park here.

Embark upon the route signed for both Herman Creek Trail 406 and Pacific Crest Trail 2000. After a fairly steep walk for 0.3 mile, crossing some powerlines along the way, you reach a junction. The trail on the right goes toward Dry Creek Falls (described earlier), so bear left. The way is less steep for the next 0.2 mile, where you encounter a most confusing junction of multiple paths. Stay straight, bearing eastward, where the route steepens considerably as an old dirt road.

A horse camp is 0.5 mile farther down the way, with another junction maze. Once again, proceed straight ahead although your bearing is now toward the southeast. As Herman Creek Trail parallels its namesake, you reach this entry in 0.9 mile. I erroneously called this falls Camp Creek Falls in the previous edition because I thought it was on that stream. The Trailkeepers of Oregon have popularized the Nick Eaton moniker.

MORE ONLINE:

Pacific Crest Falls (u) ★ USGS *Carson* (1994 nl)

Insipient Falls (u) ★ USGS *Carson* (1994 ns), called Falls Creek Falls in the last edition

8 WYETH

1 GORTON CREEK FALLS ★★★

MAGNITUDE: 70
ELEVATION: 500 feet
WATERSHED: Small

APPROACH: Trail (fairly easy)
LAT/LONG: 45.681832° N / 121.772111° W
USGS MAP: *Carson* (1994 ns)

Gorton Creek pours 120 to 140 feet from cliffs within the Columbia Gorge NSA. Some vantage points reveal a 20- to 30-foot upper tier along the stream. Depart Interstate 84 at Wyeth (Exit 51), and drive 0.4 mile through Wyeth Camp. Proceed to the route's end at the parking area for Wyeth Trail 411 and begin walking; after a few hundred yards the way becomes a dirt road. Do not take either of the two signed trails (400 or 411); instead, continue along the dirt road. In 0.3 mile the road again becomes a path, crossing the creek once. After another 0.2 mile, you will need to negotiate a few large boulders before reaching the base of the cataract.

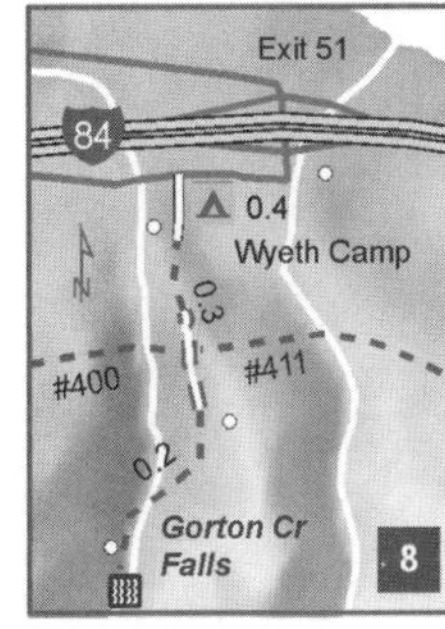

9 STARVATION CREEK STATE PARK

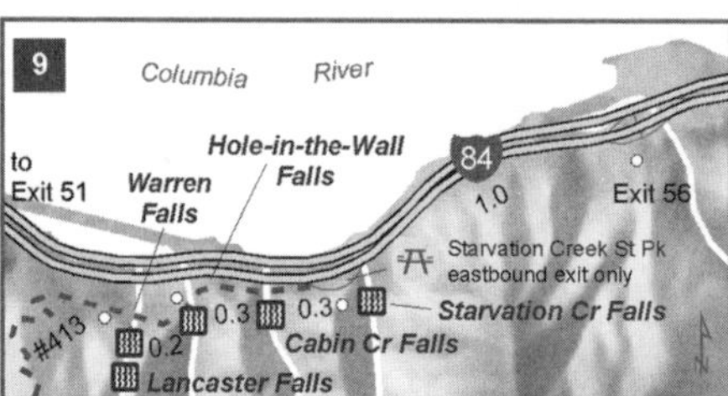

Turn off Interstate 84 at the eastbound-only exit for day-use Starvation Creek State Park and rest area. Westbounders must make a U-turn at Wyeth (Exit 51) to enter, then make a similar turn at Viento Park (Exit 56) when leaving.

STARVATION CREEK FALLS ★★★★

MAGNITUDE: 62
ELEVATION: 280 feet
WATERSHED: Small
APPROACH: Auto
LAT/LONG: 45.687588° N / 121.688426° W
USGS MAP: *Mount Defiance* (1994 nl)

The name of this 186-foot waterfall and its stream came from an event that happened in December 1884. Two trains were snowbound nearby on the recently completed railroad. The stranded passengers called the area "Starveout," although no one perished during the incident. Walk a short distance from the southeast side of the picnic area (far end to your left) to view the falls.

Starvation Creek Falls

CABIN CREEK FALLS ★★

MAGNITUDE: 32 (l)
ELEVATION: 300 feet
WATERSHED: Very small
APPROACH: Trail (easy)
LAT/LONG: 45.687394° N / 121.696537° W
USGS MAP: *Mount Defiance* (1994 nl)

Water trickles 175 to 200 feet from Cabin Creek. Starting at the rest area, hike 0.3 mile west along Mount Defiance Trail 413 to a trailside view in front of the cataract.

HOLE-IN-THE-WALL FALLS ★★★

MAGNITUDE: 42
ELEVATION: 200 feet
WATERSHED: Small
APPROACH: Trail (fairly easy)
LAT/LONG: 45.686269° N / 121.70203° W
USGS MAP: *Mount Defiance* (1994 nl)

This 75- to 100-foot descent once sprayed onto the old highway, so the course of Warren Creek was diverted by blasting a tunnel through the adjacent basaltic cliff. The falls was originally named Warren Falls. Walk 0.3 mile past Cabin Creek Falls (described earlier) along Mount Defiance Trail 413.

WARREN FALLS ★★

MAGNITUDE: 29 (l)
ELEVATION: 320 feet
WATERSHED: Very small
APPROACH: Trail (moderate)
LAT/LONG: 45.684725° N / 121.706021° W
USGS MAP: *Mount Defiance* (1994 ns)

The lowest 30- to 35-foot portion of Lancaster Falls, USGS *Mount Defiance* (1994) now officially carries this name. Continue 0.2 mile past Hole-in-the-Wall Falls (described earlier) for a total of 0.8 mile along Mount Defiance Trail 413. Samuel C. Lancaster was the engineer who designed the beautiful Historic Columbia River Highway prior to World War I. There are no trails to the larger 200- to 250-foot cataract farther up Wonder Creek; only distant views are available from the highway.

10 HOOD RIVER VALLEY

The area around Hood River is known for windsurfing and fruit orchards. The town and its surrounding valley can be accessed from Interstate 84 via Exits 62 and 64 or from Mount Hood via State Route 35.

WAH GWIN GWIN FALLS ★★★

MAGNITUDE: 65
ELEVATION: 280 feet
WATERSHED: Medium
APPROACH: Auto
LAT/LONG: 45.711732° N / 121.55358° W
USGS MAP: *Hood River* (1994)

Punchbowl Falls

This 207-foot plunge along Phelps Creek is located on the grounds of the luxuriant Columbia Gorge Hotel. *Wah Gwin Gwin* is an American Indian phrase meaning "tumbling or rushing waters." Leave I-84 at West Hood River and Westcliff Drive (Exit 62). Turn left (west) at Westcliff Drive, and reach the hotel and falls in 0.2 mile.

1 PUNCHBOWL FALLS ★★★

MAGNITUDE: 41 (h)
ELEVATION: 840 feet
WATERSHED: Large

APPROACH: Auto
LAT/LONG: 45.602067° N / 121.635833° W
USGS MAP: *Dee* (1994)

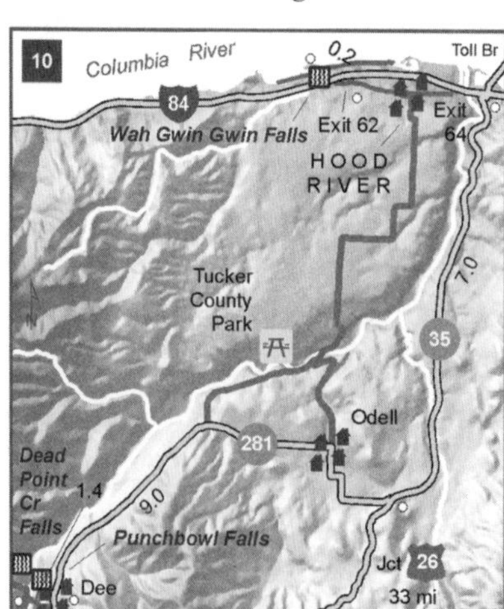

Hood River drops 10 to 15 feet into a large pool flanked by sheer cliffs of columnar basalt. Drive to the lumber processing facility at Dee, located on State Route 281. Turn right on Punchbowl Road, and continue 1.4 miles to an unsigned parking area on the near (east) side of the river. Take a short walk down the dirt road to pathways leading to unguarded vistas at the rim of the small canyon.

DEAD POINT CREEK FALLS (U) ★★

MAGNITUDE: 23 (l)
ELEVATION: 840 feet
WATERSHED: Medium
APPROACH: Auto
LAT/LONG: 45.602457° N / 121.636112° W
USGS MAP: *Dee* (1994 nl)

Look across the Hood River to view this 40- to 50-foot double falls. It is located immediately downstream from Punchbowl Falls (described earlier) and can be seen from the same viewpoints. The USGS topographic map erroneously labels this previously unnamed cataract as Punchbowl Falls.

11 MOSIER

MOSIER CREEK FALLS (U) ★★★

MAGNITUDE: 57
ELEVATION: 160 feet
WATERSHED: Large
APPROACH: Trail (easy)
LAT/LONG: 45.682537° N / 121.390465° W
USGS MAP: *White Salmon* (1994 nl)

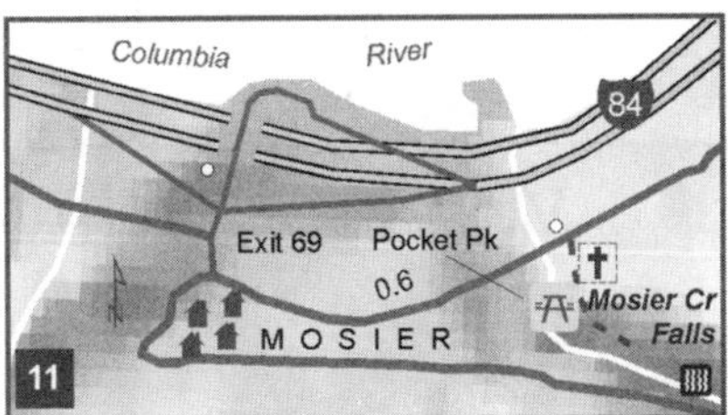

Mosier Creek slides into a small gorge, dropping a total of 125 to 150 feet. Turn off Interstate 84 at Mosier (Exit 69), and drive 0.6 mile east, passing the town of Mosier. A short, easy path on the right (east) side of Mosier Creek Bridge leads past Pioneer Cemetery to an unguarded overlook at Pocket Park.

MORE ONLINE:
Rowena Dell Falls (u) ★ USGS *Lyle* (1994 nl)

12 THE DALLES

Perched upon basalt, the city The Dalles stands as the eastern sentinel to the Columbia Gorge. Turn off Interstate 84 at The Dalles East and U.S. Highway 197 (Exit 87). Drive south 0.2 mile, then turn right (west) and go 0.2 mile to Southeast Frontage Road.

CUSHING FALLS ★★

MAGNITUDE: 13
ELEVATION: 140 feet
WATERSHED: Large
APPROACH: Auto
LAT/LONG: 45.611584° N / 121.119701° W
USGS MAP: *Petersburg* (1994)

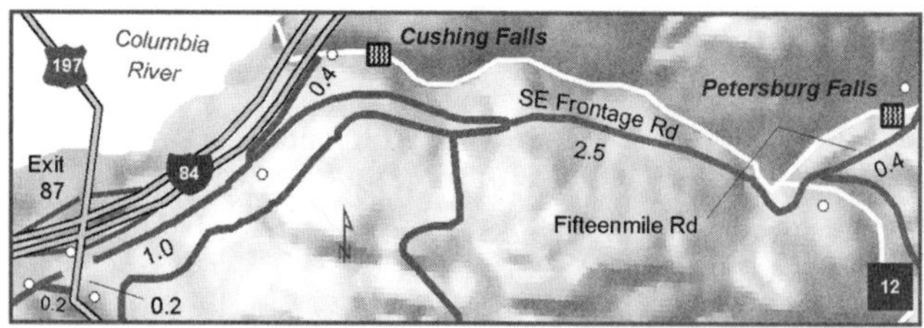

This modest 10- to 15-foot drop along Fifteenmile Creek occurs in a setting that is markedly drier than those of its counterparts to the west. The eastern flank of the Columbia Gorge is characterized by a climatological phenomenon known as the rain-shadow effect. The rain shadow results from the fact that most of the region's precipitation falls on the western, windward side of the Cascade Mountains.

Drive 1 mile along Southeast Frontage Road, then turn left and continue for 0.4 mile. Cross the bridge and turn right on an unimproved road. The descent is a very short, easy walk heading upstream.

MORE ONLINE:

Petersburg Falls (u) ★ USGS *Petersburg* (1994 nl)

13 WHITE SALMON

☐ HUSUM FALLS ★★

MAGNITUDE: 41 (h)
ELEVATION: 400 feet
WATERSHED: Large
APPROACH: Auto
LAT/LONG: 45.799195° N / 121.485394° W
USGS MAP: *Husum* (1994 nl)

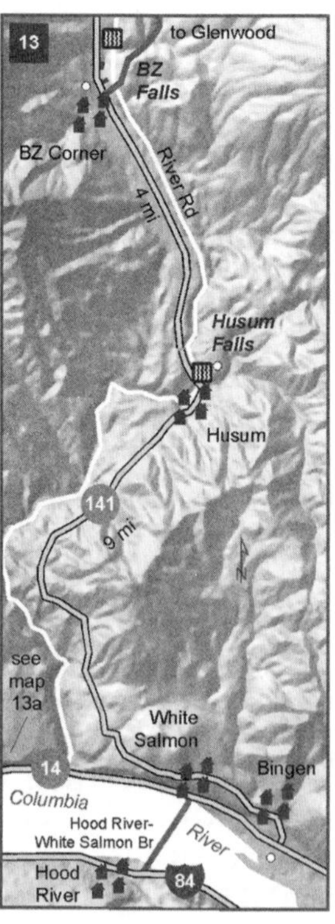

White Salmon River rushes 10 to 15 feet right in downtown Husum. The community is located 9 miles north of Bingen along State Route 141, also known as River Road. The falls can be seen from the bridge; park at the turnout on the north side where there is an interpretive sign about rafting on the White Salmon National Scenic River.

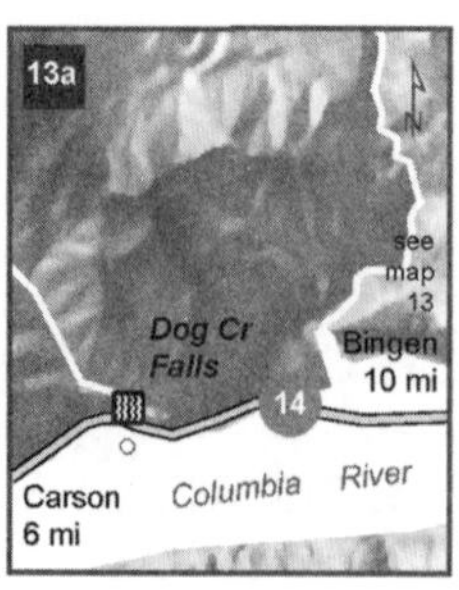

1 BZ FALLS ★★

MAGNITUDE: 38
ELEVATION: 680 feet
WATERSHED: Large
APPROACH: Trail (fairly easy)
LAT/LONG: 45.856656° N / 121.508536° W
USGS MAP: *Northwestern Lake* (1994 ns)

A pinch in the White Salmon River froths 20 to 25 feet into a tight gorge. Drive 0.1 mile north of BZ Corner along State Route 141 (4 miles north of Husum Falls), then turn right into the parking area for White Salmon River Launch Point. Walk down the access trail to the river, which is equipped with a pair of rails to aid persons who are taking their rafts down to the river. After a short distance down the route, an opening occurs along the left rail. Turn here and follow the side trail upstream 0.4 mile through a lovely gorge. There is a vista of the falls from a deck at the end of the route.

DOG CREEK FALLS (U) ★★

MAGNITUDE: 32 (h)
ELEVATION: 120 feet
WATERSHED: Small
APPROACH: Auto
LAT/LONG: 45.711267° N / 121.671078° W
USGS MAP: *Mount Defiance* (1994 nl)

Dog Creek sprays 15 to 20 feet downward in a narrow fan shape within the Columbia Gorge NSA. Stop at the unsigned parking area just west of mile marker 56, located 6 miles east of Carson and 10 miles west of Bingen. Walk a short distance upstream to a view.

14 CARSON

Isadore St. Martin discovered hot springs in this area in 1876. Bathhouses, cabins, and a hotel were subsequently constructed during the early 1900s and have recently been renovated. The area is currently maintained by the owners of the Carson Mineral Hot Springs Spa and Golf Resort. Visitors can enjoy these facilities and also hike to a nearby waterfall. There is a day-use parking fee for persons wishing only to roam around. The resort is located 1.2 miles east of Carson off Hot Springs Avenue, or 1.3 miles north of State Route 14.

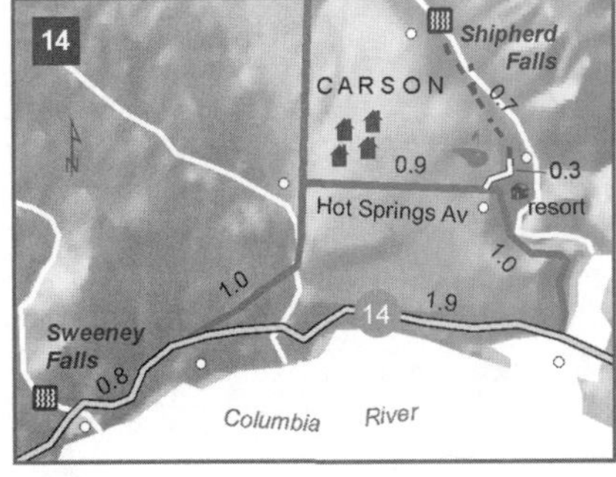

 SHIPHERD FALLS ★★

MAGNITUDE: 55
ELEVATION: 160 feet
WATERSHED: Large
APPROACH: Trail (fairly easy)
LAT/LONG: 45.737946° N / 121.805746° W
USGS MAP: *Carson* (1994)

This 40- to 60-foot series of cascades along the Wind River is next to a fishway, gauging station, and (locked) footbridge. After paying the day-use fee at the office, find the trailhead behind the historic Hotel St. Martin, and proceed 0.7 mile paralleling the Wind River to multiple vantage points along the way.

 SWEENEY FALLS ★★

MAGNITUDE: 45
ELEVATION: 300 feet
WATERSHED: Small
APPROACH: Bushwhack (moderate)
LAT/LONG: 45.709305° N / 121.843769° W
USGS MAP: *Carson* (1994 ns)

Motorists zipping along State Route 14 will certainly miss this 45- to 60-foot cataract, since it is camouflaged from the highway by vegetation and there are no signs. Drive to a turnout on the cliff side of the road, located at mile 46.6 based on mile markers 46 and 47. Find the path next to the turnout. You must first negotiate a steep slope—the most difficult part of the journey. When I last visited the area, there was a rope to make the descent easier. From there, it's an easy 0.1 mile along the path that ends at the base of the falls along Smith Creek.

15 STEVENSON

ROCK CREEK FALLS (U) ★★★

MAGNITUDE: 39 (l)
ELEVATION: 240 feet
WATERSHED: Large
APPROACH: Trail (easy)
LAT/LONG: 45.699669° N / 121.899602° W
USGS MAP: *Bonneville Dam* (1994 nl)

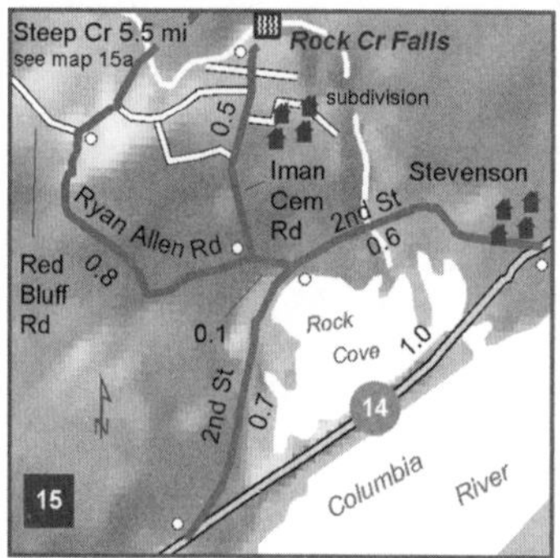

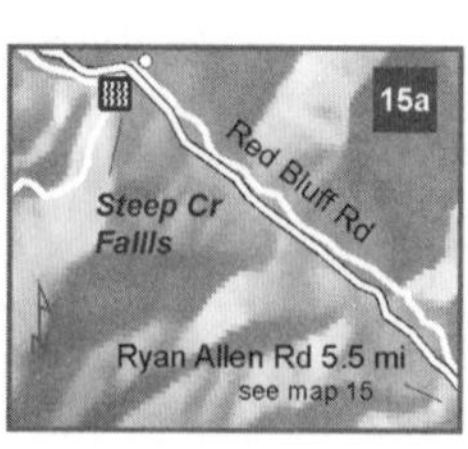

A short, well-worn path leads to side views of Rock Creek, shimmering as it drops 35 to 50 feet over a wide ledge. Turn off State Route 14 onto Second Street either in Stevenson or 1 mile west of town. Turn west off Second Street onto Ryan Allen Road. In 0.1 mile, turn

Rock Creek Falls

right on Iman Cemetery Road. Continue on this road to its end in 0.5 mile. Look for a path leading down to the stream. Residential development has encroached upon this location, so public access may change.

7 STEEP CREEK FALLS (U) ★★

MAGNITUDE: 48
ELEVATION: 1160 feet
WATERSHED: Small
APPROACH: Auto
LAT/LONG: 45.74768° N / 121.982536° W
USGS MAP: *Bonneville Dam* (1994 nl)

Gain a roadside view of Steep Creek tumbling 30 to 40 feet into Rock Creek. Follow the directions to Rock Creek Falls (described earlier), but instead of turning on Iman Cemetery Road, continue along Ryan Allen Road for 0.8 mile. Turn left on Red Bluff Road, and drive 5.5 miles to the point where the gravel road crosses Rock Creek next to the cataract.

16 BEACON ROCK

The 600-foot projection of Beacon Rock is one of the major landmarks of the Columbia River Gorge. Beacon Rock State Park is located next to State Route 14 about 18 miles west of Washougal and 4 miles east of North Bonneville.

RODNEY FALLS ★★

MAGNITUDE: 51
ELEVATION: 1000 feet
WATERSHED: Small
APPROACH: Trail (moderate)
LAT/LONG: 45.643337° N / 122.014443° W
USGS MAP: *Beacon Rock* (1994)

Hardy Creek plunges and cascades a total of 100 to 150 feet in two major sections. Drive 0.3 mile from the highway to the picnic area of Beacon Rock State Park. Begin hiking along Hamilton Mountain Trail. After a moderate climb of nearly 1.3 miles, you will encounter two short spur paths. The lower spur provides a view of the lower tier of the falls. Proceed on the main trail to a footbridge crossing and another short spur to the upper portion.

HARDY FALLS ★★★

MAGNITUDE: 63
ELEVATION: 800 feet
WATERSHED: Small
APPROACH: Trail (moderate)
LAT/LONG: 45.642152° N / 122.015302° W
USGS MAP: *Beacon Rock* (1994)

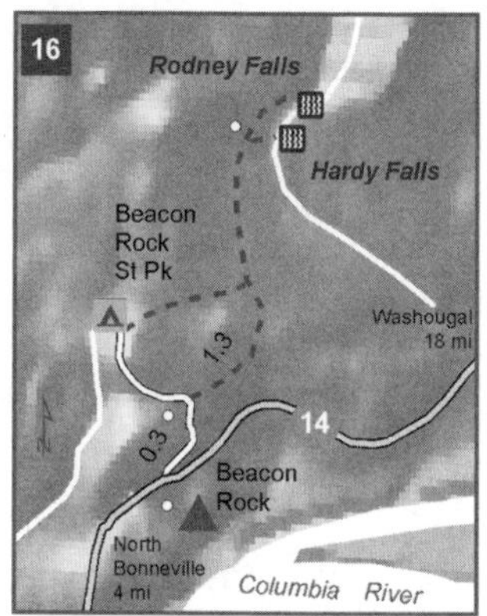

The more scenic of two descents along Hardy Creek, this one pours 80 to 120 feet downward. Instead of taking the lower spur to Rodney Falls (described earlier), choose the upper way to the far right. This spur leads quickly to a viewpoint for this entry.

17 WASHOUGAL RIVER

Remember how hot it was in the Northwest during the summer of 2003? When I visited the region that June, bathers were *en masse* along the Washougal River, cooling off in its refreshing waters. To my delight, all but the first of the following quintet of modest waterfalls are next to swimming holes.

SALMON FALLS ★★

MAGNITUDE: 29
ELEVATION: 380 feet
WATERSHED: Large
APPROACH: Auto
LAT/LONG: 45.615562° N / 122.201769° W
USGS MAP: *Bridal Veil* (1994 ns)

Obtain a bridge-side view of Washougal River pouring 10 to 15 feet into a pool below. A cement structure on the left side of the falls detracts from the scenery. Turn north off State Route 14 onto State Route 140, 10 miles east of Washougal or 12 miles west of North Bonneville. Drive up the hill, and after 4 miles, turn right (north) onto Washougal River Road. Proceed 1.7 miles and turn right onto Salmon Falls Road. Cross the bridge and park at the unmarked turnout. This entry is probably located on private property.

DOUGAN FALLS ★★

MAGNITUDE: 32
ELEVATION: 640 feet
WATERSHED: Large
APPROACH: Auto
LAT/LONG: 45.672642° N / 122.152802° W
USGS MAP: *Bobs Mtn.* (2000)

This stairstep series of block-type falls totals 30 to 60 feet along the Washougal River. Water also slides 20 to 30 feet into the river from nearby Dougan Creek. Located on public land maintained by the State of Washington, the waterfall is located 5.5 miles upstream from Salmon Falls (described earlier), where the Washougal River Road crosses the river for a second time.

NAKED FALLS ★★

MAGNITUDE: 43
ELEVATION: 730 feet
WATERSHED: Large
APPROACH: Bushwhack (fairly easy)
LAT/LONG: 45.684711° N / 122.131817° W
USGS MAP: *Bobs Mtn.* (2000 ns)

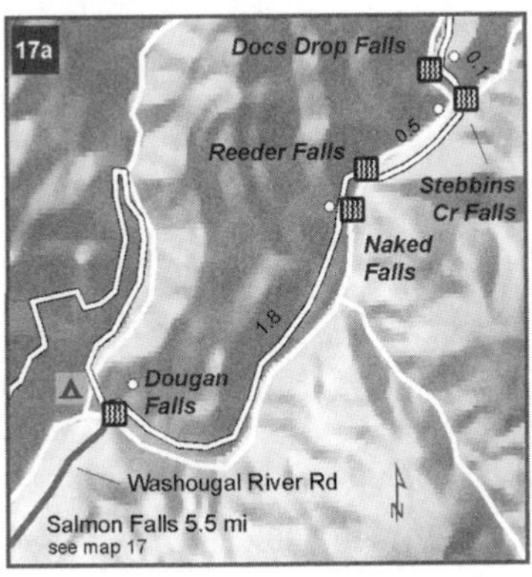

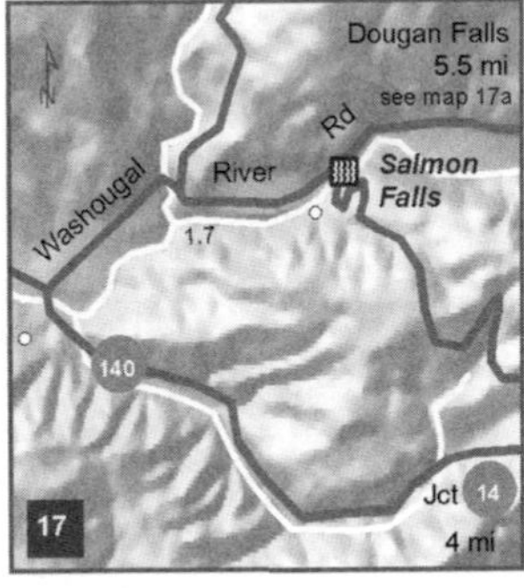

This is a series of small falls and cascades as the Washougal River tumbles a total of 15 to 25 feet. Turn right at the road junction immediately past the bridge at Dougan Falls (described earlier). Proceed 1.8 miles and park along a wide spot in the road. You have gone a few hundred yards too far if you meet another bridge, which incidentally provides a view upstream of Reeder Falls USGS *Bobs Mtn.* (2000 ns). Looking downstream from the bridge, you can see the top of Naked Falls.

Meanwhile back along the road, look for a path that initially requires a brief descent with "root-holds" (the hardest part), then leads quickly 0.1 mile to rock slabs above and adjacent to the main display. Reportedly its name is based on the bare rock rather than some cultural phenomenon.

STEBBINS CREEK FALLS (U) ★★

MAGNITUDE: 25
ELEVATION: 820 feet
WATERSHED: Medium
APPROACH: Auto
LAT/LONG: 45.691021° N / 122.121582° W
USGS MAP: *Beacon Rock* (1994 ns)

Also unofficially known as Mad Dog Falls, this 15- to 20-foot display pours directly into the Washougal River. Continue 0.5 mile past Naked Falls (described earlier) to turnouts next to a bridge crossing over this entry.

DOCS DROP FALLS (U) ★★

MAGNITUDE: 27
ELEVATION: 780 feet
WATERSHED: Large
APPROACH: Auto
LAT/LONG: 45.693015° N / 122.124714° W
USGS MAP: *Beacon Rock* (1994 ns)

Drive or walk 0.1 mile beyond Stebbins Creek Falls (described earlier) to rivulets of water descending 15 to 25 feet along the Washougal River.

MORE ONLINE:

Reeder Falls ★, mentioned earlier

18 CAMAS

Lacamas Park, located within the lumber town of Camas, harbors three modest falls. From downtown, drive 1.4 miles north on State Route 500 from its junction with Business State Route 14. Turn right into the parking area.

THE POTHOLES ★★

MAGNITUDE: 30
ELEVATION: 240 feet
WATERSHED: Large (d)
APPROACH: Trail (fairly easy)
LAT/LONG: 45.598194° N / 122.401776° W
USGS MAP: *Camas* (1994 ns)

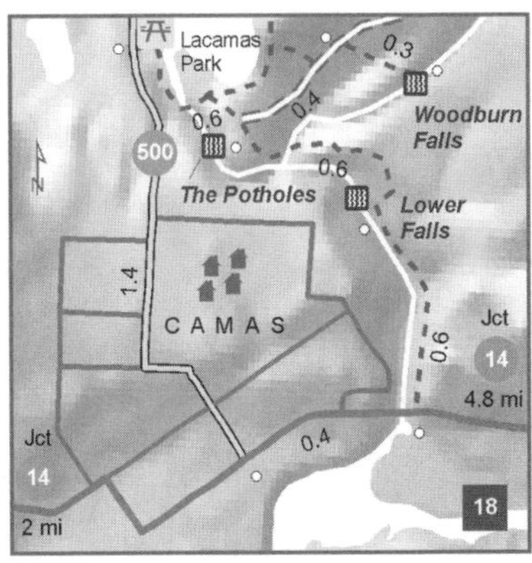

Rivulets of Lacamas Creek pour 15 to 20 feet along a wide expanse of bedrock. Views are obscured when the foliage is in leaf. Walk past the park's small playground and turn right, taking a path following tiny Round Lake. Cross a footbridge over a generator, then in 0.3 mile walk over the concrete dam. Parallel the lake for another 0.2 mile, then select the middle trail at a three-pronged fork. Proceed 0.1 mile to a grassy area above the cataract.

LOWER FALLS ★★

MAGNITUDE: 29
ELEVATION: 120 feet
WATERSHED: Large (d)
APPROACH: Trail or bushwhack (fairly easy)
LAT/LONG: 45.596993° N / 122.394502° W
USGS MAP: *Camas* (1994 nl)

Lacamas Creek slides 25 to 35 feet over an escarpment in two segments. Continue past The Potholes (described earlier), following Lacamas Creek downstream. In 0.6 mile reach a footbridge over the top of the falls. Better views require some bushwhacking. Backtrack from the bridge, looking for a faint path where the trail begins to leave the creek. Follow it down to open views below the base of the falls.

MORE ONLINE:
Woodburn Falls ★ USGS *Camas* (1994 ns)

Lower Falls

OREGON

NORTHERN COAST RANGE

The Coast Range extends from the northwestern lobe of Oregon southward to California. For convenience, the region has been divided into two chapters, Northern Coast Range and Southern Coast Range. This northern chapter describes waterfalls found in association with the moist, montane environment stretching from the Columbia River, between Portland and Astoria, to an arbitrarily chosen southern limit along U.S. Highway 20, which connects Newport and Corvallis.

During my travels along the coast, I found evidence suggesting that the Pacific Northwest has an enormous number of unmapped waterfalls. The density of mapped falls in the Northern Coast Range is comparable to the other regions of the Northwest (topographic maps and other sources document 67 features, of which 23 are mentioned in the following pages). However, many more falls likely occur in the area. Cal Baker, an employee of Siuslaw National Forest, has surveyed and recorded 99 drops exceeding 5 feet in the Hebo Ranger District alone.

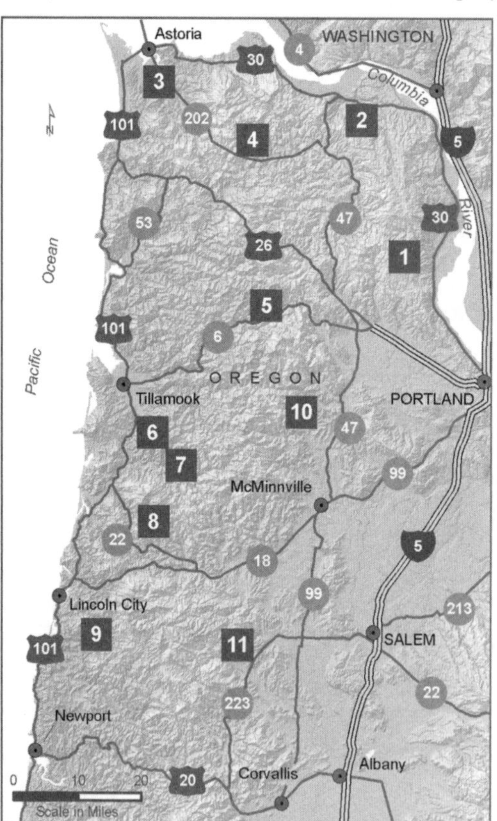

Much of Idaho, Oregon, and Washington are more rugged and wild than the Coast Range, so if a similar proportion of cataracts is unlisted in those areas, the entire Northwest probably has well more than 10,000 waterfalls versus the 1583 falls I have personally mapped. It would require an encyclopedia-sized document to describe every cataract!

1 SCAPPOOSE

BONNIE FALLS ★★

MAGNITUDE: 44
ELEVATION: 330 feet
WATERSHED: Large
APPROACH: Auto
LAT/LONG: 45.804019° N / 122.937735° W
USGS MAP: *Chapman* (1990)

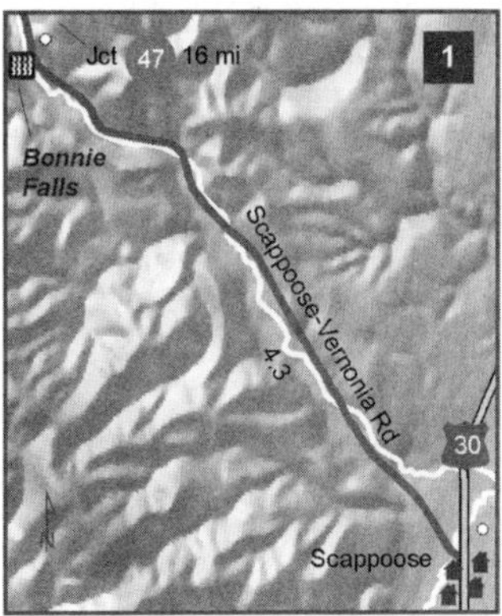

North Scappoose Creek tumbles 15 to 25 feet over a basalt escarpment. Turn off U.S. Highway 30 at the north end of Scappoose, and drive 4.3 miles northwest along Scappoose-Vernonia Road. A small unsigned parking turnout immediately precedes the falls. A fish ladder has been built next to them.

2 BEAVER CREEK

Motorists driving along old U.S. Highway 30 pass by two waterfalls between Rainier and Clatskanie. The route changed long ago, so few travelers see them unless they turn off the main highway. Drive 6.2 miles west from Rainier on US 30 to the marked Delena turnoff, located 1.2 miles west of the turnoff to Vernonia.

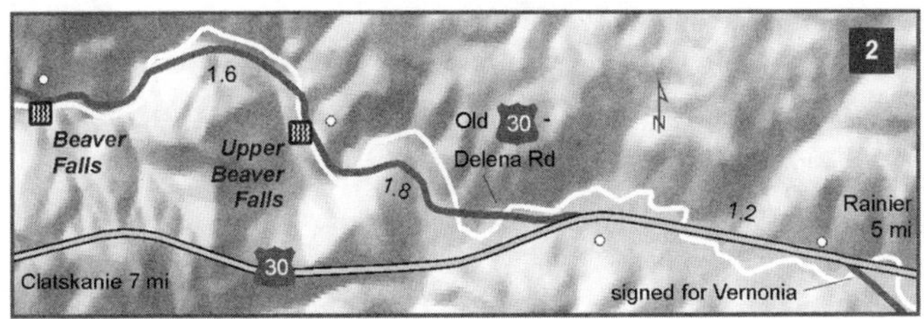

BEAVER FALLS ★★★

MAGNITUDE: 64
ELEVATION: 230 feet
WATERSHED: Large
APPROACH: Trail (easy)
LAT/LONG: 46.104379° N / 123.124245° W
USGS MAP: *Delena* (1985)

Water pours 60 to 80 feet from Beaver Creek. Be careful. There are no guardrails at the viewpoint from the top of the waterfall. Turn westward off U.S. Highway 30 onto Old U.S. Highway 30 (Delena Road). Drive 3.4 miles to an unsigned parking area to the left (south). Walk down the short dirt road to a path leading shortly to side views above the descent.

MORE ONLINE:

Upper Beaver Falls (u) ★ USGS *Delena* (1985 ns)

3 OLNEY

YOUNGS RIVER FALLS ★★★

MAGNITUDE: 54
ELEVATION: 90 feet
WATERSHED: Large
APPROACH: Auto or trail (easy)
LAT/LONG: 46.066896° N / 123.79027° W
USGS MAP: *Olney* (1981)

Youngs River curtains 30 to 50 feet into the Klaskanine Valley. I remember years ago seeing a commercial showing Clydesdales high-stepping near the base of the falls. Drive 10 miles southeast from Astoria on State Route 202, or 20 miles northwest from Jewell. At the Olney junction drive 3.8 miles down the road marked for the falls. Turn left upon the old roadgrade to its end in 0.1 mile. Enjoy the recently built roadside vista, or walk 0.1 mile down to the base of the cataract.

Youngs River Falls

BARTH FALLS ★★

MAGNITUDE: 16
ELEVATION: 300 feet
WATERSHED: Medium
APPROACH: Auto
LAT/LONG: 46.061968° N / 123.687273° W
USGS MAP: *Green Mtn.* (1977)

Water pours 5 to 10 feet into a small gorge along the Klaskanine River. From Olney junction (described earlier for Youngs River Falls), drive 4.7 miles eastward

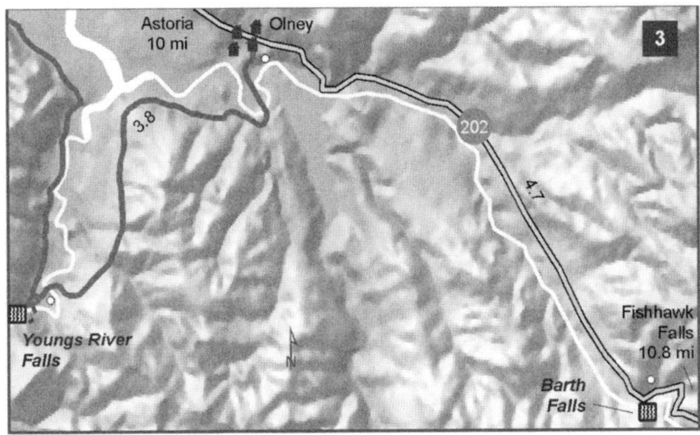

along State Route 202 to a small unmarked turnout adjacent to the falls. The topographic map shows this waterfall nearby along a very short intermittent stream. Visiting the site revealed no evidence of a cataract at that location, but I found this entry nearby. The US Geographic Names Information System lists the coordinate at the river location, so this is likely the true Barth Falls.

4 JEWELL

FISHHAWK FALLS ★★

MAGNITUDE: 33
ELEVATION: 770 feet
WATERSHED: Medium
APPROACH: Auto or trail (fairly easy)
LAT/LONG: 45.958325° N / 123.583718° W
USGS MAP: *Vinemaple* (1984)

Fishhawk Creek ripples 40 to 60 feet downward within Lee Wooden County Park. Located between Jewell and Fishhawk Falls is Jewell Meadows Wildlife Area. Elk and deer are often seen browsing in this state game refuge. There are marked viewpoints next to the highway.

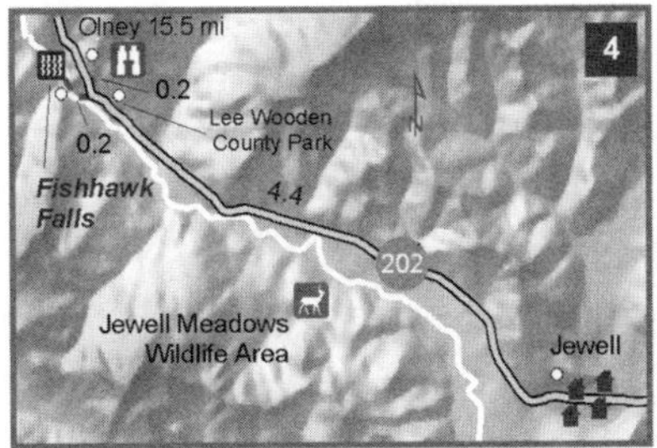

Drive 4.4 miles northwest from Jewell along State Route 202 to the park. A trail leads upstream to the base of the falls in 0.2 mile. You can also drive 0.2 mile farther to an unsigned viewpoint above the descent.

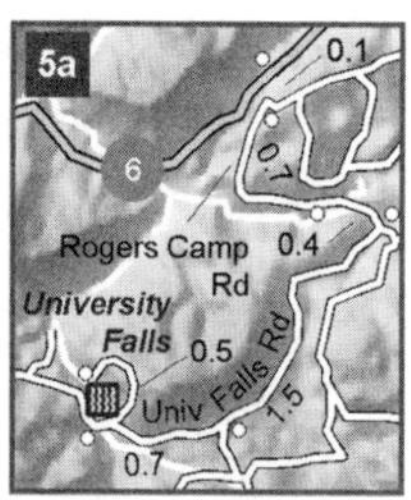

5 WILSON RIVER

State Route 6 is *the* highway for travelers accessing the coast from Portland. And drivers tend to speed on it, so be careful when turning on and off for the following trio of pleasant waterfalls.

UNIVERSITY FALLS ★★★

MAGNITUDE: 59
ELEVATION: 1640 feet
WATERSHED: Small
APPROACH: Trail (moderate)
LAT/LONG: 45.599566° N / 123.393668° W
USGS MAP: *Woods Point* (1979)

Water curtains 40 to 50 feet within Tillamook State Forest. Be cognizant of the signs for the falls as you drive, as there are a lot of road junctions along the way. Take SR 6 for 9 miles west of its junction with State Route 8. Just past mile marker 33, turn onto Rogers Camp Road, also marked for University Falls. Go 0.1 mile and bear right. Proceed 0.7 mile, bearing right again, and drive 0.4 mile to University Falls Road. Turn right and right again in 1.5 miles to one last right-hand turn.

Reach the sign for the trailhead in 0.7 mile. Find a wide spot to park. Hike for 0.5 mile, avoiding the dirt road junctions that are used by all-terrain vehicles. The footpath ends at the base of this delightful display along Elliot Creek.

FERN ROCK CREEK FALLS ★★

MAGNITUDE: 35
ELEVATION: 1100 feet
WATERSHED: Very small
APPROACH: Auto
LAT/LONG: 45.607508° N / 123.437334° W
USGS MAP: *Woods Point* (1979 ns)

A small stream veils 15 to 25 feet adjacent to the highway. Drive 3.9 miles southwest of the junction for University Falls (described earlier) along SR 6. Look for the large turnout on the south side of the road with the generic sign sheepishly signed as "falls." It is situated 0.2 mile east of mile marker 29.

Fern Rock Creek Falls

BRIDGE CREEK FALLS ★★

MAGNITUDE: 25
ELEVATION: 480 feet
WATERSHED: Very small
APPROACH: Trail (fairly easy)
LAT/LONG: 45.56193° N / 123.585628° W
USGS MAP: *Jordan Creek* (1984 ns)

Bridge Creek tumbles a total of 40 to 60 feet over three ledges of rock. Take SR 6 for 9.2 miles southwest of Fern Rock Creek Falls (described earlier), 20 miles northeast of Tillamook, to a large turnout on the south side of the highway just west of mile marker 20. A nice trail with a series of concrete and wooden steps quickly leads to the base of the cataract. Such features make you wonder why the place is not signed.

MORE ONLINE:
Little Falls ★ USGS *Elsie* (1984)
Nehalem Falls ★ USGS *Foley Peak* (1985)
Lester Creek Falls, USGS *Jordan Creek* (1984 ns) EXPLORE!
Umbrella Falls, USGS *Soapstone Lake* (1985 ns) EXPLORE!
Wilson Falls, USGS *Jordan Creek* (1984 ns) EXPLORE!

6 TILLAMOOK

Compared to the relatively modest falls of this region, the following entry will surely impress you. Buy some crackers and the famous Tillamook cheese, and take in the highest waterfall of the entire Coast Range.

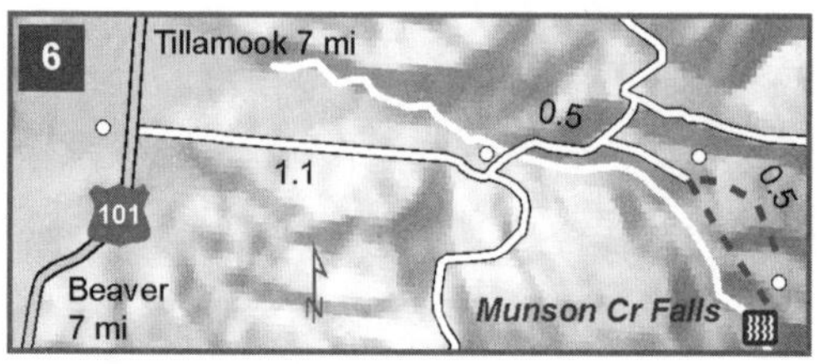

MUNSON CREEK FALLS ★★★★

MAGNITUDE: 75
ELEVATION: 760 feet
WATERSHED: Small
APPROACH: Trail (fairly easy)
LAT/LONG: 45.362481° N / 123.769327° W
USGS MAP: *Beaver* (1985)

This fine-lined cataract drops 266 feet as a triple horsetail. The descent and its stream are named after Goran Munson, a native of Michigan who settled nearby in 1889. Turn off U.S. Highway 101 about halfway between Tillamook and Beaver at the sign for Munson Creek Falls County Park. Follow the signs 1.6 miles to the parking area and trailhead.

The easily hiked Lower Trail traverses through a lush forest to the base of the falls. For full views, follow the Upper Trail for 0.5 mile to an excellent gorge vista. (Reportedly, this way has not been maintained and is overgrown with vegetation.) The steep trails were built as part of youth programs in 1960–62 and 1978–79.

7 BLAINE

CLARENCE CREEK FALLS (U) ★★

MAGNITUDE: 27
ELEVATION: 560 feet
WATERSHED: Medium
APPROACH: Auto
LAT/LONG: 45.263114° N / 123.641096° W
USGS MAP: *Blaine* (1984 nl)

Clarence Creek slides 46 feet next to the road. Turn left (north) off U.S. Highway 101 at Beaver onto the Blaine–Little Nestucca River Road (Forest Service Road 85). Drive for 11.8 miles, then turn left (north) on Clarence Creek Road (Forest Service Road 83). The gravel route ascends steeply before leveling off to a gentle slope in 0.9 mile at the falls.

NIAGARA FALLS AND PHEASANT CREEK FALLS ★★★

MAGNITUDE: 26 (l)
ELEVATION: 680 feet
WATERSHED: Small
APPROACH: Trail (moderate)
LAT/LONG: 45.221233° N / 123.642791° W
USGS MAP: *Niagara Creek* (1979 ns)

View a pair of waterfalls in tandem as a tiny unnamed creek originating near Niagara Point plunges 107 feet beside Pheasant Creek cascading 112 feet downward within Siuslaw National Forest. Their impressiveness decreases as a dry summer ensues.

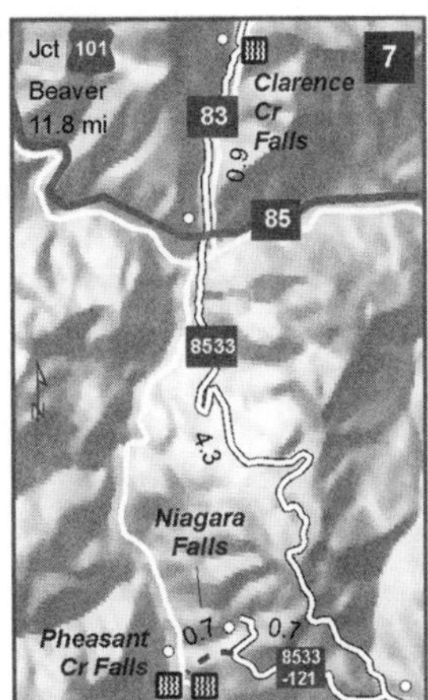

Follow the directions for Clarence Creek Falls (described earlier), but instead of turning left on Clarence Creek Road (Forest Service Road 83), turn right (south) on Forest Service Road 8533. Proceed 4.3 miles to Forest Service Road 8533-121, and turn right; the trailhead is located 0.7 mile along this secondary route. The trail ends in 0.7 mile at the base of the falls. I was once almost struck by a falling boulder here and later found out it had been dislodged by an earthquake.

MORE ONLINE:
Alder Glen Falls (u) ★ USGS *Dovre Peak* (1984 ns)

8 DOLPH

GUNALDO FALLS ★★

MAGNITUDE: 66
ELEVATION: 520 feet
WATERSHED: Medium
APPROACH: Bushwhack (moderate)
LAT/LONG: 45.1016° N / 123.77452° W
USGS MAP: *Dolph* (1985 ns)

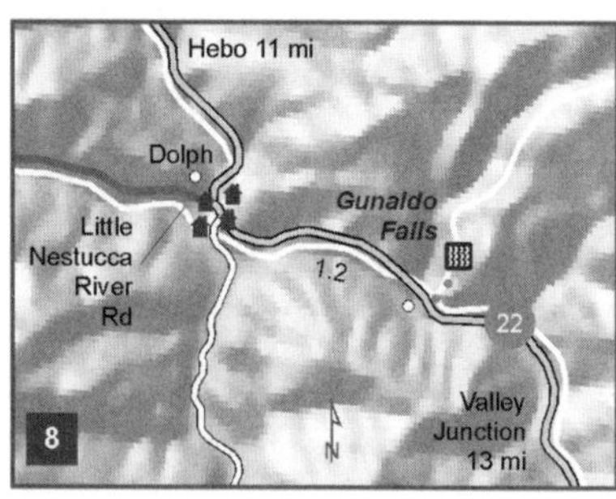

An unnamed tributary sprays 66 feet into Sourgrass Creek. Drive toward Dolph Junction, located where State Route 22 and Little Nestucca River Road meet, 11 miles south of Hebo and 14.2 miles northwest of Valley Junction. Take SR 22 from Dolph southeast for 1.2 miles to a wide expanse of the road immediately preceding a dirt road to the right (south). Listen for the falls. Scramble down the adjacent slope to the stream.

9 LINCOLN CITY

Many outdoor enthusiasts believe that recreational opportunities are slighted in the forests of the Coast Range. This situation has improved over the past couple of decades, especially for hiking to waterfalls. The following cataract is one of the hidden gems within Siuslaw National Forest.

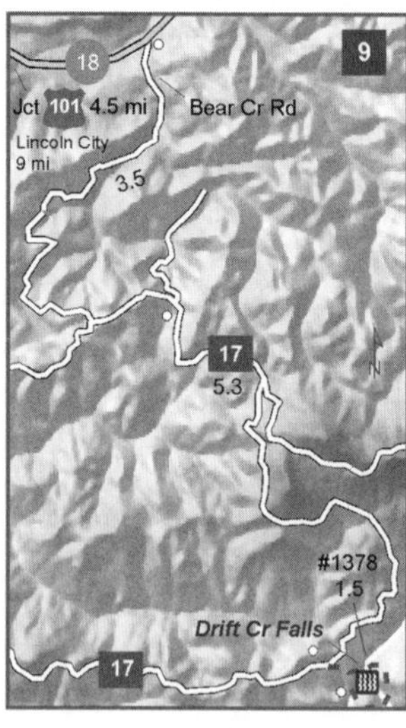

DRIFT CREEK FALLS ★★★★

MAGNITUDE: 62
ELEVATION: 640 feet
WATERSHED: Small

APPROACH: Trail (moderate)
LAT/LONG: 44.933209° N / 123.850351° W
USGS MAP: *Stott Mtn.* (1984 ns)

Water pours 75 feet off the side of a cliff, with an outstanding bird's-eye view of the display from a suspension footbridge. From the junction of U.S. Highway 101 and State Route 18, take the latter highway eastward for 4.5 miles. Turn right onto Bear Creek Road, and follow it for 3.5 miles. Stay straight where the way becomes Forest Service Road 17. The signed parking area and trailhead are 5.3 miles farther.

It's a 1.5-mile hike from here along Drift Creek Falls Trail 1378. A salute goes out to the trailblazers who constructed an extremely consistent grade over the entire route. Eventually arrive at the footbridge, which affords views to the right looking down into the cataract and at the gorge bottom 100 feet below.

Here we have what appears to be a waterfall with an unconventional name, as it descends into Drift Creek from a tributary rather than dropping along its course. Further investigation shows topographic maps have also labeled the tributary as Drift Creek, a duplication that is likely a misnomer.

10 CHERRY GROVE

Nestled in the eastern foothills of the Coast Range is the insular community of Cherry Grove. Two small waterfalls descend nearby along the refreshing waters of the Tualatin River. Unfortunately some of the town's residents have reportedly hassled visitors, so if you decide to go, leave the children at home.

LEE FALLS ★★

MAGNITUDE: 37
ELEVATION: 390 feet
WATERSHED: Large

APPROACH: Trail (fairly easy)
LAT/LONG: 45.465141° N / 123.284684° W
USGS MAP: *Turner Creek* (1979)

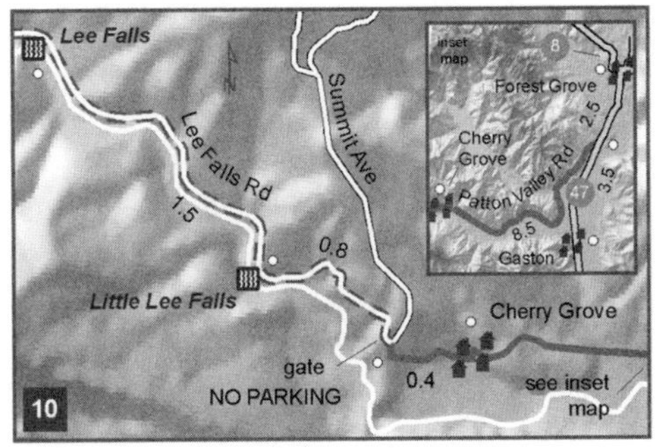

The Tualatin River pours 10 to 20 feet from a rocky escarpment adjacent to the dirt road. Turn west off State Route 47 upon Patton Valley Road, located 2.5 miles south of Forest Grove (where SR 47 meets State Route 8) and 3.5 miles north of Gaston. Drive 8.5 miles to Cherry Grove, staying on the main road through the hamlet. After 0.4 mile, at a sweeping curve to the right, the route becomes Summit Avenue. A short distance farther the paved surface ends. Lee Falls Road is to your left, but reportedly now has "No Parking" signs.

Turn around, find somewhere back in town where it is safer to park, and walk back. From the start of Lee Falls Road, it's a 2.3-mile trek, passing Little Lee Falls ★ USGS *Turner Creek* (1979) 0.8 mile along the way.

MORE ONLINE:

Little Lee Falls, mentioned earlier

11 FALLS CITY

☐ FALLS CITY FALLS (U) ★★

MAGNITUDE: 57
ELEVATION: 380 feet
WATERSHED: Large

APPROACH: Auto
LAT/LONG: 44.867222° N / 123.438643° W
USGS MAP: *Falls City* (1974 nl)

The Little Luckiamute River sharply drops 25 to 35 feet into a tight gorge. This descent is located within Michael Harding Park, where only partially obscured side views are possible. Turn off State Route 223 onto a road signed for Falls City, 6 miles south of Dallas and 20 miles north of U.S. Highway 20. Drive 4 miles to town. After crossing a bridge over the river, turn right at the South Main Street sign, and drive 0.1 mile to the park.

OREGON

SOUTHERN COAST RANGE

The southern portion of Oregon's Coast Range extends from the north along State Route 34, which connects Waldport and Corvallis, south to the California border, where the range transitions into the Klamath Mountains. There are 98 waterfalls mapped in this region; 36 of them are included here.

The landscape of the Southern Coast Range is geomorphically youthful. Its geology includes each of the three major classes of rocks. Igneous rocks, such as basalt, are common, as are sedimentary layers of sandstone and siltstone. Heat and pressure have transformed some of these rocks into the third category, metamorphic rocks, of which gneiss and quartzite are examples. Each type of rock has a varying degree of resistance to the erosive effects of running water.

This region was once characterized by low relief, but between 1 million and 3 million years ago internal earth forces uplifted and deformed the flat, coastal plains. The courses of most of the rivers flowing to the Pacific Ocean from the western flank of the Cascade Range were altered by this evolution of the Coast Range. Only two waterways, the Rogue River and the Umpqua River, were powerful enough to maintain their passages to the sea. On these two rivers falls were shaped where rising bedrock with a slow rate of erosion met the less resistant streambeds.

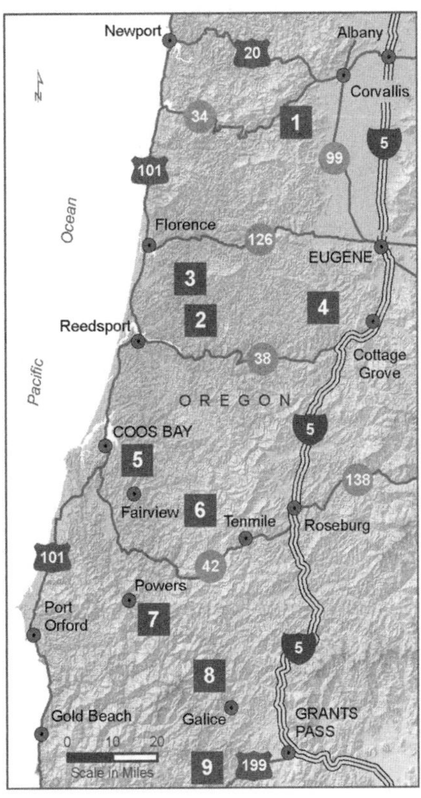

Additional descents formed where tributary creeks connected with larger rivers. As uplifting progressed, smaller streams generally eroded the rock beneath them less effectively than the main channels did. Therefore, a vertical drop is often seen near a tributary's confluence with the larger waterway. Elk Creek Falls is an example.

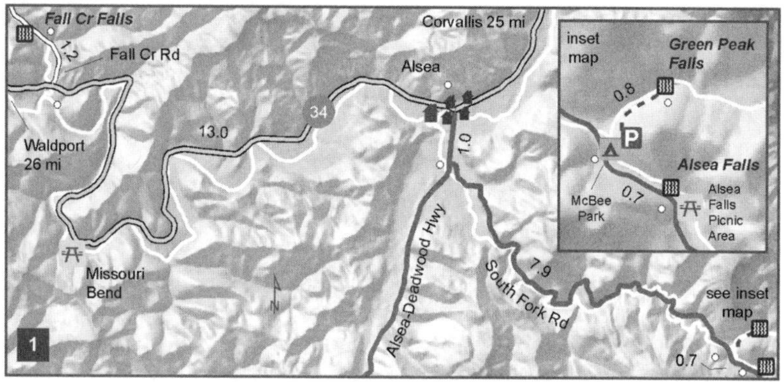

1 ALSEA

Alsea is located near three waterfalls along the eastern flank of the Coast Range. The town is 25 miles southwest of Corvallis and 26 miles east of Waldport on State Route 34.

1 FALL CREEK FALLS ★★

MAGNITUDE: 14
ELEVATION: 160 feet
WATERSHED: Large
APPROACH: Auto
LAT/LONG: 44.391801° N / 123.739812° W
USGS MAP: *Grass Mtn.* (1984 nl)

Although Fall Creek drops less than 10 feet, a fish ladder has been constructed to bypass it. Follow SR 34 west of Alsea for 13 miles, and turn right (north) on Fall Creek Road. Look for the cataract to the left in 1.2 miles.

2 GREEN PEAK FALLS ★★

MAGNITUDE: 55
ELEVATION: 740 feet
WATERSHED: Medium
APPROACH: Trail (fairly easy)
LAT/LONG: 44.335762° N / 123.494572° W
USGS MAP: *Glenbrook* (1984)

Water veils 30 to 40 feet downward along the South Fork Alsea River. Turn off SR 34 at Alsea, and drive south along Alsea-Deadwood Highway for 1 mile. Then turn left (east) onto South Fork Road, continue 7.9 miles, and turn into Herbert K. McBee Memorial Park. Drive to the trailhead at the far end of the parking area. Walk 0.8 mile down its length to the small plunge pool at the base of the falls.

ALSEA FALLS ★★

MAGNITUDE: 30
ELEVATION: 780 feet
WATERSHED: Medium
APPROACH: Trail (easy)
LAT/LONG: 44.326399° N / 123.491911° W
USGS MAP: *Glenbrook* (1984)

South Fork Alsea River cascades 30 to 50 feet downward. Continue southward along South Fork Road beyond McBee Memorial Park (described earlier) for 0.7 mile to Alsea Falls Picnic Area. A short trail leads to the river at the base of the descent.

2 SMITH RIVER

SMITH RIVER FALLS ★★

MAGNITUDE: 54
ELEVATION: 70 feet
WATERSHED: Large
APPROACH: Auto
LAT/LONG: 43.788325° N / 123.817231° W
USGS MAP: *Smith River Falls* (1984)

This 5- to 10-foot drop along the otherwise placid Smith River is located on publicly accessible Bureau of Land Management property. The features are named for

Smith River Falls

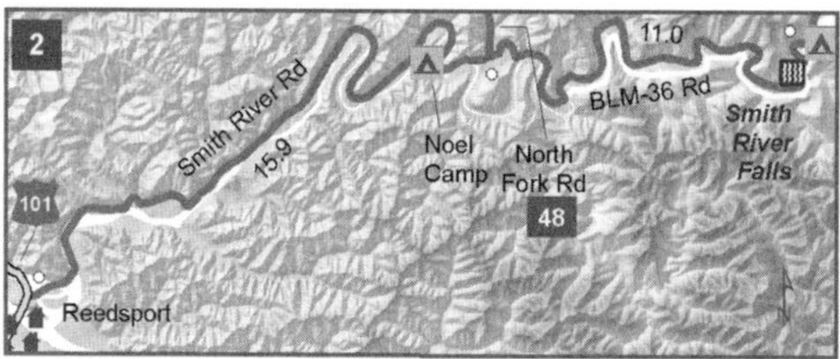

Jedediah Strong Smith, an early nineteenth-century fur trader and explorer. From the north end of Reedsport turn east off U.S. Highway 101 onto Smith River Road. Continue east for 26.9 miles, passing the junction with North Fork Road (Forest Service Road 48) (do not turn at the junction) after 15.9 miles. The waterfall, which is less impressive in summer, is located just before Smith River Falls Campground.

3 CENTRAL COAST RANGER DISTRICT

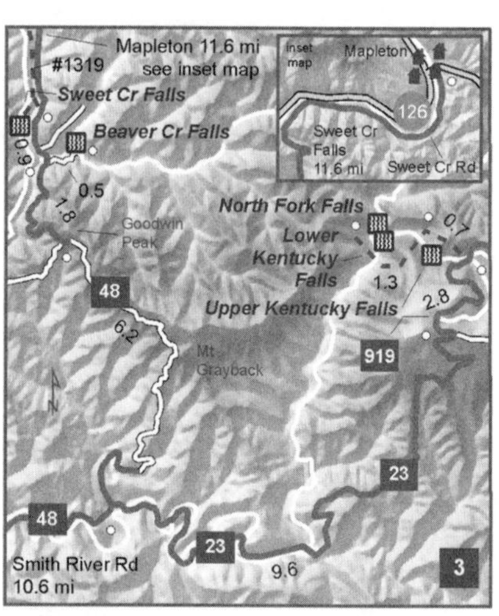

Seven scenic waterfalls are nestled deep within the Central Coast Ranger District (formerly named Mapleton Ranger District), Siuslaw National Forest. Be sure to note the turns you make when driving in these backwoods, as it is easy to become disoriented. Decades before a trail was constructed to North Fork Falls, I remember being unable to tell one hill or road from another and giving up on the quest that afternoon.

1 SWEET CREEK FALLS ★★

MAGNITUDE: 40
ELEVATION: 440 feet
WATERSHED: Large
APPROACH: Trail (fairly easy)
LAT/LONG: 43.946225° N / 123.903083° W
USGS MAP: *Goodwin Peak* (1984)

Depart State Route 126 in the town of Mapleton, next to the Siuslaw Bridge, southward onto Sweet Creek Road. Follow it 11 miles to the Homestead-Sweet Creek Trailhead. Drive another 0.6 mile, and park in the area signed for the Sweet Creek Falls Trailhead. A short spur trail leads quickly down to Sweet Creek Trail 1319. Turn left at the junction, and head 0.3 mile upstream to the lower 25- to 35-foot segment of the cataract spilling over igneous rock. The way continues up another 0.1 mile to a fenced vista of the 50- to 60-foot upper portion, but the narrow gorge prevents a full view.

A US Forest Service flyer mentions that nine additional waterfalls can be seen along the trail. According to other sources, they drop from slabs of sandstone over a 1-mile stretch downstream from the main falls.

BEAVER CREEK FALLS ★★★

MAGNITUDE: 44
ELEVATION: 630 feet
WATERSHED: Medium
APPROACH: Trail (easy)
LAT/LONG: 43.942224° N / 123.892097° W
USGS MAP: *Goodwin Peak* (1984)

Beaver Creek and Sweet Creek combine to create this interestingly shaped 25- to 35-foot waterfall. (It's probably named after the first stream because the other joins it halfway down the descent.) Drive southward beyond the trailhead for Sweet Creek Falls (described earlier) for 0.9 mile. Turn left (east) onto the spur road signed for Beaver Creek Trailhead. Park near the road's end in 0.5 mile. Embark upon the path where there is a close-up vantage point in 0.1 mile.

UPPER KENTUCKY FALLS ★★★

MAGNITUDE: 66
ELEVATION: 1400 feet
WATERSHED: Small
APPROACH: Trail (fairly easy)
LAT/LONG: 43.928502° N / 123.803477° W
USGS MAP: *Baldy Mtn.* (1984 ns)

This is the first of three waterfalls to be found along Kentucky Falls Trail 1376. This route is not recommended for young children, as part of the way is unprotected on the side of cliffs. From the junction of the Beaver Creek Falls access road (described earlier), drive 1.8 miles southward on Sweet Creek Road, then continue 6.2 miles along North Fork Road (Forest Service Road 48) to Forest Service Road 23. For those coming from the south, follow Smith River Road (described in the previous section) east from U.S. Highway 101 for 11 miles to FS Road 48; turn north and continue 10.6 miles to FS Road 23.

Turn east on FS Road 23. After an additional 9.6 miles, turn left (northwest) on Forest Service Road 919, and proceed 2.8 miles to the trailhead.

The first 0.7 mile of the hike is fairly easy, then it begins to follow the small gorge of Kentucky Creek. Here you will gain a trailside view of the 80- to 100-foot upper descent of the stream.

LOWER KENTUCKY FALLS ★★★★

MAGNITUDE: 48
ELEVATION: 920 feet
WATERSHED: Small
APPROACH: Trail (moderate)
LAT/LONG: 43.931176° N / 123.817124° W
USGS MAP: *Baldy Mtn.* (1984 ns)

Kentucky Creek plunges 50 to 60 feet before diverging into a pair of 15- to 20-foot horsetails. A viewing platform has been built near the base of the falls.

Lower Kentucky Falls

Kentucky Creek Trail (described earlier) steepens considerably from the upper falls to its end 1.3 miles farther, 2 miles from the trailhead.

NORTH FORK FALLS ★★★

MAGNITUDE: 26 (l)
ELEVATION: 820 feet
WATERSHED: Medium
APPROACH: Trail (moderate)
LAT/LONG: 43.932257° N / 123.817725° W
USGS MAP: *Baldy Mtn.* (1984)

The North Fork Smith River curtains 60 to 80 feet over a large escarpment. During periods of low discharge, these falls appear in a segmented form. This entry is also visible from the end of Kentucky Creek Trail (described earlier). The cataract can be seen in tandem with Lower Kentucky Falls from selected vantage points.

MORE ONLINE:

The Horn ★ USGS *Mapleton* (1984 nl)

Lake Creek Falls, USGS *Triangle Lake* (1984 ns) EXPLORE!

4 LORANE

☐ SIUSLAW FALLS ★★

MAGNITUDE: 22
ELEVATION: 570 feet
WATERSHED: Large
APPROACH: Trail (easy)
LAT/LONG: 43.854586° N / 123.364152° W
USGS MAP: *Letz Creek* (1984)

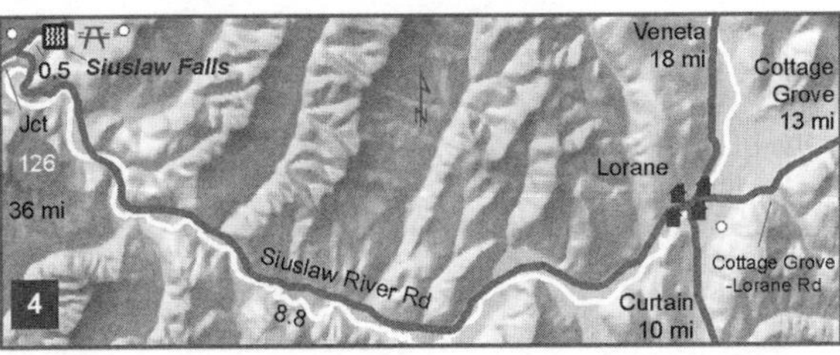

Water stairsteps 5 to 10 feet over a 70-foot-wide expanse of the Siuslaw River. From Cottage Grove drive 13 miles southwest on the Cottage Grove–Lorane Road to the hamlet of Lorane. Continue west on Siuslaw River Road for 8.8 miles to an unnamed county park. Stop after 0.5 mile along the park access road. The falls is a short walk away. Look for a fish ladder along the south side of the falls.

5 MILLICOMA RIVER

Waterfalls are abundant on the various tributaries of the Millicoma River. Unfortunately, most of them are inaccessible. But all is not lost. The most impressive falls of the area and indeed of the region are the star attractions at Golden and Silver Falls State Park. Turn eastward off U.S. Highway 101 south of downtown Coos Bay on a road signed for Eastside and the state park. Drive through Eastside, and continue on to the logging community of Allegany in 14 miles. The day-use state park is at the road's end 10 miles farther.

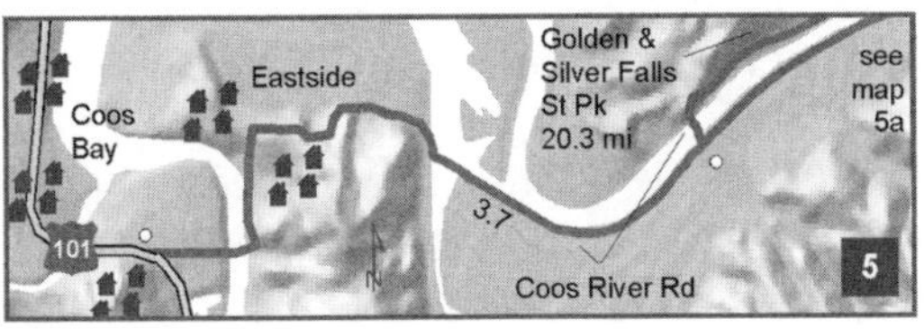

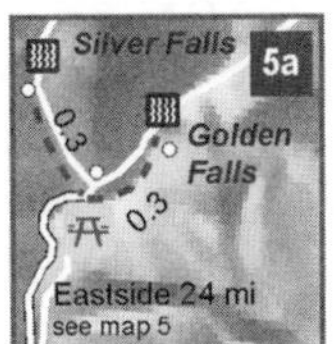

Golden Falls

SILVER FALLS ★★

MAGNITUDE: 21 (t)
ELEVATION: 520 feet
WATERSHED: Small
APPROACH: Trail (easy)
LAT/LONG: 43.486419° N / 123.934927° W
USGS MAP: *Golden Falls* (1990)

Silver Creek trickles 80 to 120 feet over an unusual dome-shaped projection of weathered bedrock. Follow the marked trail from the picnic area for a gently sloped 0.3 mile to the falls. It is deserving of a higher rating if you catch it during peak stream flow.

7 GOLDEN FALLS ★★★

MAGNITUDE: 34
ELEVATION: 480 feet
WATERSHED: Medium
APPROACH: Trail (easy)
LAT/LONG: 43.485531° N / 123.92894° W
USGS MAP: *Golden Falls* (1990)

Glenn Creek plummets 125 to 160 feet over a rock wall. It is named after Dr. C. B. Golden, first grand chancellor of the Knights of Pythias of Oregon. Take the second marked trail from the end of the park road, an easy 0.3 mile to the base of the falls.

6 EAST FORK COQUILLE RIVER

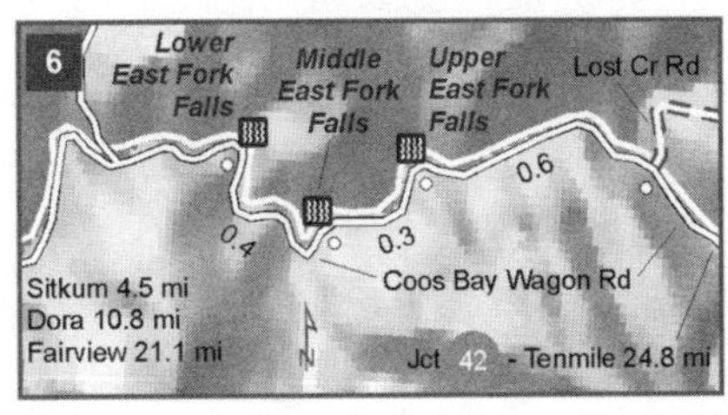

There are many small waterfalls along the scenic East Fork Coquille River, and the historic Coos Bay Wagon Road follows beside it. Be careful when driving this narrow route: Logging trucks have replaced horse-drawn buggies! Be sure to find a safe place to park off the road when you locate each descent. The Wagon Road can be accessed from the west at Fairview and from the east at Tenmile.

LOWER EAST FORK FALLS (U) ★★

MAGNITUDE: 19
ELEVATION: 880 feet
WATERSHED: Large
APPROACH: Auto
LAT/LONG: 43.148275° N / 123.787689° W
USGS MAP: *Sitkum* (1990 nl)

East Fork Coquille River tumbles 15 to 20 feet along a bend in the stream. The farthest downstream of a trio of descents, this waterfall is located 4.5 miles east of Sitkum, 10.8 miles east of Dora, and 26.1 miles west of Tenmile.

MIDDLE EAST FORK FALLS (U) ★★

MAGNITUDE: 36
ELEVATION: 920 feet
WATERSHED: Large
APPROACH: Auto
LAT/LONG: 43.146052° N / 123.783226° W
USGS MAP: *Sitkum* (1990 nl)

Water pours 15 to 20 feet over a small rock escarpment. Drive 0.4 mile upstream from the lower falls (described earlier).

MORE ONLINE:
Upper East Fork Falls (u) ★ USGS *Sitkum* (1990 nl)
Laverne Falls ★ USGS *Daniels Creek* (1971)

Coquille River Falls

7 POWERS

The western portion of Rogue River-Siskiyou National Forest is a largely primitive area of southwest Oregon's Coast Range. Many waterfalls here are currently inaccessible and unmapped. Also, seasonal descents are often seen along canyon roads during moist periods. Three of the most easily accessible cataracts located in the Powers Ranger District area are listed here.

ELK CREEK FALLS ★★★

MAGNITUDE: 32 (l)
ELEVATION: 480 feet
WATERSHED: Small

APPROACH: Trail (fairly easy)
LAT/LONG: 42.815586° N / 124.011579° W
USGS MAP: *China Flat* (1996)

Elk Creek drops 80 to 120 feet over a bluff, next to which is a picnic table. This entry is not as impressive during dry spells. Turn south off State Route 42 onto South Fork Coquille River Road (Forest Service Road 33), 3 miles southeast of Myrtle Point. Drive 19 miles to the ranger station at Powers, then continue 8.7 miles south to the parking area for Elk Creek Falls Trail 1150. Follow the path to the left, toward the stream. It is a short stroll to the falls.

COQUILLE RIVER FALLS ★★★

MAGNITUDE: 46
ELEVATION: 1280 feet
WATERSHED: Large

APPROACH: Trail (fairly hard)
LAT/LONG: 42.717384° N / 124.021449° W
USGS MAP: *Illahe* (1998)

This waterfall is superb year-round, as water crashes 40 to 60 feet along the Coquille River. At the trail's end, miniature falls can also be seen sliding into the river from Drowned Out Creek. Drive 10.5 miles past Elk Creek Falls (described earlier), and turn left (east) on Forest Service Road 3348 soon after crossing the river. Continue for 1.5 miles to the trailhead. Coquille River Trail 1257 steadily switchbacks down the steep valley side for 0.5 mile to a streamside vantage point below the falls.

WOODEN ROCK CREEK FALLS (U) ★★

MAGNITUDE: 45
ELEVATION: 2480 feet
WATERSHED: Medium

APPROACH: Auto
LAT/LONG: 42.829861° N / 123.926048° W
USGS MAP: *Eden Valley* (1998 nl)

A curtain of water slides 40 to 60 feet over bulging bedrock. Continue eastward 10.4 miles past Coquille River Falls Trailhead (described earlier) along Forest Service Road 3348. Turn left (north) onto Forest Service Road 240. Proceed 2.1 miles to an unsigned turnout just before the bridge crossing Wooden Rock Creek. Peer over the rim of the small gorge for partial views.

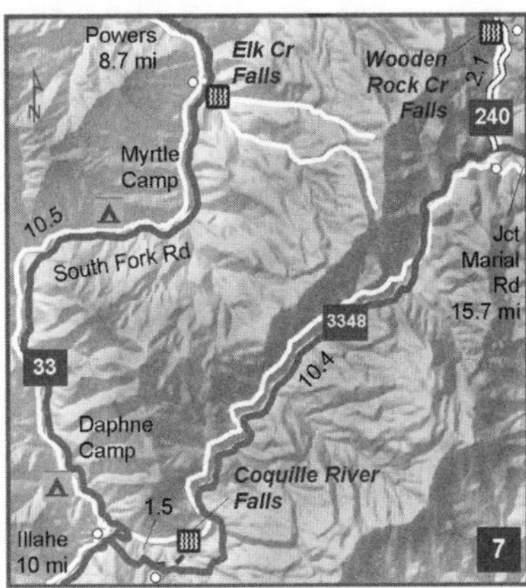

8 THE WILD ROGUE

The lower Rogue River cuts through the Klamath Mountains portion of the Coast Range, creating a 2000-foot-deep canyon. A 35-mile stretch of it is designated a national wild and scenic river, a federal classification intended to provide river recreation in a primitive setting and to preserve the natural, untamed integrity of a river and its surrounding environment. The following waterfalls can all be visited within a half-day's hike.

Access the area by departing from Interstate 5 at Merlin (Exit 61). Drive westward along Merlin–Galice Road, where you reach the small hamlet of Galice after 16.5 miles. The road has now turned north; continue 1.5 miles to the Smullin Visitors Center at Rand.

MOUSE CREEK FALLS (U) ★★

MAGNITUDE: 19 (l)
ELEVATION: 900 feet
WATERSHED: Very small
APPROACH: Auto
LAT/LONG: 42.624047° N / 123.601479° W
USGS MAP: *Galice* (1998 nl)

The most easily accessible waterfall in the area is ironically the most obscure. Some of the locals aren't even aware of its 35- to 45-foot descent over a wall of bedrock. Drive 2.3 miles north of Smullin Visitors Center (described earlier) to an unsigned turnout at Mouse Creek. If you look closely, you can see the cataract from the road. For better views, bushwhack about 50 yards. Best seen during wet periods, it deserves a lower rating in summer.

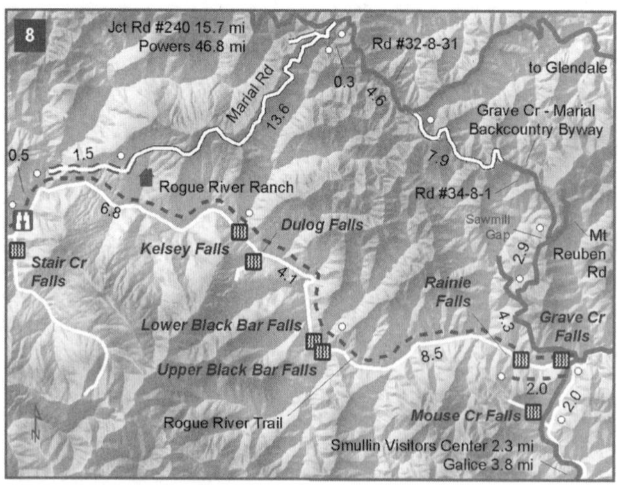

RAINIE FALLS ★★

MAGNITUDE: 32 (h)
ELEVATION: 580 feet
WATERSHED: Large
APPROACH: Moderate
LAT/LONG: 42.649478° N / 123.615169° W
USGS MAP: *Mount Reuben* (1998)

Five falls occur along the Rogue River within this canyon. All but this one are more like rapids than waterfalls. Drive 2 miles beyond Mouse Creek Falls (described earlier), and park along the turnout just before the bridge crossing the Rogue. Rainie Falls Trail begins toward the left. After walking an easy 0.3 mile, you will see a 2- to 5-foot interruption known as Grave Creek Falls USGS *Mount Reuben* (1998). After an additional 1.7 miles of moderate hiking, you can see this 10- to 15-foot drop extending 120- to 150-feet wide near the trail's end.

STAIR CREEK FALLS ★★★

MAGNITUDE: 65
ELEVATION: 340 feet
WATERSHED: Large
APPROACH: Trail (fairly easy)
LAT/LONG: 42.695829° N / 123.901672° W
USGS MAP: *Marial* (1998)

The drive to this falls is rugged, but it's a good adventure. Fill up your tank before leaving, because there are no gas stations anywhere in this wilderness-like area. From the bridge crossing (described earlier), proceed over the Rogue, then turn left onto the Grave Creek-Marial Backcountry Byway (BLM Road 34-8-1). Proceed 4.3 miles to Mount Reuben Road and bear right. After another 2.9 miles, turn left toward Sawmill Gap (BLM Road 34-8-1). This road ends 7.9 miles farther; turn left (west) onto BLM Road 32-8-31. Drive 4.6 miles, and turn left for the access road to the backcountry outpost of Marial. Take another left in 0.3 mile.

Travel is quite slow from this point onward, but usually passable for passenger vehicles. Pass Rogue River Ranch in 13.6 miles. The route turns to dirt the final 1.5 miles beyond Mule Creek Bridge to the road's end at a parking area for hiking on the Rogue River Trail.

Embark upon the trail, where it soon parallels the river in a narrow gorge. Watch rafters and kayakers shoot the many rapids in this picturesque reach. After 0.5 mile in the downstream direction, Stair Creek enters across the gorge as a double punchbowl totaling 40 to 60 feet. Here the trail is cut into the gorge, so those fearful of heights need to be wary. It is suggested that you don't stray very far from the trail.

MORE ONLINE:

Grave Creek Falls, mentioned earlier
Dulog Falls, USGS *Kelsey Peak* (1998 ns) EXPLORE!
Lower Black Bar Falls, USGS *Bunker Creek* (1998) EXPLORE!
Upper Black Bar Falls, USGS *Bunker Creek* (1998) EXPLORE!
Kelsey Falls, USGS *Kelsey Peak* (1998 ns) EXPLORE!

Flora Dell Falls, USGS *Illahe* (1998 ns) EXPLORE!
Fall Creek Falls, USGS *Marial* (1998) EXPLORE!
Silver Falls, USGS *York Butte* (1998) EXPLORE!
Tate Creek Falls, USGS *Marial* (1998 nl) EXPLORE!

9 ILLINOIS RIVER

Though it doesn't carry the notoriety of the Rogue, the Illinois River also carries the status of national wild and scenic river. One modest drop occurs along its reaches, with two other rather nondescript entries also in the general vicinity.

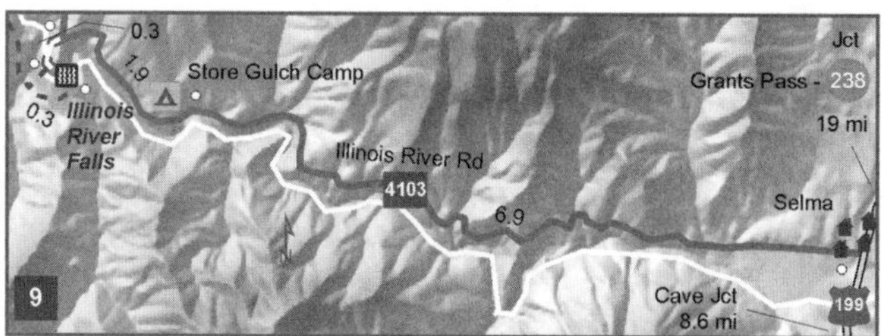

 ILLINOIS RIVER FALLS ★★

MAGNITUDE: 40
ELEVATION: 1000 feet
WATERSHED: Large
APPROACH: Trail (fairly easy)
LAT/LONG: 42.303042° N / 123.774128° W
USGS MAP: *Pearsoll Peak* (1998)

A 15- to 20-foot drop occurs where the river negotiates an extensive jumble of igneous rock. Drive to the crossroads named Selma, located along U.S. Highway 199 approximately 19 miles south of State Route 238 in Grants Pass and 8.6 miles north of Cave Junction. At the crossroads, turn west onto Illinois River Road (Forest Service Road 4103), following it 8.8 miles (1.9 miles past Store Gulch Camp) to an unsigned dirt road on the left. People in passenger cars can carefully drive down it for 0.3 mile to the parking area and trailhead.

The walk begins across an attractive wooden suspension footbridge. Notice the scars on the landscape on the other side of the canyon; fires in 1992 and 2002 have ravished many tracts of Rogue River-Siskiyou National Forest. After crossing, turn left, following Fall Creek Trail 1221 upstream. Don't go down the path immediately to the left, as that only goes to the riverbank. Walk just a bit farther before turning. From here it is 0.3 mile to a variety of rock-side vantage points of the cascades.

MORE ONLINE:
Little Illinois River Falls ★ USGS *Cave Junction* (1996)
Cave Creek Falls (u) ★ USGS *Oregon Caves* (1996 ns)

OREGON

THE MIDDLE CASCADES

This chapter describes waterfalls located in an area that ranges from Mount Hood, which is a few miles south of the Columbia Gorge, through the Cascades to Mount Washington, 75 miles to the south. There are 166 cataracts known to occur throughout the region, with 58 of them mentioned here.

The major peaks of the Cascades are actually volcanoes. The appearance of each snow-topped mountain shows the relative time since it last experienced volcanic activity. The smooth slopes of Mount Hood (11,236 feet) indicate its youth, while Mount Jefferson (10,496 feet) is slightly older and hence more rugged. Three-Fingered Jack (7841 feet) and Mount Washington (7802 feet) have very jagged features, suggesting that their volcanic activity ceased even longer ago, allowing glacial erosion to greatly modify their once-smooth form.

Glaciation created most of the waterfalls associated with the volcanic mountains of the high Cascades. The alpine glaciers that top these peaks today once extended to lower elevations. Today, streams descend from adjacent rock

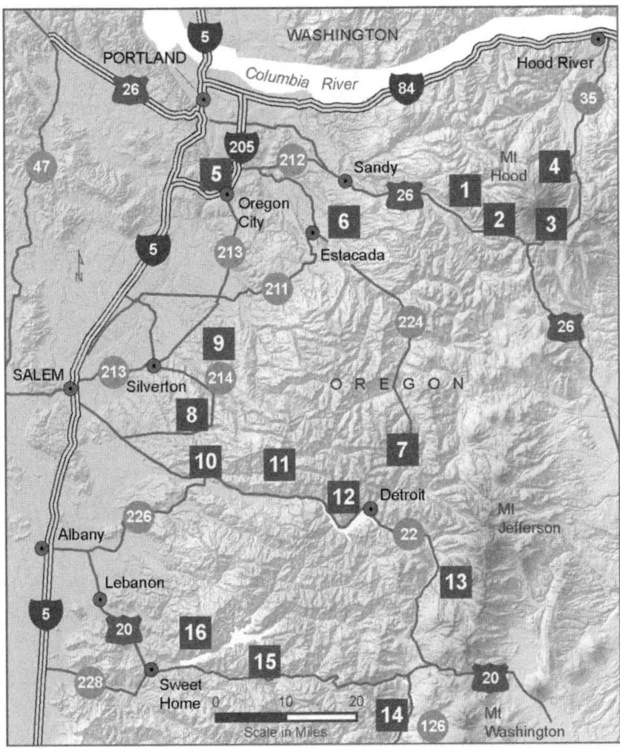

walls into these glacially carved valleys. Switchback Falls is an example. Some cataracts are found on valley floors where glaciers eroded unevenly, as at Gooch Falls, or where the present stream cuts over a highly resistant rock escarpment, as at Downing Creek Falls.

The many falls along the western flank of the Cascades reflect the circumstances of the development of the entire range. About 20 million to 30 million years ago, lava flows and accumulations of ashfalls alternately covered the region. The lava hardened to become basaltic bedrock, while the volcanic ash mixed with dust to create rock layers called tuffaceous sandstone. Twelve million years ago the area was uplifted and folded, forming the Cascade Range.

As streams carved courses from the high Cascades westward, their flowing waters eroded the softer sandstone much more rapidly than the resistant basalt. Good examples of this process are the descents at Silver Falls State Park and along the McKenzie River, which plunge over ledges of basalt. Recesses beneath the falls are open amphitheaters where running water has eroded away sandstone layers.

1 MOUNT HOOD WILDERNESS

One of twelve wilderness areas in Oregon, Mount Hood Wilderness preserves more than 35 square miles of pristine sanctuary only a few miles from metropolitan Portland. The following entry is located within this wilderness, a part of Zigzag Ranger District of Mount Hood National Forest.

RAMONA FALLS ★★★

MAGNITUDE: 54
ELEVATION: 3520 feet
WATERSHED: Small (g)
APPROACH: Trail (fairly hard)
LAT/LONG: 45.379998° N / 121.776167° W
USGS MAP: *Bull Run Lake* (1980)

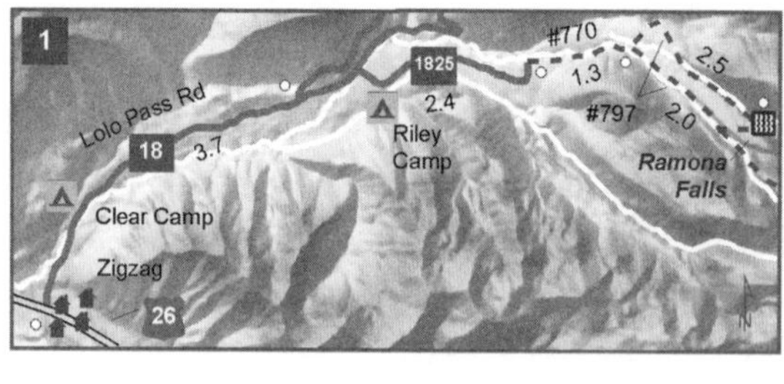

Beauty trumps power where Sandy River veils downward 60 to 80 feet in an idyllic setting. Turn north off U.S. Highway 26 at Zigzag onto Lolo Pass Road (Forest Service Road 18). In 3.7 miles bear right on Muddy Fork Road (Forest Service Road 1825), driving to its end in 2.4 miles. Sandy River Trail 770 begins here. Take it its entire 1.3-mile length to the looped Ramona Falls Trail 797. Hike 2 miles to the falls via the lower section, with a return option along the upper loop that adds 0.5 mile to the journey.

2 ZIGZAG RIVER

All of the following cataracts are in the southwest sector of Mount Hood Wilderness in the Zigzag Ranger District of Mount Hood National Forest.

 DEVIL CANYON FALLS (U) ★★

MAGNITUDE: 54
ELEVATION: 2840 feet
WATERSHED: Small
APPROACH: Auto
LAT/LONG: 45.318456° N / 121.860045° W
USGS MAP: *Government Camp* (1997 nl)

An unnamed stream plunges 60 to 75 feet within Devil Canyon. Only a distant view is possible. Drive 1.6 miles east of Rhododendron along U.S. Highway 26 to Zigzag Mountain Road (Forest Service Road 27-2627) and turn north. The road deteriorates into a dirt surface, but it is usually navigable by automobiles during the summertime. Drive 4 miles to an overlook of the Zigzag River Valley and the falls.

LITTLE ZIGZAG FALLS ★★★

MAGNITUDE: 45
ELEVATION: 3200 feet
WATERSHED: Small (g)
APPROACH: Trail (easy)
LAT/LONG: 45.312858° N / 121.79123° W
USGS MAP: *Government Camp* (1997 ns)

The Little Zigzag River tumbles 35 to 45 feet downward. Turn off U.S. Highway 26 onto signed Forest Service Road 2639, located 2.4 miles east of the turn for Devil Canyon (described earlier) and 2.2 miles west of the Oregon Trail sign (see the Yocum Falls description). Drive 2.2 miles to the road's end at Little Zigzag Falls Trail 795C. Hike 0.3 mile to a vista immediately in front of the cataract.

YOCUM FALLS (U) ★★★

MAGNITUDE: 46
ELEVATION: 3250 feet
WATERSHED: Small
APPROACH: Trail (fairly hard)
LAT/LONG: 45.307063° N / 121.793097° W
USGS MAP: *Government Camp* (1997)

Yocum Falls consists of a series of cataracts. Long ago there was a vista along a now abandoned part of the highway that enabled sightseers to view them collectively. The road has been reconfigured and the timber has matured, masking the falls at the former viewpoint. What remains accessible is the upper portion (described later) and this lowest drop, which spreads 25 to 35 feet over a ledge

Yocum Falls

along Camp Creek. This falls is named after Oliver C. Yocum, who in 1900 opened a hotel and resort in nearby Government Camp. The difficulty rating assigned to this waterfall is due to a combination of lack of clear signage and the steep path near the destination.

Drive along U.S. Highway 26 eastward for 2.2 miles beyond Forest Service Road 2639 (described earlier). Park here, where a sign indicates that the Oregon Trail once passed through here. Walk down the trail to the pavement of the old highway and turn right. You will soon reach a part of The Chute, where wagons had to be roped down Laurel Hill. Continue along the old highway 0.1 mile past this point. When you begin to hear the falls, find the footpath to your right, which had a series of orange ribbons when I scouted the area showing the way 0.1 mile down to the base of the descent. From here it is 0.3 mile back to your vehicle.

UPPER YOCUM FALLS (U) ★★

MAGNITUDE: 48
ELEVATION: 3360 feet
WATERSHED: Small
APPROACH: Auto
LAT/LONG: 45.306626° N / 121.792668° W
USGS MAP: *Government Camp* (1997 ns)

Camp Creek slides more than 100 feet down into the valley. Drive along U.S. Highway 26 to a Sno-Park wayside 0.9 mile east of the trailhead for Yocum Falls (described earlier), and 1 mile west of the entrance to Ski Bowl Resort. The cataract is immediately downstream from Mirror Lake Trailhead. The only view is from the parking area, where you can look down upon the upper portion of the falls. Called Yocum Falls in earlier editions of the guidebook.

3 BENNETT PASS

Since earlier editions of this guidebook, highway reconfiguration has changed the directions and mileages for accessing the following waterfalls within Hood River Ranger District of Mount Hood National Forest. The updates are provided here.

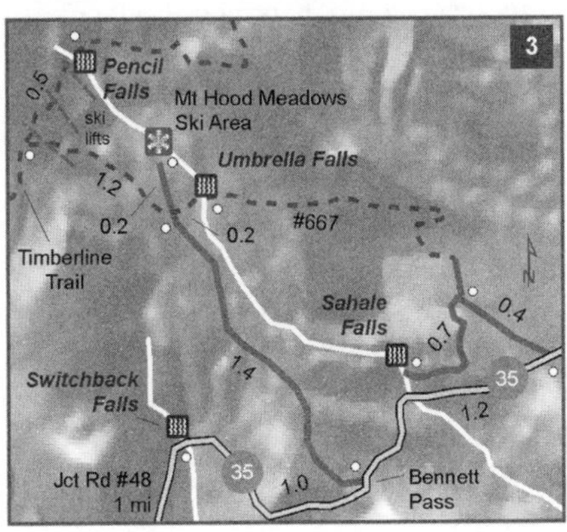

SAHALE FALLS ★★★

MAGNITUDE: 67
ELEVATION: 4590 feet
WATERSHED: Small (g)
APPROACH: Auto
LAT/LONG: 45.318637° N / 121.640619° W
USGS MAP: *Mt. Hood South* (1980)

Bright water tumbles 60 to 100 feet along the East Fork Hood River. The cataract was named many decades ago by George Holman as part of a competition sponsored by the Portland Telegram. Also spelled "Sahalie," it is a Chinook word meaning "high." Drive along State Route 35 for 1.2 miles eastward beyond the entrance at Bennett Pass for Mount Hood Meadows Ski Area. Turn left here, proceeding 0.4 mile and turning left again to the road's end 0.7 mile farther at the old bridge overlooking the falls.

UMBRELLA FALLS ★★

MAGNITUDE: 51
ELEVATION: 5250 feet
WATERSHED: Small (g)
APPROACH: Trail (fairly easy)
LAT/LONG: 45.329364° N / 121.660317° W
USGS MAP: *Mt. Hood South* (1980)

Just a bit of imagination is needed to see that this 40- to 60-foot waterfall along the East Fork Hood River is aptly named. Drive 1.4 miles up the access road for Mount Hood Meadows Ski Area (described earlier) to a sign marking Umbrella Falls Trail 667 on the right (east) side of the road. Follow the trail 0.2 mile to the base of the falls.

PENCIL FALLS ★★

MAGNITUDE: 25
ELEVATION: 5800 feet
WATERSHED: Very small (g)
APPROACH: Trail (moderate)
LAT/LONG: 45.337147° N / 121.672247° W
USGS MAP: *Mt. Hood South* (1980 nl)

A headwater tributary of the East Fork Hood River pours 25 to 35 feet amidst the ski lifts of Mount Hood Meadows. From Umbrella Falls Trailhead (described earlier), walk up the road a bit to access the trail's western segment. Hike up this moderately steep trail for 1.2 miles to its end at Timberline Trail. Take the right fork, crossing a maintenance road for the ski area, and continue along the trail for 0.5 mile to the cataract. It is located just beyond the passing of the third ski lift. Cross a creek on the main trail, then turn right down a path to a close-up vantage point directly into the falls.

This falls deserves a lower rating when its stream flow decreases as summer progresses. A series of small falls also occur the next several hundred feet downstream. Reaching them requires a moderately easy bushwhack.

MORE ONLINE:

Switchback Falls ★ USGS *Mt. Hood South* (1980)

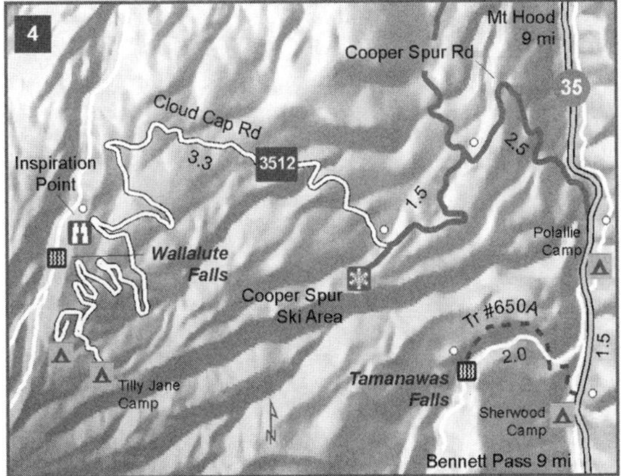

4 NORTHEAST MOUNT HOOD

This fourth section completes the waterfall tour around Mount Hood within Mount Hood National Forest. The following pair of cataracts occur in its Hood River Ranger District.

TAMANAWAS FALLS ★★★★

MAGNITUDE: 82
ELEVATION: 3440 feet
WATERSHED: Medium (g)
APPROACH: Trail (moderate)
LAT/LONG: 45.401411° N / 121.589206° W
USGS MAP: *Dog River* (1996)

Cold Spring Creek plunges 100 to 150 feet over a rock ledge in a deep woods setting. *Tamanawas* is a Chinook word for "friendly or guardian spirit." Drive on State Route 35 to the parking area for Tamanawas Trail 650A, located 0.2 mile north of Sherwood Camp, 9 miles north of Bennett Pass and 10.5 miles south of the town of Mount Hood. The gently sloping route leads 2 miles to the falls.

WALLALUTE FALLS ★★

MAGNITUDE: 77 (h)
ELEVATION: 5000 feet
WATERSHED: Small (g)
APPROACH: Auto
LAT/LONG: 45.411474° N / 121.656283° W
USGS MAP: *Mt. Hood North* (1980)

Although the view from the road is a distant one, the stream named Eliot Branch can still be heard roaring more than 100 feet downward with the specter of Mount Hood in the background. Its waterfall was named in 1893 by Miss A. M. Long. She is believed to be the first white person to have seen the falls, the name of which is a Wasco Indian term meaning "strong water." This waterfall straddles Mount Hood Wilderness.

Turn west off State Route 35 onto Cooper Spur Road. After 4 miles, turn right (northwest) on Cloud Cap Road (Forest Service Road 3512). Follow this steep, winding road to a viewpoint in 3.3 miles that should be signed for Inspiration Point. Look at the northeast base of the mountain (to your lower left) to locate the cataract.

5 OREGON CITY

Waterfalls and cities are not mutually exclusive. Indeed, it is not uncommon for cataracts along large rivers to be harnessed for industry, which in turn attracts settlement. The following entry is a classic example.

❑ WILLAMETTE FALLS ★★★

MAGNITUDE: 61 (h)
ELEVATION: 50 feet
WATERSHED: Large

APPROACH: Auto
LAT/LONG: 45.35247° N / 122.617436° W
USGS MAP: *Oregon City* (1985 ns)

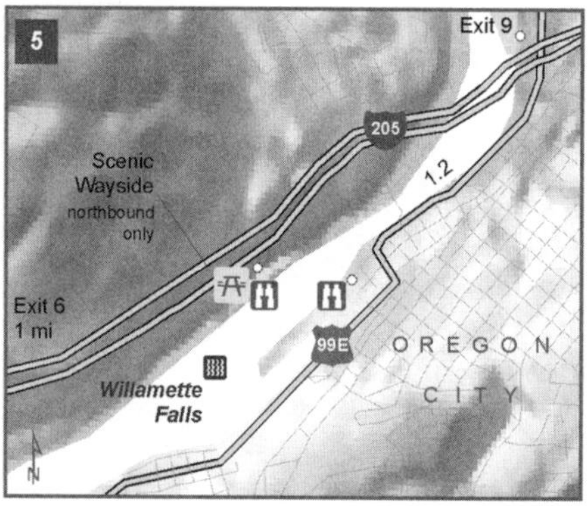

Despite its appearance being altered by the construction of a lock system for navigating the Willamette River, this 15- to 20-foot drop is still impressive due to its several-hundred-foot breadth. Several picturesque vistas are available. One vantage point is afforded by departing Interstate 205 at Oregon City (Exit 9). Go south on State Route 99E, and drive 1.2 miles to the signed viewpoint. To see a perspective from the opposite side of the river, stop at the marked scenic wayside 1 mile past Exit 6 on I-205; this option is accessible only to northbounders.

6 EAGLE CREEK

The following pair of small cataracts lies outside the national forests. Turn southeast off State Route 211 onto Southeast Eagle Creek Road, which is located 0.1 mile east of the junction of SR 211 with State Route 224. Proceed 1.2 miles, and turn left (east) on Southeast Wildcat Road. Continue 1.8 miles, then bear right (south) on County Road 40.

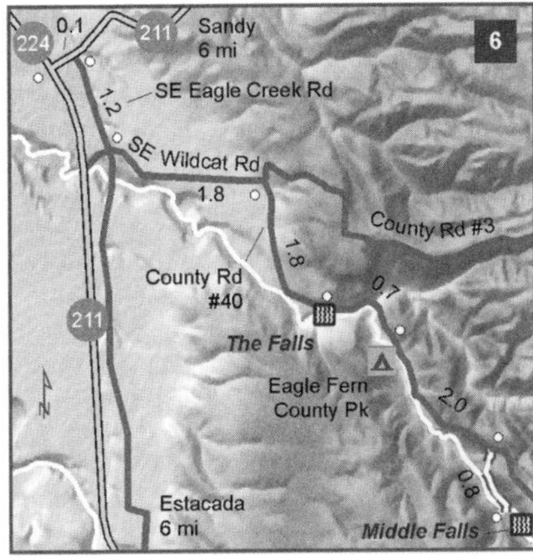

MIDDLE FALLS ★★

MAGNITUDE: 62 (h)
ELEVATION: 660 feet
WATERSHED: Large
APPROACH: Trail (fairly easy)
LAT/LONG: 45.294898° N / 122.25684° W
USGS MAP: *Estacada* (1985 nl)

Water pours 20 to 30 feet over a wide breadth of Eagle Creek. Take County Road 40 for 4.5 miles, and park at a yellow-gated road to the right (south). Walk along the dirt road for 0.8 mile until you can hear the descent. A short path leads to its base. Fishing is prohibited in Eagle Creek.

MORE ONLINE:
The Falls ★ USGS *Estacada* (1985)

7 BAGBY HOT SPRINGS

Hikers can enjoy the therapeutic effects of Bagby Hot Springs, located deep within Clackamas River Ranger District, Mount Hood National Forest. Motorists cannot drive to the hot springs, but everyone can visit the following pair of modest descents.

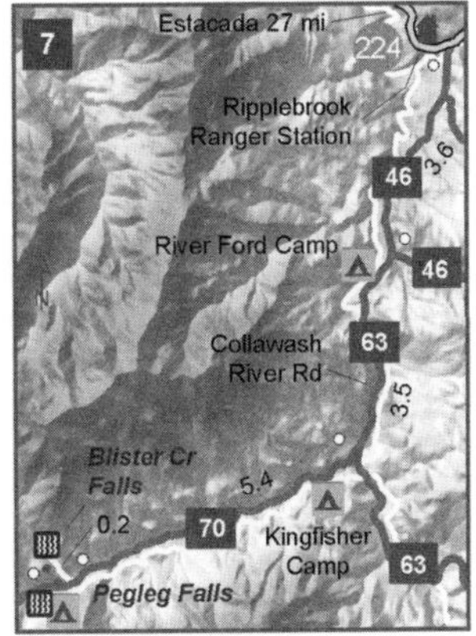

PEGLEG FALLS ★★

MAGNITUDE: 38
ELEVATION: 2030 feet
WATERSHED: Large
APPROACH: Auto
LAT/LONG: 44.95682° N / 122.162813° W
USGS MAP: *Bagby Hot Springs* (1997)

Water descends 10 to 15 feet along Hot Springs Fork, with a fish ladder bypassing the falls. Drive 27 miles southeast from Estacada on State Route 224 to Clackamas River Road (Forest Service Road 46), which is 0.5 mile past Ripplebrook Ranger Station. Turn right (south) on Forest Service Road 46, and after 3.6 miles bear right (south) on Collawash River Road (Forest Service Road 63). Turn right once more in another 3.5 miles onto Forest Service Road 70, and reach Pegleg Falls Camp in 5.6 miles.

Drive into the camp, and stop at the first parking area. The falls is located just upstream. Bagby Hot Springs Camp is 0.4 mile farther, and it offers trail access to the springs.

BLISTER CREEK FALLS (U) ★★

MAGNITUDE: 33
ELEVATION: 2190 feet
WATERSHED: Small
APPROACH: Bushwhack (moderate)
LAT/LONG: 44.959052° N / 122.159101° W
USGS MAP: *Bagby Hot Springs* (1997 nl)

Blister Creek streams 25 to 35 feet into a small pool. The falls can be seen from a bridge 0.2 mile before Pegleg Falls Camp (described earlier). Angler's paths offer closer views of the cataract.

8 SILVER FALLS STATE PARK

Silver Creek Canyon is a waterfall lover's paradise, all of the falls are within moderate walking distances of State Route 214 via the Trail of Ten Falls. The highway passes through the state park 14 miles southeast of Silverton and 25 miles east of Salem.

UPPER NORTH FALLS ★★★

MAGNITUDE: 68
ELEVATION: 1520 feet
WATERSHED: Large
APPROACH: Trail (easy)
LAT/LONG: 44.883174° N / 122.614175° W
USGS MAP: *Elk Prairie* (1985)

North Silver Creek drops 65 feet in the first of a series of nice falls that get better as you progress through the park. Find the trail at the south side of the parking lot at the east end of the park. Cross under the highway, and walk east 0.3 mile to the path's end at the falls.

NORTH FALLS ★★★★

MAGNITUDE: 76
ELEVATION: 1400 feet
WATERSHED: Large
APPROACH: Trail (fairly easy)
LAT/LONG: 44.884892° N / 122.623273° W
USGS MAP: *Elk Prairie* (1985)

North Falls

There are exciting views both beside and behind this impressive 136-foot waterfall, located along North Silver Creek. Take the trail mentioned in the previous entry 0.3 mile westward to trailside vantage points.

TWIN FALLS ★★

MAGNITUDE: 45
ELEVATION: 1230 feet
WATERSHED: Large
APPROACH: Trail (fairly easy)
LAT/LONG: 44.885166° N / 122.637156° W
USGS MAP: *Drake Crossing* (1985)

North Silver Creek diverges as it tumbles 31 feet over weathered bedrock. Follow the trail 0.9 mile downstream from North Falls (described earlier), a total of 1.2 miles from the trailhead.

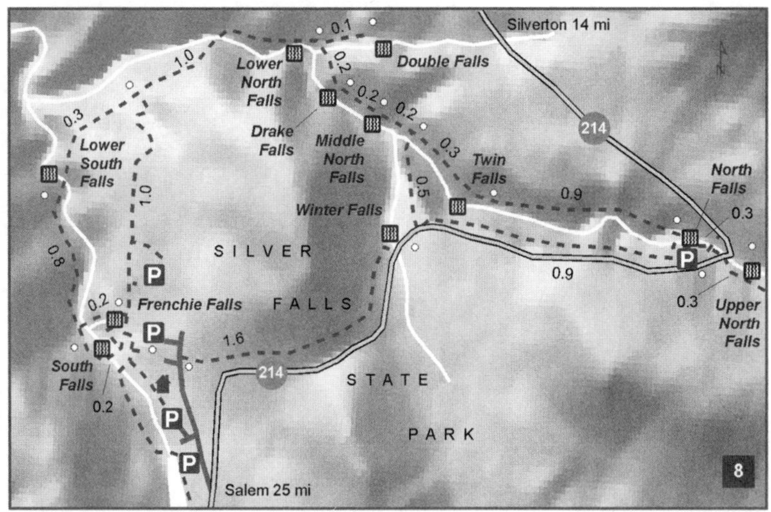

MIDDLE NORTH FALLS ★★★

MAGNITUDE: 42
ELEVATION: 1120 feet
WATERSHED: Large
APPROACH: Trail (fairly easy)
LAT/LONG: 44.888708° N / 122.643057° W
USGS MAP: *Drake Crossing* (1985)

This unique waterfall hurtles through the air for two-thirds of its 106-foot drop and then veils over bedrock along the final portion. A side trail goes behind and around this descent from North Silver Creek. Walk 0.5 mile downstream from Twin Falls (described earlier), a total of 1.7 miles from the trailhead, or 0.7 mile past Winter Falls (described later) to view this entry.

DRAKE FALLS ★★

MAGNITUDE: 35
ELEVATION: 1060 feet
WATERSHED: Large
APPROACH: Trail (moderate)
LAT/LONG: 44.890016° N / 122.646276° W
USGS MAP: *Drake Crossing* (1985)

North Silver Creek drops 27 feet in a curtain of water. Gain trailside views by hiking 0.2 mile downstream from Middle North Falls (described earlier) to this entry.

 DOUBLE FALLS ★★★

MAGNITUDE: 37 (l)
ELEVATION: 1220 feet
WATERSHED: Small
APPROACH: Trail (moderate)
LAT/LONG: 44.892068° N / 122.64501° W
USGS MAP: *Drake Crossing* (1985)

Water drops a total of 178 feet in tiered fashion as part of this falls along North Silver Creek. The lower portion descends four times as far along Hullt Creek as the upper part. Walk 0.3 mile past Drake Falls (described earlier) to the signed spur trail. Walk up the side path a short distance for views.

LOWER NORTH FALLS ★★

MAGNITUDE: 63
ELEVATION: 1030 feet
WATERSHED: Large
APPROACH: Trail (moderate)
LAT/LONG: 44.891703° N / 122.646855° W
USGS MAP: *Drake Crossing* (1985)

This is the last major falls, descending 30 feet, along North Silver Creek. Walk a few yards downstream from the spur path for Double Falls (described earlier) along the main trail. It is 1.1 miles back to Winter Falls Trailhead, or 2.1 miles to the trailhead near North Falls.

WINTER FALLS ★★

MAGNITUDE: 33 (l)
ELEVATION: 1360 feet
WATERSHED: Very small
APPROACH: Trail (fairly easy)
LAT/LONG: 44.88436° N / 122.641019° W
USGS MAP: *Drake Crossing* (1985)

Winter Creek falls 134 feet in two forms. Initially it plunges down, then it becomes a horsetail. Drive 0.9 mile west of the trailhead for North Falls (described earlier) and walk 0.1 mile to a vista.

SOUTH FALLS ★★★★

MAGNITUDE: 82
ELEVATION: 1200 feet
WATERSHED: Medium
APPROACH: Trail (fairly easy)
LAT/LONG: 44.87875° N / 122.659086° W
USGS MAP: *Drake Crossing* (1985)

This is the highlight of the park. South Silver Creek drops 177 feet over a ledge of basalt. Several vistas, including a trailside view behind the cataract, reveal the many faces of this entry. Walk about 0.4 mile west from the parking areas in the western portion of the park.

LOWER SOUTH FALLS ★★★

MAGNITUDE: 75
ELEVATION: 980 feet
WATERSHED: Medium
APPROACH: Trail (moderate)
LAT/LONG: 44.885349° N / 122.661082° W
USGS MAP: *Drake Crossing* (1985)

The trail passes behind this 93-foot plummet along South Silver Creek. Continue 0.8 mile downstream from South Falls (described earlier), a total of 1.2 miles from the trailhead.

MORE ONLINE:
Frenchie Falls ★ USGS *Drake Crossing* (1985 ns)

9 SCOTTS MILLS

MCKAY FALLS (U) ★★

MAGNITUDE: 38
ELEVATION: 420 feet
WATERSHED: Large
APPROACH: Auto
LAT/LONG: 45.041046° N / 122.664622° W
USGS MAP: *Scotts Mills* (1985 ns)

Within Scotts Mills Park, water pours 10 to 15 feet over a 35- to 50-foot breadth of Butte Creek. Drive to Scotts Mills via State Route 213 and Scotts Mills Road. Turn right on Third Street, then proceed a couple blocks and turn left into the park. Views are a very short distance away. Waterfall lover Bryan Swan unofficially named this falls after Thomas McKay, who long ago built a mill (now gone) for which the town is named.

ABIQUA FALLS ★★★★

MAGNITUDE: 64
ELEVATION: 1200 feet
WATERSHED: Large
APPROACH: High-clearance & trail (fairly hard)
LAT/LONG: 44.926185° N / 122.567762° W
USGS MAP: *Elk Prairie* (1985)

Abiqua Creek pours 90 to 100 feet over a classic exposure of columnar basalt into a large pool. When I last visited it and according to more recent reports, the private landowners allowed access. If the situation has changed, *please don't trespass.*

Drive 11.0 miles beyond McKay Falls (described earlier) as Third Street in Scotts Mills becomes Crooked Finger Road. Turn right (west) upon an unnamed gravel road signed for an all-terrain vehicle parking area. Proceed 1 mile to the playground for off-road enthusiasts. The road roughens considerably for the remaining 1.1 miles. Park along the right side of the road next to a gate.

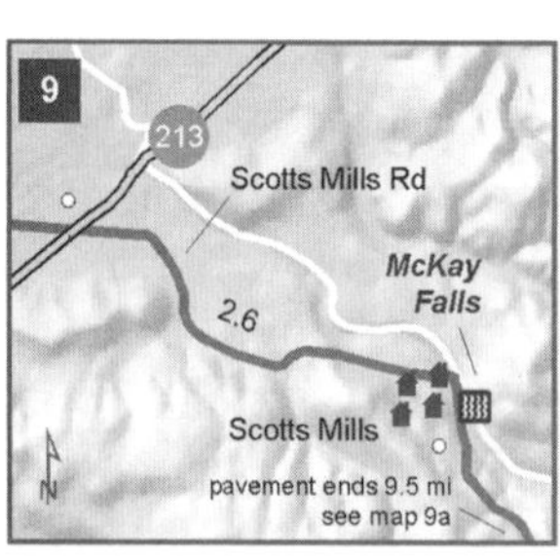

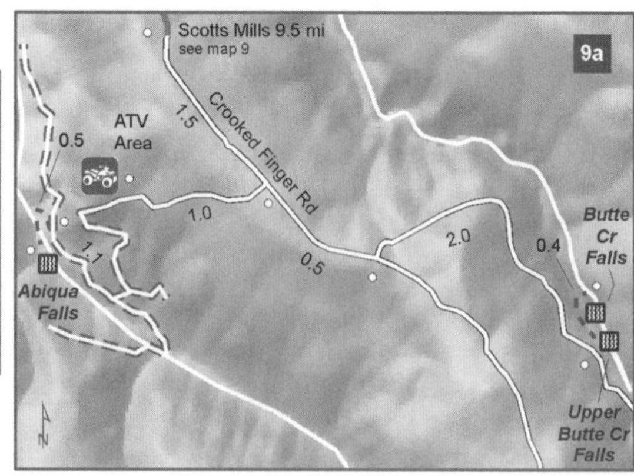

Abiqua Falls

Find a faint path in back of you on the opposite side of the road. Follow it about 30 yards to an old abandoned road. Turn left, go 10 feet, and enter the woods to the left. Proceed a few more feet and turn right. Hopefully you can now see the trail descending steeply 0.3 mile to the creek. Once you are at the bottom, follow the rocky path 0.2 mile upstream, ending at a large, natural amphitheater harboring the waterfall.

☐ UPPER BUTTE CREEK FALLS ★★★

MAGNITUDE: 49
ELEVATION: 1760 feet
WATERSHED: Medium
APPROACH: Trail (moderate)
LAT/LONG: 44.923146° N / 122.511822° W
USGS MAP: *Elk Prairie* (1985 ns)

Within Santiam State Forest, Butte Creek plunges 15 to 25 feet into a pool. From the turn for the all-terrain vehicle area (described earlier), continue 0.5 mile, then turn left onto another gravel road (not signed). Travel 2 miles down this route to a turnout to the left. A sign now exists at the trailhead. After a short distance, take the right fork at a junction. The path descends 0.2 mile down to an excellent vista. Behind the falls is a grotto, or cavernlike recess, that you can explore.

BUTTE CREEK FALLS ★★★★

MAGNITUDE: 56
ELEVATION: 1720 feet
WATERSHED: Medium
APPROACH: Trail (moderate)
LAT/LONG: 44.9238° N / 122.512402° W
USGS MAP: *Elk Prairie* (1985)

Water plummets 60 to 80 feet in a lush setting in Santiam State Forest. From the Upper Falls (described earlier), hike another 0.2 mile down the trail. The viewpoints are beautiful, as they are from the top of unguarded rock outcrops. Be careful.

10 MEHAMA

Vehicular access to this area has changed. From June through October, you can travel as follows. In Mehama, depart State Route 22 northward upon Wagner Road Southeast. After 2.4 miles, you reach a three-way intersection. Take the way that goes straight on Ayers Creek Road, signed for Shellburg Falls. Proceed 0.8 mile, then turn left upon AC100 Road. Continue 2.8 miles, and turn left upon Shellburg Road. You will reach a campground within Santiam State Forest's Shellburg Falls Recreation Area in another 2.6 miles.

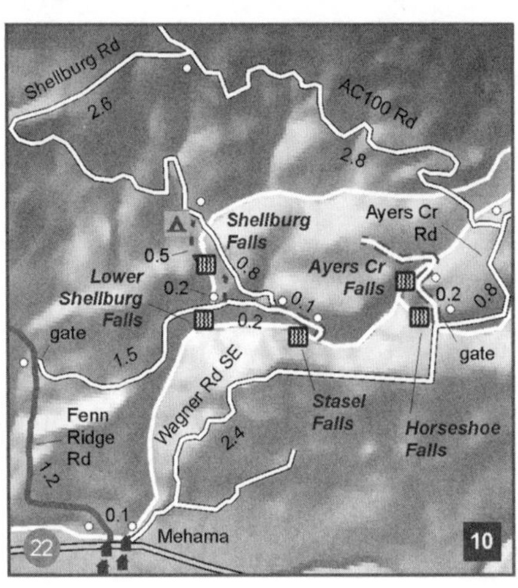

Any time of the year, you can alternatively drive 1.2 miles up Fenn Ridge Road, but you will need to hike 1.5 miles along the gated access road to reach the southern end of the recreation area.

STASEL FALLS ★★

MAGNITUDE: 45
ELEVATION: 1220 feet
WATERSHED: Medium
APPROACH: Trail (fairly easy)
LAT/LONG: 44.808668° N / 122.600609° W
USGS MAP: *Lyons* (1985)

Drive 0.8 mile southward beyond the campground (described earlier) to an unsigned turnout to the left. Walk a little more than 0.1 mile along an old jeep trail, then depart it at the well-worn path to the right. Use the sound of rushing water as a clue to turn. The path quickly leads to a vista above and looking directly into the cataract. Note the pillar of rock to the right of the upper tier.

The sheer cliffs at this location restrict this entry to responsible adults. The falls would deserve a higher rating if it were possible to see both tiers from a single vantage point.

LOWER SHELLBURG FALLS ★★

MAGNITUDE: 46
ELEVATION: 1250 feet
WATERSHED: Small
APPROACH: Auto
LAT/LONG: 44.810251° N / 122.608333° W
USGS MAP: *Lyons* (1985)

Shellburg Creek pours 20 to 40 feet. Continue driving beyond the turnout for Stasel Falls (described earlier) for 0.2 mile, and park next to the gated road. The falls are immediately in front of you, with some vegetation cleared that once greatly obscured the view.

SHELLBURG FALLS ★★★★

MAGNITUDE: 61
ELEVATION: 1340 feet
WATERSHED: Small
APPROACH: Trail (fairly easy)
LAT/LONG: 44.81261° N / 122.60872° W
USGS MAP: *Lyons* (1985)

This 80- to 100-foot plume along Shellburg Creek descends over bulging basalt so you can walk behind the waterfall. From Lower Shellburg Falls (described

Shellburg Falls

earlier), find the unmarked trail on the north side of the road. The gentle trail reaches this upper counterpart in 0.2 mile, with the way continuing another 0.5 mile to the campground (described earlier).

l HORSESHOE FALLS ★★

MAGNITUDE: 57
ELEVATION: 1500 feet
WATERSHED: Medium
APPROACH: Bushwhack (fairly hard)
LAT/LONG: 44.81022° N / 122.586704° W
USGS MAP: *Lyons* (1985)

Located on property owned by Longview Fibre Company, Stout Creek pours 40 to 50 feet into a semicircular, natural amphitheater. When I visited in July 2006, the timber company allowed responsible adults access to the area. Drive as if you were headed to Shellburg Falls Recreation Area (described earlier), but bear left after driving 2.4 miles along Wagner Road SE, right after you cross the stream. Make sure you park where you don't block the company gate.

Walk about 0.1 mile up the road, then veer through the clear-cut to the left where the road widens. Walk a couple of hundred feet down to the tree line, then listen for the falls and watch for the appearance of a small gorge. Proceed along the tree line in the appropriate direction, dependent on your point of entry. Find a decent rimside view of the falls and its horseshoe-shaped amphitheater. This fall deserves a higher rating, if you can find the moderately steep, thin path that reportedly makes its way down to the floor of the gorge. Longview only allows adults to visit this falls.

MORE ONLINE:
Ayers Creek Falls ★ USGS *Lyons* (1985)

11 LITTLE NORTH SANTIAM RIVER

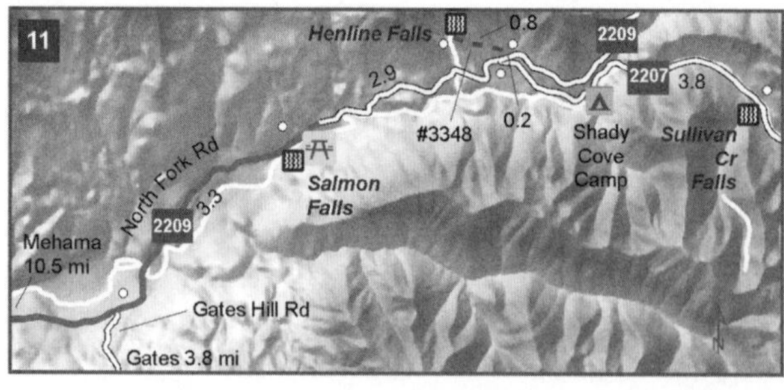

Access to the pleasant Elkhorn Valley and the waterfalls upstream is easiest via Forest Service Road 2209, which joins State Route 22, 1 mile east of Mehama. Alternatively, adventurous drivers with reliable brakes may wish to tackle (in low gear) Gates Hill Road. Beginning in the town of Gates, this gravel route proceeds up, up, up, then down, down, down on its route to the Elkhorn Valley.

SALMON FALLS ★★★

MAGNITUDE: 56 (h)
ELEVATION: 1120 feet
WATERSHED: Large
APPROACH: Auto
LAT/LONG: 44.831301° N / 122.369831° W
USGS MAP: *Elkhorn* (1994)

Located within Salmon Falls County Park, this high-volume 25- to 35-foot waterfall drops down along the Little North Santiam River. A fish ladder bypasses the cataract. Drive 3.3 miles up the valley (east) from the junction of Gates Hill Road and FS Road 2209. Turn at the sign for the county park.

SULLIVAN CREEK FALLS ★★

MAGNITUDE: 22
ELEVATION: 1980 feet
WATERSHED: Small
APPROACH: Auto
LAT/LONG: 44.840963° N / 122.265375° W
USGS MAP: *Elkhorn* (1994 ns)

A former clear-cut has healed nicely around the entry, increasing the scenic beauty of this 40- to 60-foot roadside display. Continue 2.9 miles past Salmon Falls (described earlier) along FS Road 2209, making a right turn onto Forest Service Road 2207. Proceed along this road for 3.8 miles to a view from the bridge spanning Sullivan Creek. This entry is located on a square-mile section of private land surrounded by Willamette National Forest.

Henline Falls

HENLINE FALLS ★★★★

MAGNITUDE: 74
ELEVATION: 1880 feet
WATERSHED: Small
APPROACH: Trail (fairly easy)
LAT/LONG: 44.849011° N / 122.339447° W
USGS MAP: *Elkhorn* (1994)

Henline Creek shimmers 75 to 100 feet over the mountainside. The falls is located within Opal Creek Wilderness, Detroit Ranger District of Willamette National Forest. The entrance to the old Silver King Mine is near the base of the falls. Look, but do not enter! A listing for Silver King Falls USGS *Elkhorn* (1985 ns) can be found in the federal government's Geographic Names Information System. But because it shows the same geographic coordinate, this is almost surely a second official name for Henline, which is a rarity.

Continue past Salmon Falls (described earlier) for 2.9 miles, then bear left, staying on FS Road 2209 and go 0.2 mile. Embark upon Henline Falls Trail 3348, reaching this wonderful display in 0.8 mile.

12 NIAGARA PARK

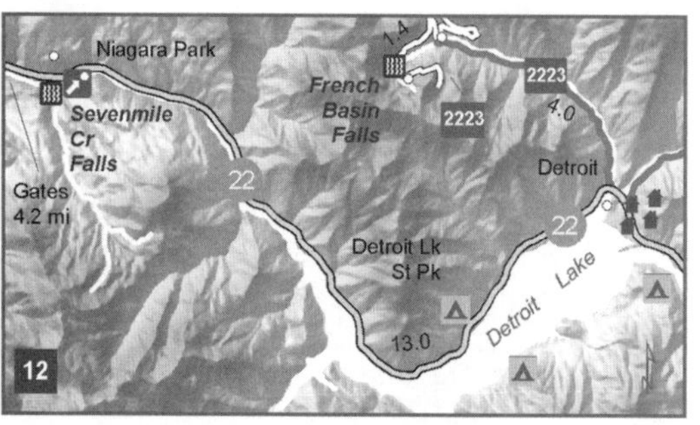

Niagara Park was the site of a small town from 1890 to 1934. A rubble masonry dam was built in the late 1890s to provide power for a paper mill, but difficulties in constructing the dam caused the mill project to be abandoned and the village faded. Historic remnants of the town can be seen at a marked turnout along State Route 22, 4.2 miles east of Gates and 13 miles west of Detroit.

1 SEVENMILE CREEK FALLS (U) ★★

MAGNITUDE: 29
ELEVATION: 1050 feet
WATERSHED: Small
APPROACH: Bushwhack (moderate)
LAT/LONG: 44.755361° N / 122.333718° W
USGS MAP: *Elkhorn* (1994 ns)

Look across the North Santiam River where Sevenmile Creek slides into the main river. Walk down a short pathway from Niagara Park to the river. Scramble on interesting rock formations to get a view of the falls.

MORE ONLINE:
Whispering Falls ★ USGS *Idanha* (1994 ns)
French Basin Falls ★ USGS *Battle Ax* (1994 nl)

13 MARION FORKS

As you head farther up the drainage basin of Marion Forks, located within the Detroit Ranger District of Willamette National Forest, the waterfalls become increasingly scenic.

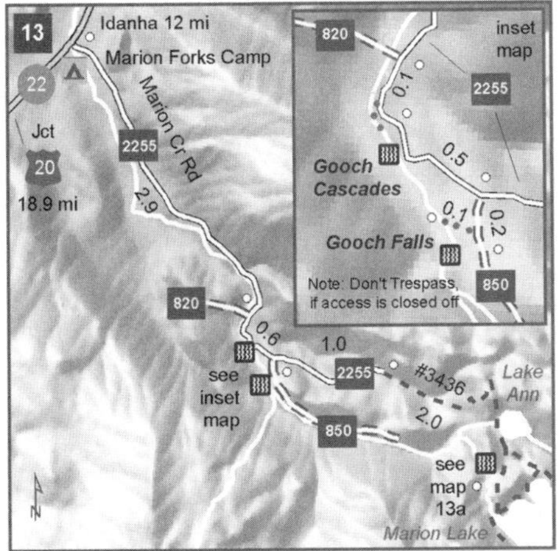

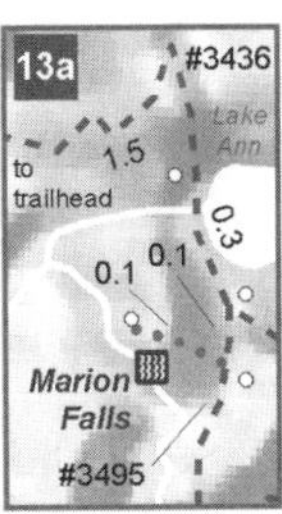

☐ GOOCH CASCADES (U) ★★

MAGNITUDE: 20
ELEVATION: 2860 feet
WATERSHED: Large
APPROACH: Bushwhack (fairly easy)
LAT/LONG: 44.580842° N / 121.918019° W
USGS MAP: *Marion Forks* (1994 ns)

Marion Creek spreads out as it descends about 10 feet within a deep woods setting. Depart State Route 22 at Marion Forks Camp upon Marion Creek Road (Forest Service Road 2255). Drive 2.9 miles along FS Road 2255, passing the turn at a bridge for Forest Service Road 820. Proceed 0.1 mile farther, and turn into an unsigned campsite at the bend in the road on the right. A cairn (small stack of rocks) signified its location when I last visited the area. Walk 100 feet to the riverside, then follow an angler's path another 100 feet to the base of the descent.

☐ GOOCH FALLS ★★★★

MAGNITUDE: 85
ELEVATION: 2810 feet
WATERSHED: Large
APPROACH: Bushwhack (moderate)
LAT/LONG: 44.576211° N / 121.913749° W
USGS MAP: *Marion Forks* (1994)

An absolutely beautiful 75- to 100-foot display drops from Marion Creek, but the terrain makes it only for adults. Continue 0.5 mile beyond the turnout for Gooch Cascades (described earlier), and turn right upon Forest Service Road 850. Park where the dirt road widens in less than 0.2 mile. If "No Trespassing" signs are posted on a small private landholding between the access road and the falls, then move on to Marion Falls (described later). Otherwise walk carefully 0.1 mile toward the creek for a natural, unfenced view above and into the falls.

MARION FALLS ★★★

MAGNITUDE: 81 (h)
ELEVATION: 3980 feet
WATERSHED: Medium
APPROACH: Trail & bushwhack (fairly hard)
LAT/LONG: 44.566443° N / 121.875597° W
USGS MAP: *Marion Lake* (1998)

The outlet of Marion Lake plunges 120 to 160 feet in the form of two powerful descents along Marion Creek. Reportedly the lower drop is the true identity of Gatch Falls, whose actual location has eluded waterfall enthusiasts for decades. Located within Mount Jefferson Wilderness, which is part of the national forest, the thunderous falls is recommended for adults only. Drive 1 mile past the turnoff for Gooch Falls (described earlier) to the end of Marion Creek Road (Forest Service Road 2255).

Hike 1.5 miles along Marion Lake Trail 3436 to Lake Ann. Continue 0.3 mile farther to a trail junction; bear right on Marion Outlet Trail 3495. Proceed about 0.1 mile to an unsigned path to the right. If you encounter a rocky slope along Trail 3495, you have passed the junction by 100 to 200 yards and will need to backtrack. Follow the path 0.1 mile to its end at an unguarded cliff at the top of the falls. The best views are from a faint path along the east side of the canyon.

MORE ONLINE:
Downing Creek Falls (u) ★ USGS *Marion Forks* (1994 nl)

14 McKENZIE RIVER

The waterfalls along the McKenzie River descend with fury, except for Tamolitch Falls, which has been artificially turned off. They all occur within the McKenzie River Ranger District, Willamette National Forest.

SAHALIE FALLS ★★★★

MAGNITUDE: 99 (h)
ELEVATION: 2800 feet
WATERSHED: Large (d)
APPROACH: Auto
LAT/LONG: 44.349067° N / 121.996919° W
USGS MAP: *Clear Lake* (1998)

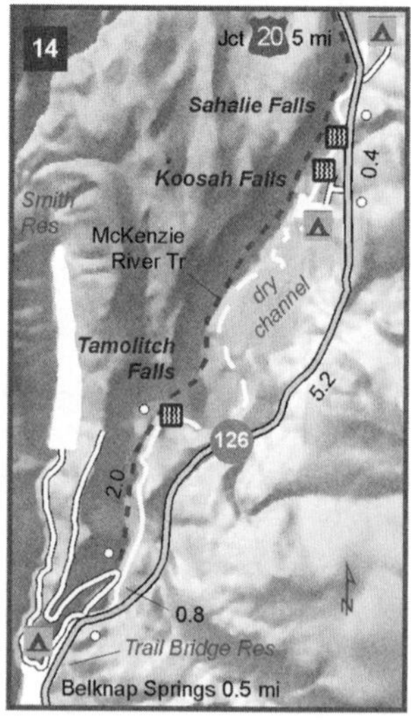

This roaring 140-foot torrent can be seen from several developed viewpoints. The smaller of the two segments disappears during periods of lower discharge. *Sahalie* is a Chinook word meaning "high." Depart State Route 126 at the point-of-interest sign located 5 miles south of U.S. Highway 20 and 6.1 miles north of Belknap Springs.

KOOSAH FALLS ★★★★

MAGNITUDE: 95 (h)
ELEVATION: 2680 feet
WATERSHED: Large (d)
APPROACH: Auto
LAT/LONG: 44.344525° N / 122.000523° W
USGS MAP: *Clear Lake* (1998)

The McKenzie River thunders 80 to 120 feet over a sharp escarpment. The cataract usually appears in a segmented form during late summer. Drive 0.4 mile south of Sahalie Falls (described earlier) along State Route 126 to the entrance marked Ice Cap Campground. Turn here and proceed to the parking area and developed viewpoints in 0.3 mile.

TAMOLITCH FALLS ★★

MAGNITUDE: 0
ELEVATION: 2380 feet
WATERSHED: none
APPROACH: Trail (moderate)
LAT/LONG: 44.312229° N / 122.026573° W
USGS MAP: *Tamolitch Falls* (1997)

A 60-foot dry rock wall is the only thing left where water once poured from the McKenzie River. But by all means, visit this location! This circular basin inspired the name "Tamolitch," which is Chinook for "tub" or "bucket." At this site, you will see a rare phenomenon: a full-sized river beginning at a single point. Springs feed the plunge pool at the base of the dry cataract. What happened to the falls? The river's water has been diverted 3 miles upstream at Carmen Reservoir, where a tunnel directs the water to Smith Reservoir and the power-generating facilities in the adjacent drainage.

Turn off State Route 126 at the north end of Trail Bridge Reservoir, 0.5 mile north of Belknap Springs or 5.2 miles south of Koosah Falls (described earlier). Drive about 0.8 mile to the McKenzie River Trailhead. Hike up the trail along the river for 2 miles to a crystal-clear, cyan-colored pool with the dry falls at its head (and a dry channel above it).

MORE ONLINE:

House Rock Falls (u) ★ USGS *Harter Mtn.* (1994 nl)

15 CASCADIA

LOWER SODA FALLS ★★★

MAGNITUDE: 25 (l)
ELEVATION: 1270 feet
WATERSHED: Small
APPROACH: Trail (moderate)
LAT/LONG: 44.407944° N / 122.475339° W
USGS MAP: *Cascadia* (1985)

Soda Creek tumbles 150 to 180 feet in three tiers among moss-covered rocks. The falls is located within Cascadia State Park. Start at the state park, located 13 miles east of Sweet Home along U.S. Highway 20. Find the unmarked trail at the far north end of the campsite area, and hike a moderately steep 0.5 mile to the descent.

RAINBOW FALLS ★★

MAGNITUDE: 40
ELEVATION: 1460 feet
WATERSHED: Small
APPROACH: Bushwhack (moderate)
LAT/LONG: 44.375652° N / 122.46858° W
USGS MAP: *Cascadia* (1994)

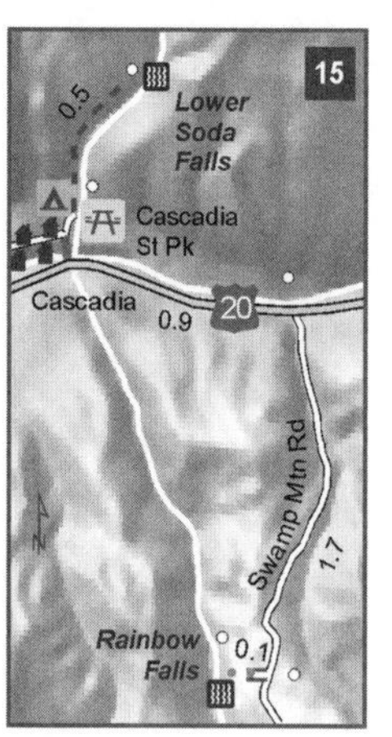

Dobbin Creek pours 20 to 30 feet into a pool. The waterfall lies outside national forest land, most likely on private property. Drive 0.9 mile east of the community of Cascadia, then turn right (south) off U.S. Highway 20 onto Swamp Mountain Road. Follow this gravel route for 1.7 miles, parking at an unsigned, old dirt road to the right. Follow the dirt road for about 100 feet, then descend along the top of a small ridge to an open view of the falls.

MORE ONLINE:
High Deck Falls (u) ★ USGS *Cascadia* (1994 ns)

16 McDOWELL CREEK FALLS COUNTY PARK

Four of the five waterfalls described in this section are within McDowell Creek Falls County Park, a pleasant and thoughtfully planned day-use recreation area. Turn off U.S. Highway 20 at Fairview Road. Proceed east for 1 mile, then turn left onto McDowell Creek Road. The county park and first parking turnout are 6.5 miles farther east.

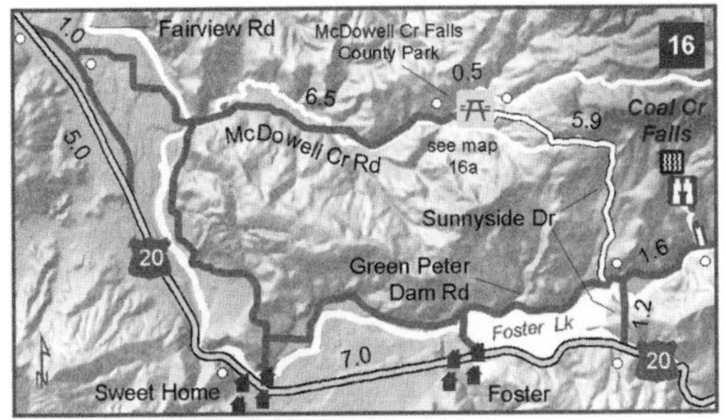

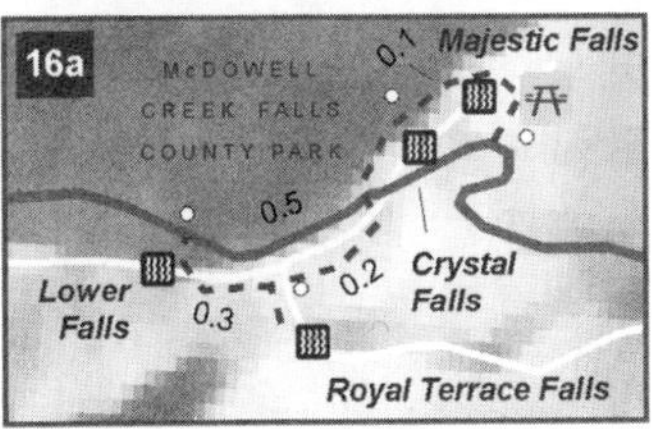

LOWER FALLS ★★

MAGNITUDE: 45
ELEVATION: 800 feet
WATERSHED: Medium
APPROACH: Trail (easy)
LAT/LONG: 44.463929° N / 122.682642° W
USGS MAP: *Sweet Home* (1984 nl)

This minor pair of descents drops about 10 feet along McDowell Creek. Park at the western access point of the park's trail system. This entry is located a very short walk away, immediately downstream from the first footbridge.

ROYAL TERRACE FALLS ★★★

MAGNITUDE: 39 (l)
ELEVATION: 1000 feet
WATERSHED: Very small
APPROACH: Trail (fairly easy)
LAT/LONG: 44.46376° N / 122.67938° W
USGS MAP: *Sweet Home* (1984 ns)

Fall Creek sprays 119 feet down in a fountainlike tiered display. A marked spur path ascends to a viewpoint above the top of the cataract. Walk an easy 0.3 mile upstream from Lower Falls (described earlier) to this waterfall.

MAJESTIC FALLS ★★★

MAGNITUDE: 58
ELEVATION: 980 feet
WATERSHED: Medium
APPROACH: Auto or trail (fairly easy)
LAT/LONG: 44.468125° N / 122.674552° W
USGS MAP: *Sweet Home* (1984 nl)

A porchlike overlook allows a close-up view of this 30- to 40-foot drop tumbling from McDowell Creek. Drive to the north end of the park. A stairway leads a short distance to the vista. Hikers can also reach it by continuing northward 0.3 mile along the main trail from Royal Terrace Falls (described earlier).

COAL CREEK FALLS (U) ★★

MAGNITUDE: 32 (l)
ELEVATION: 920 feet
WATERSHED: Small
APPROACH: Bushwhack (fairly hard)
LAT/LONG: 44.440677° N / 122.591232° W
USGS MAP: *Green Peter* (1984 nl)

Coal Creek drops 40 to 60 feet outside of McDowell Creek Falls County Park. It is most likely situated on private property. Depart US 20 at the east end of Foster Lake and drive north on Sunnyside Drive for 1.2 miles to Green Peter Dam Road. You can also reach this road by following Sunnyside Drive for 5.9 miles southeast of McDowell Creek Falls County Park. From the Dam Road, drive east 1.6 miles and park at the dirt road to the left (north).

Walk to the end of the road, then scramble up the crumbly slope to a faint path. A short distance farther is a fairly distant view of this entry.

MORE ONLINE:

Crystal Falls ★ USGS *Sweet Home* (1984 nl)

Coal Creek Falls

OREGON

THE SOUTH CASCADES

South-central Oregon presents a collage of scenic outdoor settings typical of the Cascade Range. The area's major peaks include Three Sisters, Bachelor Butte, Diamond Peak, and Mount McLoughlin—all of which are volcanic in origin. The region also boasts five national forests, four wilderness areas, an abundance of mountain lakes, and Crater Lake National Park. Waterfalls are well distributed throughout the South Cascades. Most of the 121 recognized falls in the region are relatively accessible; 82 of them are documented in this book.

Many of this region's waterfalls are among the most majestic of the Pacific Northwest. They often occur streaming down the walls of canyons carved by alpine glaciers. During the last major ice age, 10,000 to 14,000 years ago, these glaciers extended their range to areas below 2500 feet in elevation in the South Cascades. Large, U-shaped glacial troughs remain as evidence of the intense erosive powers of these glaciers. Today, rivers follow the valleys abandoned by the retreating glaciers. As tributary streams flow into the troughs, they often drop sharply as waterfalls. Rainbow Falls, Proxy Falls, and Vidae Falls are examples. Many physical geographers and geologists refer to this type of descent as ribbon falls.

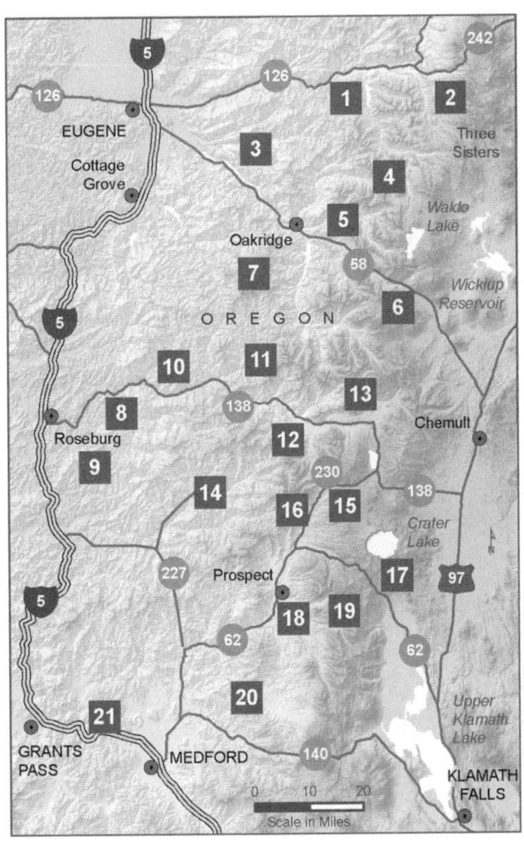

The western portion of the South Cascades formed in the same manner as the central portion described in the preceding chapter. Where layers of resistant basalt and weak sandstone meet along a stream's course, the sandstone erodes faster than the basalt. The graceful Toketee Falls and idyllic Grotto Falls are good examples of cataracts shaped in this way.

1 COUGAR RESERVOIR

Several years ago I did not spot any waterfalls when I drove along Aufderheide Forest Drive, which parallels Cougar Reservoir within McKenzie River Ranger District of Willamette National Forest. Imagine my surprise when the following cataract was documented to be next to the highway. It turns out the descent is oriented in such a way it's not likely to be noticed by northbound drivers, but it is plainly seen by folks driving in the opposite direction. What's that saying? *It's all a matter of your point of view.*

TERWILLIGER FALLS ★★★

MAGNITUDE: 50
ELEVATION: 1760 feet
WATERSHED: Small

APPROACH: Auto or watercraft
LAT/LONG: 44.080912° N / 122.23483° W
USGS MAP: *Cougar Reservoir* (1997 ns)

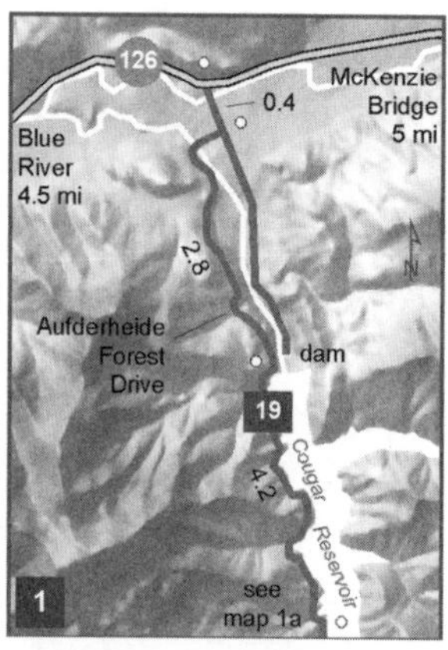

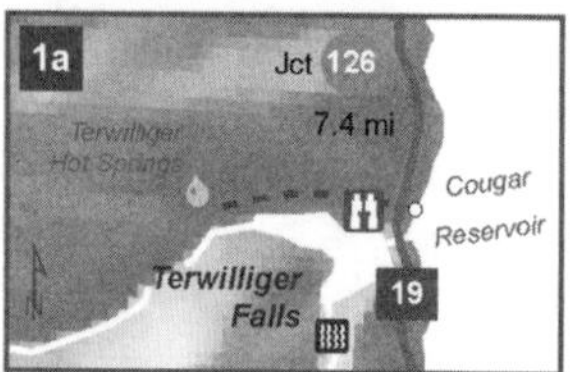

An unnamed stream ribbons 60 to 80 feet down a hillside into a cove of Cougar Reservoir. Turn south off of State Route 126 upon Aufderheide Forest Drive. The turn, which is also signed for the reservoir, is 4.5 miles east of Blue River townsite and 5 miles west of the hamlet of McKenzie Bridge. After 0.4 mile, bear right, rather than staying straight at the stop sign. You reach the top of Cougar Dam in another 2.8 miles. Turn right here onto the road signed as Forest Service Road 19. After 4.2 more miles, find a parking space to your left signed for Terwilliger Hot Springs.

Walk across the road to the entrance into the hot springs area. A stump partway up the cove makes a good vantage point, but you might have to pay to get there. If so, you may as well take a dip in the hot springs (swimwear optional). If you have a portable watercraft, ask for permission to paddle in the cove, enabling close-up views.

2 McKENZIE HIGHWAY

The peaks of North Sister (10,085 feet), Middle Sister (10,047 feet), and South Sister (10,358 feet) dominate the Cascade scenery along State Route 242, also known as McKenzie Highway. The following waterfalls are readily accessible just inside Three Sisters Wilderness, which is located within the McKenzie River Ranger District of Willamette National Forest.

Terwilliger Falls

7 RAINBOW FALLS ★★★

MAGNITUDE: 85 (h)
ELEVATION: 2960 feet
WATERSHED: Medium

APPROACH: Trail (fairly easy)
LAT/LONG: 44.131349° N / 122.000464° W
USGS MAP: *Linton Lake* (1997)

The peaks of the Three Sisters provide a background to a cross-valley view of Rainbow Creek distantly descending 150 to 200 feet. About 0.5 mile east of McKenzie Bridge Ranger Station, turn south off State Route 126 onto Foley Ridge Road (Forest Service Road 2643). Follow it for 6.4 miles, turn right on

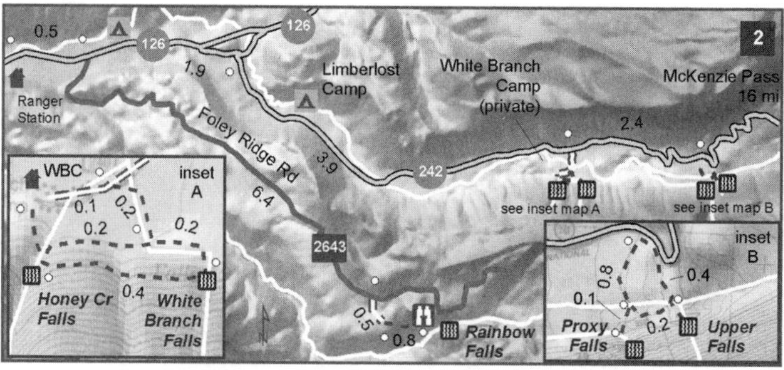

the marked dirt road, and proceed 0.5 mile to the start of Rainbow Falls Trail 3543. The moderately gentle trail ends in 0.8 mile at an unfenced, distant view of the cataract.

WHITE BRANCH FALLS ★★

MAGNITUDE: 21 (l)
ELEVATION: 2560 feet
WATERSHED: Very small (s)
APPROACH: Trail (fairly easy)
LAT/LONG: 44.161266° N / 121.962162° W
USGS MAP: *Linton Lake* (1997 nl)

It's okay to visit this moss-framed 35- to 50-foot veil located on private property as long as you check in first. Depart State Route 126 for SR 242, and drive 3.9 miles to White Branch Camp. Turn right and proceed 0.3 mile to an unsigned turnout and trailhead along the road's south side. Walk 0.1 mile up to the camp buildings, and ask permission to hike.

Go back down where you parked. Follow the path 0.2 mile to a loop. Taking the left fork, it is another 0.2 mile to this display, with the loop also providing access to Honey Creek Falls USGS *Linton Lake* (1997 ns).

UPPER FALLS ★★

MAGNITUDE: 28 (l)
ELEVATION: 3000 feet
WATERSHED: Very small (s)
APPROACH: Trail (fairly easy)
LAT/LONG: 44.163021° N / 121.923345° W
USGS MAP: *Linton Lake* (1997 ns)

Water cascades steeply 100 to 125 feet from springs issuing from a high canyon wall. Continue 2.4 miles eastward past White Branch Camp (described earlier) along SR 242 to the signed parking area for Proxy Falls trailheads. The trails have recently been reconfigured into an interpretive loop. In order to save the best falls for last, start on the entrance to the left and hike clockwise. After 0.4 mile, a short spur quickly leads you to the base of the Upper Falls.

2 PROXY FALLS ★★★★

MAGNITUDE: 91
ELEVATION: 3000 feet
WATERSHED: Medium (s)
APPROACH: Trail (fairly easy)
LAT/LONG: 44.161681° N / 121.92753° W
USGS MAP: *Linton Lake* (1997)

As trees surround you, you gain a windowlike view of Proxy Creek, also called Lower Falls, pouring 200 feet in impressive fashion. From the Upper Falls (described earlier), continue 0.2 mile to another spur to the left, ending 0.1 mile farther at the vista. From here, it is 0.8 mile to complete the trail loop at the west end of the parking area.

MORE ONLINE:

Honey Creek Falls ★, mentioned earlier

3 BIG FALL CREEK

1 CHICHESTER FALLS ★★★

MAGNITUDE: 34
ELEVATION: 1100 feet
WATERSHED: Medium
APPROACH: Auto
LAT/LONG: 43.970095° N / 122.537893° W
USGS MAP: *Saddleblanket Mtn.* (1997)

This idyllic 20- to 30-foot drop along Andy Creek is located within Middle Fork Ranger District, Willamette National Forest. The easiest way to view it is from the highway bridge. Look closely to observe an interesting grotto around the plunge pool. Moss and plants enhance the setting.

There are several interesting scenes on the way to this entry. Turn off State Route 58 at the Lowell Exit, where an old covered bridge looks out of place above the reservoir of Lookout Point Lake. To reach the falls, follow the Lowell–Jasper Road through town. Just before reaching a second covered bridge, turn right (east) in 2.9 miles on Big Fall Creek Road. Take this secondary road, which becomes Forest Service Road 18, for 15.9 miles to an unsigned turnout at Andy Creek.

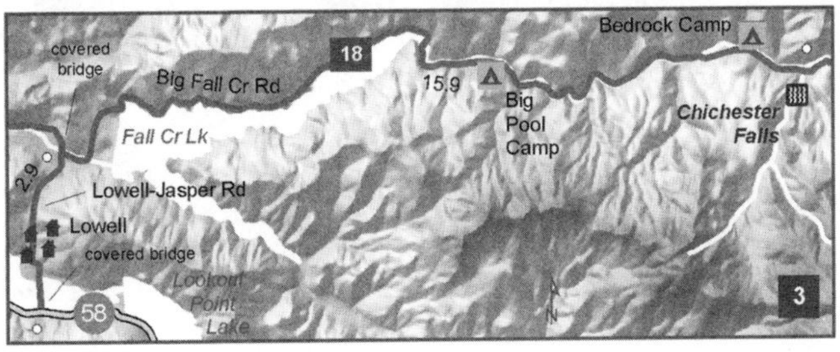

Chichester Falls

4 ERMA BELL LAKES

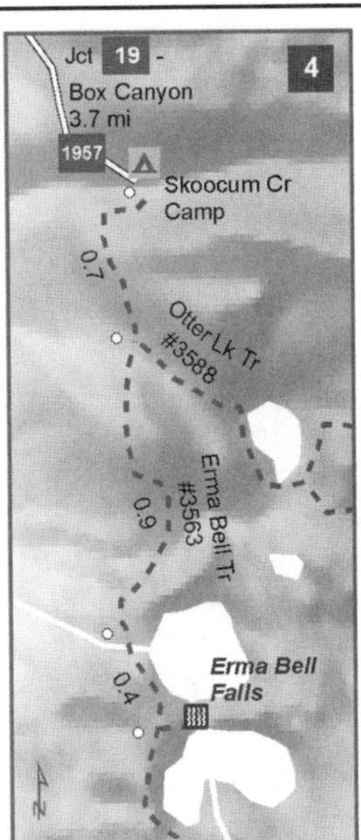

Who would have thought a waterfall could exist on top of a mountain? One occurs here, as a stream pours between Middle and Lower Erma Bell Lakes in glacially scoured terrain. Drive to Forest Service Road 1957 from the south by departing State Route 58 at Westfir upon Aufderheide Scenic Byway (Forest Service Road 19). Follow this route for 35 miles, and turn right onto FS Road 1957 at Box Canyon. Southbounders depart U.S. Highway 126 about 5 miles west of McKenzie Bridge onto the same byway. Proceed southward 27 miles, passing Cougar Reservoir along the way, to the left turn on FS Road 1957 at Box Canyon. The trailhead for the lakes is located at the end of the 3.7-mile length of FS Road 1957 at Skookum Creek Camp.

☐ ERMA BELL FALLS (U) ★★★

MAGNITUDE: 57
ELEVATION: 4580 feet
WATERSHED: Small

APPROACH: Trail (moderate)
LAT/LONG: 43.837592° N / 122.041904° W
USGS MAP: *Waldo Mtn.* (1986 nl)

The outlet to Middle Erma Bell Lake descends 30 to 40 feet in a fountainlike display. The falls is located within Three Sisters Wilderness of Willamette National Forest. From Skookum Creek Camp, start hiking along Erma Bell Trail 3563. The first 0.7 mile is fairly level until it meets Otter Lake Trail 3588. Stay on Trail 3563, bearing right, where you meet Lower Erma Bell Lake in another 0.9 mile. At the south end of the lake, in 0.3 mile more the trail steepens considerably. Look for an unsigned path 0.1 mile farther, to the left soon after you first hear the roar of the falls. This path quickly leads to the top of the cataract, with several vantage points below.

5 SALMON CREEK

Reach the following trio of waterfalls by turning north off State Route 58 at Fish Hatchery Road, which is located on the east side of Oakridge. Follow the route 1.4 miles to its end, then proceed right (east) on Salmon Creek Road (Forest Service Road 24). They are all located within Middle Fork Ranger District, Willamette National Forest.

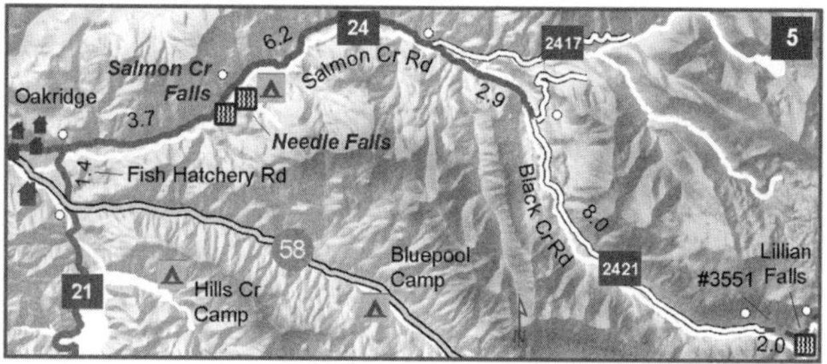

SALMON CREEK FALLS ★★

MAGNITUDE: 47 (h)
ELEVATION: 1450 feet
WATERSHED: Large
APPROACH: Auto
LAT/LONG: 43.76165° N / 122.373892° W
USGS MAP: *Huckleberry Mtn.* (1997)

Water tumbles a total of 10 to 15 feet along a 60- to 80-foot breadth of Salmon Creek. Drive 3.7 miles east of Fish Hatchery Road (described earlier) along Salmon Creek Road (Forest Service Road 24) to Salmon Creek Falls Camp. Vantage points are available from both the picnic area and the campground.

NEEDLE FALLS (U) ★★

MAGNITUDE: 21 (l)
ELEVATION: 1460 feet
WATERSHED: Very small
APPROACH: Auto
LAT/LONG: 43.762471° N / 122.372025° W
USGS MAP: *Huckleberry Mtn.* (1997 nl)

An unnamed creek skirts 35 to 50 feet into Salmon Creek behind campsite 4 in Salmon Creek Falls Camp (mentioned earlier). This entry deserves a lower rating during dry spells.

 LILLIAN FALLS ★★

MAGNITUDE: 25
ELEVATION: 3980 feet
WATERSHED: Small
APPROACH: Trail (fairly hard)
LAT/LONG: 43.698108 / 122.092003° W
USGS MAP: *Waldo Lake* (1997)

Nettie Creek steeply cascades 60 to 80 feet. Follow Forest Service Road 24 eastward past Salmon Creek Falls (described earlier). After 6.2 miles, the paved road crosses Salmon Creek and becomes a single lane. Continue 2.7 additional miles to a crossing at Black Creek. About 0.2 mile farther, bear right (south) on Black Creek Road (Forest Service Road 2421). The road ends in 8 more miles at the start of Black Creek Trail 3551.

Hike the moderately steep route to a trailside view of the falls in 2 miles. It was named after Lillian Ryker McGillvrey, who was a cook on the trail construction crew. Prior editions of this book list the entry as Lithan Falls, as that is how it is labeled on the 1986 USGS map, which has since been updated. Apparently the name was transcribed incorrectly, with "lli" mistaken as "th."

MORE ONLINE:

Pine Creek Falls (u) ★ USGS *Warner Mtn.* (1997 nl)

6 SALT CREEK

Six impressive cataracts are concentrated within an area of only 2 square miles in the Middle Fork Ranger District of Willamette National Forest. Drive 21 miles east from Oakridge or 6 miles west from Willamette Pass along State Route 58. Park at the Salt Creek Falls turnout or in Salt Creek Falls Picnic Area.

SALT CREEK FALLS ★★★★★

MAGNITUDE: 98 (h)
ELEVATION: 4000 feet
WATERSHED: Large
APPROACH: Auto
LAT/LONG: 43.611977° N / 122.128609° W
USGS MAP: *Diamond Peak* (1997)

This cascade is the gem of the South Cascades, as Salt Creek plummets 286 feet into a gorge. Trails and a fenced vista provide a variety of views of the cataract, which was first seen by anglos (Frank S. Warner and Charles Tufti) in March 1887. The falls is easily accessible from the turnout or the picnic area (described earlier).

LOWER DIAMOND CREEK FALLS ★★

MAGNITUDE: 82
ELEVATION: 4000 feet
WATERSHED: Medium
APPROACH: Trail (fairly easy)
LAT/LONG: 43.612691° N / 122.140282° W
USGS MAP: *Diamond Peak* (1997 nl)

Although it is 200 to 250 feet tall, its obscure views diminish this entry's scenic rating. In past visits, a couple of trees prevented a clear vantage point of the bottom portion of the falls. From Salt Creek Picnic Area (described earlier), follow Diamond Creek Falls Trail 3598 for a gentle 0.7 mile along the rim of Salt Creek Canyon to one of several viewpoints.

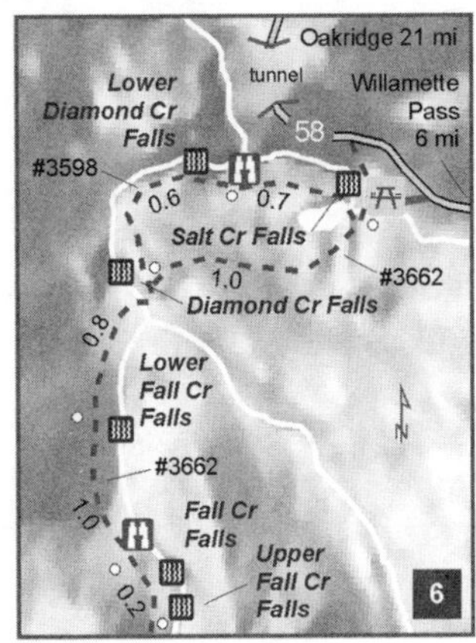

DIAMOND CREEK FALLS ★★★★

MAGNITUDE: 72
ELEVATION: 4240 feet
WATERSHED: Medium
APPROACH: Trail (moderate)
LAT/LONG: 43.607223° N / 122.14363° W
USGS MAP: *Diamond Peak* (1997 nl)

This superb cataract occurs where Diamond Creek pours 70 to 90 feet downward. Follow Trail 3598 for 0.6 mile beyond Lower Diamond Creek Falls (described earlier). A trail provides a good viewpoint above the descent, plus a short spur trail quickly leads to its base. You can take a loop route back to Salt Creek Picnic Area by continuing a short distance, bearing left onto Vivian Lake Trail 3662, and walking 1 mile.

LOWER FALL CREEK FALLS (U) ★★

MAGNITUDE: 45
ELEVATION: 4440 feet
WATERSHED: Small
APPROACH: Trail (fairly hard)
LAT/LONG: 43.59375° N / 122.139982° W
USGS MAP: *Diamond Peak* (1997 ns)

This double waterfall along Fall Creek totals 30 to 50 feet. At the junction of Diamond Creek Falls Trail 3598 with Vivian Lake Trail 3662 (described earlier), turn right onto Trail 3662. Cross some railroad tracks, and proceed 0.8 mile up the moderately steep path to views just off the trail.

FALL CREEK FALLS ★★

MAGNITUDE: 54
ELEVATION: 4780 feet
WATERSHED: Small
APPROACH: Trail (hard)
LAT/LONG: 43.592802° N / 122.138501° W
USGS MAP: *Diamond Peak* (1997)

Fall Creek plunges 40 to 60 feet. Continue climbing steeply for 1 mile past Lower Fall Creek Falls (described earlier). A sign tacked to a tree points to a moderately distant view of this entry.

UPPER FALL CREEK FALLS (U)★★★

MAGNITUDE: 69
ELEVATION: 5000 feet
WATERSHED: Small
APPROACH: Trail (hard)
LAT/LONG: 43.591606° N / 122.138416° W
USGS MAP: *Diamond Peak* (1997 ns)

This is the best of the cataracts along Fall Creek, descending 50 to 80 feet. Hike 0.2 mile past Fall Creek Falls (described earlier) to a trailside vantage point. From here, it is 3 miles back to Salt Creek Picnic Area.

Opposite: *Salt Creek Falls*

7 ROW RIVER

The recreation staff at Umpqua National Forest is a waterfall lover's best friend. They always seem to be blazing trails to more and more descents. They have even copublished a 20-page color pamphlet entitled *Thundering Waters* with the Roseburg Bureau of Land Management District, guiding travelers to the area's falls. (I am pleased to note that it cites this guidebook.)

The Row River drainage basin of the Cottage Grove Ranger District of Umpqua National Forest contains several waterfalls. Access the area by departing Interstate 5 at Cottage Grove (Exit 174) and driving east on Cottage Grove–Dorena Road for 17 miles to the community of Culp Creek. All these entries but Wildwood Falls are situated within the national forest.

WILDWOOD FALLS ★★

MAGNITUDE: 34
ELEVATION: 1000 feet
WATERSHED: Large
APPROACH: Auto
LAT/LONG: 43.699846° N / 122.81886° W
USGS MAP: *Culp Creek* (1986)

The course of the Row River is interrupted by this 10- to 15-foot drop. Drive to the east side of Culp Creek townsite, then bear left in 0.3 mile onto an unsigned road, remaining on the north side of the Row River. Views of the descent are available at the Wildwood Falls Picnic Area in 0.8 mile and at a developed roadside vista just before that.

SPIRIT FALLS ★★★

MAGNITUDE: 34 (l)
ELEVATION: 1920 feet
WATERSHED: Small
APPROACH: Trail (moderate)
LAT/LONG: 43.730771° N / 122.641619° W
USGS MAP: *Rose Hill* (1998)

This aptly named 60-foot veil, located where Alex Creek gouges into a bulging mass of moss-covered substrate, has a surrealistic feel. From Wildwood Falls (described earlier), drive 2.4 miles to the crossroads of Disston. Stay on the north side of the Row River; the route changes its name to Layng Creek Road (Forest Service Road 17). Proceed 9 miles to a signed trailhead and a path that leads moderately steeply 0.5 mile to a picnic table at the base of this entry.

MOON FALLS ★★

MAGNITUDE: 24 (t)
ELEVATION: 3000 feet
WATERSHED: Very small
APPROACH: Trail (fairly easy)
LAT/LONG: 43.735702° N / 122.611192° W
USGS MAP: *Holland Point* (1997)

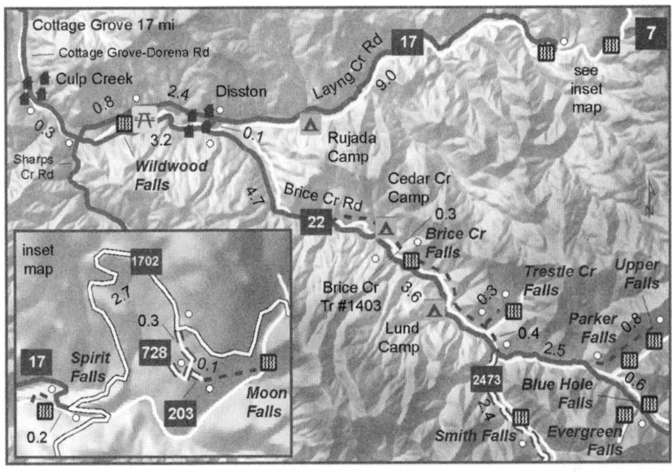

The upper reaches of Alex Creek drop 120 feet. The approach is an easy 0.5-mile walk, complete with a picnic table. Continue 0.2 mile past the trailhead for Spirit Falls (described earlier) to Forest Service Road 1702. Turn left and drive 2.7 miles; then bear right on Forest Service Road 1702-728. Drive along this unimproved surface for 0.3 mile before turning left on Forest Service Road 1702-203; in another 0.1 mile you reach the trailhead.

1 BRICE CREEK FALLS ★★

MAGNITUDE: 29
ELEVATION: 1510 feet
WATERSHED: Large
APPROACH: Trail (easy)
LAT/LONG: 43.668377° N / 122.70389° W
USGS MAP: *Rose Hill* (1998 ns)

A sequence of falls and cascades occurring along this particular reach of Brice Creek is highlighted by this 5- to 10-foot segmented punchbowl. At the junction of Layng Creek Road (Forest Service Road 17) and Brice Creek Road (Forest Service Road 22, described earlier), continue along the latter route for 4.7 miles to Cedar Creek Camp. Park here and walk across the footbridge to Brice Creek Trail 1403. It's a 0.3-mile march to the right (upstream) for this particular entry.

2 TRESTLE CREEK FALLS ★★★

MAGNITUDE: 58
ELEVATION: 2240 feet
WATERSHED: Small
APPROACH: Trail (moderate)
LAT/LONG: 43.647792° N / 122.656962° W
USGS MAP: *Rose Hill* (1998 ns)

Water sprays downward 60 feet in a moss-covered setting. Continue 3.6 miles past Cedar Creek Camp (described earlier) along Brice Creek Road (Forest

Service Road 22). Park at the turnout near the bridge crossing. Walk across the bridge, meeting Brice Creek Trail 1403. Turn left (west), and hike 0.4 mile to Trestle Creek Falls Trail 1403C to the right. The hike steepens considerably the final 0.3 mile up Trestle Creek to viewpoints of the cataract.

SMITH FALLS ★★

MAGNITUDE: 42
ELEVATION: 2640 feet
WATERSHED: Medium
APPROACH: High-clearance
LAT/LONG: 43.616264° N / 122.641019° W
USGS MAP: *Fairview Peak* (1997)

Champion Creek tumbles 15 to 25 feet along a route dubbed the "Tour of the Golden Past," which was once a thoroughfare leading to the historic Bohemia Mining District, only remnants of which remain. A sign indicating the location of Jerome #9 Placer Claim is posted near the falls. Adjacent to the parking area for Trestle Creek Falls (described earlier) is Champion Creek Road (Forest Service Road 2473). Vehicles with decent clearance can usually drive up the road during summer, though the 2.4-mile journey is slow.

PARKER FALLS ★★★

MAGNITUDE: 41
ELEVATION: 2620 feet
WATERSHED: Small
APPROACH: Trail (moderate)
LAT/LONG: 43.636519° N / 122.606279° W
USGS MAP: *Holland Point* (1997 nl)

Parker Creek splits into two rivulets dropping 35 feet off a rock escarpment. From the parking area for Trestle Creek Falls (described earlier), continue along Brice Creek Road (Forest Service Road 22) for 2.5 miles, and stop just before the next bridge crossing. Trek up Parker Falls Trail 1415 for 0.5 mile to this entry, also known as Lower Parker Falls.

UPPER PARKER FALLS ★★

MAGNITUDE: 22
ELEVATION: 2700 feet
WATERSHED: Small
APPROACH: Trail (fairly hard)
LAT/LONG: 43.637621° N / 122.603918° W
USGS MAP: *Holland Point* (1997 nl)

Water slides 40 feet along Parker Trail in this upper falls. Proceed beyond Parker Falls (described earlier); the trail steepens for 0.3 mile to a viewpoint of this display.

EVERGREEN FALLS (U) ★★

MAGNITUDE: 35
ELEVATION: 2600 feet
WATERSHED: Very small
APPROACH: Auto
LAT/LONG: 43.632372° N / 122.605764° W
USGS MAP: *Holland Point* (1997 ns)

An unnamed creek skips a total of 30 to 40 feet among the mosses. Waterfall enthusiast Bryan Swan coined this unofficial name during one of his waterfall excursions. Drive 0.6 mile past the trailhead for Parker Falls (described earlier) along Brice Creek Road (Forest Service Road 22) to this roadside cataract.

BLUE HOLE FALLS (U) ★★★

MAGNITUDE: 39
ELEVATION: 2540 feet
WATERSHED: Medium
APPROACH: Trail (fairly easy)
LAT/LONG: 43.632186° N / 122.603575° W
USGS MAP: *Holland Point* (1997 ns)

This is one of the prettiest punchbowls in the Northwest. From the turnout at Evergreen Falls (described earlier), walk a short distance up Brice Creek Road (Forest Service Road 22) to angler's paths that lead a short 0.1 mile to the river. A variety of natural vantage points of this entry are available, with another nice descriptive name given by waterfall lover Bryan Swan.

MORE ONLINE:

Pinard Falls USGS *Holland Point* (2011 ns) EXPLORE!

8 LITTLE RIVER

As you progress up the Little River Valley, you will pass one waterfall after another. Access the area by turning southeast off State Route 138 at Glide onto Little River Road (Forest Service Road 27). All but the next descent are located within North Umpqua Ranger District, Umpqua National Forest.

WOLF CREEK FALLS ★★★

MAGNITUDE: 26 (l)
ELEVATION: 1280 feet
WATERSHED: Medium
APPROACH: Trail (moderate)
LAT/LONG: 43.218384° N / 122.94782° W
USGS MAP: *Red Butte* (1997)

Water slides down a mountainside in two parts. The upper portion drops 75 feet, and the lower, 50 feet. The trail to the falls is courtesy of the Bureau of Land Management. Drive southeast 10.6 miles from SR 138 along Little River Road (FS Road 27), and stop at the signed parking area across the road from Wolf Creek Trailhead. It is a gently sloping 2-mile trip to the falls.

HEMLOCK FALLS ★★

MAGNITUDE: 63
ELEVATION: 2800 feet
WATERSHED: Medium
APPROACH: Trail (fairly hard)
LAT/LONG: 43.216241° N / 122.728695° W
USGS MAP: *Quartz Mtn.* (1997)

Water rushes 80 feet along the lower reaches of Hemlock Creek. Drive along Little River Road (FS Road 27) for 14.8 miles past Wolf Creek Falls (described earlier). Turn into Lake in the Woods Camp. Hemlock Falls Trail 1520 begins just before you reach the campsites. Follow a steep path for 0.5 mile down to this entry.

7 TRIBUTARY FALLS (U) ★★

MAGNITUDE: 40
ELEVATION: 3260 feet
WATERSHED: Very small
APPROACH: Trail (moderate)
LAT/LONG: 43.212332° N / 122.715713° W
USGS MAP: *Quartz Mtn.* (1997 ns)

Dropping 20 to 30 feet along an unnamed creek, this is the first of a trio of waterfalls visible along the recently reconstructed Hemlock Trail 1505. Drive 0.1 mile eastward past Lake in the Woods Camp (described earlier). Turn right (south) on an obscure road, and proceed an additional 0.1 mile to the trailhead. Hike up the moderately steep route for 0.5 mile to a viewing platform.

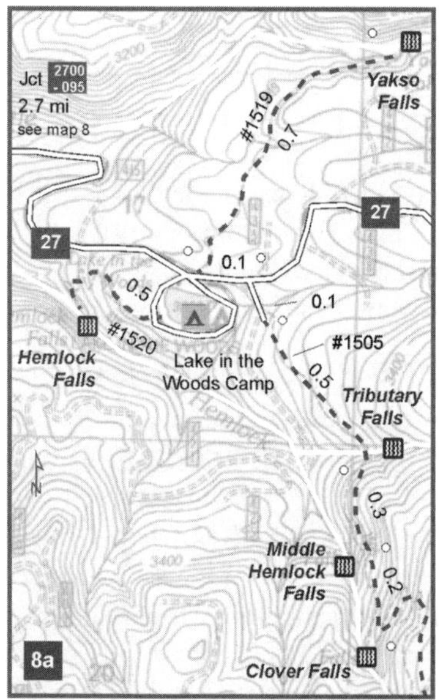

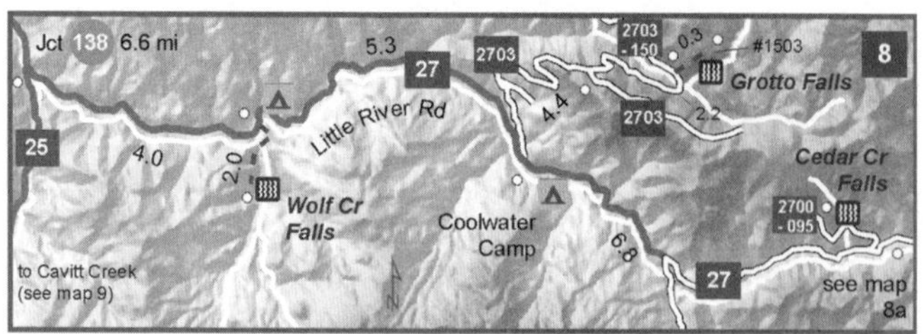

MIDDLE HEMLOCK FALLS (U) ★★

MAGNITUDE: 41
ELEVATION: 3340 feet
WATERSHED: Small
APPROACH: Trail (fairly hard)
LAT/LONG: 43.208938° N / 122.716592° W
USGS MAP: *Quartz Mtn.* (1997 nl)

From the trail, only the upper portion of this descent can be seen tumbling 30 to 40 feet from Hemlock Creek. Hike the steep trail past Tributary Falls (described earlier) for 0.3 mile to trailside vantage points.

CLOVER FALLS ★★★

MAGNITUDE: 43
ELEVATION: 3580 feet
WATERSHED: Small
APPROACH: Trail (fairly hard)
LAT/LONG: 43.206029° N / 122.715863° W
USGS MAP: *Quartz Mtn.* (1997 nl)

This is the best of the cataracts along Hemlock Trail 1505, as water hurtles 30 to 40 feet along Hemlock Creek. Follow the steep trail another 0.2 mile past Middle Hemlock Falls (described earlier) to a trailside view. It is 1 mile back down the mountain to the trailhead. This entry was unofficially named Upper Hemlock Falls in earlier editions of the guidebook.

YAKSO FALLS ★★★

MAGNITUDE: 71
ELEVATION: 3100 feet
WATERSHED: Small
APPROACH: Trail (moderate)
LAT/LONG: 43.224607° N / 122.715369° W
USGS MAP: *Quartz Mtn.* (1997)

This is a classic example of a fan form, as the Little River takes a 70-foot drop. Yakso Falls Trail 1519 starts across the road from the entrance to Lake in the Woods Camp (described earlier). Proceed 0.7 mile down to the base of the falls.

GROTTO FALLS ★★★

MAGNITUDE: 37 (l)
ELEVATION: 3120 feet
WATERSHED: Medium
APPROACH: Trail (fairly easy)
LAT/LONG: 43.250244° N / 122.821242° W
USGS MAP: *Mace Mtn.* (1997)

The shimmering waters of this pleasant waterfall plunge 100 feet along Emile Creek. Some have also referred to it as Emile Falls USGS *Mace Mtn.* (1985), which is actually another cataract farther downstream and was inaccessible when I field-truthed the area. The creek and its namesake falls, plus Shivigny Mountain, are named after Emile Shivigny, who homesteaded nearby in 1875.

Backtrack 9.5 miles from Lake in the Woods Camp, or continue 5.3 miles past Wolf Creek Falls along Little River Road (FS Road 27, described earlier).

Grotto Falls

Turn north onto Forest Service Road 2703, drive 4.4 miles, then turn left on Forest Service Road 2703-150. Follow this gravel route up the mountain 2.2 miles farther to Grotto Falls Trail 1503, located on the far side of Emile Creek Bridge. The trail goes behind the descent in 0.3 mile.

MORE ONLINE:

Cedar Creek Falls ★ USGS *Taft Mtn.* (1997 ns)

9 CAVITT CREEK

SHADOW FALLS ★★★

MAGNITUDE: 42
ELEVATION: 2200 feet
WATERSHED: Medium
APPROACH: Trail (moderate)
LAT/LONG: 43.152249° N / 122.949923° W
USGS MAP: *Red Butte* (1997)

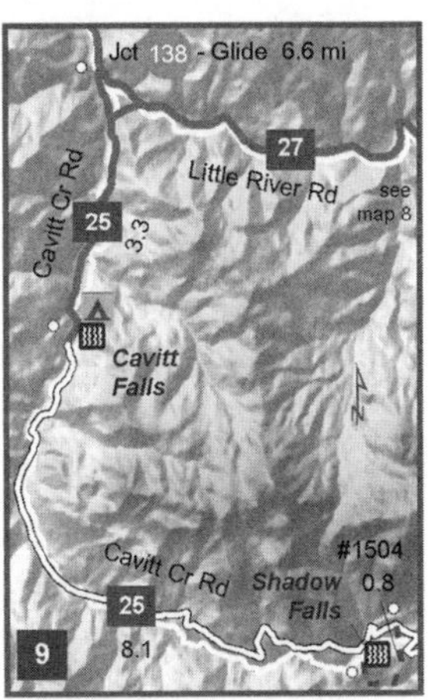

This triple waterfall totaling 80 to 100 feet along Cavitt Creek is aptly named. Over time the falls has worked its way upstream through a rock fracture, forming a narrow, natural grotto that always offers some shade. Immediately downstream from the falls, next to the trail, are interesting weathered bedrock formations.

Turn right (south) off Little River Road (Forest Service Road 27, described earlier) onto Cavitt Creek Road (Forest Service Road 25), which is located 6.6 miles from Glide. After 3.3 miles, you can turn into Cavitt Falls Park and visit Cavitt Falls USGS *Lane Mtn.* (1998). Take a footbath in the refreshing pool at the base of this 10- to 15-foot descent. The park is administered by the Bureau of Land Management.

For Shadow Falls, continue along FS Road 25 for another 8.1 miles, stopping at the signed turnout. Follow Shadow Falls Trail 1504 to the cataract in 0.8 mile. This falls is located within North Umpqua Ranger District, Umpqua National Forest.

MORE ONLINE:
Cavitt Falls ★, mentioned earlier

10 IDLEYLD PARK

Scenic State Route 138 serves as a convenient corridor between Glide and Crater Lake, making the following waterfalls easily accessible to the traveler. Be sure to use your turn signal, as the traffic tends to speed through here. I have been honked at more than once, despite using that contraption attached to the steering wheel.

Shadow Falls

7 COBBLE CREEK FALLS ★★

MAGNITUDE: 33
ELEVATION: 1380 feet
WATERSHED: Small
APPROACH: Auto
LAT/LONG: 43.43341° N / 122.90329° W
USGS MAP: *Harrington Creek* (1989 nl)

Peer a fair distance into a small, tight gorge from which Cobble Creek can be seen descending at least 30 to 50 feet. Drive 5.8 miles east of Glide, 0.8 mile east of Idleyld Park along SR 138, and turn left (north) upon Rock Creek Road, also called County Road 78. You missed the turn by 0.2 mile if you see Swiftwater Bridge crossing the North Umpqua River to your right. Pass BLM Rock Creek Camp Site in 6.7 miles, and stay straight at the junction 1.3 miles farther. From here drive 2 miles to a small unsigned turnout on your left.

DEADLINE FALLS ★★

MAGNITUDE: 39
ELEVATION: 770 feet
WATERSHED: Large
APPROACH: Trail (easy)
LAT/LONG: 43.324609° N / 122.998756° W
USGS MAP: *Old Fairview* (1997 ns)

If you are as fortunate as I am, you will see salmon attempting to jump this 5- to 10-foot-tall and 50- to 70-foot-wide North Umpqua River cataract. The best time to visit is May through October. Depart SR 138, and drive to the signed parking just south of the Swiftwater Bridge (described earlier), located 1 mile east of Idleyld Park and 16 miles west of Steamboat. This handicapped-accessible segment of North Umpqua Trail proceeds 0.3 mile to a short spur ending at the viewing area for the falls.

SUSAN CREEK FALLS ★★★

MAGNITUDE: 50
ELEVATION: 1060 feet
WATERSHED: Medium
APPROACH: Trail (fairly easy)
LAT/LONG: 43.305202° N / 122.907453° W
USGS MAP: *Old Fairview* (1997)

This 30- to 40-foot cataract along Susan Creek is situated on a Bureau of Land Management parcel. Those hiking beyond the falls can see American Indian mounds. Drive east from Swiftwater Bridge (described earlier) along SR 138 for 6 miles to Susan Creek Camp. The trailhead is across the road from the parking area. Reach the falls by hiking 1 mile along a relatively gentle path.

FALL CREEK FALLS ★★★

MAGNITUDE: 57
ELEVATION: 1400 feet
WATERSHED: Small
APPROACH: Trail (moderate)
LAT/LONG: 43.319024° N / 122.83999° W
USGS MAP: *Mace Mtn.* (1997 nl)

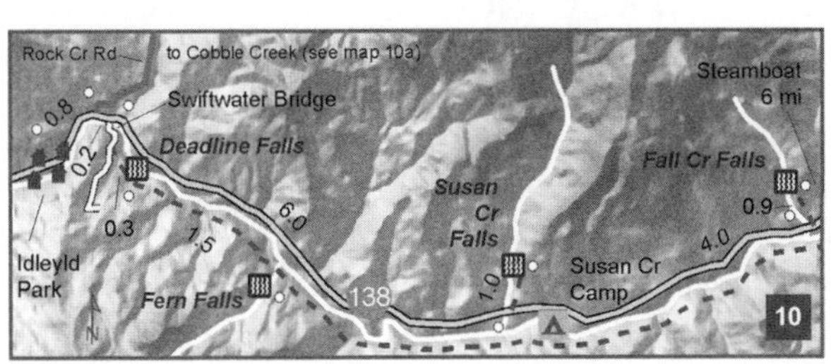

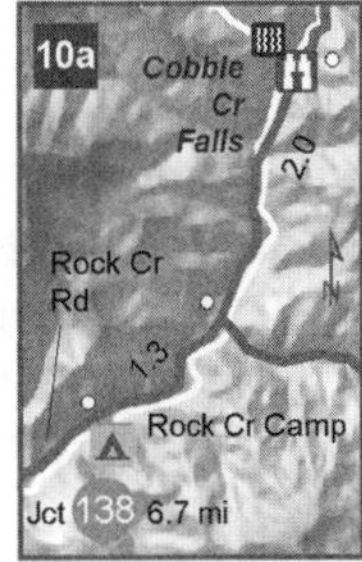

Fall Creek tumbles twice, with each tier dropping 35 to 50 feet. It is located within the North Umpqua Ranger District of Umpqua National Forest. Reach this entry by walking around and through slabs of bedrock and past the natural, lush vegetation of Jobs Garden.

Drive 4 miles east from Susan Creek Picnic Area (described earlier) on SR 138 to the marked turnout for Fall Creek Falls National Recreation Trail. This beautiful path leads 0.9 mile to the falls.

MORE ONLINE:

Fern Falls ★ USGS *Old Fairview* (1997 ns)

11 STEAMBOAT

Fishing is prohibited in the entire basin encompassing Steamboat Creek in order to provide undisturbed spawning grounds for the salmon and steelhead trout of the North Umpqua River drainage. The following waterfalls are all situated within North Umpqua Ranger District, Umpqua National Forest.

STEAMBOAT FALLS ★★★

MAGNITUDE: 47
ELEVATION: 1380 feet
WATERSHED: Large
APPROACH: Auto
LAT/LONG: 43.373639° N / 122.640906° W
USGS MAP: *Steamboat* (1997)

A developed viewpoint showcases this 20- to 30-foot drop along Steamboat Creek. Some fish attempt to jump the falls, while others use the adjacent ladder. Turn northeast off State Route 138 onto Steamboat Road (Forest Service Road 38) at Steamboat Junction. After 1.1 miles you can visit more modest Little Falls USGS *Steamboat* (1997), where you have even a better chance of seeing fish jump. Look for an unsigned turnout next to the falls and the adjacent bedrock slabs. Continuing onward for the main display, drive an additional 4.2 miles, and turn right (southeast) onto Forest Service Road 3810. Proceed 0.6 mile to the entrance of Steamboat Falls Camp and the cataract.

JACK FALLS ★★

MAGNITUDE: 32 (l)
ELEVATION: 1460 feet
WATERSHED: Small
APPROACH: Bushwhack (fairly hard)
LAT/LONG: 43.317947° N / 122.689207° W
USGS MAP: *Steamboat* (1997)

This set of three falls is closely grouped along Jack Creek. The lower descent slides 20 to 30 feet in two segments. The middle and upper falls are of the horsetail type, descending 25 to 40 feet and 50 to 70 feet, respectively. From Steamboat Junction, drive southeast along State Route 138 for 3.1 miles, and park at an unsigned turnout at mile marker 42. Walk 100 yards farther to Jack Creek. Follow the brushy streambank to the base of the lower falls.

CANTON CREEK FALLS ★★

MAGNITUDE: 41
APPROACH: Trail (moderate)
ELEVATION: 2480 feet
LAT/LONG: 43.505014° N / 122.718196° W
WATERSHED: Small
USGS MAP: *Fairview Peak* (1997 nl)

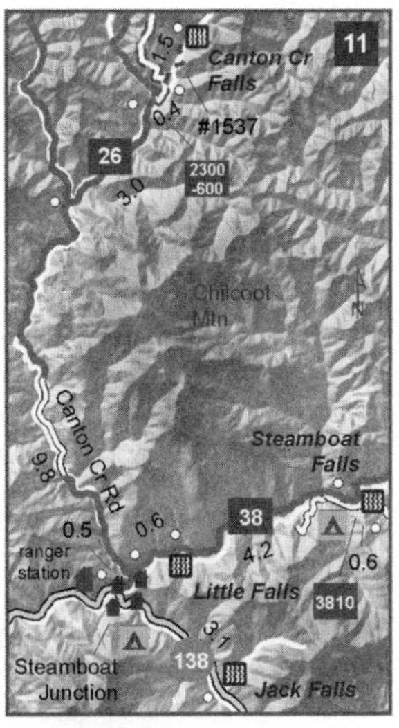

Walk to a gorge-rim vista of this 60- to 80-foot slide along Canton Creek. From State Route 138, turn northeast on Steamboat Road (Forest Service Road 38), then left in 0.5 mile onto Canton Creek Road. Follow this route for 9.8 miles to Upper Canton Road (Forest Service Road 26), and turn right. Take FS Road 26 for 3 miles, and turn right (east) on Saddle Camp Road (Forest Service Road 2300-600). Reach the trailhead in 0.4 mile. Hike 1.5 miles along Canton Creek Falls Trail 1537 to your destination.

MORE ONLINE:
Little Falls ★, described earlier

12 TOKETEE

The following two waterfalls are among the most impressive in the South Cascades and are not very difficult to access. Both are located within Diamond Lake Ranger District, Umpqua National Forest.

TOKETEE FALLS ★★★★

MAGNITUDE: 61
ELEVATION: 2340 feet
WATERSHED: Large (d)
APPROACH: Trail (fairly easy)
LAT/LONG: 43.263156° N / 122.43341° W
USGS MAP: *Toketee Falls* (1997)

These falls are an inspiring sight, as the North Umpqua River drops 30 feet before plunging 90 feet over a sheer wall of basalt. *Toketee* is an American Indian word meaning "graceful." The Toketee Pipeline can be seen along the walk to the falls. Pacific Power diverts water from Toketee Lake via its 12-foot redwood-stave pipe. A portion of the North Umpqua River is bypassed for

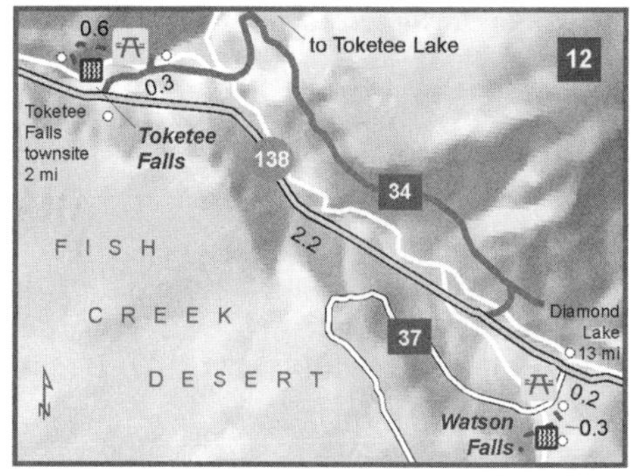

1663 feet via a mile-long tunnel. The water then plunges down a steel penstock pipe to the Toketee Powerhouse, where it can generate as much as 210,000 kilowatts of electricity.

Turn north off State Route 138 onto Forest Service Road 34, heading toward Toketee Lake. Drive 0.3 mile to the left (west) turn marked Toketee Falls Trail 1495. Follow the easily hiked path 0.6 mile to a viewpoint looking into the falls.

Toketee Falls

WATSON FALLS ★★★★★

MAGNITUDE: 99 (h)
ELEVATION: 3200 feet
WATERSHED: Medium
APPROACH: Trail (fairly easy)
LAT/LONG: 43.241855° N / 122.391074° W
USGS MAP: *Fish Creek Desert* (1997)

Peer up at Watson Creek plummeting 272 feet from a mesa of basalt and andesite known locally as Fish Creek Desert. The first good vantage point is from a footbridge, with the trail continuing more steeply to the base of the waterfall. Drive east 2.2 miles past Toketee Lake along State Route 138 to Fish Creek Road (Forest Service Road 37); turn right (south). Proceed 0.2 mile to Watson Falls Picnic Ground. Follow Watson Falls Trail 1495 to the first vista in 0.3 mile.

MORE ONLINE:
Surprise Falls, USGS *Potter Mountain* (1998 ns) EXPLORE!
Columnar Falls, USGS *Potter Mountain* (1998 ns) EXPLORE!

13 NORTHEAST UMPQUA

The cataracts never seem to end in the North Umpqua River watershed. This section describes four more descents within Diamond Lake Ranger District, Umpqua National Forest.

WHITEHORSE FALLS ★★

MAGNITUDE: 37
ELEVATION: 3660 feet
WATERSHED: Large
APPROACH: Auto
LAT/LONG: 43.247681° N / 122.305067° W
USGS MAP: *Garwood Butte* (1985)

Relax at the viewing area overlooking this 10- to 15-foot punchbowl along the course of the Clearwater River. Depart State Route 138 at the signed turn for Whitehorse Falls Camp, which is located 4.5 miles east of Toketee Falls townsite. Park at the picnic area adjacent to the cataract.

CLEARWATER FALLS ★★

MAGNITUDE: 48
ELEVATION: 4200 feet
WATERSHED: Medium
APPROACH: Trail (easy)
LAT/LONG: 43.248712° N / 122.227926° W
USGS MAP: *Diamond Lake* (1998)

The Clearwater River tumbles 30 feet. Drive 3.5 miles east from Whitehorse Falls (described earlier) along State Route 138 to the marked turn for Clearwater Falls Camp. Follow the access road 0.2 mile to a picnic area, from which a path quickly leads to the falls.

7 LEMOLO FALLS ★★★★

MAGNITUDE: 75 (h)
ELEVATION: 3720 feet
WATERSHED: Large (d)
APPROACH: Trail (fairly hard)
LAT/LONG: 43.345694° N / 122.22018° W
USGS MAP: *Lemolo Lake* (1998)

While the prior pair of entries is conducive to meditation, this 75- to 100-foot monster along the North Umpqua River does not allow for such tranquility. *Lemolo* is a Chinook word meaning "wild" or "untamed." Depart State Route 138 by turning north onto Lemolo Lake Road (Forest Service Road 2610), located 3 miles east of Clearwater Falls (described earlier).

Proceed toward Lemolo Lake and bear left (north) after 4.3 miles onto Thorn Prairie Road (Forest Service Road 3401). Go 0.4 mile, then turn right on Lemolo Falls Road (Forest Service Road 3401-800). The trailhead is 1.8 miles farther. Lemolo Falls Trail 1468 descends steeply, reaching the base of the thunderous falls in 1 mile.

Lemolo Falls

☐ WARM SPRINGS FALLS ★★★

MAGNITUDE: 68
ELEVATION: 3580 feet
WATERSHED: Medium
APPROACH: Trail (easy)
LAT/LONG: 43.357537° N / 122.244277° W
USGS MAP: *Lemolo Lake* (1998 ns)

Warm Springs Creek plummets 50 to 70 feet over cliffs of basalt. Follow the directions to Lemolo Falls (described earlier), but instead of turning at Road 3401, continue 0.9 mile on Lemolo Lake Road (Forest Service Road 2610) to the far side of Lemolo Dam. Turn left (northwest) on Forest Service Road 600, and drive 3 miles to Forest Service Road 680. Bear left here, and proceed 1.7 miles to the start of Warm Springs Falls Trail 1499. At the trail's end in 0.3 mile is a viewing deck above and looking into the cataract.

MORE ONLINE:

Cow Creek Falls ★ USGS *Cedar Springs Mtn.* (1998 ns)

14 SOUTH UMPQUA

The following trio of modestly pleasing waterfalls occurs within the watershed of the South Umpqua River, Tiller Ranger District, Umpqua National Forest. Access the area by driving along State Route 227 to the hamlet of Tiller.

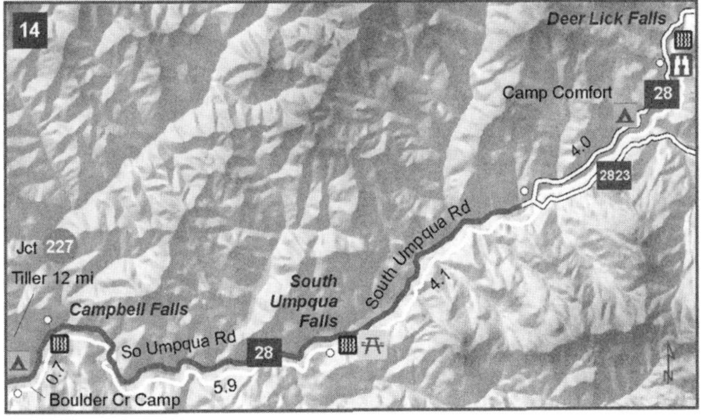

CAMPBELL FALLS ★★

MAGNITUDE: 36 (h)
ELEVATION: 1430 feet
WATERSHED: Large
APPROACH: Trail (fairly easy)
LAT/LONG: 43.052341° N / 122.770334° W
USGS MAP: *Dumont Creek* (1998)

The South Umpqua River tumbles 10 to 15 feet. The falls is named in honor of Robert G. Campbell, a former US Forest Service employee who was killed in action during World War II. Turn off SR 227 onto South Umpqua Road (Forest Service Road 28), located just northwest of the ranger station at Tiller. Proceed 12.7 miles to the signed turnout, 0.7 mile past Boulder Creek Camp. A trail leads quickly to the river in 0.2 mile.

SOUTH UMPQUA FALLS ★★

MAGNITUDE: 25
ELEVATION: 1640 feet
WATERSHED: Large
APPROACH: Auto
LAT/LONG: 43.054458° N / 122.686456° W
USGS MAP: *Acker Rock* (1998)

Water slides 10 to 15 feet over wide slabs of bedrock along the South Umpqua River. A fish ladder bypasses the falls. Drive eastward on South Umpqua Road (Forest Service Road 28), 5.9 miles past Campbell Falls (described earlier) to South Umpqua Falls Picnic Area and Observation Point.

DEER LICK FALLS ★★

MAGNITUDE: 43
ELEVATION: 2280 feet
WATERSHED: Large
APPROACH: Auto
LAT/LONG: 43.127511° N / 122.584103° W
USGS MAP: *Twin Lakes Mtn.* (1997)

Peer from a moderate distance into a series of five blocky descents ranging from 5 to 20 feet in height along Black Rock Fork. Drive 4.1 miles northeast past South Umpqua Falls (described earlier) along South Umpqua Road (Forest Service Road 28). Do not cross the river at the junction, but instead bear left on FS Road 28 toward Camp Comfort. Four miles farther there are unsigned vantage points along the road. A trail reportedly now leads up the creek to the falls.

MORE ONLINE:
Cathedral Falls, USGS *Tiller* (1998 ns) EXPLORE!

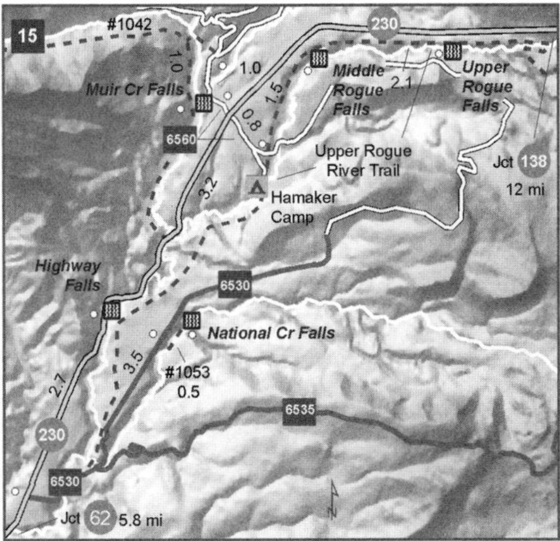

15 UPPER ROGUE RIVER

The following entries are all situated within High Cascades Ranger District, Rogue River-Siskiyou National Forest.

 UPPER ROGUE FALLS (U) ★★

MAGNITUDE: 44
ELEVATION: 4590 feet
WATERSHED: Medium
APPROACH: Trail (moderate)
LAT/LONG: 43.087003° N / 122.277408° W
USGS MAP: *Hamaker Butte* (1999 nl)

Upper Rogue River Trail 1034 passes two falls along its northerly route. This entry descends steeply 30 to 50 feet along the Rogue River. Depart State Route 230 upon Forest Service Road 6560, located 11.7 miles north of State Route 62 and 12 miles west of State Route 138. Drive along FS Road 6560, bearing left at the fork rather than turning toward Hamaker Camp to the right.

Park where the trail crosses the road in 0.8 mile. Start hiking northward. You will meet Middle Rogue Falls (u) USGS *Hamaker Butte* (1999 nl) after 1.5 miles and encounter this entry 2.1 miles farther.

NATIONAL CREEK FALLS ★★

MAGNITUDE: 50
ELEVATION: 3860 feet
WATERSHED: Medium
APPROACH: Trail (moderate)
LAT/LONG: 43.031405° N / 122.344737° W
USGS MAP: *Hamaker Butte* (1999 nl)

National Creek pours 30 to 50 feet downward in three segments. Drive 5.9 miles south of Forest Service Road 6560 (mentioned earlier) along State Route 230, and turn left (east) on Forest Service Road 6530. Follow this way 3.5 miles to the marked parking area for National Creek Falls Trail 1053. The path descends fairly steeply to the base of the cataract in 0.5 mile.

MORE ONLINE:

Middle Rogue Falls (u) ★, mentioned earlier

Muir Creek Falls ★ USGS *Hamaker Butte* (1999 nl)

Highway Falls ★ USGS *Hamaker Butte* (1999 nl), formerly Lower Rogue Falls (u)

Alkali Creek Falls USGS *Hamaker Butte* (1999 nl) EXPLORE!

16 NATURAL BRIDGE

Near the community of Union Creek 200 feet of the Rogue River disappears underground, providing a "natural bridge" over it. The stream drops into a landform known as a lava tube, whereby an old lava flow solidified creating an outer crust while the rest of the flow continued downslope, resulting in a subterranean cavity. Drive 1.1 miles south of Union Creek along State Route 62 to the signed turn, then another 1.1 miles along the access road to this geologic oddity and Rogue River Trail 1034. Three waterfalls occur within this portion of High Cascades Ranger District, Rogue River-Siskiyou National Forest.

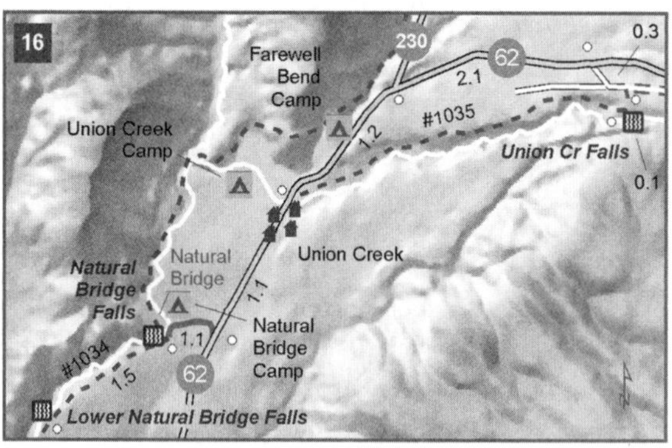

 NATURAL BRIDGE FALLS (U) ★★

MAGNITUDE: 33
ELEVATION: 3200 feet
WATERSHED: Large
APPROACH: Auto
LAT/LONG: 42.888443° N / 122.466407° W
USGS MAP: *Union Creek* (1997 ns)

The Rogue River tumbles 20 to 30 feet near Natural Bridge. The waterfall is adjacent to a wooden footbridge that crosses Rogue River Trail 1034 (described earlier).

LOWER NATURAL BRIDGE FALLS (U)★★

MAGNITUDE: 24
ELEVATION: 3020 feet
WATERSHED: Large
APPROACH: Trail (moderate)
LAT/LONG: 42.879244° N / 122.486036° W
USGS MAP: *Union Creek* (1997 nl)

Water froths 10 to 15 feet along the Rogue River. Follow Rogue River Trail 1034 (described earlier) for 1.5 miles downstream from Natural Bridge. An old four-wheel-drive road serves as the trail for the last 0.3 mile.

MORE ONLINE:
Union Creek Falls (u) ★, USGS *Union Creek* (1997 nl)

17 CRATER LAKE NATIONAL PARK

The center of attraction in Crater Lake National Park is the enormous depression, known as a caldera, presently occupied by Crater Lake. A cataclysmic eruption of the 12,000-foot peak of volcanic Mount Mazama 6600 years ago left a crater whose rim now stands approximately 8100 feet in elevation. Heavy annual precipitation maintains the lake level. In addition to the lake, Vidae Falls and Annie Falls are readily accessible within the park.

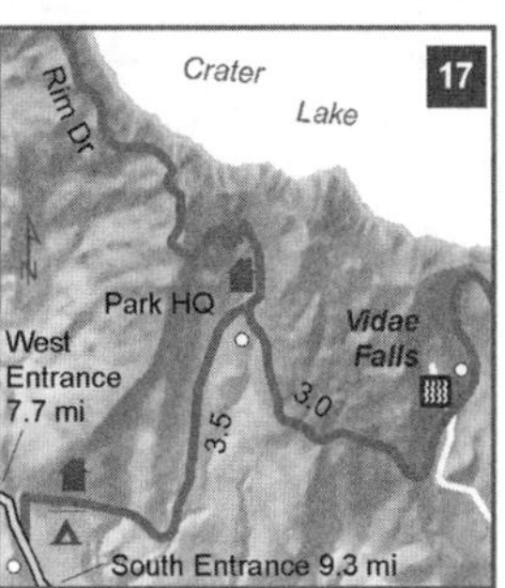

VIDAE FALLS ★★★

MAGNITUDE: 48
ELEVATION: 6700 feet
WATERSHED: Very small
APPROACH: Auto
LAT/LONG: 42.884529° N / 122.100039° W
USGS MAP: *Crater Lake East* (1999 nl)

Vidae Creek sprays 70 to 90 feet from Crater Lake's south rim near Applegate Peak. From the park headquarters drive 3 miles southeast to a turnout next to the falls.

MORE ONLINE:
Annie Falls ★ USGS *Maklaks Crater* (1998)

18 MILL CREEK

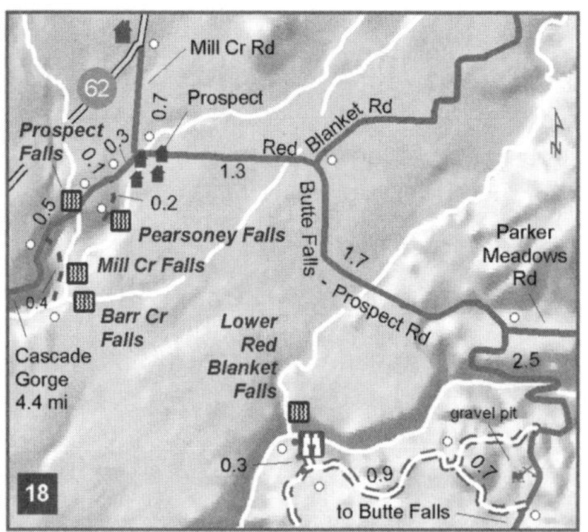

Three of the following five waterfalls are part of the Boise Cascade Corporation's Mill Creek Falls Scenic Area. The timber company has constructed public trails on a tract of pristine land. Turn off State Route 62 onto Mill Creek Road at either Cascade Gorge or Prospect. Park at the turnout marked by a large trail system sign 0.9 mile west of Prospect and 4.4 miles east of Cascade Gorge.

 MILL CREEK FALLS ★★★★

MAGNITUDE: 71
ELEVATION: 2360 feet
WATERSHED: Large

APPROACH: Trail (easy)
LAT/LONG: 42.740282° N / 122.495391° W
USGS MAP: *Prospect South* (1988)

Look across the canyon cut by the Rogue River to this thundering 173-foot plunge along Mill Creek. Follow the interpretive trail immediately south of the parking area (described earlier), and walk 0.3 mile to the viewpoint.

BARR CREEK FALLS ★★★★

MAGNITUDE: 94 (h)
ELEVATION: 2360 feet
WATERSHED: Medium

APPROACH: Trail (fairly easy)
LAT/LONG: 42.737918° N / 122.495799° W
USGS MAP: *Prospect South* (1999 nl)

This waterfall makes a beautiful display as Barr Creek shimmers 175 to 200 feet into Rogue River Canyon. In historical documents this cataract is also called Bear Creek Falls. Follow the trail 0.1 mile past Mill Creek Falls (described earlier) to a rocky outcrop providing a superb cross-canyon vista.

 PROSPECT FALLS (U) ★★★

MAGNITUDE: 40 (h)
ELEVATION: 2500 feet
WATERSHED: Large

APPROACH: Trail (fairly easy)
LAT/LONG: 42.745829° N / 122.495971° W
USGS MAP: *Prospect South* (1999 ns)

Prospect Falls

The Rogue River rushes 50 to 100 feet, neatly framed by the bridge spanning its gorge. I unofficially named this falls after the nearby community. Drive 0.5 mile east of the Mill Creek parking area (described earlier) to an unsigned turnout on the east side of the Rogue River Bridge. A well-trodden path leads to many good, unfenced views. It is worth the stop, considering it is readily accessible but not advertised.

PEARSONEY FALLS ★★

MAGNITUDE: 45
ELEVATION: 2480 feet
WATERSHED: Large
APPROACH: Trail (easy)
LAT/LONG: 42.744994° N / 122.489834° W
USGS MAP: *Prospect South* (1999 ns)

This waterfall, named after two pioneer families, the Pearsons and the Mooneys, drops 15 to 25 feet along Mill Creek. Continue 0.1 mile northeast of the Rogue River Bridge (described earlier) to the signed parking area off Mill Creek Road. Follow the main trail 0.2 mile to a trailside view of this entry.

LOWER RED BLANKET FALLS (U) ★★

MAGNITUDE: 75
ELEVATION: 2440 feet
WATERSHED: Large
APPROACH: High-clearance & bushwhack (hard)
LAT/LONG: 42.729392° N / 122.468355° W
USGS MAP: *Prospect South* (1999 nl)

Red Blanket Creek plummets a total of 90 to 140 feet in a secluded setting. The moderately distant cross-canyon vista is recommended for experienced adventurers only. The falls is probably located on private land. Take Red Blanket Road east from Prospect, and turn right after 1.3 miles on Butte Falls–Prospect Road. Continue another 1.7 miles, then bear right (south) toward Butte Falls.

After the route switchbacks for 2.5 miles uphill, look for a jeep trail to the right (west). It is the first road past a short gravel road ending at a gravel pit. Follow the jeep trail for 1.6 miles as shown on the accompanying map. Park at a short, abandoned jeep trail, which leads toward the canyon rim.

Follow the trail for a few hundred yards, then cut through the woods toward the roaring sound of the falls. Pick a route partway down the moderately steep slope until the falls come into view on the opposite side of the gorge. It is 0.3 mile to get back to your vehicle.

19 SKY LAKES WILDERNESS

Access to the following waterfalls is via Upper Red Blanket Trail 1090. Reach the trailhead by driving east of Prospect along Red Blanket Road for 15 miles to the road's end. All of the falls are located within Sky Lakes Wilderness, Rogue River-Siskiyou National Forest.

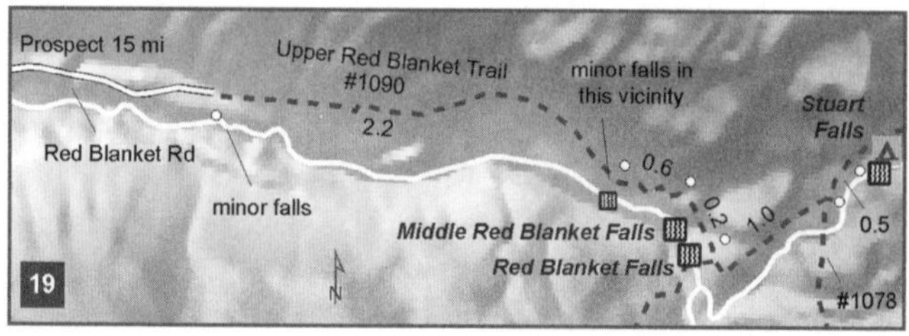

RED BLANKET FALLS ★★

MAGNITUDE: 50
ELEVATION: 5060 feet
WATERSHED: Medium
APPROACH: Trail (fairly hard)
LAT/LONG: 42.79349° N / 122.228731° W
USGS MAP: *Union Peak* (1998)

Red Blanket Creek takes a double drop, with the upper portion descending 50 to 70 feet. Only the top of the lower tier is visible from the trail. Begin hiking the moderately steep Upper Red Blanket Trail 1090. Just beyond the trailhead and at 2.2 miles, you pass small falls along tributaries. At 2.8 miles, you meet Middle Red Blanket Falls (u) USGS *Union Peak* (1998 ns). Proceed another 0.2 mile to trailside views of the main entry.

STUART FALLS ★★★

MAGNITUDE: 47
APPROACH: Trail (fairly hard)
ELEVATION: 5460 feet
LAT/LONG: 42.799127° N / 122.212938° W
WATERSHED: Medium
USGS MAP: *Union Peak* (1998)

Butte Falls

Refresh yourself in the cool mist of water veiling 25 to 40 feet along Red Blanket Creek. Continue 1 mile past Red Blanket Falls (described earlier) to the end of Trail 1090. Follow Stuart Falls Trail 1078 to the left (north), and proceed 0.5 mile to the cataract.

MORE ONLINE:
Middle Red Blanket Falls (u) ★, mentioned earlier

20 BUTTE FALLS

BUTTE FALLS ★★

MAGNITUDE: 54
ELEVATION: 2340 feet
WATERSHED: Large
APPROACH: Trail (fairly easy)
LAT/LONG: 42.545156° N / 122.562205° W
USGS MAP: *Butte Falls* (1999)

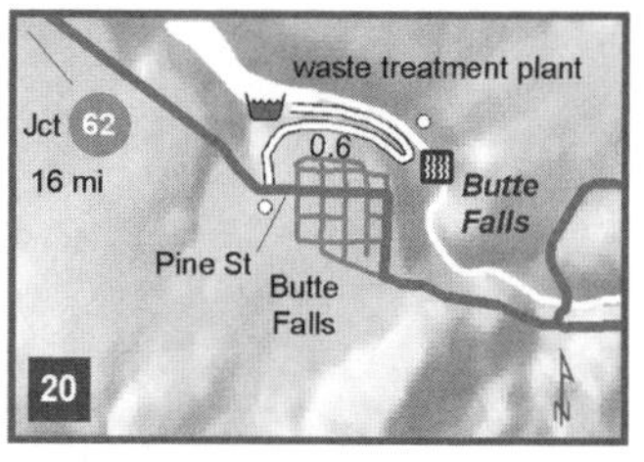

The nearby community is named after this 10- to 15-foot waterfall, which slices diagonally across South Fork Butte Creek. Turn off State Route 62 at Butte Falls junction, located 5 miles north of Eagle Point. Reach the town of Butte Falls in 16 miles. Upon entering the village, look for Pine Street to the left (north). Backtrack one block to an unmarked gravel road. Take this unpaved route north past a waste treatment plant to an unsigned parking area in 0.6 mile. Well-worn paths quickly lead to the falls.

21 GOLD BAR

Place names in this vicinity of southern Oregon were coined in the early 1800s by miners looking to strike it rich after a large gold nugget was found around here.

 DILLON FALLS ★★

MAGNITUDE: 25 (h)
ELEVATION: 1090 feet
WATERSHED: Large
APPROACH: Trail (easy)
LAT/LONG: 42.457751° N / 123.025948° W
USGS MAP: *Gold Hill* (1983)

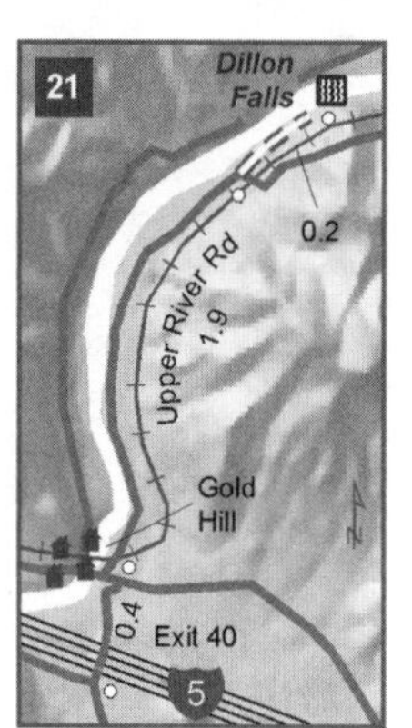

This is one of the lesser-known cascades along the extensive Rogue River. Depart Interstate 5 at Gold Hill (Exit 40). Drive north along Upper River Road for 0.4 mile, where it jogs briefly with the road to Gold Hill. Continue 1.9 miles farther to a dirt road just before a railroad crossing. Navigate around the potholes for 0.2 mile toward the road's end and park. Follow the walkway across the sluice, then take the angler's path that quickly leads to the base of this 10- to 15-foot challenge to salmon. Also known as Hayes Falls, it is split into two segments by an island.

OREGON

THE COLUMBIA PLATEAU

The landscape of eastern Oregon is dominated by a broad region of generally low relief called the Columbia Plateau. This region, which extends into southeastern Washington, northern Nevada, and southwestern Idaho, is composed of thick layers of basalt that formed from widespread lava flows 30 million years ago. Waterfalls are scarce in the Oregon portion of the plateau. Because of the consistent erosion resistance of the basaltic bedrock, cataracts are lacking along most of the region's major rivers. In addition, low annual precipitation means that few tributary streams flow over the rims of the larger river canyons. Of the region's 93 known waterfalls, 32 are listed in this chapter.

Most of the cataracts in this region are found where other geomorphic processes have contributed to waterfall formation. Recent lava flows inundated

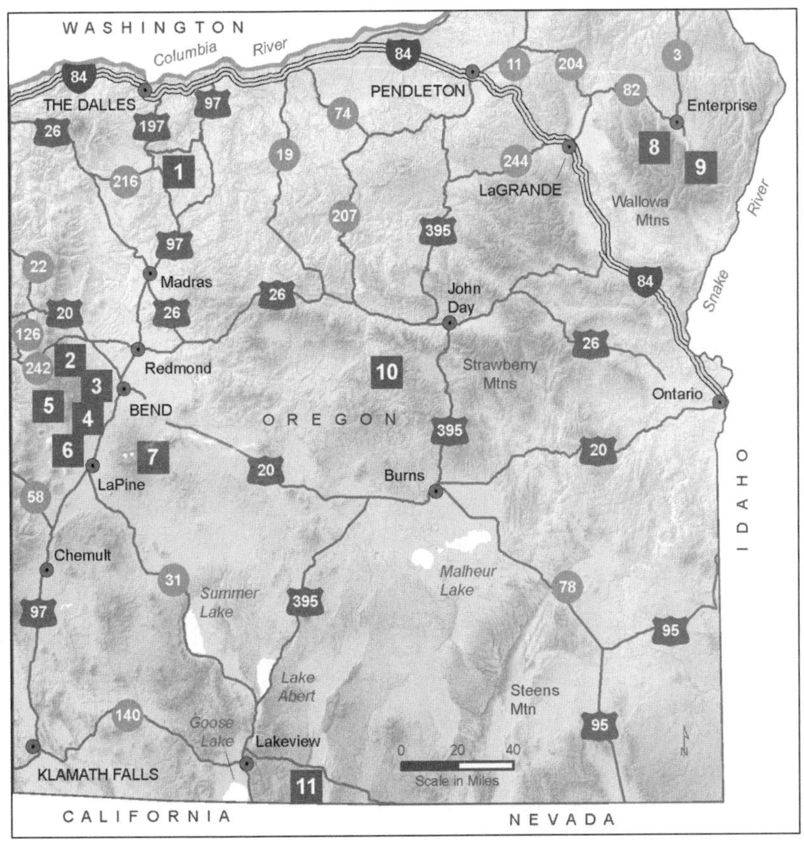

the course of the Deschutes River 5000 to 6000 years ago. When the lava cooled, jumbled basaltic rock was formed. The river cuts into and tumbles over these rocky obstructions.

The Strawberry Mountains near the town of John Day were shaped by the accumulation of basalt, rhyolite, and breccia due to volcanic activities 10 million to 13 million years ago. The extreme differences in the erosional resistance of these rock types produce waterfalls in places where streams flow across the contact point between two or more different varieties of rock.

The Wallowa Mountains of northeastern Oregon are one of the few nonvolcanic areas of the region. Here large masses of granite and sedimentary rocks were displaced thousands of feet above the surrounding plain 100 million to 150 million years ago. The range's high relief stopped subsequent lava at its western perimeter. Since the Wallowas rise more than 8000 feet above sea level, their climate was sufficiently cold and moist to support alpine glaciation. The erosive work of these glaciers left vertical breaks for stream courses to plunge over.

A few of this chapter's waterfalls are actually in the South Cascades. They have been placed here because accessibility is from highways along the plateau.

1 TYGH VALLEY

Both the Deschutes and White rivers appear as oases in the dry climate of central Oregon. Scientifically, they are known as exotic streams because they are fed by the waters of the cooler, moister Cascade Mountains. The following cataracts are sure to quench the scenic thirst of any traveler.

☐ SHERARS FALLS ★★★

MAGNITUDE: 46 (h)
ELEVATION: 680 feet
WATERSHED: Large
APPROACH: Auto
LAT/LONG: 45.257565° N / 121.038956° W
USGS MAP: *Sherars Bridge* (1987 ns)

Watch American Indian anglers net for salmon where the Deschutes River roars 15 to 20 feet in a sagebrush setting. The Confederated Tribes of Warm Springs owns this waterfall. The State Department of Natural Resources and the tribe cooperate to regulate fishing on the river.

Drive along State Route 216 to Sherars Bridge over the Deschutes River. The bridge is located 7.4 miles east of U.S. Highway 197 and 21.5 miles west of U.S. Highway 97. Stop for views of this entry 0.2 mile south of the bridge. Supervise your children, as the tumultuous river is extremely dangerous.

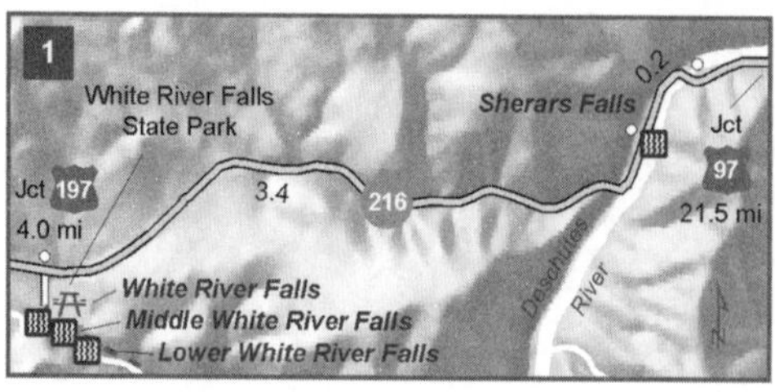

WHITE RIVER FALLS ★★★

MAGNITUDE: 72
ELEVATION: 1000 feet
WATERSHED: Large
APPROACH: Auto
LAT/LONG: 45.242881° N / 121.097343° W
USGS MAP: *Maupin* (1996 ns)

A viewing platform offers an outstanding vista of rivulets of the White River pouring 70 to 80 feet downward off a 150- to 175-foot-wide escarpment. Also known as Tygh Valley Falls, this waterfall is located within White River Falls State Park. Drive 3.4 miles westward past Sherars Falls (described earlier) along State Route 216 to the signed turnout for this day-use park. Proceed another 0.2 mile to the parking area, and walk 150 feet to the fenced overlook.

MIDDLE WHITE RIVER FALLS (U) ★★★★

MAGNITUDE: 75
ELEVATION: 920 feet
WATERSHED: Large
APPROACH: Trail (fairly easy)
LAT/LONG: 45.24267° N / 121.09657° W
USGS MAP: *Maupin* (1996 ns)

This second of a trio of falls is actually a single 25- to 35-foot plunge. The trailside vantage point, however, includes the upper falls (described earlier), revealing a dramatic tiered combination. Walk downstream on the paved trail into the small canyon. The trail quickly turns to dirt, with this entry coming into view after 0.1 mile.

LOWER WHITE RIVER FALLS (U) ★★

MAGNITUDE: 50
ELEVATION: 760 feet
WATERSHED: Large
APPROACH: Trail (fairly easy)
LAT/LONG: 45.241884° N / 121.09539° W
USGS MAP: *Maupin* (1996 ns)

The last of the falls in White River State Park tumbles 25 to 35 feet into a large amphitheater. Continue past Middle White River Falls (described earlier), down some wooden steps past an old powerhouse. Follow the trail through the high desert vegetation for 0.2 mile just beyond the falls for the best views.

2 SISTERS

Adventurous waterfall enthusiasts will love this relatively obscure journey, which requires a high-clearance vehicle to gain access on foot to a satisfying trio of waterfalls. These falls are in the eastern portion of Three Sisters Wilderness, which occurs within Sisters Ranger District of Deschutes National Forest. From downtown Sisters at the intersection of U.S. Highway 20 (Cascade Avenue) and Elm Street, head south on Elm, which becomes Three Creek Road. After

7.2 miles turn right on Forest Service Road 1514, signed for Whychus Creek (formerly called Squaw Creek). Proceed 3 miles and bear right at the fork in the road.

After another 1.9 miles, turn left on rough (dirt) Forest Service Road 600 immediately before the main road crosses the creek on a bridge. You almost immediately encounter a fork; bear left. After 2 bumpy miles, you reach a T intersection with Forest Service Road 680. Turn left. Creep another 0.4 mile to the trailhead at the end of the road.

CHUSH FALLS ★★★★

MAGNITUDE: 56
APPROACH: High-clearance vehicle & trail (fairly hard)
ELEVATION: 4980 feet
LAT/LONG: 44.149712° N / 121.682965° W
WATERSHED: Medium
USGS MAP: *Trout Creek Butte* (1988 nl)

Whychus Creek appears like nature's fountain, spreading out along its 45- to 55-foot drop. Hike 1 mile along the trail to an unfenced canyon-rim vista. Several coniferous trees obscure a full view. For a full mist-side vantage point near its base, find the path to the right, and make your way 0.1 mile steeply down to the stream, which is federally designated as a national wild and scenic river.

THE CASCADES ★★

MAGNITUDE: 49
APPROACH: High-clearance vehicle & trail (fairly hard)
ELEVATION: 5200 feet
LAT/LONG: 44.146032° N / 121.684575° W
WATERSHED: Medium
USGS MAP: *Trout Creek Butte* (1988 ns)

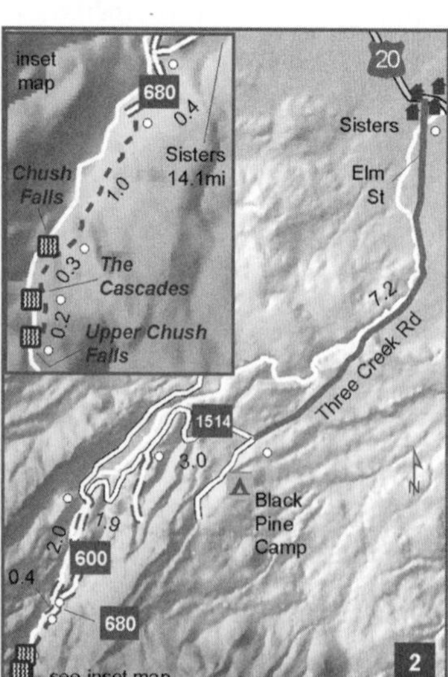

Water pours 25 to 35 feet along Whychus Creek. Depending upon flow, this descent can morph into tiered and fan forms. From the canyon-rim vista at Chush Falls (described earlier), continue upstream along the main trail. The path thins considerably, but if you stay just left of the gorge rim, you will be fine. Hike 0.3 mile to a clear trailside vantage point.

Chush Falls

7 UPPER CHUSH FALLS ★★★★★

MAGNITUDE: 67
ELEVATION: 5600 feet
WATERSHED: Medium
APPROACH: High-clearance vehicle & trail (fairly hard)
LAT/LONG: 44.142891° N / 121.684918° W
USGS MAP: *Trout Creek Butte* (1988)

Gawk from an awesome vista next to Whychus Creek looking up into this 200- to 250-foot giant. It was formerly known as Squaw Creek Falls, but its name was officially changed, no doubt for political correctness. Continue along the path for 0.2 mile beyond The Cascades (described earlier) where it terminates in front of this torrent.

3 TUMALO CREEK

All of the following waterfalls are located within the Bend-Fort Rock Ranger District of Deschutes National Forest. Head toward the eastern flank of the Cascade Range by turning off U.S. Highway 97 in Bend upon westbound Franklin Avenue. After crossing the bridge downtown over the Deschutes River, the road becomes Galveston Avenue. After 1.6 miles, stay on the main road, now named Skyliner Road. Proceed west 10.4 miles, and bear right (continuing westward) upon Forest Service Road 1828. From here it is 3 miles to Tumalo Falls Picnic Area at the road's end.

TUMALO FALLS ★★★

MAGNITUDE: 81
ELEVATION: 5080 feet
WATERSHED: Large
APPROACH: Auto
LAT/LONG: 44.033864° N / 121.566987° W
USGS MAP: *Tumalo Falls* (1988)

This 97-foot plummet is framed by stark tree snags—brown remnants of a forest fire during the summer of 1979. While managed fire is an important component in modern forestry, this particular blaze was unplanned. The scarred scene is a reminder of the old maxim "Only you can prevent forest fires."

From the picnic area, look upstream along Tumalo Creek into the falls. Closer views are also possible from Tumalo Creek Trail.

MIDDLE TUMALO FALLS (U) ★★

MAGNITUDE: 52
ELEVATION: 5240 feet
WATERSHED: Large
APPROACH: Trail (moderate)
LAT/LONG: 44.041623° N / 121.578467° W
USGS MAP: *Tumalo Falls* (1988 nl)

Tumalo Creek tumbles a total of 46 to 65 feet in tiered fashion. Follow Tumalo Creek Trail (described earlier) upstream for 1.1 miles to a vista. The trail formerly ended below this entry, but it has since been extended and reportedly enables access to additional cataracts another mile or so upstream.

Tumalo Falls

7 BRIDGE CREEK FALLS (U) ★★

MAGNITUDE: 46
ELEVATION: 5270 feet
WATERSHED: Small
APPROACH: Trail (fairly easy)
LAT/LONG: 44.030424° N / 121.580054° W
USGS MAP: *Tumalo Falls* (1988 nl)

Watch water pouring 25 to 35 feet along Bridge Creek. From Tumalo Falls Picnic Area (described earlier), locate the trailhead to Bridge Creek Trail. Proceed along this moderately gentle route for 1 mile to this entry.

MORE ONLINE:
Cline Falls ★ USGS *Cline Falls* (1962)
Canal Falls (u) ★ USGS *Bend* (1981 nl)
Steelhead Falls, USGS *Steelhead Falls* (1992) EXPLORE!

4 LAVA BUTTE GEOLOGICAL AREA

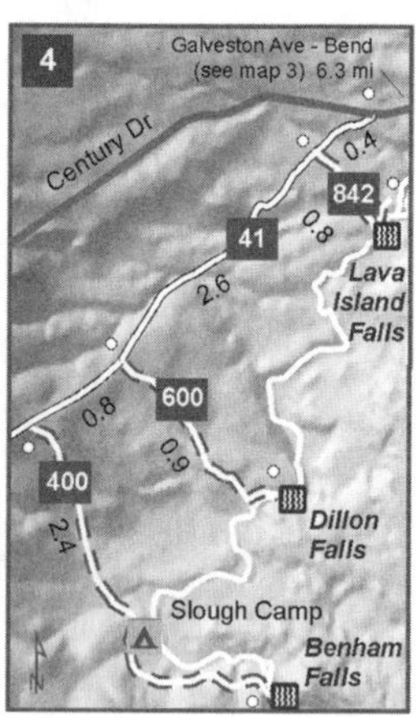

The aptly named Deschutes River (*Deschutes* is French for "of the falls") has ten cataracts along its course from La Pine to the Columbia River. It drops three times along the western fringe of Lava Butte Geological Area, which is located within Bend-Fort Rock Ranger District, Deschutes National Forest.

From downtown Bend, drive west on Franklin Avenue toward Tumalo Falls (described earlier), except instead of staying on the main road, turn left (south) in 1.6 miles on Century Drive (also known as Cascade Lakes Highway). Continue 6.3 miles, and turn left (south) on gravel Forest Service Road 41 for the sign to Dillon Falls.

LAVA ISLAND FALLS ★★

MAGNITUDE: 24
ELEVATION: 3920 feet
WATERSHED: Large
APPROACH: Auto
LAT/LONG: 43.986763° N / 121.397235° W
USGS MAP: *Benham Falls* (1981)

This entry is simply a set of small cascades, but the fact that the Deschutes River splits the jumbled lava rock makes the site intriguing. Follow Forest Service Road 41 south for 0.4 mile from Century Drive (described earlier). Turn left (east) on dirt Forest Service Road 842, and continue to its end in 0.8 mile.

 DILLON FALLS ★★★

MAGNITUDE: 37 (h)
ELEVATION: 4040 feet
WATERSHED: Large
APPROACH: Trail (easy)
LAT/LONG: 43.957438° N / 121.411612° W
USGS MAP: *Benham Falls* (1981)

The Deschutes River froths 40 to 60 feet within a quarter-mile chasm cut into the basaltic bedrock. The waterfall is named for local homesteader Leander Dillon. Take Forest Service Road 41 southward 2.6 miles past its junction for Lava Island Falls (described earlier). Turn left (southeast) on dirt Forest Service Road 600, and drive to its end in 0.9 mile. A trail goes from the parking area to views of the gorge and its cascade. The observation points at the rim are unprotected, so be careful.

Dillon Falls

 BENHAM FALLS ★★★

MAGNITUDE: 36 (h)
ELEVATION: 4130 feet
WATERSHED: Large
APPROACH: Trail (easy)
LAT/LONG: 43.93774° N / 121.411719° W
USGS MAP: *Benham Falls* (1981)

The Deschutes River shoots down 40 to 60 feet through a narrow canyon. The cataract is named for J. R. Benham, who unsuccessfully filed a homesteading claim for land nearby in 1885. Continue along Forest Service Road 41 for 0.8 mile beyond the turn for Dillon Falls (described earlier). Turn left (south) onto Forest Service Road 400, and drive 2.4 miles, parking where the road meets the river. Benham Falls is immediately downstream. A short pathway leads to secure, but unfenced views.

5 CASCADE LAKES HIGHWAY

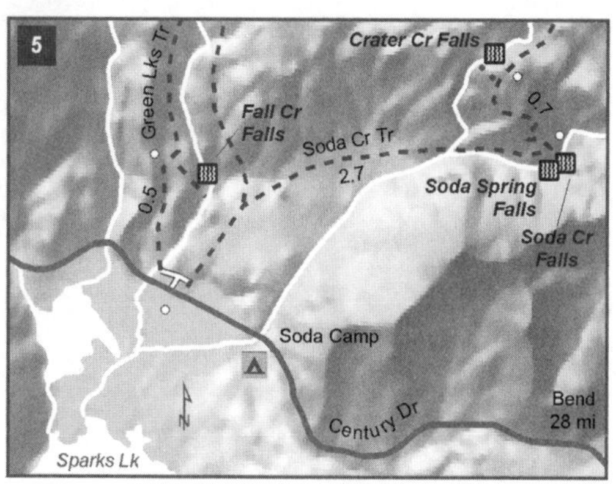

Access this scenic highway by first departing U.S. Highway 97 in Bend upon westbound Franklin Avenue. Turn left in 1.6 miles upon Century Drive, which is another name for Cascade Lakes Highway (see map 3 of this chapter). After 26.4 miles farther, turn right into the signed access for Green Lakes Trail. There are two parking areas: The one to the right (east) accesses waterfalls along Soda Creek Trail; the other leads to Green Lakes Trail and its cataract. This area is a part of Bend-Fort Rock Ranger District, Deschutes National Forest.

SODA CREEK FALLS (U) ★★

MAGNITUDE: 39
ELEVATION: 5900 feet
WATERSHED: Small

APPROACH: Trail (moderate)
LAT/LONG: 44.040513° N / 121.69562° W
USGS MAP: *Broken Top* (1988 nl)

Soda Creek drops 5 to 10 feet in block form before fanning another 20 to 30 feet downward. Hike along Soda Creek Trail for 2.1 miles through a lava field and then a meadow. After the trail reaches a wooded area, it is 0.6 mile farther to the minor drop of Soda Spring Falls (u), USGS *Broken Top* (1988 ns). Continue hiking a bit farther up the trail to a viewpoint of the main falls where the route begins to depart the stream and switchbacks uphill.

CRATER CREEK FALLS (U) ★★

MAGNITUDE: 41
ELEVATION: 6240 feet
WATERSHED: Small

APPROACH: Trail & bushwhack (hard)
LAT/LONG: 44.047731° N / 121.703667° W
USGS MAP: *Broken Top* (1988 nl)

Water sprays 40 to 50 feet downward along Crater Creek. This route is recommended for adults only. After passing Soda Creek Falls (described earlier), the trail steepens considerably. After 0.7 mile, Crater Creek comes into view. Leave the trail, and proceed down the ridge top for about 100 yards. Stay off the steep slopes in the canyon!

FALL CREEK FALLS ★★★

MAGNITUDE: 61
ELEVATION: 5500 feet
WATERSHED: Medium
APPROACH: Trail (fairly hard)
LAT/LONG: 44.038476° N / 121.731326° W
USGS MAP: *Broken Top* (1988 nl)

Fall Creek explodes 25 to 35 feet over a rock escarpment. Starting at Green Lakes Trail (described earlier), walk up the moderately steep path for 0.5 mile. You can plainly hear the falls. Find the short side trail, which leads above the cataract and to several paths that take you below to full views.

MORE ONLINE:
Soda Spring Falls (u) ★, mentioned earlier

6 LA PINE

FALL RIVER FALLS ★★

MAGNITUDE: 22
ELEVATION: 4120 feet
WATERSHED: Large
APPROACH: Trail (easy)
LAT/LONG: 43.794518° N / 121.527612° W
USGS MAP: *Pistol Butte* (1981)

Fall River tumbles 10 to 15 feet next to grassy banks surrounded by pine trees. The falls is located within La Pine State Recreation Area. Leave U.S. Highway 97 at Vandevert Road, 15.5 miles south of Bend. Drive west 1 mile, then turn left (south) on South Century Drive. Proceed 6 miles and turn left on Forest Service Road 4360. Continue 0.8 mile, then park at the wide turnout preceding the Fall River Bridge. Follow the jeep trail 0.2 mile to this pleasant setting.

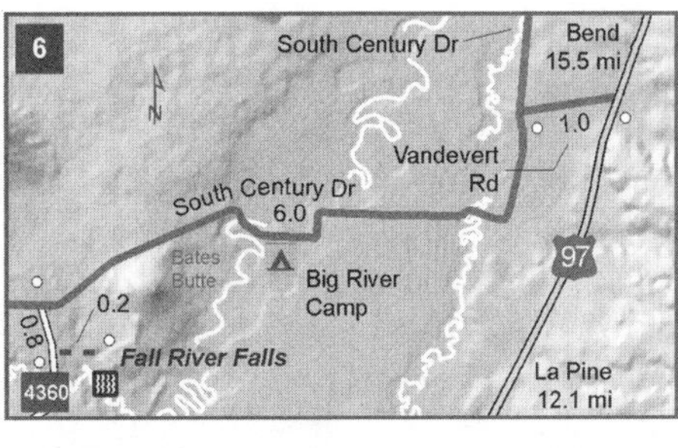

MORE ONLINE:
Pringle Falls ★ USGS *La Pine* (1981)

7 NEWBERRY CRATER

A dominant feature of the geology south of Bend is a large, gently sloping shield volcano. Atop this mound is a caldera, the Newberry Crater, where the central portion of the volcano collapsed about 200,000 years ago. Paulina Lake and East Lake currently fill the depression. The erosive power of Paulina Creek as it flows from Paulina Lake has cut through the volcano's layers of basalt at a greater rate than through the more resistant rhyolite layers. Waterfalls occur where these two rock layers meet along the stream's course. The area is now the centerpiece of the Newberry National Volcanic Monument, a part of Deschutes National Forest.

 FOOTBRIDGE FALLS ★★★

MAGNITUDE: 51
ELEVATION: 5340 feet
WATERSHED: Medium
APPROACH: Trail (moderate)
LAT/LONG: 43.71341° N / 121.335566° W
USGS MAP: *Paulina Peak* (1981 nl)

Paulina Creek descends a total of 50 to 80 feet as the creek diverges along its upper portion before fanning out below. The scenic rating decreases during low-water periods in late summer. Turn east off U.S. Highway 97 at Paulina Lake Road, 6 miles north of La Pine. Drive 10 miles to a large parking area to the left (north), reportedly now signed as 10 Mile Sno-Park.

Paulina Creek Falls

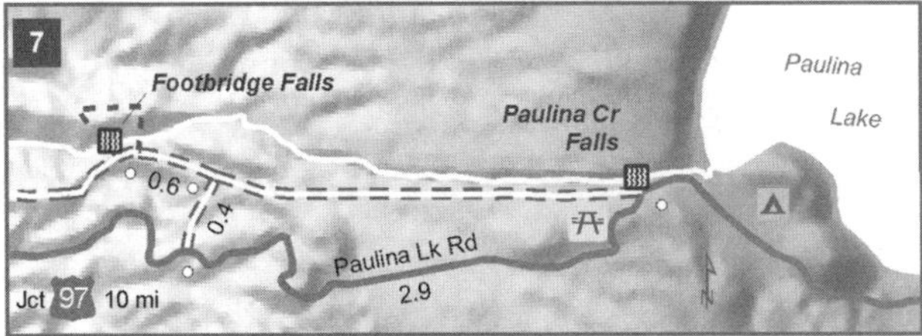

Hike along an old jeep trail beginning at the far end of the turnout. At a junction in 0.4 mile, bear left (west), and walk 0.6 mile until you can hear the falls. Here an unsigned trail leads across a footbridge over the creek and downstream to views of the falls. I unofficially called it Lower Paulina Creek Falls in earlier editions of this book.

PAULINA CREEK FALLS ★★★★★

MAGNITUDE: 84
ELEVATION: 6200 feet
WATERSHED: Medium
APPROACH: Trail (easy)
LAT/LONG: 43.712294° N / 121.282523° W
USGS MAP: *Paulina Peak* (1981)

This 100-foot dual segmented cataract is best seen in early summer when Paulina Creek has substantial flow. Drive along the paved road for 2.9 miles past the turnout for Footbridge Falls (described earlier). Park at the parking lot signed for Paulina Falls. A short trail leads to a developed vista offering superb vantage points of the falls. Hikers can also trek to more views below the falls.

8 ENTERPRISE

Waterfalls, many officially named, have been mapped throughout the Wallowa Mountains. Unfortunately, unless you are a backpacker, most are inaccessible since they lie deep within the Eagle Cap Wilderness, Wallowa National Forest. The exceptions are the five cataracts on the north end. They are described in this section and the one that follows.

HUNTER FALLS ★★★

MAGNITUDE: 56 (h)
ELEVATION: 5700 feet
WATERSHED: Medium
APPROACH: Trail (moderate)
LAT/LONG: 45.333625° N / 117.404134° W
USGS MAP: *North Minam Meadows* (1990)

Lake Creek forcefully squeezes a total of 50 to 60 feet through eroded bedrock. From State Route 82 in the hamlet of Lostine, turn off the highway, and head south along Lostine River Road. A visitor information station is 9 miles in. Continue 2.8 additional miles, and park at Lostine Guard Station.

Find the unsigned trailhead by walking back across the creek crossing to a wide spot in the road. The path initially ascends steeply before leveling off over 0.3 mile. A very short spur goes to close-up side views of the lower tier.

UPPER HUNTER FALLS (U) ★★

MAGNITUDE: 28 (h)
ELEVATION: 5780 feet
WATERSHED: Medium
APPROACH: Trail (moderate)
LAT/LONG: 45.33361° N / 117.403748° W
USGS MAP: *North Minam Meadows* (1990 ns)

Water stairsteps 40 to 50 feet along Lake Creek. Continue steeply past Hunter Falls (described earlier) along the main path. You attain a trailside vantage point in another 0.1 mile.

Falls Creek Falls

FALLS CREEK FALLS ★★★★

MAGNITUDE: 53 (h)
ELEVATION: 5420 feet
WATERSHED: Medium
APPROACH: Trail (fairly easy)
LAT/LONG: 45.307644° N / 117.312574° W
USGS MAP: *Chief Joseph Mtn.* (1990 nl)

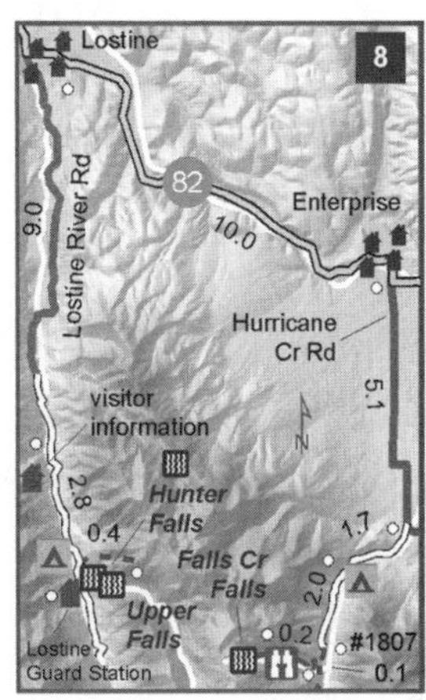

What a picturesque scene as Falls Creek plummets 60 to 80 feet with usually snow-laden Sawtooth Peak in the background. From State Route 82 in Enterprise, turn south onto Hurricane Creek Road. Bear right after 5.1 miles, which takes you up Hurricane Creek. Pass a campground in 1.7 additional miles, with the road's end and trailhead 2 miles farther.

Embark upon Hurricane Creek Trail 1807. Hike 0.1 mile, and turn right on the spur marked as Falls Creek. Go another 0.2 mile to a somewhat distant view of the waterfall. Depending upon stream discharge, you may or may not be able to bushwhack upstream to its base. Others have previously reported a path ascending alongside the stream, but the scoured-out appearance of the place suggests an event such as an avalanche or major flood destroyed it.

MORE ONLINE:
Lookingglass Falls ★ USGS *Rondowa* (1995)

9 WALLOWA LAKE

Wallowa Lake is a stunningly beautiful example of a form of a large paternoster lake, a body of water formed by a natural dam of deposits blocking part of a glacial valley. Drive 6 miles past the town of Joseph along State Route 82 to Wallowa Lake State Park, which is located within Wallowa-Whitman National Forest. Turn left (south) toward the picnic area and away from the main boating and camping facilities. Access to the High Wallowas Gondola is 0.2 mile away, with the road's end for trail hiking 0.8 mile farther.

WALLOWA FALLS ★★★

MAGNITUDE: 52 (h)
ELEVATION: 4660 feet
WATERSHED: Large
APPROACH: Trail & bushwhack (moderate)
LAT/LONG: 45.267752° N / 117.216205° W
USGS MAP: *Joseph* (1990 nl)

Peer down at the West Fork Wallowa River pouring over a 30- to 50-foot escarpment. This falls is not recommended for children or skittish adults. To reach the falls, follow West Fork Trail 1820, which starts at the picnic area, toward Ice Lake. A footbridge crosses the East Fork Wallowa River and then ascends shortly to a rocky outcrop adjacent to the West Fork in 0.1 mile. From this natural vista, follow the ridge a short distance downstream to a well-worn path above the river.

ADAM CREEK FALLS ★★★

MAGNITUDE: 66
ELEVATION: 7200 feet
WATERSHED: Small
APPROACH: Gondola or trail (hard)
LAT/LONG: 45.231058° N / 117.261857° W
USGS MAP: *Eagle Cap* (1990 ns)

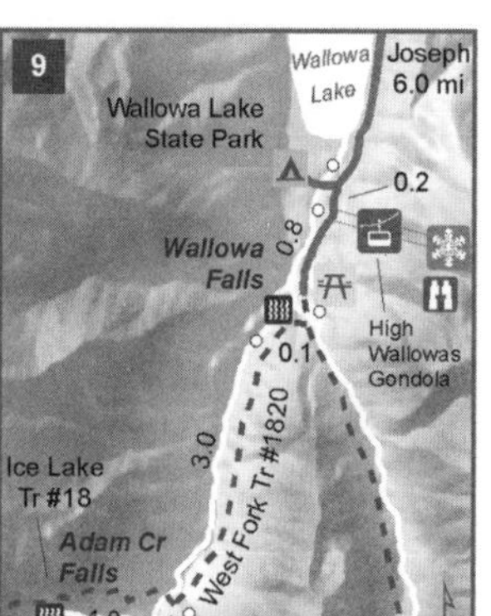

This series of falls descends hundreds of feet along Adam Creek and can be seen collectively or individually, depending upon whether you hike to them or take the aerial tram. Hikers should proceed 3 miles along West Fork Trail 1820 (described earlier) and then turn right (west) on Ice Lake Trail 18. You will encounter the tiers of this cataract one at a time, as you make the 4-mile trek to its end at Ice Lake. Tourists atop Mount Howard see this entry as silvery threads along the mountainside, looking southwest. (Access is via the High Wallowas Gondola, which ascends 3700 feet above the valley.)

Atop the mountain, you will have unforgettable views of Eagle Cap Wilderness, Wallowa Lake, and the Columbia Plateau. Look for the falls toward the southwest.

10 OCHOCO

SOUTH FORK FALLS ★★

MAGNITUDE: 28
ELEVATION: 3540 feet
WATERSHED: Large
APPROACH: Auto
LAT/LONG: 44.184674° N/ 119.524579° W
USGS MAP: *Suplee Butte* (1992)

Water tumbles 75 feet over a 200- to 300-foot reach of the South Fork John Day River. Located on Bureau of Land Management land, the cascades are locally known as Izee Falls. The surrounding steep canyon walls are composed of impressive columns of basalt.

Deep Creek Falls

Drive 32 miles west from U.S. Highway 395 on County Road 63, or 32 miles east from Paulina along County Roads 112 and 67, to BLM Road 6207. Proceed north, following the river, for 5.5 miles to Forest Service Road 58. Bear right, staying on BLM Road 6207, for 0.8 mile to an unsigned turnout next to the top of the cataract.

11 ADEL

DEEP CREEK FALLS ★★★

MAGNITUDE: 56
ELEVATION: 4800 feet
WATERSHED: Large
APPROACH: Auto
LAT/LONG: 42.173877° N / 119.949945° W
USGS MAP: *Adel* (1968)

Columns of basalt frame this 30- to 50-foot drop along Deep Creek in a sagebrush setting. It is likely situated on either private property or Bureau of Land Management land. For a roadside view of this entry, drive 2.7 miles west from Adel or 30 miles east from Lakeview along State Route 140.

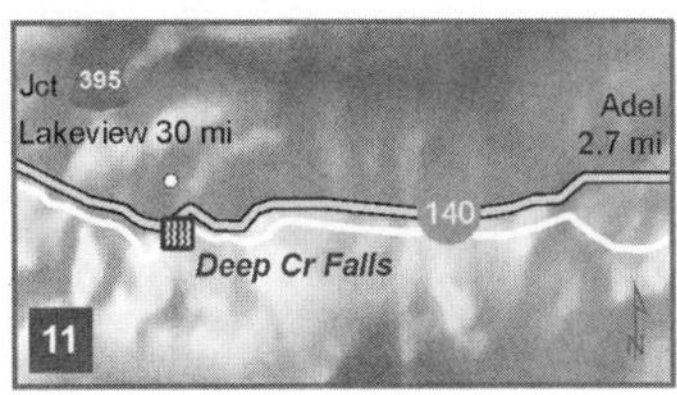

IDAHO

THE PANHANDLE

The Panhandle of northern Idaho separates Washington from Montana. Stretching 170 miles southward from the Canadian border to Lewiston, its width varies from 45 to 125 miles. Although many states have unusual shapes, Idaho's is unique in its historical and political significance. No other state was shaped wholly by boundaries originally set by its neighbors. Idaho is made up of land not annexed by Montana, Wyoming, Utah, Nevada, Oregon, or Washington.

The Idaho Panhandle has 54 recognized waterfalls, of which 40 are described here. This is a region of large lakes and rolling to rugged mountains. Lake Coeur d'Alene, Lake Pend Oreille, Priest Lake, and Dworshak Reservoir cover

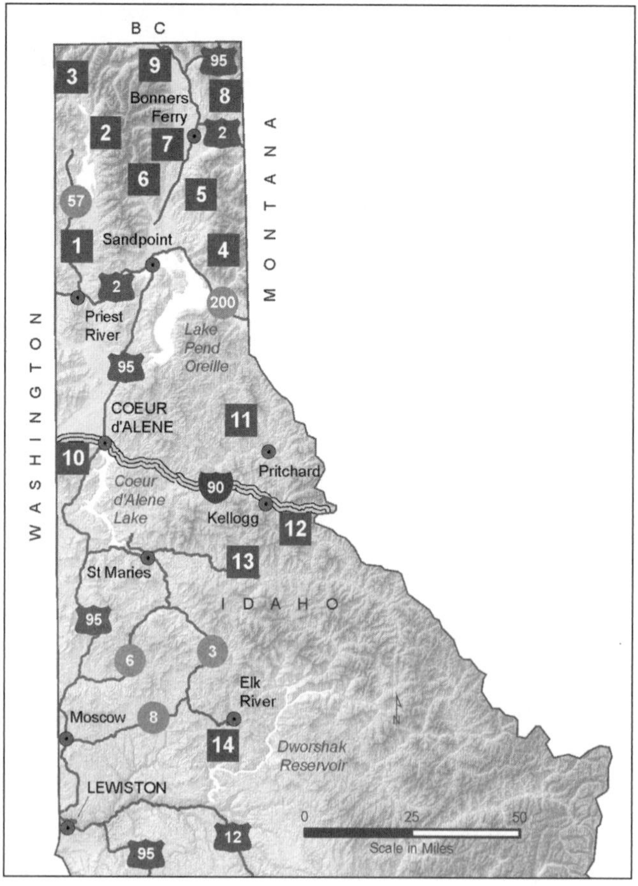

Torrelle Falls

large areas. All but Dworshak are natural. Mountain ranges such as the Selkirks, the Purcells, the Bitterroots, and the Clearwaters are distributed through the region. National forests formerly named Coeur d'Alene, Kaniksu, and St. Joe have recently been consolidated into . . . wait for it . . . Idaho Panhandle National Forests.

Geomorphologists, scientists who study landforms, classify waterfalls as destructive or constructive. Most cataracts, including almost all of those in the Pacific Northwest, are of the destructive variety. The force of running water slowly erodes the streambeds, usually causing the falls to recede upstream over geologic time. Constructive descents, on the other hand, mostly flow over mineral deposits and migrate downstream as the deposits accumulate. (Fall Creek Falls, listed in the Snake River Plain chapter, for example, is a constructive falls.)

Destructive falls are further classified by how they developed. Consequent falls are located where a preexisting break occurs along the course of a stream.

An example is water plunging into a glacier-carved valley, as at Copper Falls. When streams erode along rock materials of varying rates of erosional resistance, subsequent falls may form, as at Lower Snow Creek Falls.

The waterfalls of the Northwest can be enjoyed for their beauty alone, but they are even more interesting when you ponder the variety of ways in which they were created.

1 PRIEST RIVER

Access this area from the town of Priest River by departing U.S. Highway 2 onto State Route 57.

1 TORRELLE FALLS ★★

MAGNITUDE: 32
ELEVATION: 2300 feet
WATERSHED: Large

APPROACH: Auto
LAT/LONG: 48.284529° N / 116.958694° W
USGS MAP: *Quartz Mtn.* (1996)

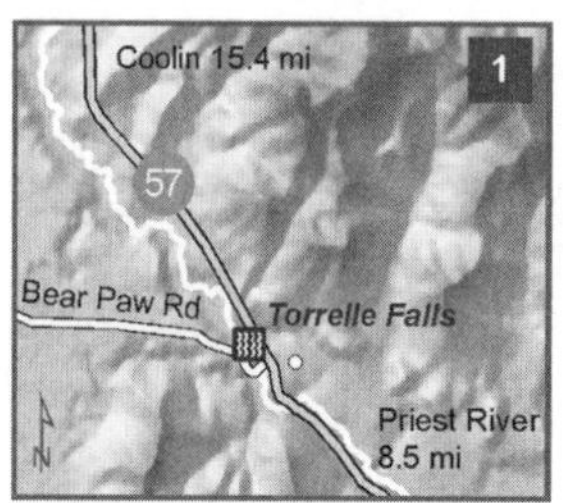

A rustic restaurant spans the West Branch Priest River at the base of this 10- to 15-foot descent. Drive 8.5 miles north from the town of Priest River along SR 57. Find this unique site on the left (west) side of the highway.

MORE ONLINE:
McAbee Falls ★ USGS *Prater Mtn.* (1996)
Mission Falls ★ USGS *Outlet Bay* (1996)

2 PRIEST LAKE EAST

Despite what is considered the more frequented side of Priest Lake, its waterfalls are all relatively unknown. The ones in the Lionhead Unit of Priest Lake State Park have the added benefit of occurring within a memorable landscape of exfoliation domes. These sheets of granitic mountains, reminiscent of the Yosemite high country, also provide the bedrock for several cataracts to slide over. The gateway to this area is via the lakeside hamlet of Coolin.

Drive 14 miles northward beyond Torrelle Falls (described previously) along State Route 57, and turn right upon Coolin Road. Proceed 5.4 miles, and just as you reach the town, turn right upon East Lakeshore Road. All of the following entries are located within property administered by the Idaho Department of Lands (IDL).

HUNT CREEK FALLS ★★★

MAGNITUDE: 42
ELEVATION: 2500 feet
WATERSHED: Medium
APPROACH: Trail (easy)
LAT/LONG: 48.566562° N / 116.82428° W
USGS MAP: *Priest Lake SE* (1996 ns)

Before heading onward to Lionhead, stop at this somewhat forceful 25- to 35-foot spray along Hunt Creek. From Coolin, drive 6.9 miles northward upon East Lakeshore Road, and turn right upon Forest Service Road 23. Proceed 0.1 mile up the road, and turn left at the IDL Endowment Lands sign. Continue another 0.1 mile, and when you feel your vehicle can no longer handle the bumps and potholes, park along the side of the road. From here, walk the rest of the way (one more 0.1 mile) to the falls.

LOWER LION CREEK FALLS (U) ★★★

MAGNITUDE: 40
ELEVATION: 3820 feet
WATERSHED: Large
APPROACH: High-clearance & trail (moderate)
LAT/LONG: 48.76061° N / 116.72459° W
USGS MAP: *Smith Peak* (1996 ns)

Here is the first of several falls within the Lion Creek drainage, as the stream slides over a granite slab before shooting 25 to 35 feet into a pool. From its junction with Forest Service Road 23 (described earlier), take East Lakeshore Road northward for 15.5 miles to the area signed as Lionhead Unit. Turn right upon State Forest Road 42, and crawl 5 miles to its end at a small parking area. The road once extended farther, but it now serves as the trail upon which you will embark.

Walk 0.5 mile to a minor waterfall pouring from a tiny creek on your immediate left. Soon beyond this point you should hear the sound of this entry, whereby off-trail close-up vantage points are readily accessed.

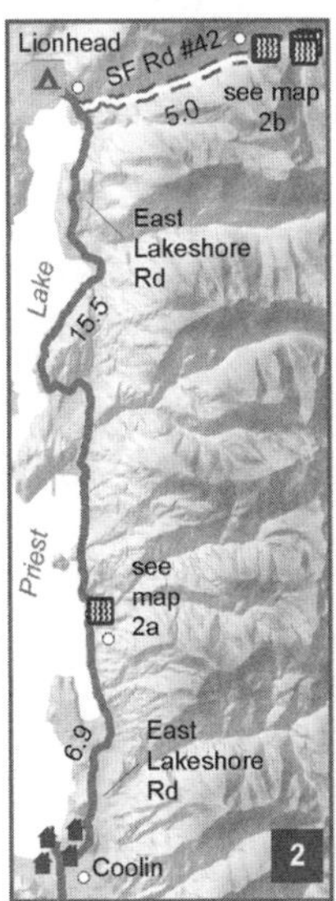

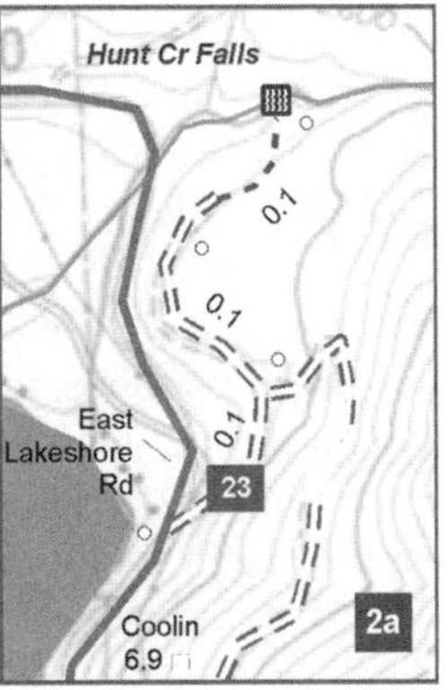

Lower Lion Creek Falls

 MIDDLE LION CREEK FALLS (U) ★★

MAGNITUDE: 15
ELEVATION: 3850 feet
WATERSHED: Large
APPROACH: High-clearance & trail (moderate)
LAT/LONG: 48.760836° N / 116.723968° W
USGS MAP: *Smith Peak* (1996 ns)

Water curls 15 to 20 feet downward within a bedrock incision. As with all the descents within the Lion Creek drainage, they are located for public enjoyment within undeveloped Idaho State Lands. Walk upon the granite slabs a couple of hundred feet upstream from the Lower Falls (described earlier).

 SLIPPERY ROCKS (U) ★★★

MAGNITUDE: 33
ELEVATION: 4220 feet
WATERSHED: Medium
APPROACH: High-clearance & trail (fairly hard)
LAT/LONG: 48.761345° N / 116.702725° W
USGS MAP: *Smith Peak* (1996 ns)

Kent Creek literally slides 40 to 60 feet over a 100- to 150-foot reach of the stream. The rating of this entry is earned by watching people scoot down the slick granite. Join in if you dare. When I visited this area, a rope was strung across the creek at the base of this entry to help protect people from being pulled farther downstream where the bedrock surfaces are more precarious.

From the Middle Falls (described earlier) head on up the trail for 1.2 miles to the crossing of Lion Creek. The shallowest, likely knee-high, ford is immediately to your right. Water shoes or old tennis shoes are recommended to get across the ice-cold water. Once on the opposite side, trudge up the path, which will likely be soggy due to all the fun everyone had 0.2 mile upstream.

Along this stretch, gain a moderately distant sighting of Lion Creek Falls (u), USGS *Smith Peak* (1996 ns), made through the trees. When I visited this area, daylight was waning and I ran out of time to investigate further. Online narratives report that the descent is accessible by continuing upstream along the trail on the north side of the creek. Additionally, there are quite likely several more cataracts off trail both upstream and downstream from here along Lion Creek.

KENT CREEK FALLS (U) ★★★★

MAGNITUDE: 56
ELEVATION: 4560 feet
WATERSHED: Medium
APPROACH: High-clearance & bushwhack (hard)
LAT/LONG: 48.760001° N / 116.702296° W
USGS MAP: *Smith Peak* (1996 ns)

Kent Creek drops fairly steeply 80 to 120 feet down a mountainside. From Slippery Rocks (described earlier), slog 0.1 mile up one of the thin footpaths to the base of this descent. From here, it's 2.0 miles back to the trailhead.

3 PRIEST LAKE WEST

Recreational activities occur year-round near 26,000-acre Priest Lake. The area's waterfalls are remote, however, and are easiest to visit from early summer through late autumn. All of them exist within Priest Lake Ranger District, Idaho Panhandle National Forests.

GRANITE FALLS ★★★

MAGNITUDE: 55 (h)
ELEVATION: 3460 feet
WATERSHED: Medium
APPROACH: Auto or trail (fairly easy)
LAT/LONG: 48.767894° N / 117.065274° W
USGS MAP: *Helmer Mtn.* (1996)

Although Granite Creek slides 50 to 75 feet within the state of Washington, it is listed in this chapter because the primary access is from Idaho. Drive 37 miles north of Priest River along State Route 57 to Nordman. Continue 13 miles, and turn into the entrance road to Stagger Inn Camp and Granite Falls. (Note: SR 57 becomes Granite Creek Road, Forest Service Road 302, about 2 miles past Nordman.)

There are two viewpoints. The closest occurs below the base of the falls and is only steps away from the parking area; turn left at the kiosk. An upper vista is also available by taking a right turn at the kiosk. Walk along Roosevelt Trail 301 for a couple hundred feet. Then turn left upon the signed Overlook Trail, and switchback a bit for 0.2 mile to a wooden platform extending beyond the cliff for a great vantage point of the descent, also known as Lower Falls. Look for the copper dedication sign next to the vista.

UPPER GRANITE FALLS ★★

MAGNITUDE: 33
ELEVATION: 3500 feet
WATERSHED: Medium
APPROACH: Trail (moderate)
LAT/LONG: 48.769591° N / 117.066347° W
USGS MAP: *Helmer Mtn.* (1996 ns)

Peer through the trees into a small gorge to see this 15- to 20-foot drop along Granite Creek, which is also called Upper Falls. Hike beyond the upper viewpoint of Granite Falls (described earlier) for 0.3 mile. Look for the descent where the trail bends away from the creek. From here it is 0.5 mile back to the trailhead by either completing a loop or backtracking.

UPPER PRIEST FALLS ★★★★

MAGNITUDE: 71 (h)
ELEVATION: 3420 feet
WATERSHED: Large
APPROACH: High-clearance & trail (hard)
LAT/LONG: 48.993151° N / 116.940798° W
USGS MAP: *Continental Mtn.* (1996)

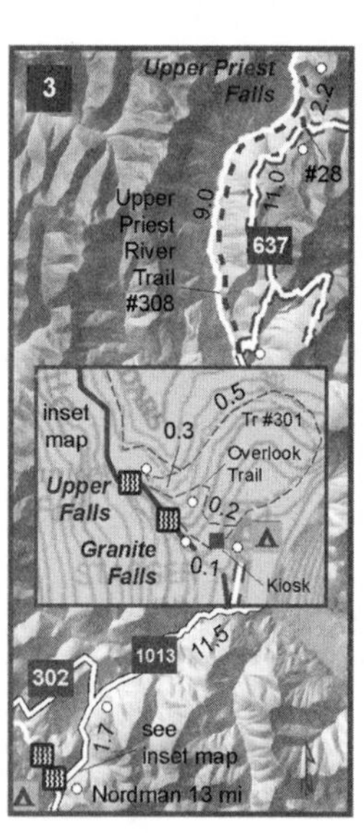

Upper Priest River noisily crashes 100 to 125 feet within this secluded northwest tip of Idaho. It is also known as American Falls to distinguish it from Canadian Falls, located farther upstream in British Columbia.

Drive 1.7 miles north of Stagger Inn Camp (described earlier) on Granite Creek Road (Forest Service Road 302), and turn right (northeast) on Forest Service Road 1013, which eventually turns into Forest Service Road 637. Proceed approximately 11.5 miles to the Upper Priest River Trailhead 308. This path follows the river for 9 miles, ending at the falls.

If your vehicle has good road clearance, continue along FS Road 637 for another 11 miles to Continental Trail 28, which is also designated as a part of the Idaho Centennial Trail. Collectively comprised of several trails and old road, its 1200-mile extent winds through the state from this northernmost location southward to the state line with Nevada. Hike 0.7 mile north on Trail 28, and turn right on Trail 308 for another 1.5 miles to the descent.

4 PEND OREILLE

The following waterfalls are located northeast of glacial Lake Pend Oreille, one of the largest natural lakes in the western conterminous United States. Both cataracts occur within Sandpoint Ranger District, Idaho Panhandle National Forests.

Char Falls

CHAR FALLS ★★★

MAGNITUDE: 61 (h)
ELEVATION: 4140 feet
WATERSHED: Medium
APPROACH: Trail (fairly hard)
LAT/LONG: 48.366365° N / 116.170875° W
USGS MAP: *Trestle Peak* (1996)

Lightning Creek descends powerfully for 50 to 75 feet, with a viewpoint framed by coniferous trees. Turn east off U.S. Highway 2/95 onto State Route 200, and drive 12.2 miles along SR 200 to Trestle Creek Road (Forest Service Road 275). Turn left (east), and proceed 13 miles to Lightning Creek Road (Forest Service Road 419). Turn right (south), and continue 0.6 mile to a primitive road to the left.

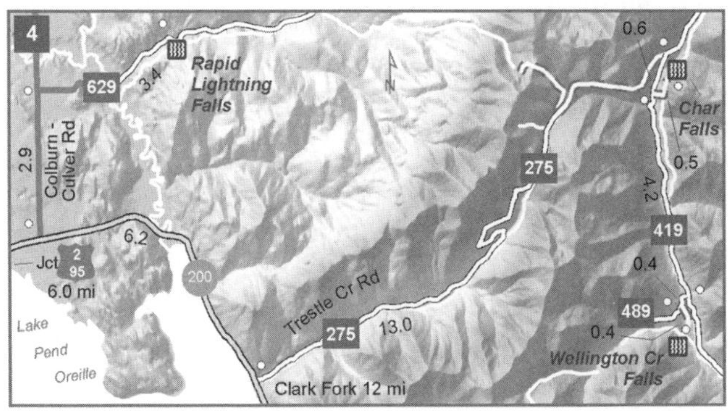

Park here, and follow the rocky road 0.5 mile to a wide trail at its end. Take the trail only 20 yards, then find a faint path to the right. It leads to an unfenced overlook of the falls in less than 100 yards.

WELLINGTON CREEK FALLS (U) ★★★

MAGNITUDE: 56
ELEVATION: 3120 feet
WATERSHED: Medium
APPROACH: High-clearance
LAT/LONG: 48.293052° N / 116.169502° W
USGS MAP: *Trestle Peak* (1996 ns)

Lush vegetation surrounds this wonderful 50- to 75-foot waterfall along Wellington Creek. Be careful near the edge of the vista's unfenced precipice in this undeveloped area.

Continue 4.2 miles past Char Falls (described earlier) along Lightning Creek Road (Forest Service Road 419) to Augor Road (Forest Service Road 489), and turn right (west). Cross Lightning Creek, and either drive or hike down the primitive road to the left. Bear left at the fork in 0.4 mile, and continue 0.4 mile on this bumpy road to its end. Walk toward the creek and a bit upstream, listening for the falls. Continue toward Wellington Creek for good overviews of this obscure entry.

MORE ONLINE:
Rapid Lightning Falls (u) ★ USGS *Elmira* (1996 ns)

5 COLBURN

GROUSE CREEK FALLS ★★

MAGNITUDE: 18
ELEVATION: 2670 feet
WATERSHED: Large
APPROACH: Trail (fairly easy)
LAT/LONG: 48.458118° N / 116.338159° W
USGS MAP: *Wylie Knob* (1996)

Grouse Creek cuts through bedrock in a small series of descents totaling 15 to 20 feet, situated within Sandpoint Ranger District, Idaho Panhandle National Forests. Turn east off U.S. Highway 2/95 at Colburn onto Colburn–Culver Road. Drive east 4.5 miles, and turn left on the gravel Forest Service Road 280. Continue 6 miles up Grouse Creek Valley to a turnout near a dirt road to the right. Park

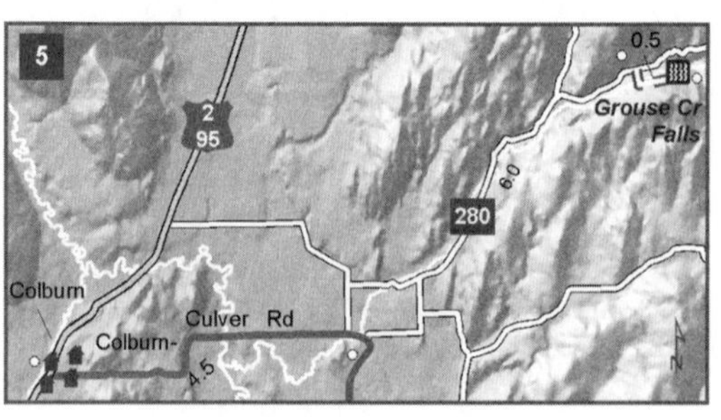

and follow the road, which becomes a trail in 0.3 mile. The waterfall is 0.2 mile farther.

6 PACK RIVER

JERU CREEK FALLS (U) ★★★

MAGNITUDE: 59
ELEVATION: 3060 feet
WATERSHED: Small
APPROACH: Trail & bushwhack (moderate)
LAT/LONG: 48.529417° N / 116.613998° W
USGS MAP: *Dodge Peak* (1996 nl)

Jeru Creek slides 100 to 150 feet down a mountainside. The waterfall is probably located on private property. Turn northwest off U.S. Highway 2/95 at Samuels onto Pack River Road (Forest Service Road 231). Drive 9 miles to the unsigned turnout on the north side of Jeru Creek. The 1-mile trek from the road starts on an obsolete four-wheel-drive route and eventually turns into a seldom-used, unmaintained trail. You encounter the descent soon after where the path seems to end.

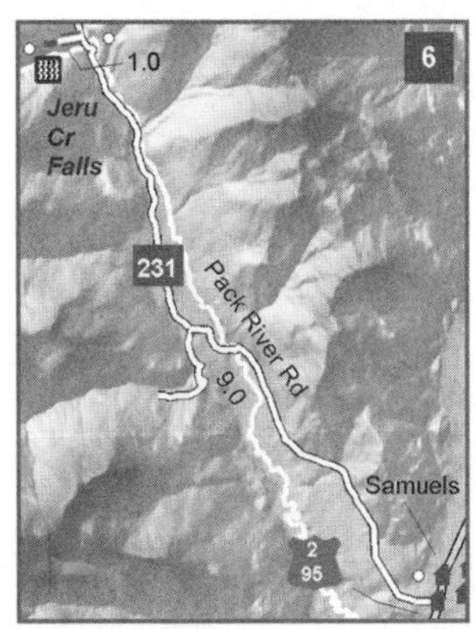

7 BONNERS FERRY

The following waterfalls occur within a fairly undeveloped area of Bonners Ferry Ranger District, Idaho Panhandle National Forests. Access the area from the small city of Bonners Ferry by departing U.S. Highway 2/95 westward upon Riverside Street, located just south of the highway's bridge crossing of Kootenai River. The way soon becomes Lions Den Road. Take it 5.1 miles to its end at a T junction with West Side Road (Forest Service Road 417).

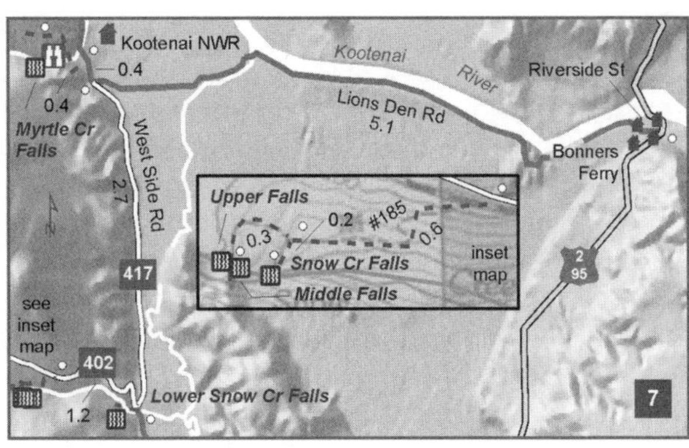

Snow Creek Falls

 LOWER SNOW CREEK FALLS (U) ★★

MAGNITUDE: 64
ELEVATION: 1900 feet
WATERSHED: Large
APPROACH: Trail (fairly easy)
LAT/LONG: 48.66487° N / 116.410772° W
USGS MAP: *Moravia* (1996 ns)

Snow Creek splits as it descends 50 to 75 feet over an escarpment. From the T junction (described earlier), drive 2.7 miles south along West Side Road (Forest Service Road 417) to an unsigned turnout on the north side of the stream. Find the unmarked trail that leads 0.1 mile to the base of the cataract. Note: Residential development has been occurring in the vicinity; don't trespass if access is no longer granted.

SNOW CREEK FALLS ★★

MAGNITUDE: 40
ELEVATION: 2260 feet
WATERSHED: Large
APPROACH: Trail (moderate)
LAT/LONG: 48.667492° N / 116.429032° W
USGS MAP: *Moravia* (1996)

Formerly only a bird's-eye glimpse was possible of this multitiered descent. Trails now let you get up close. Depart West Side Road (Forest Service Road 417) upon Forest Service Road 402, immediately north of the turnout for the previous entry. Travel 1.2 miles, and park along a wide spot along the left side of the route near the signed trailhead.

Walk 0.6 mile down the trail, and turn left at spur signed "Lower Falls," another name for the 25- to 35-foot drop for this tier of the cataract. From here, it is 0.2 mile farther to a deckside view. Notice the spray from above the falls. Read on to discover its identity.

UPPER SNOW CREEK FALLS ★★★

MAGNITUDE: 51
ELEVATION: 2340 feet
WATERSHED: Large
APPROACH: Trail (moderate)
LAT/LONG: 48.667421° N / 116.430169° W
USGS MAP: *Moravia* (1996 nl)

Snow Creek spreads downward 35 to 50 feet in a wooded setting. From the trail split (described earlier), bear right at the sign labeled "Upper Falls." You meet the base of the cataract at the path's end in 0.3 mile. From here, it's 0.9 mile back to the road. Don't leave yet though. What about that spray that I mentioned earlier? Continue reading.

MIDDLE SNOW CREEK FALLS ★★

MAGNITUDE: 46
ELEVATION: 2300 feet
WATERSHED: Large
APPROACH: Trail (moderate)
LAT/LONG: 48.667407° N / 116.42959° W
USGS MAP: *Moravia* (1996 ns)

Snow Creek pours 60 to 80 feet into a bedrock slot, sending spray into Snow Creek Falls (described previously). Precarious views make it suitable for mature persons only. From the Upper Falls (described previously), walk downstream a short distance to a thin path. Peer from the edge for an obstructed, partial view of the drop.

MYRTLE CREEK FALLS ★★★

MAGNITUDE: 66
ELEVATION: 1900 feet
WATERSHED: Large
APPROACH: Trail (moderate)
LAT/LONG: 48.706533° N / 116.419569° W
USGS MAP: *Moravia* (1996 ns)

Located adjacent to Kootenai National Wildlife Refuge, peer into a small gorge carved by Myrtle Creek, containing a 15- to 25-foot punchbowl followed by its waters thundering 35 to 50 feet downward. From its junction with Lions Den Road (described previously), proceed northward 0.4 mile along West Side Road (Forest Service Road 417) to the signed turn and parking area on the left. The trail is deceptive as its first 0.2 mile is paved to a footbridge. Then the blacktop ends with a fairly steep ascent for the final 0.2 mile to an open, unguarded vista. Keep your wits, as the terrain is precarious here.

8 MOYIE RIVER

Moyie Falls is purported to be one of Idaho's great scenic attractions—no argument here. But contrary to what most directions imply, you can't get good views from the main highway. The following description, however, will direct you to a picture-perfect vista.

MOYIE FALLS ★★★★★

MAGNITUDE: 71 (h)
ELEVATION: 2020 feet
WATERSHED: Large
APPROACH: Auto
LAT/LONG: 48.732779° N / 116.175489° W
USGS MAP: *Moyie Springs* (1996)

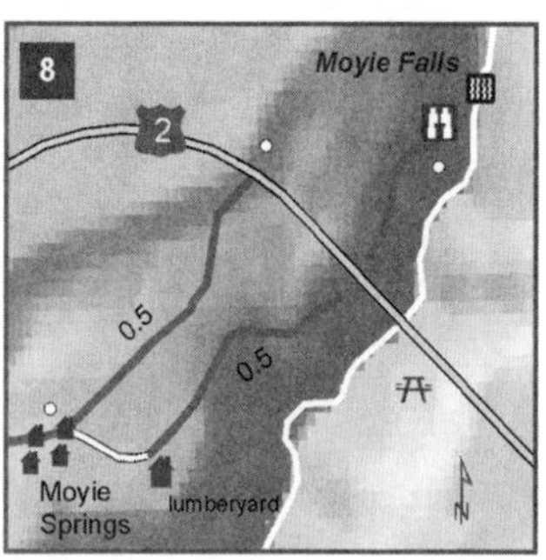

Moyie River absolutely thunders through a small gorge in tiered form. The upper portion crashes 60 to 100 feet beneath an antiquated span crossing the canyon. The lower portion cascades 20 to 40 feet. The falls is probably located on private property.

Turn off U.S. Highway 2 at the Moyie Springs exit immediately west of the Moyie River Bridge. In 0.5 mile, turn left on the street adjacent to a lumberyard. Follow this residential road 0.5 mile to various turnouts offering good views into the canyon.

9 BOUNDARY LINE

Located in proximity to Idaho's border with British Columbia is the following pair of scenic waterfalls.

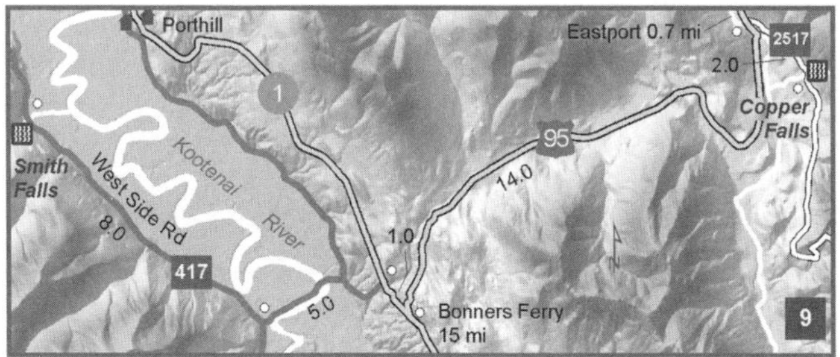

SMITH FALLS ★★★

MAGNITUDE: 67
ELEVATION: 1800 feet
WATERSHED: Large
APPROACH: Auto
LAT/LONG: 48.959941° N / 116.556834° W
USGS MAP: *Smith Falls* (1996)

A high volume of water plummets 60 feet along Smith Creek. The falls and the viewpoint are situated on private property. Please obey the posted restrictions so that others can continue to enjoy this entry.

About 15 miles north of Bonners Ferry, turn north onto State Route 1 from U.S. Highway 95. Drive 1 mile, then turn left (west) on an unsigned paved road. Continue for 5 miles, crossing the Kootenai River at the halfway point. Turn right (north) onto West Side Road (Forest Service Road 417), and proceed 8 miles to a marked turnout at the falls.

COPPER FALLS ★★★★

MAGNITUDE: 77
ELEVATION: 3400 feet
WATERSHED: Small
APPROACH: Trail (moderate)
LAT/LONG: 48.971971° N / 116.142122° W
USGS MAP: *Eastport* (1996)

Copper Creek hurtles 160 feet from a cliff within Bonners Ferry Ranger District, Idaho Panhandle National Forests. Turn east off U.S. Highway 95 onto Forest Service Road 2517 less than 0.7 mile south of the Eastport border crossing or 14 miles northeast of the junction with State Route 1. Follow this bumpy gravel road for 2 miles to Copper Falls Trail 20. Hike 0.3 mile along the moderately steep trail to the falls.

10 POST FALLS

Back in the early 1980s when I looked at the topographic map for this area, it did not show any waterfalls, only dams. A fellow student from the area confirmed that hydroelectric facilities had replaced the falls. Fast-forward to 2011. While I was performing yet another online search for "new" cataracts, up came this area. While field-truthing that area, I found two falls that most people thought had disappeared. Eastbounders depart Interstate 90 at Spokane Street (Exit 5); westbounders have to leave the interstate 1 mile eastward and drive 1 mile along Seltice Way to reach Spokane Street.

Q'EMILN FALLS (U) ★★

MAGNITUDE: 36
ELEVATION: 2190 feet
WATERSHED: Large (d)
APPROACH: Trail (easy)
LAT/LONG: 47.703741° N / 116.955883° W
USGS MAP: *Post Falls* (1981 ns)

Water slides 20 to 25 feet over a dam along the south channel of the Spokane River before dropping a few feet across a 100- to 150-foot slab of bedrock. From the Spokane Street exit (described earlier), turn south. Drive 0.8 mile beyond I-90, then turn right upon Parkway Drive. Proceed 0.1 mile, and turn right into Q'emiln Park. Drive 0.1 mile, passing the sign on the left showing the trail system (which does not lead to the descent). Rather, don't stop until the park road bends to the right.

You should see two gated paths. Take the one on the left. (The one on the right goes above the dam). After a 0.1-mile stroll, the path meets a fence protecting visitors at the top of a cliff, with views of the dam and its falls. It deserves a lesser rating when its flow is low.

POST FALLS ★★★

MAGNITUDE: 27 (l)
ELEVATION: 2190 feet
WATERSHED: Large (d)
APPROACH: Trail (easy)
LAT/LONG: 47.708853° N / 116.95378° W
USGS MAP: *Post Falls* (1981 ns)

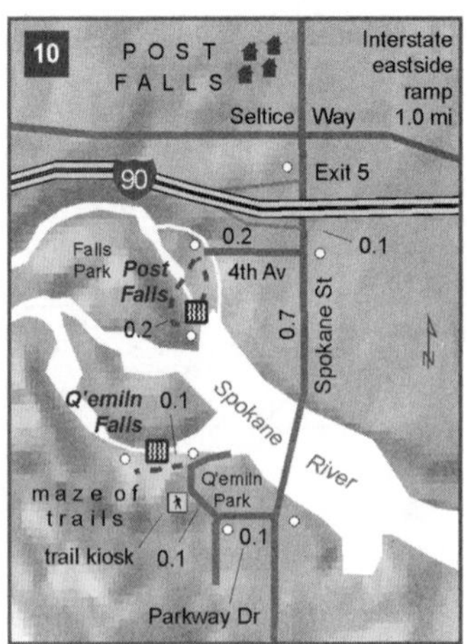

Strands of Spokane River tumble 40 to 60 feet over a jumble of bedrock. From Q'emiln Park (described earlier), turn back north along Spokane Street. After 0.7 mile, turn left upon 4th Avenue. Proceed 0.2 mile, and turn left into Falls Park. From the parking area, head toward the river through the landscaped grounds. After reaching the gorge in 0.1 mile, go 0.1 mile downstream to viewpoints of the V-shaped dam and its falls. You can complete a loop walk back to your vehicle in less than 0.1 mile.

Opposite: *Fern Falls*

11 PRICHARD

Prichard is listed among the many old mining towns in northern Idaho. Unlike those communities still surviving in the Silver Valley, paralleling Interstate 90, about the only building left in this outpost is the historic and still operating Prichard Tavern. Depart I-90 at Kingston (Exit 43). Head north on Forest Service Road 9, and drive 23 miles to the sign on the right for the tavern. Check it out before or after visiting the following three waterfalls, all of which are situated within Idaho Panhandle National Forests.

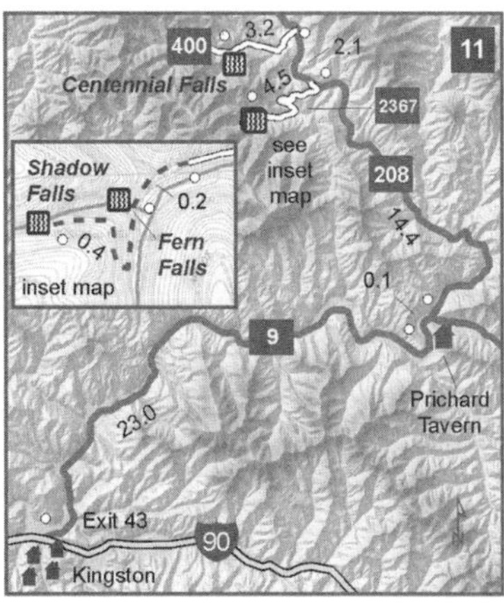

FERN FALLS ★★

MAGNITUDE: 34
ELEVATION: 3230 feet
WATERSHED: Small

APPROACH: Trail (easy)
LAT/LONG: 47.759948° N / 116.105408° W
USGS MAP: *Pond Peak* (1996)

Water pours 10 to 15 feet from a tributary of Yellow Dog Creek. Adventurers can walk behind it if they so choose. From the turnoff for the tavern (described earlier), continue 0.1 mile, then bear straight upon Forest Service Road 208. (FS Road 9 continues to the right.) Proceed 14.4 miles, and turn left upon Beetle Creek Road (Forest Service Road 2367). Go 4.5 miles to the road's end at the trailhead. From here, it's 0.2 mile to a footbridge just downstream from the base of the descent. *Note:* The USGS map labels Fern Falls 500 feet upstream from the location signed by the US Forest Service.

11 SHADOW FALLS ★★

MAGNITUDE: 43
ELEVATION: 3340 feet
WATERSHED: Small
APPROACH: Trail (moderate)
LAT/LONG: 47.760049° N / 116.10697° W
USGS MAP: *Pond Peak* (1996)

Upstream from Fern Falls (described earlier), a tributary of Yellow Dog Creek drops 20 to 25 feet into a small grotto. You can walk behind this descent. Continue 0.1 mile along the trail, then switchback up a bit before ending at a footbridge near the base of this entry 0.3 mile farther. From here, it's 0.6 mile back to the trailhead. *Note:* The USGS map labels Fern Falls where Shadow Falls is signed on site by the US Forest Service. I did not find anything resembling a waterfall where the USGS map depicts Shadow Falls.

MORE ONLINE:
Centennial Falls ★ USGS *Pond Peak* (1996 ns)

12 MULLAN

As you travel east from Coeur d'Alene along Interstate 90, you will pass the historic mining towns of Kellogg, Wallace, and Mullan. The following waterfalls, accessible from late summer to early autumn, are located near the Bitterroot Divide, which separates Idaho from Montana. Both are situated within Coeur d'Alene Ranger District, Idaho Panhandle National Forests. Depart the interstate at Exit 69, and drive 0.1 mile to Friday Avenue. Turn right, signed for Shoshone County Park, and proceed 0.8 mile. Bear right upon Willow Creek Road. Drive 1.7 miles, crossing underneath I-90, to the end of the road.

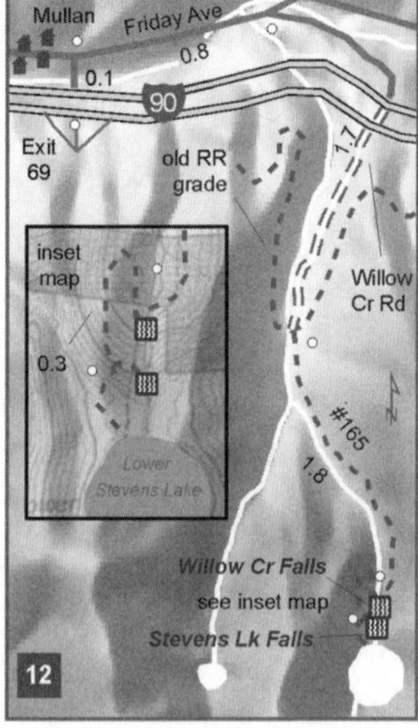

Stevens Lake Falls

WILLOW CREEK FALLS (U) ★★

MAGNITUDE: 29
ELEVATION: 5140 feet
WATERSHED: Small

APPROACH: Trail (fairly hard)
LAT/LONG: 47.438199° N / 115.759382° W
USGS MAP: *Mullan* (1995 ns)

From the parking area at the end of Willow Creek Road (described earlier), you will see an old railroad grade, especially popular with mountain bikers. Don't take it; rather head straight up Trail 165. Hike the moderately strenuous route for 1.8 miles to this 20- to 30-foot tumble where the trail crosses East Fork Willow Creek.

STEVENS LAKE FALLS (U) ★★★

MAGNITUDE: 53
ELEVATION: 5440 feet
WATERSHED: Small
APPROACH: Trail (fairly hard)
LAT/LONG: 47.43653° N / 115.759639° W
USGS MAP: *Mullan* (1995 ns)

From the trail crossing the creek (described earlier), a long switchback takes you through a field of talus (boulders) and then up into the forest. After a 0.3-mile ascent, find the unfenced cliffside vista of the 80- to 100-foot plunge into a bedrock cleft. An upper tier also exists, but when I last visited the area, it was mostly masked by vegetation. From this juncture, it's only 0.1 mile up to glacial Lower Stevens Lake and then 2.2 miles back down to the trailhead.

13 ST. JOE RIVER

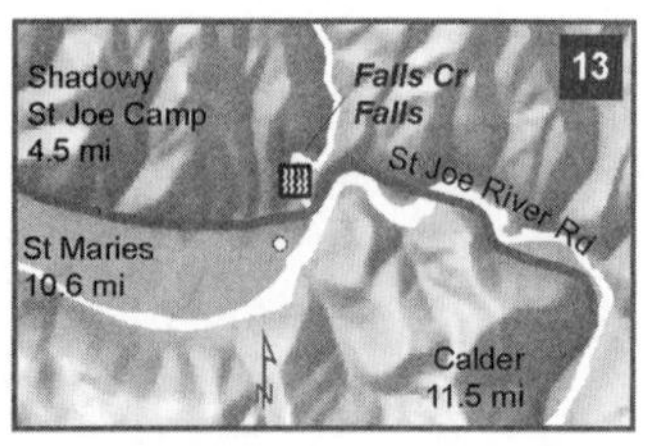

St. Joe River is known for two particular facts. First, it is navigable to one of the highest elevations of any river in North America. Second, its sport fishing is regarded as excellent, especially along the remote upper reaches where you can practically jump across the "mighty" St. Joe.

FALLS CREEK FALLS ★★

MAGNITUDE: 46 (h)
ELEVATION: 1980 feet
WATERSHED: Medium
APPROACH: Auto
LAT/LONG: 47.320884° N / 116.297819° W
USGS MAP: *Saint Joe* (1996 ns)

Unsuspecting travelers are likely to miss this 20- to 30-foot drop of Falls Creek into the St. Joe River. It is located on private property surrounded by St. Joe Ranger District, Idaho Panhandle National Forests. Turn east off State Route 3 onto the St. Joe River Road, 0.5 mile northeast of St. Maries. The falls is 10.6 miles beyond St. Maries or 4.5 miles past Shadowy St. Joe Camp. Park at the turnout closest to the bridge over Falls Creek.

MORE ONLINE:
Scribner Falls, USGS *Pole Mtn.* (1994) EXPLORE!

14 ELK CREEK

Many waterfalls are to be found within this portion of Palouse Ranger District, Clearwater National Forest. Drive south from Bovill toward the Elk River on State Route 8. After 16 miles, turn right (south) onto Forest Service Road 1452, signed for Elk Creek Falls Recreation Area. Proceed 1.6 miles along FS Road 1452, then go another 0.5 mile via FS Road 1452B to the parking area.

1 UPPER ELK FALLS ★★

MAGNITUDE: 31
ELEVATION: 2660 feet
WATERSHED: Large

APPROACH: Trail (moderate)
LAT/LONG: 46.739633° N / 116.173472° W
USGS MAP: *Elk Creek Falls* (1994 nl)

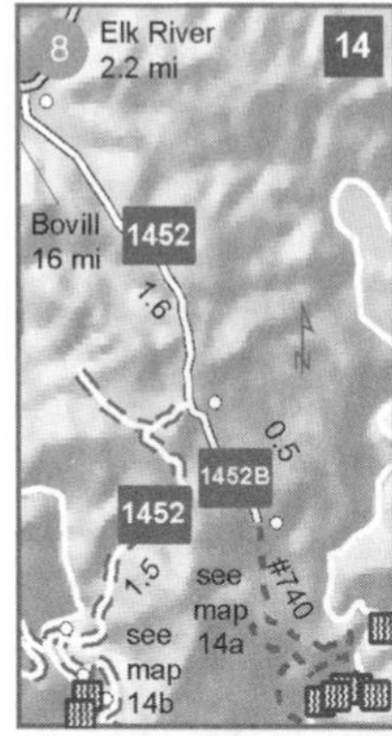

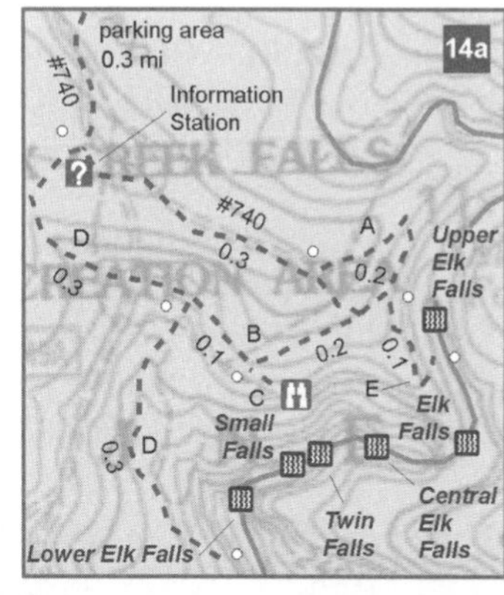

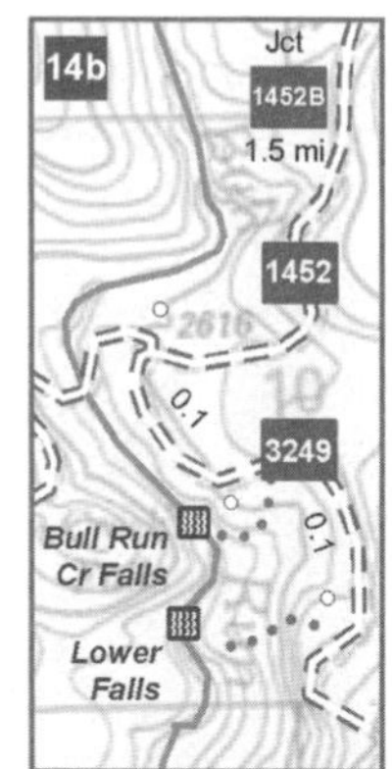

Elk Falls

The uppermost descent along Elk Creek drops 30 to 50 feet into a circular basin. From the parking area (described earlier), embark upon Elk Creek Falls Trail 740. Follow it 0.6 mile to Upper Falls Loop Trail 740A. Proceed 0.2 mile to Upper Falls Overlook Trail 740E, which ends in 0.1 mile at the descent.

ELK FALLS ★★★★

MAGNITUDE: 72
ELEVATION: 2550 feet
WATERSHED: Large
APPROACH: Trail (moderate)
LAT/LONG: 46.736207° N / 116.174416° W
USGS MAP: *Elk Creek Falls* (1994)

This 125- to 150-foot cataract, also called Elk Creek Falls and Middle Falls, is the highest of the six waterfalls along Elk Creek. From Upper Elk Falls (described earlier), take Trail 740E back to Trail 740A and turn left. Proceed a short distance, and take the left fork upon Middle Falls Trail 740B. After 0.2 mile, turn left upon Middle Falls Overlook Trail 740C. Take the path a short distance to the overlook.

While you are hiking, look down the gorge for a view of Central Elk Falls (u) USGS *Elk Creek Falls* (1994 ns), where water pours 20 to 30 feet along Elk Creek. Avid anglers and other nimble individuals often bushwhack down to this reach of the stream.

TWIN FALLS (U) AND SMALL FALLS (U) ★★

MAGNITUDE: 45
ELEVATION: 2400 feet
WATERSHED: Large
APPROACH: Trail (moderate)
LAT/LONG: 46.736354° N / 116.176819° W
USGS MAP: *Elk Creek Falls* (1994 ns)

This pair of waterfalls can be viewed in tandem. Twin Falls is a 10- to 20-foot segmented descent, while Small Falls drops 10 to 20 feet in a punchbowl form. Look for them about 0.1 mile downstream from Central Elk Falls (described earlier).

LOWER ELK FALLS ★★★★

MAGNITUDE: 72
ELEVATION: 2350 feet
WATERSHED: Large
APPROACH: Trail (fairly hard)
LAT/LONG: 46.735972° N / 116.178192° W
USGS MAP: *Elk Creek Falls* (1994 nl)

This 75- to 100-foot plunge is the most powerful of the waterfalls along Elk Creek. From the Trail 740C overlook, walk back to Trail 740B, and turn left. Go 0.1 mile, and turn left upon Lower Falls Extension Trail 740D. Take it to its end in 0.3 mile. From here, it is 0.9 mile back to the parking area; take Trail 740D its entire length back to the first leg of Elk Creek Falls Trail 740.

BULL RUN CREEK FALLS ★★★

MAGNITUDE: 60
ELEVATION: 2480 feet
WATERSHED: Medium
APPROACH: Bushwhack (moderate)
LAT/LONG: 46.737104° N / 116.195852° W
USGS MAP: *Elk Creek Falls* (1994)

Bull Run Creek tumbles a total of 75 to 100 feet. This and the following entry straddle timber company property and an undeveloped portion of Elk Creek Falls Recreation Area. From the parking area (described earlier), backtrack with your vehicle for 0.5 mile, and drive southwestward along FS Road 1452 for 1.5 miles to its junction with Forest Service Road 3249. Park in a wide spot. Walk about 0.1 mile along FS Road 3249, looking for a faint path to the right, which leads quickly to this cataract.

Part of the road might be gated. If it is, park where you won't block the way, and take a trek to your destination.

LOWER BULL RUN CREEK FALLS (U) ★★

MAGNITUDE: 45
ELEVATION: 2420 feet
WATERSHED: Medium
APPROACH: Bushwhack (hard)
LAT/LONG: 46.736192° N / 116.196431° W
USGS MAP: *Elk Creek Falls* (1994 nl)

Water pours 30 to 50 feet along Bull Run Creek. This entry is recommended for determined bushwhackers only. Return to the road from Bull Run Creek Falls (described earlier), and continue walking along the ridge in the downstream direction for 0.1 mile. After passing a small marshy area, scramble down the steep timbered slope to the creek below the base of the falls.

MORE ONLINE:
Central Elk Falls (u) ★, mentioned earlier; previously named Middle Elk Falls

Lower Bull Run Creek Falls

IDAHO

CENTRAL WILDERNESS AREAS

The interior of Idaho is dominated by swift rivers cutting deep canyons through rugged mountains. This sparsely populated region contains the largest tracts—3 million acres—of wilderness in the contiguous United States. Adventurers can explore the Selway-Bitterroot, Frank Church River of No Return, Gospel Hump, and Sawtooth Wildernesses; the Hells Canyon and Sawtooth National Recreation Areas; and the Wild and Scenic Salmon River.

The geology of this region is largely determined by the history of its igneous rocks. During the late Mesozoic era, 75 million to 100 million years ago,

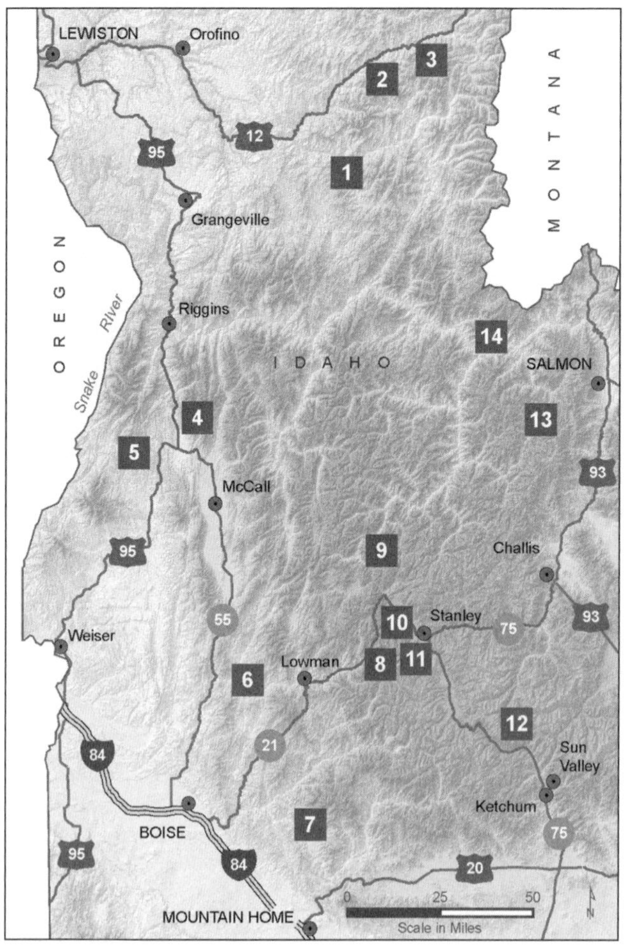

Selway Falls

extensive masses of magma crystallized in the subsurface of central Idaho. Rocks ranging from igneous granite and diorite to metamorphic gneisses were formed. Over the next 50 million years, these masses, collectively called a batholith, were uplifted to form mountains.

The mountainous terrain of the Idaho interior has been shaped mostly by erosion. Alpine glaciers carved the batholith at least four times over the last 2 million years, sharpening peaks and widening valleys. Most waterfalls in the region were created by glaciation. Warbonnet Falls descends from a mountainside into a glacial valley. Other streams follow along valleys and encounter obstacles called moraines (linear rock deposits left by glacial activity). Lady Face Falls, for instance, breaks through and drops over a moraine.

Stream erosion also contributes to the configuration of the batholith. The Salmon, Snake, Selway, and Lochsa rivers have carved impressive canyons and gorges. Waterfalls tumble into these powerful waterways from tributaries that erode at a slower rate than the main rivers (Fountain Creek Falls and Tumble Creek Falls are examples). Cascades such as Selway Falls and Carey Falls are cases where rivers have eroded heterogeneous rock material unevenly.

Because of the wild nature of central Idaho, large descents remain to be found, described, and mapped. Many of these cataracts are accessible only by plane, but a good share await discovery by hikers and backpackers. This book describes 30 of the 58 falls known to occur within the central interior.

1 SELWAY RIVER

The Selway River begins in the interior of the Selway-Bitterroot Wilderness. As it flows from the wilderness area, its waters become a river of substantial magnitude. Farther downstream at Lowell, the Selway meets the Lochsa River to become the Middle Fork Clearwater River.

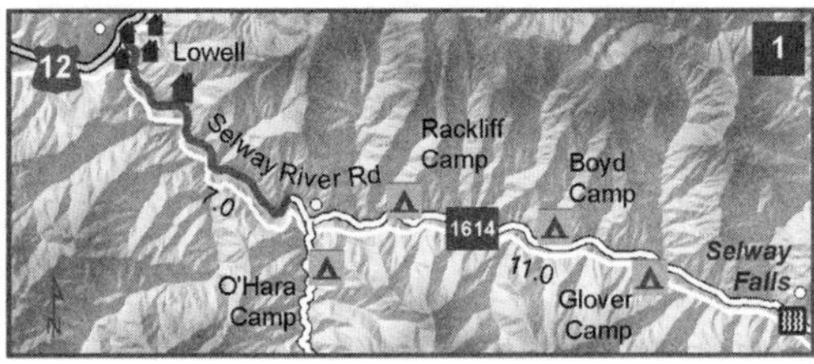

SELWAY FALLS ★★

MAGNITUDE: 39 (h)
ELEVATION: 1700 feet
WATERSHED: Large
APPROACH: Auto
LAT/LONG: 46.051962° N / 115.307505° W
USGS MAP: *Selway Falls* (1995)

A long reach of the Selway River cascades a total of 50 feet within Moose Creek Ranger District, Nez Perce National Forest. Turn southeast off U.S. Highway 12 at Lowell, and drive 18 miles to the end of Selway River Road (Forest Service Road 1614). The cataract is visible beside the gravel roadway.

2 LOCHSA RIVER

U.S. Highway 12 faithfully parallels the Lochsa River from its beginning near Lolo Pass to its confluence with the Selway River 78 miles downstream. There are plenty of campsites along this stretch of the highway, but no vehicle services are available from Lolo Hot Springs to Lowell. Be sure your automobile has a full tank of gas before you start. Several waterfalls pour from tributary streams into the Lochsa within a 2-mile stretch 16 to 18 miles northeast of Lowell. The following waterfalls occur within the Middle Fork Clearwater Wild and Scenic River area, Lochsa Ranger District, Clearwater National Forest.

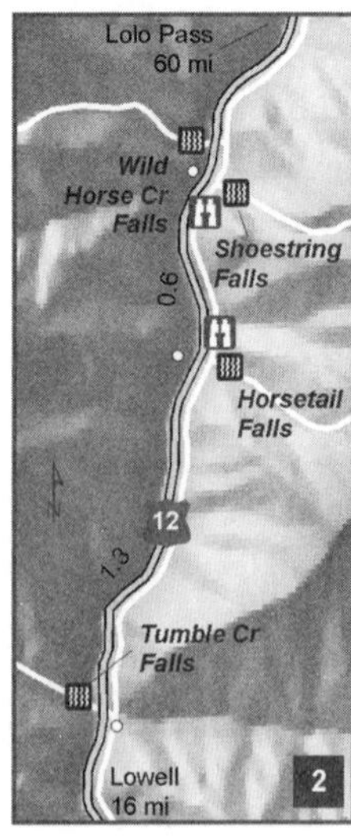

HORSETAIL FALLS ★★

MAGNITUDE: 59
ELEVATION: 2000 feet
WATERSHED: Very small
APPROACH: Auto
LAT/LONG: 46.26974° N / 115.391211° W
USGS MAP: *McLendon Butte* (1994 ns)

Peer across the Lochsa River to Horsetail Falls descending 60 to 100 feet from an unnamed stream. Drive to a marked turnoff along US 12 between mile markers 114 and 115.

SHOESTRING FALLS ★★

MAGNITUDE: 51
ELEVATION: 1920 feet
WATERSHED: Very small
APPROACH: Auto
LAT/LONG: 46.278417° N / 115.390181° W
USGS MAP: *McLendon Butte* (1994)

Water stairsteps 150 to 200 feet in five sections where an unnamed creek drops into the Lochsa River. View this waterfall from across the river at the marked turnout between mile markers 115 and 116.

WILD HORSE CREEK FALLS (U) ★★

MAGNITUDE: 48
ELEVATION: 1880 feet
WATERSHED: Small
APPROACH: Auto
LAT/LONG: 46.280893° N / 115.391147° W
USGS MAP: *McLendon Butte* (1994 ns)

Wild Horse Creek descends in a double drop totaling 40 to 60 feet. Park at the Shoestring Falls turnout (described earlier), and walk 0.1 mile along US 12 for a close-up view of this entry.

MORE ONLINE:
Tumble Creek Falls (u) ★, USGS *McLendon Butte* (1994 ns)
Snowshoe Falls USGS *Huckleberry Butte* (1994 ns) EXPLORE!

3 WARM SPRINGS CREEK

Warm Springs Creek derives its name from the thermal waters that flow into the stream from Jerry Johnson Hot Springs. Most hikers head for the rustic hot springs, often entering the waters *au naturel.* The area rapidly becomes secluded as you progress upstream past the springs.

3 JERRY JOHNSON FALLS (U) ★★★

MAGNITUDE: 56 (h)
ELEVATION: 3900 feet
WATERSHED: Large
APPROACH: Trail (fairly hard);
LAT/LONG: 46.431631° N / 114.86244° W
USGS MAP: *Tom Beal Peak* (1994 nl)

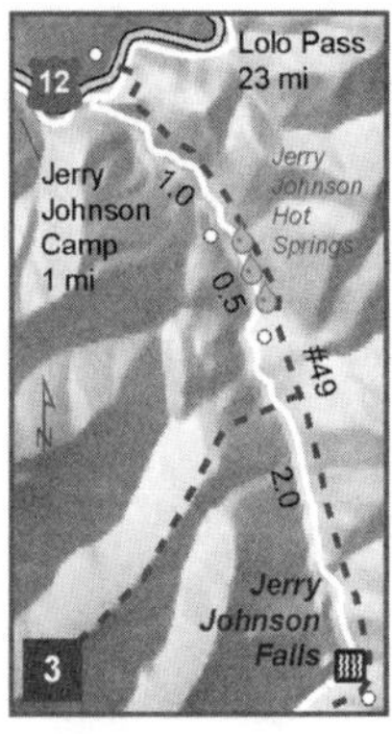

Warm Springs Creek roars 40 to 70 feet into a large basin. This entry is located within Powell Ranger District, Clearwater National Forest. Drive to the parking area for Warm Springs Creek Trail 49, located along U.S. Highway 12, 1 mile east of Jerry Johnson Camp. A footbridge crosses the Lochsa River before the trail reaches Warm Springs Creek and follows it upstream 1.5 miles to the hot springs. You pass two more thermal areas over the next 0.5 mile. One mile farther the trail crosses a small tributary creek, and then in another mile it gradually climbs above Warm Springs Creek to trailside views of the falls.

4 LITTLE SALMON RIVER

Idaho consists of two broadly settled areas—the Panhandle and the Snake River Plain—separated by the Central Wilderness. The existence of this large, mostly uninhabited area helps explain the distinctly different characters, both cultural and physical, of the two populated regions, which are connected by only one paved road, U.S. Highway 95. All of the cataracts described in this section occur on either private parcels or Bureau of Land Management lands bounded by New Meadows Ranger District, Payette National Forest.

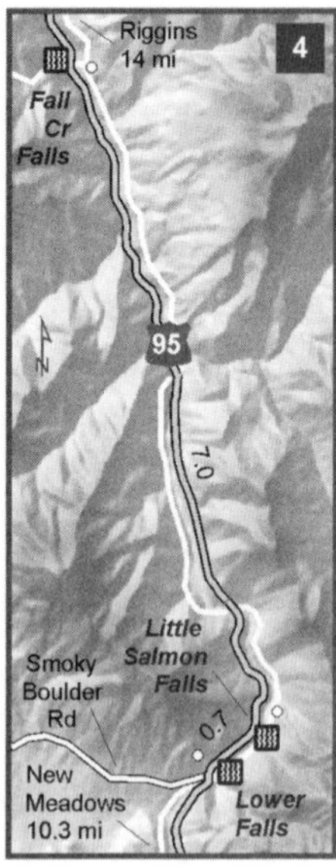

LITTLE SALMON FALLS (U) ★★

MAGNITUDE: 35
ELEVATION: 3640 feet
WATERSHED: Large
APPROACH: Auto
LAT/LONG: 45.129334° N / 116.285535° W
USGS MAP: *Indian Mtn.* (1983 ns)

Several small descents occur along the Little Salmon River where it parallels US 95. This 10- to 15-foot drop is the prettiest and easiest to visit. Drive 11 miles north of New Meadows to an unsigned turnout adjacent to this cataract.

FALL CREEK FALLS (U) ★★

MAGNITUDE: 30
ELEVATION: 2920 feet
WATERSHED: Small
APPROACH: Auto
LAT/LONG: 45.225564° N / 116.32242° W
USGS MAP: *Indian Mtn.* (1983 ns)

Fall Creek tumbles 15 to 25 feet before continuing beneath the highway and into the Little Salmon River. Drive 7 miles north of Little Salmon Falls (described earlier) to an unsigned turnout along US 95.

MORE ONLINE:
Lower Little Salmon Falls (u) ★ USGS *Bally Mtn.* (1983 ns)
Carey Falls ★ USGS *Carey Dome* (1995)
Goose Creek Falls, USGS *Meadows* (1973 ns) EXPLORE!

5 LOST VALLEY

LOST CREEK FALLS ★★

MAGNITUDE: 15
ELEVATION: 4380 feet
WATERSHED: Large
APPROACH: Auto
LAT/LONG: 44.917824° N / 116.453065° W
USGS MAP: *Tamarack* (1986)

Lost Creek drops serenely about 10 feet in a wooded setting. This falls is situated within Council Ranger District, Payette National Forest. Depart U.S. Highway 95 1 mile south of Tamarack, and turn right (west) onto Lost Valley Reservoir Road (Forest Service Road 089.) Drive 5.3 miles to the dam, then proceed south on Forest Service Road 154 for 2.7 miles to the cataract. It is visible from the road, or you can get close-up views via angler's paths.

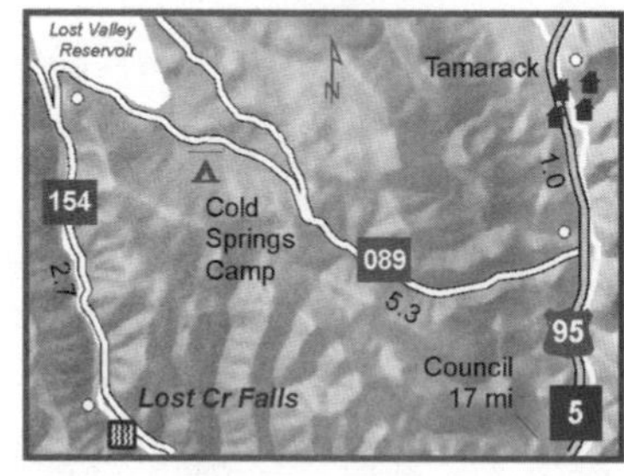

6 GARDEN VALLEY

In the town of Banks, turn off State Route 55 onto South Fork Road, heading toward Lowman. The road is now paved all the way to the town of Lowman. Along the way you will pass through an area known locally as Garden Valley, as well as many hot springs adjacent to the South Fork Payette River. The following cataracts are located within Lowman Ranger District, Boise National Forest.

LITTLE FALLS ★★

MAGNITUDE: 40
ELEVATION: 3350 feet
WATERSHED: Large
APPROACH: Auto
LAT/LONG: 44.072707° N / 115.763411° W
USGS MAP: *Grimes Pass* (1988)

This 5- to 10-foot drop along the breadth of South Fork Payette River is aptly named. There was once an abandoned mine shaft across the road from the falls, but it has been obliterated by the construction of the improved highway. Drive 9.5 miles eastward past Hot Springs Camp along South Fork Road.

Big Falls

BIG FALLS ★★

MAGNITUDE: 42
ELEVATION: 3480 feet
WATERSHED: Large
APPROACH: Auto
LAT/LONG: 44.066216° N / 115.722877° W
USGS MAP: *Pine Flat* (1972)

This 25- to 40-foot waterfall is "big" only in contrast to its downstream counterpart. The best roadside views are from a moderate distance. Continue 2.2 miles past Little Falls (described earlier). Look upstream; the falls is visible at the bottom of the canyon floor 100 to 150 feet below.

7 SOUTH FORK BOISE RIVER

Travel through rangeland, prairie, and wooded tracts into South Fork Canyon. The 300- to 400-foot-deep gorge is seldom visited. Leave Interstate 84 at Mountain Home, and drive 20 miles north on U.S. Highway 20 to Forest Service Road 134, signed for Anderson Ranch Dam and Prairie. Proceed 5 miles to the dam. After crossing the dam, turn left (west) on Forest Service Road 113, and drive 22 miles to the hamlet of Prairie. At the junction, turn left (west). The following falls are located within Mountain Home Ranger District, Boise National Forest.

SMITH CREEK FALLS (U) ★★★

MAGNITUDE: 76
ELEVATION: 3700 feet
WATERSHED: Large
APPROACH: Bushwhack (hard)
LAT/LONG: 43.520999° N / 115.679849° W
USGS MAP: *Long Gulch* (1964 nl)

The waters of this 80- to 120-foot plummet roar into an impressive grotto carved by Smith Creek. This entry is appropriate for nimble adults only. Drive westward from Prairie for 2.4 miles to the junction with FS Road 189. Bear left, staying on FS Road 189, and proceed 3.7 miles toward South Fork Canyon. About 0.1 mile before entering the canyon, you will encounter a cattle guard in the road. About 200 feet or so past this guard, park in the wide spot in the road.

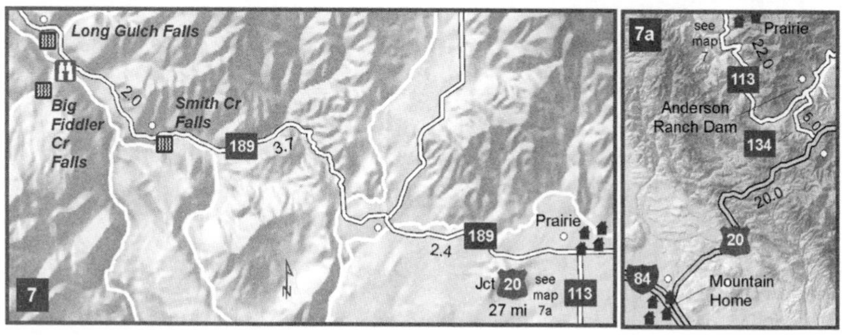

Smith Creek Falls

Cross a 5- to 10-foot-wide irrigation canal, in which the water may be from knee to waist deep, and walk carefully through the sagebrush toward Smith Creek. In about 100 feet you come to the canyon rim and its cliffs. Be careful!

7 BIG FIDDLER CREEK FALLS ★★

MAGNITUDE: 35 (l)
ELEVATION: 4000 feet
WATERSHED: Very small
APPROACH: Auto
LAT/LONG: 43.530007° / 115.707916° W
USGS MAP: *Long Gulch* (1964 ns)

This 252-foot drop is the tallest officially measured waterfall in Idaho. Unfortunately, the creek is seasonal and thus usually dry during summer. From the cattle guard on FS Road 189 (described earlier), drive 2 miles into South Fork Canyon, and look across the canyon to the falls. In summer look for evidence of water flowing along the canyon's upper tier of cliffs. Immediately upstream, on seasonal Big Fiddler Creek, you may see another small cataract pouring 60 to 80 feet from the lower canyon tier into the South Fork Boise River.

LONG GULCH FALLS (U) ★★

MAGNITUDE: 24 (l)
ELEVATION: 3600 feet
WATERSHED: Medium

APPROACH: Auto
LAT/LONG: 43.538019° N / 115.705684° W
USGS MAP: *Long Gulch* (1964 ns)

Long Gulch plunges 100 to 125 feet into the South Fork Boise River. The creek is seasonal, but it often maintains some flow throughout summer. From the same location described in the Big Fiddler Creek Falls entry (see above), look for this falls on the near side of the canyon.

8 SAWTOOTHS WEST

The rugged Sawtooth Mountains are a tribute to the strength of glacial sculpturing during the last Ice Age. The following waterfalls are all located within the Sawtooth Wilderness portion of Sawtooth National Recreation Area. Reach the following set of cataracts on the western flank of the mountains by turning off State Route 21 at the marked access road to Grandjean Camp. Drive 8 miles to the trailheads at the end of the gravel road, where self-issuing wilderness permits are available for hikers and backpackers to complete before they embark on the trail. If you camp, make sure you are at least 100 feet away from any trail, stream, or lake.

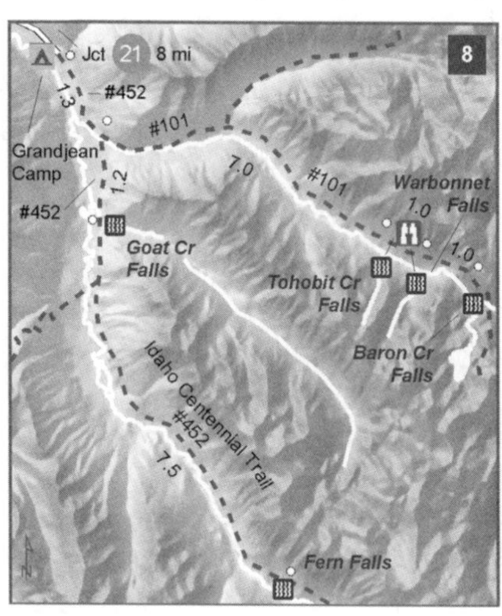

GOAT CREEK FALLS (U) ★★

MAGNITUDE: 39
ELEVATION: 5260 feet
WATERSHED: Medium

APPROACH: Trail & bushwhack (moderate)
LAT/LONG: 44.113092° N / 115.137276° W
USGS MAP: *Edaho Mtn.* (1972 ns)

Goat Creek tumbles a total of 50 feet over a series of cascades. From the trailhead near Grandjean Camp (described earlier), embark upon South Fork Trail 452, paralleling the South Fork Payette River. Reach the junction with Redfish Creek-Baron Creek Trail 101 in 1.3 miles; continue on Trail 452 to Goat Creek a moderate 1.2 miles farther. Scramble a short distance upstream to a vantage point of this descent.

FERN FALLS ★★

MAGNITUDE: 44
ELEVATION: 6380 feet
WATERSHED: Large
APPROACH: Backpack (hard)
LAT/LONG: 44.033281° N / 115.089854° W
USGS MAP: *Warbonnet Peak* (1972)

The South Fork Payette River tumbles twice in an attractive 30-foot display. Continue 7.5 miles past Goat Creek Falls (described earlier) on South Fork Trail 452, which also serves as part of the 1200-mile Idaho Centennial Trail. From the falls, it is 10 miles back to the trailhead.

TOHOBIT CREEK FALLS (U) ★★

MAGNITUDE: 42
ELEVATION: 6960 feet
WATERSHED: Very small
APPROACH: Backpack (hard)
LAT/LONG: 44.103554° N / 115.055699° W
USGS MAP: *Warbonnet Peak* (1972 ns)

This is the first of several ribbon falls dropping from tributaries into the glacial valley currently occupied by Baron Creek. From the trailhead near Grandjean Camp (described earlier), hike 1.3 miles along South Fork Trail 452 to Redfish Creek-Baron Creek Trail 101. Turn left, and follow this trail 7 miles to a cross-canyon trailside view.

WARBONNET FALLS (U) ★★

MAGNITUDE: 42
ELEVATION: 7120 feet
WATERSHED: Very small
APPROACH: Backpack (hard)
LAT/LONG: 44.099625° N / 115.044648° W
USGS MAP: *Warbonnet Peak* (1972 ns)

An unnamed stream hurtles from the lip of a hanging valley. Continue 1 mile past Tohobit Creek Falls (described earlier) along Redfish Creek-Baron Creek Trail 101. Look across the canyon to see the cataract.

BARON CREEK FALLS ★★★

MAGNITUDE: 56
ELEVATION: 7500 feet
WATERSHED: Small
APPROACH: Backpack (hard)
LAT/LONG: 44.100596° N / 115.03525° W
USGS MAP: *Warbonnet Peak* (1972)

Baron Creek pours 50 feet downward as the stream breaks through a glacial moraine of rock debris. Hike along Redfish Creek-Baron Creek Trail 101 for 1 mile past the view of Warbonnet Falls (described earlier) to this waterfall, located 10.2 miles from the trailhead. The route continues up to Baron Lakes.

9 MIDDLE FORK SALMON RIVER

Aptly nicknamed "The River of No Return," the Salmon River and its major tributaries are famous white-water rafting destinations. Hundreds of river miles flow through the Frank Church Wilderness, which is so large that it intersects five national forests. The following descent is fortuitously accessible to all, because it happens to be located next to a major launch point along the Middle Fork.

DAGGER FALLS ★★

MAGNITUDE: 26 (h)
ELEVATION: 5680 feet
WATERSHED: Large
APPROACH: Auto
LAT/LONG: 44.529438° N / 115.285468° W
USGS MAP: *Big Soldier Mtn.* (1990)

The rafting launch point for the Middle Fork Salmon River is just below this falls. Don't be deceived by the 10- to 15-foot drop that may look like a negotiable obstacle; it is rated for experts only. When visiting this falls, I was told that two experienced rivermen had perished within the past week attempting to run the falls.

Dagger Falls

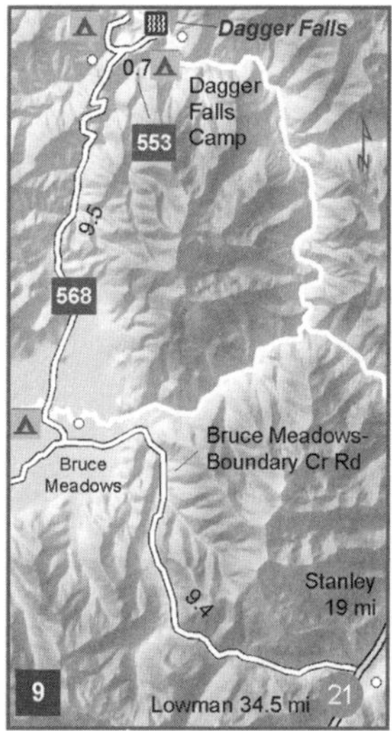

Depart State Route 21 at the sign for Bruce Meadows and Boundary Creek. You pass the meadows after 9.4 miles, where there is a junction. Turn right for Forest Service Road 568 and Dagger Falls Camp. After another 9.5 miles, turn right at the T intersection, and continue 0.7 mile along Forest Service Road 553 to the campground and the falls. Walk a short distance to the observation deck. If you see salmon jumping, consider how many hundreds of miles they have traveled from the Pacific Ocean to make it this far to spawn.

10 STANLEY LAKE CREEK

To reach the following two waterfalls, enter the Sawtooths from the north by driving 5 miles northwest of Stanley along State Route 21. Turn left at Stanley Lake Road (Forest Service Road 455), and drive 3.5 miles to Inlet Camp. The trailhead for Stanley Lake Creek Trail 640 is near Area B of the campground. Both of the falls are situated within the Sawtooth Wilderness portion of Sawtooth National Recreation Area. The route here also serves as one of the legs comprising the Idaho Centennial Trail.

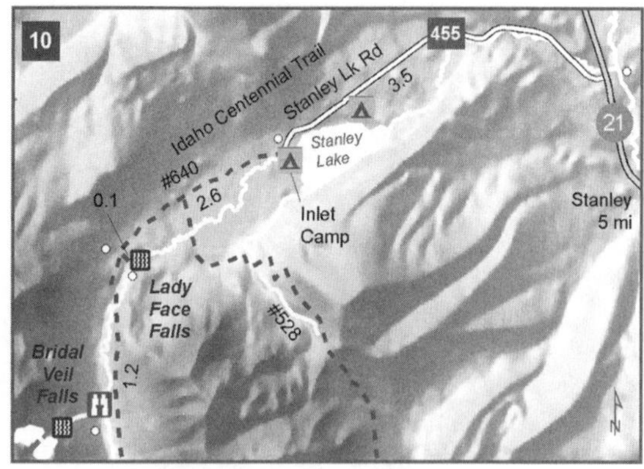

1 LADY FACE FALLS ★★

MAGNITUDE: 57
ELEVATION: 6680 feet
WATERSHED: Medium

APPROACH: Trail (moderate)
LAT/LONG: 44.231067° N / 115.096581° W
USGS MAP: *Stanley Lake* (1988)

Stanley Lake Creek breaks through a moraine and plunges 50 to 75 feet into a basin. Follow Stanley Lake Trail 640 for 2.6 miles. The first 2 miles are easy hiking, then the trail steepens. After another 0.5 mile, look for a sign marking the falls (for some reason it faces hikers walking in the opposite direction), where a spur path leads 0.1 mile farther to a partially obscured gorge-rim view of the cataract. If you cross the creek, you've gone too far.

BRIDAL VEIL FALLS ★★

MAGNITUDE: 62
ELEVATION: 7320 feet
WATERSHED: Small
APPROACH: Trail (fairly hard)
LAT/LONG: 44.211722° N / 115.107374° W
USGS MAP: *Stanley Lake* (1988)

The outlet from Hanson Lakes cascades steeply 120 to 160 feet in two distinct drops. Hike 1.2 miles past Lady Face Falls (described earlier) along Stanley Lake Trail 640 to a sign announcing the waterfall. Nearby is an open area offering a distant view up the side of the valley.

11 SAWTOOTHS EAST

Grizzly bears are among the inhabitants of the Sawtooth Wilderness. Don't let this fact intimidate you and prevent you from visiting this magnificent area. However, do remain alert and follow the guidelines posted at the campground and various trailheads.

GOAT FALLS ★★★★★

MAGNITUDE: 70
ELEVATION: 8100 feet
WATERSHED: Small
APPROACH: Auto or trail (fairly hard)
LAT/LONG: 44.176364° N / 115.018094° W
USGS MAP: *Stanley Lake* (1988)

Goat Creek veils 250 to 300 feet down the mountainside to form the best waterfall in the Sawtooths. Drive 2.3 miles west of Stanley on State Route 21 to Iron Creek Road (Forest Service Road 619). Drive 4 miles to the end of the gravel road and the beginning of Alpine Lake-Sawtooth Lake Trail 640. Hike 1 mile, then turn left (east) at the junction with Alpine Trail 528. Continue 2.5 miles to full views of the falls. Distant views of this cataract are also possible a couple of miles south of Stanley along SR 21.

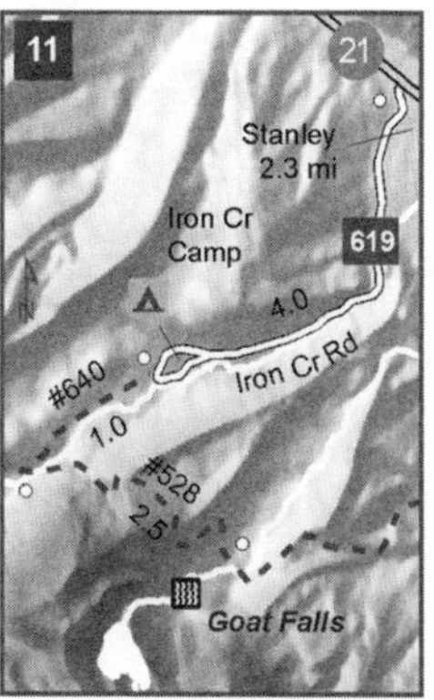

12 KETCHUM

NORTH FORK FALLS (U) ★★

MAGNITUDE: 32
ELEVATION: 7500 feet
WATERSHED: Medium
APPROACH: Trail (fairly hard)
LAT/LONG: 43.881222° N / 114.456944° W
USGS MAP: *Ryan Peak* (1967 ns)

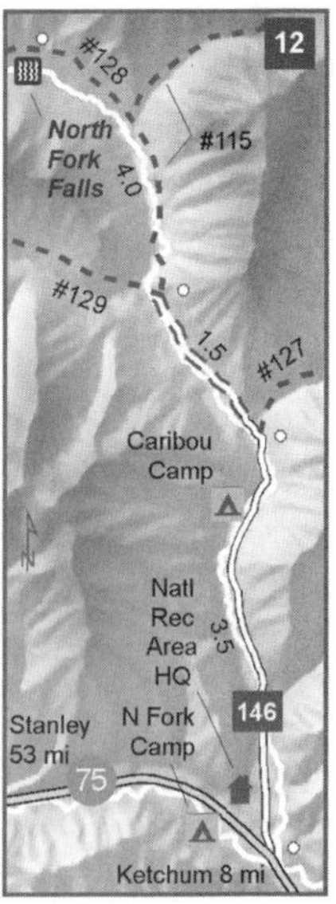

This 50- to 75-foot slide along the North Fork Big Wood River is situated inside Sawtooth National Recreation Area. Drive 8 miles north of Ketchum along State Route 75 to the recreation area headquarters. Turn right (north) on North Fork Road (Forest Service Road 146). The East Fork Big Wood River flows across the road after 3.5 miles; check the water level before attempting to cross the stream with your vehicle.

Continue 1.5 miles to the end of the road, then begin hiking along North Fork Trail 115. Bear left (northwest) on Trail 128. After a total of 4 miles, the trail rises above the canyon floor at the falls.

13 LEESBURG

The following entry is south of the historic townsite of Leesburg. The community was born during the gold rush of 1866, and its population ballooned to 7000 residents within twelve months. The rush soon subsided, and by 1870 only 180 people lived in Leesburg. Today the site is a mining outpost at best. Access to this area from U.S. Highway 93 is via Williams Creek Road (Forest Service Road 021), located 5 miles south of the city of Salmon.

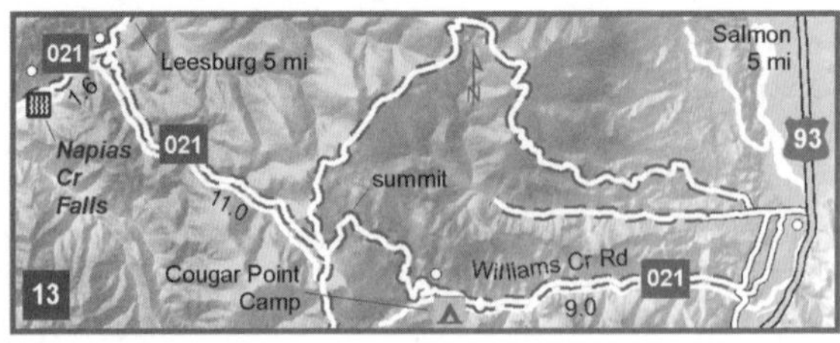

NAPIAS CREEK FALLS ★★

MAGNITUDE: 32
ELEVATION: 5120 feet
WATERSHED: Large
APPROACH: Auto
LAT/LONG: 45.141114° N / 114.201099° W
USGS MAP: *Jureano Mtn.* (1989)

This series of cascades totaling 70 feet is located within the Salmon-Colbalt Ranger District of Salmon-Challis National Forest. *Napias* is Shoshoni for "money," an appropriate name considering the history of this area. Drive 20 miles on FS Road 021 to Napias Creek. Turn left (south), and continue on FS Road 021 as it follows the creek downstream. The cataract can be seen from the road in 1.6 miles.

Fountain Creek Falls

14 NORTH FORK SALMON RIVER

The Salmon River has carved a canyon more than 1 mile deep as it flows 165 miles west through the Clearwater Mountains. There are two named falls in the eastern half of this canyon. One is accessible to motorists, while only experienced rafters can reach the other. Novices should not try to run the "The River of No Return."

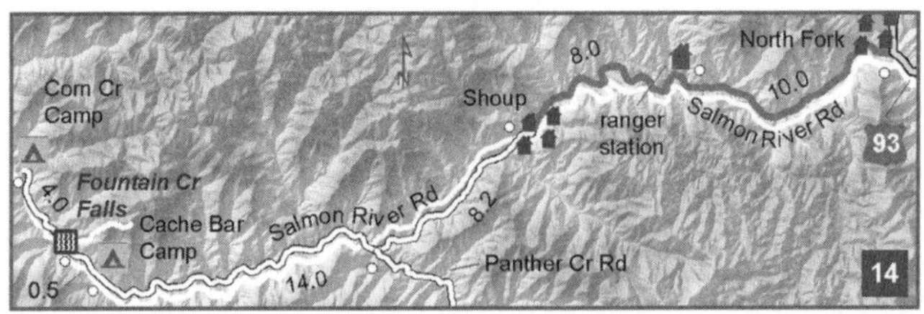

FOUNTAIN CREEK FALLS ★★

MAGNITUDE: 15 (l)
ELEVATION: 3200 feet
WATERSHED: Small
APPROACH: Auto
LAT/LONG: 45.327007° N / 114.647805° W
USGS MAP: *Butts Creek Point* (1962 ns)

Fountain Creek descends from a canyon wall in a stairstep display totaling 35 to 50 feet. It is located within North Fork Ranger District, Salmon-Challis National Forest. Turn west off U.S. Highway 93 at North Fork, and follow Salmon River Road westward. Pass a ranger station in 10 miles and then Shoup 8 miles farther. Drive past Panther Creek Road in another 8.2 miles, then reach Cache Bar Camp 14 miles farther. From this point, drive 0.5 mile past the campground to the falls.

IDAHO

THE SNAKE RIVER PLAIN

Southern Idaho presents the traveler interested in waterfalls with a dilemma. There is no best time of the year to visit its cataracts. The prime time to view individual falls varies more dramatically here than in any other region of the Pacific Northwest.

The least temperamental are streams originating from springs, since they flow continuously. Jump Creek and the Thousand Springs area offer examples. Some flows fluctuate with the demand for hydroelectric power. The falls near Hagerman and Clear lakes change depending on how much water is being diverted to the nearby power stations. The waterfalls along the Snake River near Twin Falls stop flowing most summers because Milner Dam, located farther upstream, impounds water to irrigate agricultural lands.

Some hydroelectric projects along the Snake have destroyed waterfalls. American Falls Dam and Swan Falls Dam have replaced the original descents, and the waters of C. J. Strike Reservoir cover Crane Falls. The highland waterfalls northeast of Rexburg flow perennially but are easily accessible only during summer. Cross-country skis or snowmobiles are required to reach them from November to May.

The Snake River Plain has 70 recognized falls, of which 29 are described here. The majority of these were created by stream courses eroding heterogeneous bedrock at varying rates. The falls along the Snake River formed because bedrock such as rhyolite resists stream erosion more effectively than basalt, its

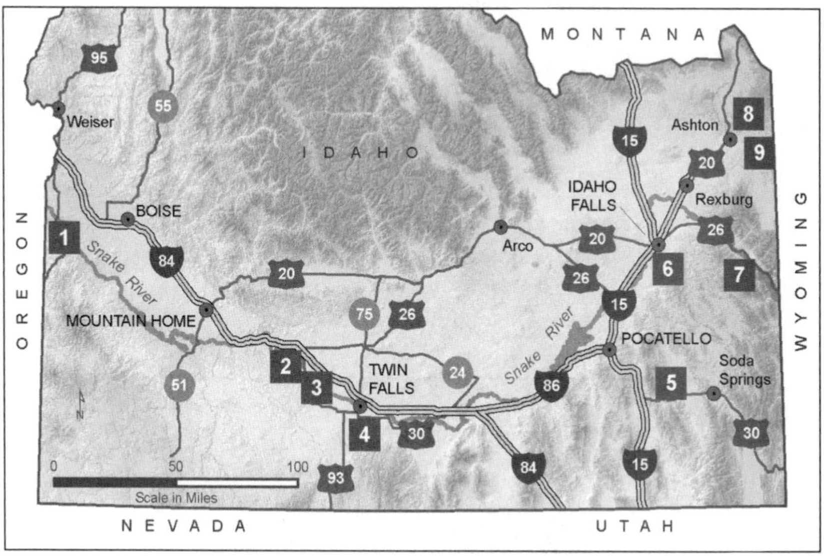

igneous counterpart, does. Most of the falls in the eastern highland areas were shaped in the same way.

Waterfalls descend from the canyon rims of the Snake River for two reasons. Runoff from irrigation finds its way into channels, which in some locales empty over solidified lava flows into the Snake. Along other reaches of the river, waterfalls descend from springs issuing forth from the canyon walls. Details of this latter phenomenon are provided later in the chapter.

1 JUMP CREEK CANYON

This small canyon is one of Idaho's hidden gems. Follow U.S. Highway 95 to Poison Creek Road, which is 2.5 miles south of the junction of US 95 with State Route 55. In 3.5 miles, where the paved road takes a sharp right, turn left (south) on an unnamed gravel road. Follow it for 0.5 mile, then turn right (west) onto a dirt road. Do not get discouraged if you see a "No Trespassing" sign; this route is the correct public access to the canyon. In 0.4 mile, the road forks. The low road leads to a private homestead, and the high road to the right ends at the mouth of the canyon in another mile. Take the high road. The land is administered by the Bureau of Land Management.

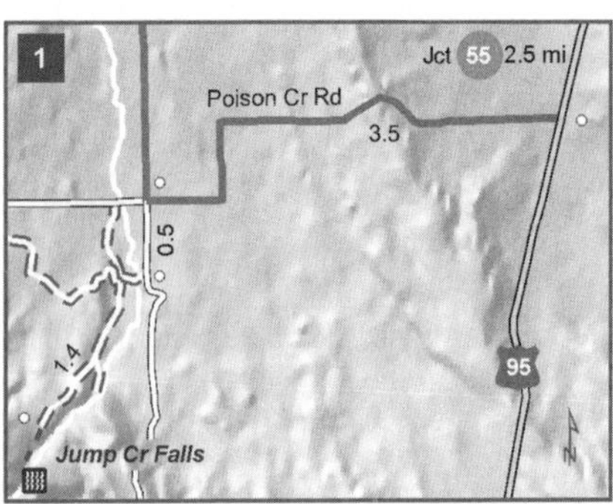

JUMP CREEK FALLS ★★★★

MAGNITUDE: 55
ELEVATION: 2640 feet
WATERSHED: Large
APPROACH: Trail (fairly easy)
LAT/LONG: 43.476701° N / 116.925113° W
USGS MAP: *Jump Creek Canyon* (1989)

Water splashes 40 to 60 feet from Jump Creek into a small canyon. Interesting rock formations frame the cataract. Follow the pathway that begins at the end of the road into the canyon. Proceed along the canyon floor, hopping from stone to stone across the creek and climbing over, around, and under large boulders that have fallen into the gorge. The destination is at the end of the trail in 0.2 mile.

2 HAGERMAN

There are dams and power plants next to each of the falls along this section of the Snake River, which means that their scenic quality varies depending on the amount of water allowed to flow over their natural courses, which in turn

Jump Creek Falls

is determined by the region's electrical demand. The area is accessible via U.S. Highway 30, which is also called Thousand Springs Scenic Route.

☐ LOWER SALMON FALLS ★★

MAGNITUDE: 50
ELEVATION: 2790 feet
WATERSHED: Large
APPROACH: Auto
LAT/LONG: 42.842005° N / 114.903221° W
USGS MAP: *Hagerman* (1992)

A portion of the Snake River tumbles 10 to 15 feet downward. Turn off US 30 at the marked entrance to Lower Salmon Power Plant, located 1.5 miles north of downtown Hagerman. Drive 0.7 mile to the best vantage point. Look for the descent along the far side of the river below the Idaho Power Plant substation.

UPPER SALMON FALLS ★★★

MAGNITUDE: 70
ELEVATION: 2880 feet
WATERSHED: Large
APPROACH: Trail (easy)
LAT/LONG: 42.766722° N / 114.898243° W
USGS MAP: *Hagerman* (1992)

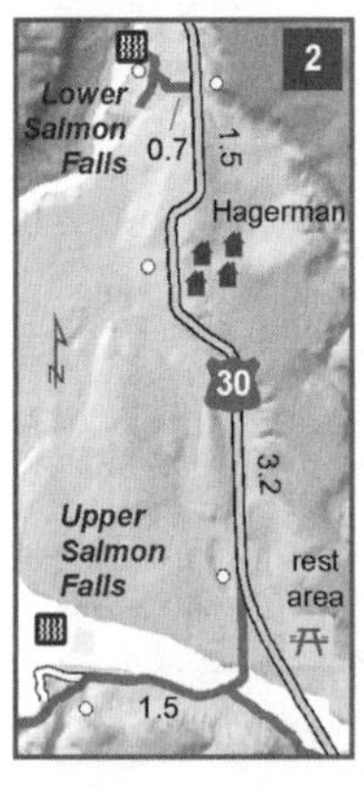

The water in this entry diverges into four main blocks, each descending 15 to 25 feet along the Snake River. Drive 3.2 miles south of Hagerman on US 30, and turn right (west) at the Upper Salmon Falls access sign. If you pass the rest area, you have missed the turnoff. Follow this secondary road 1.5 miles to the power plant. There is an obscured vista of the falls from the gravel road.

For closer views, park at the east end of the road, cross an unmarked catwalk to an island halfway across the Snake, and then proceed down the cement walkway to the falls. *Warning:* Periodically, Idaho Power floods the walkway area; the company is not liable if unwary visitors become trapped on the island.

MORE ONLINE:
Indian Bathtub Falls (u) ★ USGS *Hot Springs* (1992 nl)
Deadman Falls ★ USGS *Glenns Ferry* (1992)
Clover Creek Falls (u) ★ USGS *King Hill* (1986 nl)

3 SNAKE PLAINS AQUIFER

The Snake River Plain northeast of Hagerman harbors one of the world's greatest groundwater resources. The mountain ranges in the southeastern part of central Idaho receive large amounts of precipitation, particularly during the winter. But the streams flowing south from these mountains fail to reach the Snake River because they sink into lava formations on the plain. Water collects in the pores of the subsurface bedrock, and since these rock layers gently dip southwestward, gravity pushes the groundwater toward Hagerman.

The course of the Snake River has been eroded to such an extent that it intersects with the aquifer. As a result, numerous springs gush from the river canyon's north wall. Most of these springs are high above the floor of the canyon, which means they are seen as waterfalls descending into the river.

FALLS FROM THOUSAND SPRINGS (U) ★★★

MAGNITUDE: 73
ELEVATION: 3000 feet
WATERSHED: Large (s)
APPROACH: Auto
LAT/LONG: 42.745122° N / 114.841466° W
USGS MAP: *Thousand Springs* (1992 ns)

There are eight major falls and many minor falls ranging in height from 40 to 100 feet and flowing from springs along the north wall on this 1-mile stretch of the Snake River Canyon located between 15 and 16 miles northwest of Buhl. The springs increase the river's volume by up to tenfold along this reach of the river.

You can see all the horsetail forms of these cataracts from across the Snake River along U.S. Highway 30 (Thousand Springs Scenic Route). For a close-up view of the easternmost descent, turn left (north) onto Clear Lakes Road from the town of Buhl. Go 13 miles then turn left (east) at the sign to Thousand Springs Picnic Area. Proceed 3.5 miles to the destination.

MORE ONLINE:
Falls from Banbury Springs (u) ★
USGS *Thousand Springs* (1992 ns)
Devils Washboard Falls ★ USGS *Thousand Springs* (1992)

4 SNAKE RIVER CANYON

The Snake River has carved sharply through basaltic rock layers to create a narrow, 400- to 500-foot canyon near the city of Twin Falls. The area has several waterfalls, many of which are seasonal.

PILLAR FALLS ★★★

MAGNITUDE: 53
ELEVATION: 3200 feet
WATERSHED: Large (d)
APPROACH: Bushwhack (fairly easy)
LAT/LONG: 42.598619° N / 114.431603° W
USGS MAP: *Twin Falls* (1992)

Towers of rhyolitic rock ranging from 30 to 70 feet tall rise between 10- to 20-foot cascades along the Snake River. The canyon rim also offers a distant

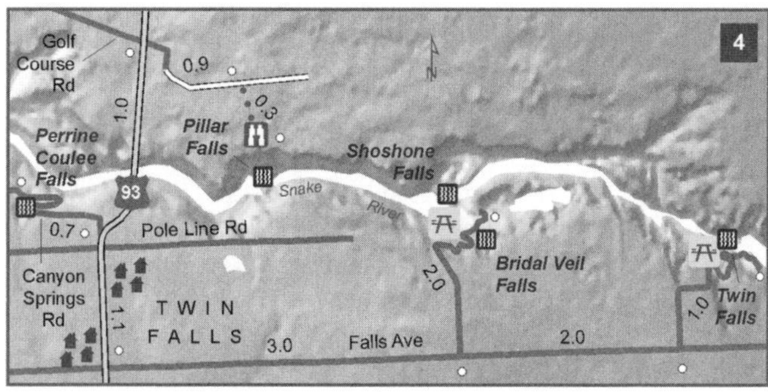

but stunning view of Shoshone Falls (see entry below). You may wonder about the huge sand pile located along the south rim halfway between the two falls. It was the launch site for Evel Knievel's ill-fated attempt to jump the canyon on a "rocket-cycle" during the early 1970s.

From the city of Twin Falls, drive north along U.S. Highway 93 for 1 mile, and turn right (east) on Golf Course Road. Continue along this dusty route for 0.9 mile and park. Walk through the old dumping grounds, comprised of decades-old junk, for about 0.3 mile to the abrupt, unguarded canyon rim. Pillar Falls is directly below with Shoshone Falls farther upstream.

PERRINE COULEE FALLS ★★★★

MAGNITUDE: 90 (h)
ELEVATION: 3500 feet
WATERSHED: Medium
APPROACH: Auto
LAT/LONG: 42.597245° N / 114.472394° W
USGS MAP: *Twin Falls* (1992)

Agricultural activities allow this otherwise seasonal waterfall to flow year-round. In fact, its discharge increases during the dry summer because the coulee collects the water that overflows from the irrigated uplands. A natural pathway goes behind the 197-foot plunge.

Drive north from the city of Twin Falls on U.S. Highway 93; just beyond Pole Line Road, then turn west onto Canyon Springs Road. Park at the unsigned turnout in 0.7 mile. The view is inspiring.

TWIN FALLS ★★★★

MAGNITUDE: 96 (h)
ELEVATION: 3400 feet
WATERSHED: Large (d)
APPROACH: Auto
LAT/LONG: 42.589773° N / 114.354849° W
USGS MAP: *Kimberly* (1992)

Only one of this pair of cataracts still flows. The larger portion has been dammed. A torrent of water hurtles down 125 feet during early spring, but it is reduced

Twin Falls

to a trickle in summer months. Milner Dam farther upstream draws off a large part of the Snake River for irrigation during the mid-year growing season.

From the city of Twin Falls follow Falls Avenue 5 miles east, passing the junction to Shoshone Falls (described later), saving the best for last. Turn left (north) at the marked road; after 1 mile it meets a picnic area adjacent to the falls.

7 BRIDALVEIL FALLS ★★

MAGNITUDE: 30
ELEVATION: 3200 feet
WATERSHED: Small
APPROACH: Auto
LAT/LONG: 42.593707° N / 114.397742° W
USGS MAP: *Twin Falls* (1992 ns)

Water tumbles 25 to 40 feet from spring-fed Dierkes Lake. The stream nearly sprays onto the road before reaching a culvert that directs the water into a pond below. Backtrack from Twin Falls (described earlier) for 3 miles to the marked turn for Shoshone Falls Park. This and the following entry are 2 miles from the junction.

☐ SHOSHONE FALLS ★★★★★

MAGNITUDE: 120
ELEVATION: 3200 feet
WATERSHED: Large (d)
APPROACH: Auto
LAT/LONG: 42.595413° N / 114.401111° W
USGS MAP: *Twin Falls* (1992)

This is the most famous waterfall in Idaho. It measures more than 1000 feet across and plunges 212 feet. The awesome display is best viewed during springtime. Later in the year, when the water is diverted upstream for agricultural uses, the river dries up and only large ledges of rhyolite can be seen. To reach the falls, located in Shoshone Falls Park, follow the directions in the previous entry.

In pioneer days a Shoshoni Indian named Quish-in-demi told the following tale to J. S. Harrington. The story is recorded in *Idaho: A Guide in Words and Pictures,* published in 1937 as part of the Federal Writers' Project:

> In the gloomy gorge above the falls there was, long ago, the trysting place of a deep-chested Shoshoni [warrior] and the slender wild girl whom he loved. Their last meeting was here on a pile of rocks that overlooked the plunging waters. He went away to scalp with deft incisions and then to lift the shaggy mane of white men with a triumphant shout; and she came daily to stand by the thundering avalanche and remember him. That he would return unharmed she did not, with the ageless resourcefulness of women, ever allow herself to doubt. But time passed, and the moons that came and ripened were many, and she still came nightly to stand on the brink and watch the changeless journeying of the water. And it was here that she stood one black night above the roar of the flood when a warrior stepped out of shadow and whispered to her and then disappeared. As quiet as the flat stone under her feet, she stood for a long while, looking down into the vault where the waters boiled up like seething white hills to fill the sky with dazzling curtains and roll away in convulsed tides. For an hour she gazed down there 200 feet to a mad pouring of motion and sound into a black graveyard of the dead. And then, slowly, she lifted her arms above her, listed her head to the fullest curve of her throat, and stood tiptoe for a moment, poised and beautiful, and then dived in a long swift arc against the falling white background . . . And the river at this point and since that hour has never been the same.

MORE ONLINE:
Auger Falls ★ USGS *Jerome* (1992)
Big Drops ★ USGS *Shoshone* (1992)

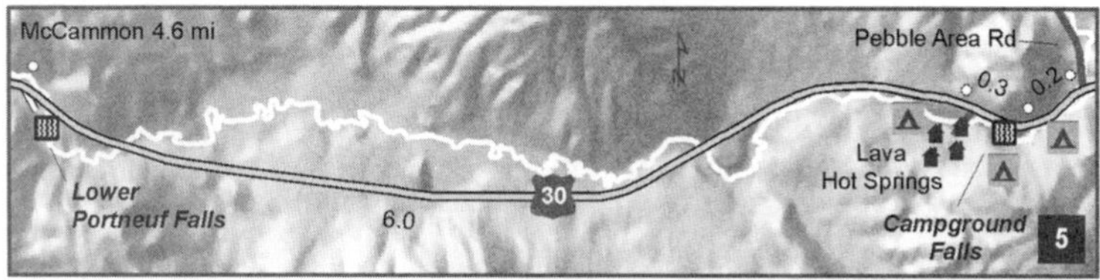

5 LAVA HOT SPRINGS

LOWER PORTNEUF FALLS (U) ★★

MAGNITUDE: 37
ELEVATION: 4840 feet
WATERSHED: Large
APPROACH: Trail (easy)
LAT/LONG: 42.62669° N / 112.12928° W
USGS MAP: *McCammon* (1968 nl)

The Portneuf River diverges into a pair of 15- to 25-foot cataracts. One appears in the form of a plunge, the other, a cascade. From the town of Lava Hot Springs drive 6 miles west along U.S. Highway 30. Park at an old jeep trail, and walk a hundred yards down to the stream and its modest display.

CAMPGROUND FALLS (U) ★★

MAGNITUDE: 37
ELEVATION: 5000 feet
WATERSHED: Large
APPROACH: Auto
LAT/LONG: 42.619048° N / 112.007208° W
USGS MAP: *Lava Hot Springs* (1968 ns)

This 10- to 15-foot drop along Portneuf River is located within a private campground, hence its unofficial name. Drive 0.3 mile past the east end of Lava Hot Springs along U.S. Highway 30.

MORE ONLINE:

Falls along the Portneuf (u) ★ USGS *Haystack Mtn.* (1976 nl)

6 CITY OF IDAHO FALLS

A low, turbulent descent on the Snake River shares its name with this community of 40,000. Stop and enjoy the falls from the adjacent city park.

IDAHO FALLS OF THE SNAKE RIVER ★★★

MAGNITUDE: 71
ELEVATION: 4670 feet
WATERSHED: Large (d)
APPROACH: Auto
LAT/LONG: 43.495026° N / 112.043771° W
USGS MAP: *Idaho Falls South* (1979 ns)

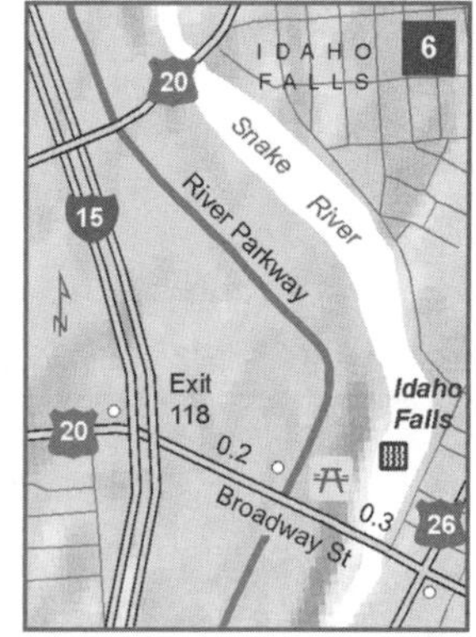

This 15- to 25-foot falls is more than 1200 feet wide and has the distinction of being artificial. In pioneer days there were only rapids at this location. A concrete dam was first built on the river in 1909 to channel some of the water to the Eagle Rock power plant for generating electricity. By the 1970s, the dam had deteriorated severely. In order to assure reliable streamflow for newer turbines, the old dam was replaced in 1981. The artificial falls was constructed as a part of the project.

Turn off Interstate 15 at Broadway Street (Exit 118), and drive toward the city center. Immediately before the bridge crossing the Snake, turn left (north) on River Parkway and find an available parking spot.

7 SWAN VALLEY

FALL CREEK FALLS ★★★★

MAGNITUDE: 78
ELEVATION: 5280 feet
WATERSHED: Large
APPROACH: Auto
LAT/LONG: 43.440862° N / 111.377296° W
USGS MAP: *Conant Valley* (1966)

Fall Creek Falls

Fall Creek plunges 60 feet over travertine into the Snake River. On either side of the central falls the water plumes to form a natural fountain that all waterfall collectors should include on their "must-see" list. This descent is the best known example in the Pacific Northwest of a constructive waterfall, a rare type that migrates downstream as minerals can no longer stay dissolved over the falling water, and thus are deposited and accumulate over time.

Drive 39 miles east of Idaho Falls or 3.2 miles west of Swan Valley along U.S. Highway 26 to Snake River–Palisades Dam Road. Turn south, and follow this gravel route 1.4 miles; park where the road widens. The best views of this cataract are a short walk farther along the roadway.

8 HENRYS FORK

Henrys Fork is a wild and scenic river in all but official federal designation. As it winds through the Ashton-Island Park Ranger District of Caribou-Targhee National Forest, the following waterfalls roar throughout its gorge.

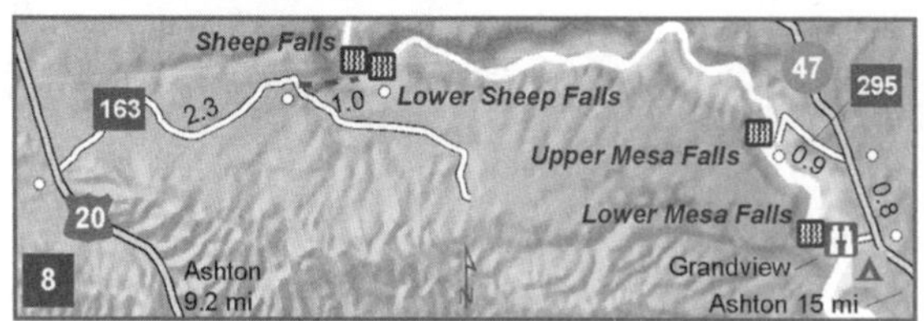

LOWER MESA FALLS ★★★

MAGNITUDE: 78
ELEVATION: 5420 feet
WATERSHED: Large
APPROACH: Auto
LAT/LONG: 44.175219° N / 111.31994° W
USGS MAP: *Snake River Butte* (1965)

The rushing waters of Henrys Fork tumble 65 chaotic feet in this waterfall some 400 feet below an overlook. Drive 15 miles northeast of Ashton on Mesa Falls Scenic Byway (State Route 47) to the signed turnout, appropriately named Grandview. This entry and the one that follows are the star attractions of Mesa Falls Recreation Area.

UPPER MESA FALLS ★★★★

MAGNITUDE: 95
ELEVATION: 5600 feet
WATERSHED: Large
APPROACH: Auto
LAT/LONG: 44.187575° N / 111.330025° W
USGS MAP: *Snake River Butte* (1965)

Lower Mesa Falls

Henrys Fork plummets 114 feet from a sheer wall of rhyolitic bedrock. It is also unofficially known as Big Falls. In 1986, the US Forest Service acquired the property, and they have restored the historic Big Falls Inn, which now houses an interpretive center and gift shop.

About 0.8 mile past Grandview (described earlier) depart State Route 47 by turning left (west) onto Upper Mesa Falls Road (Forest Service Road 295). Drive to the road's end in 0.9 mile. A view at the brink of the falls is just a short walk away along a boardwalk. Be careful at the canyon rim!

☐ SHEEP FALLS ★★★

MAGNITUDE: 50
ELEVATION: 5820 feet
WATERSHED: Large
APPROACH: Trail (moderate)
LAT/LONG: 44.199714° N / 111.394119° W
USGS MAP: *Lookout Butte* (1965)

Watch water tumble 15 to 25 feet along Henrys Fork. Drive 9.2 miles north of Ashton along U.S. Highway 20 to signed Sheep Falls Road (Forest Service Road 163). Turn right (east), and follow the route 2.3 miles to the trailhead.

Sheep Falls Trail 760, built in 1986 by Challenger Group YSC, goes down to the river and reaches the falls in 1 mile.

 LOWER SHEEP FALLS (U) ★★

MAGNITUDE: 47
ELEVATION: 5800 feet
WATERSHED: Large
APPROACH: Trail (moderate)
LAT/LONG: 44.200252° N / 111.391737° W
USGS MAP: *Lookout Butte* (1965 ns)

Water drops 15 to 25 feet along Henrys Fork. Walk fewer than 100 yards downstream from Sheep Falls (described earlier).

9 YELLOWSTONE AREA

Although two of the following falls are in Wyoming, they can be most easily reached from just across the border in Idaho. The Falls River, which flows out of the southwestern corner of Yellowstone National Park, is aptly named. A total of 27 cataracts are known to occur in its drainage basin. Four of them are described here.

SHEEP FALLS ★★★

MAGNITUDE: 51
ELEVATION: 5890 feet
WATERSHED: Large
APPROACH: Trail (moderate)
LAT/LONG: 44.079941° N / 111.090493° W
USGS MAP: *Sheep Falls* (1989)

The name of this 35-foot waterfall comes from the sheep drives that once occurred in the vicinity. It is situated within Ashton Ranger District, Caribou-Targhee National Forest. Drive 6 miles east from Ashton on State Route 47 to Cave Falls Road (Forest Service Road 582). Bear right, follow FS Road 582 for 14.6 miles, then turn right (south) at Wyoming Creek Road (Forest Service Road 124). Drive down this gravel road for 2.4 miles, and park off the side of the road at a junction with an unsigned jeep trail on the left. (Note: The gravel road ends 0.3 mile farther on.)

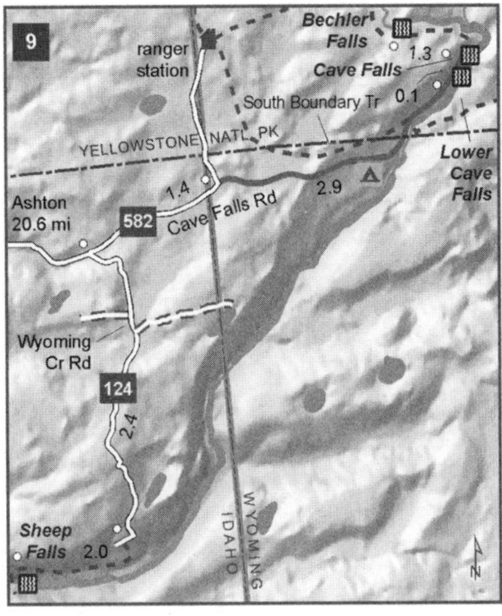

Hike down the jeep trail for 2 miles to the top of the falls. Nimble adults can follow a faint path that leads to the best views.

☐ CAVE FALLS ★★★★

MAGNITUDE: 73
ELEVATION: 6260 feet
WATERSHED: Large
APPROACH: Auto
LAT/LONG: 44.143584° N / 110.997173° W
USGS MAP: *Cave Falls* (1989)

This picturesque block waterfall descends 35 feet along the Falls River within Yellowstone National Park. It is named after a large recess beneath the stream's west bank. Follow the directions to Sheep Falls (described earlier), but stay on Cave Falls Road (Forest Service Road 582) an additional 4.4 miles to its end at the falls, a total of 25 miles from Ashton.

☐ LOWER CAVE FALLS (U) ★★

MAGNITUDE: 40
ELEVATION: 6220 feet
WATERSHED: Large
APPROACH: Auto
LAT/LONG: 44.141567° N / 110.99874° W
USGS MAP: *Cave Falls* (1989 nl)

Rushing water descends 5 to 10 feet along Falls River within Yellowstone National Park. Look for this cataract about 0.1 mile downstream from Cave Falls (described earlier).

☐ BECHLER FALLS ★★

MAGNITUDE: 31
ELEVATION: 6340 feet
WATERSHED: Large
APPROACH: Trail (moderate)
LAT/LONG: 44.149374° N / 111.011786° W
USGS MAP: *Bechler Falls* (1989)

Water tumbles 15 to 25 feet along a wide reach of the Bechler River in Yellowstone National Park. Follow the Bechler River Trail 1.3 miles beyond Cave Falls (described earlier) to this cataract.

SUGGESTED READING

Adam, Kevin. *North Carolina Waterfalls: A Hiking and Photography Guide.* Winston-Salem, NC: John F. Blair, 2005.

———. *Waterfalls of Virginia and West Virginia.* Birmingham, AL: Menasha Ridge Press, 2002.

Blouin, Nicole, Steve Bordonaro, and Marylou Wier Bordonaro. *Waterfalls of the Blue Ridge.* 3rd ed. Birmingham, AL: Menasha Ridge Press, 2003.

Bolnick, Bruce, and Doreen Bolnick. *Waterfalls of the White Mountains: 30 Hikes to 100 Waterfalls.* 2nd ed. Woodstock, VT: Countryman Press, 2003.

Brooks, Benjamin, and Tim Cook. *The Waterfalls of South Carolina.* 2nd ed. Spartanburg, SC: Palmetto Conservation Foundation, 2007.

Brown, Ann Marie. *California Waterfalls.* 4th ed. Berkeley, CA: Moon Outdoors, 2011.

Brown, Scott E. *New York Waterfalls: A Guide for Hikers and Photographers.* Mechanicsburg, PA: Stackpole Books, 2010.

———. *Pennsylvania Waterfalls: A Guide for Hikers and Photographers.* Mechanicsburg, PA: Stackpole Books, 2004.

Bushee Jr., Joseph. *Waterfalls of Massachusetts.* North Amherst, MA: New England Cartographics, 2004.

Cheng, Johnny T. *A Guide to New Zealand Waterfalls.* Artesia, CA: Story Nature Press, 2006.

Danielsson, Matt, and Krissi Danielsson. *Waterfall Lover's Guide to Northern California.* Seattle: The Mountaineers Books, 2006.

Doeffinger, Derek. *Waterfalls and Gorges of the Finger Lakes.* Ithaca, NY: McBooks Press, 2002.

——— and Keith Boas. *Waterfalls of the Adirondacks and Catskills.* Ithaca, NY: McBooks Press, 1999.

Dow, Charles Mason. *Anthology and Bibliography of Niagara Falls.* Albany, NY: State of New York, 1921.

Ernst, Tim. *Arkansas Waterfall Guidebook.* Cave Mountain, AR: Cloudland.net Publishing, 2003.

Fowler, Allan. *The Wonder of a Waterfall.* New York, NY: Children's Press, 1999.

Freeman, Rich, and Sue Freeman. *200 Waterfalls in Central and Western New York: A Finders' Guide.* Fishers, NY: Footprint Press, 2002.

Harris, Mark, and George Fisher. *Waterfalls of Ontario.* Toronto, ON: Firefly Books, 2003.

Hughes, Patricia. *Maine's Waterfalls: A Comprehensive Guide.* Atglen, PA: Schiffer Publishing, 2009.

Letcher, Gary. *Waterfalls of the Mid-Atlantic States.* Woodstock, VT: Countryman Press, 2004.

Lisi, Patrick. *Wisconsin Waterfalls: A Touring Guide.* Madison, WI: Prairie Oak Press, 2000.

Mitchell, Sam. *Pura Vida: Waterfalls and Hot Springs of Costa Rica.* 2nd ed. Birmingham, AL: Menasha Ridge Press, 1995.

Morrison, Mark. *Waterfall Walks and Drives in Georgia, Alabama, and Tennessee.* Douglasville, GA: H. F. Publishing, 1995.

Osborne, Michael. *Granite, Water and Light: Waterfalls of Yosemite Valley.* El Portal, CA: Yosemite Natural History Association, 1989.

Parsons, Greg, and Kate B. Watson. *New England Waterfalls: A Guide to More than 200 Cascades and Waterfalls.* 2nd ed. Woodstock, VT: Countryman Press, 2010.

Penrose, Laurie, Bill Penrose, and Ruth Penrose. *A Guide to 199 Michigan Waterfalls.* 3rd ed. Davison, MI: Friede Publications, 2009.

Plumb, Gregory A. "A Scale for Comparing the Visual Magnitude of Waterfalls." *Earth-Science Reviews* 34 (1993): 261–270.

———. *Waterfalls of Tennessee.* 2nd ed. Johnson City, TN: Overmountain Press, 2008.

———. *The Computer Companion to Waterfall Lover's Guide to the Pacific Northwest.* 5th ed. www.mymaps.com/nwfalls/toc.htm. Updated in May 2013.

Rubinstein, Paul, Lee H. Whittlesey, and Mike Stevens. *The Guide to Yellowstone Waterfalls and Their Discovery.* Englewood, CO: Westcliffe Publishers, 2000.

Swan, Bryan. *Northwest Waterfall Survey.* www.waterfallsnorthwest.com.

Wallinga, Eve, and Gary Wallinga. *Waterfalls of Minnesota's North Shore.* Hovland, MN: North Shore Press, 2006.

Wunder, Dick. *100 Utah Waterfalls.* Thompson Springs, UT: Arch Hunter Books, 1999.

INDEX

Page numbers in *italics* indicate photographs. The letter *C* refers to page number of color plate.

ABOUT THE AUTHOR

Greg Plumb is a geographer who has spent nearly thirty years driving and hiking tens of thousands of spray-soaked miles to document waterfalls throughout the United States. Currently an Oklahoma resident, he continues to take expeditions to the Pacific Northwest to update his database and seek out the seemingly never-ending number of cataracts in the region. Greg is Professor and Chair of the Department of Cartography and Geography at East Central University (www.ecok.edu/cartogeo) and is Director of the Oklahoma Atlas Institute (www.okatlas.org). He performs statistical mapping and analysis as the owner of Personalized Map Company (www.mymaps.com). He is also the author of *Waterfalls of Tennessee.*

The author at Turner Falls, a few miles from his home in the Arbuckle Mountains, Oklahoma (Photo by Robin Plumb)

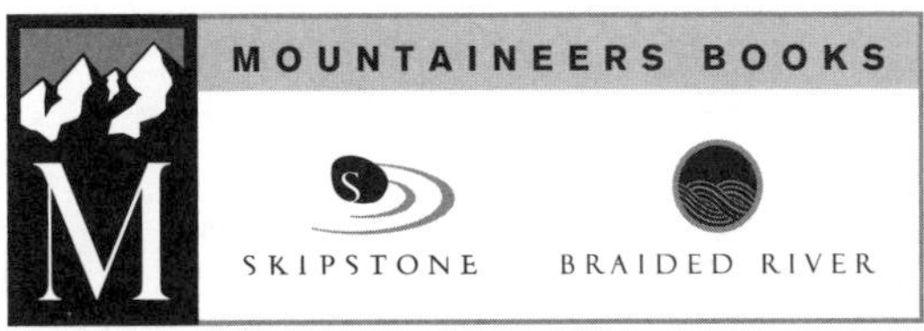

recreation • lifestyle • conservation

Mountaineers Books is a leading publisher of mountaineering literature and guides—including our flagship title, *Mountaineering: The Freedom of the Hills*—as well as adventure narratives, natural history, and general outdoor recreation. Through our two imprints, Skipstone and Braided River, we also publish titles on sustainability and conservation. We are committed to supporting the environmental and educational goals of our organization by providing expert information on human-powered adventure, sustainable practices at home and on the trail, and preservation of wilderness.

The Mountaineers, founded in 1906, is a 501(c)(3) nonprofit outdoor activity and conservation organization whose mission is "to explore, study, preserve, and enjoy the natural beauty of the outdoors." One of the largest such organizations in the United States, it sponsors classes and year-round outdoor activities throughout the Pacific Northwest, including climbing, hiking, backcountry skiing, snowshoeing, bicycling, camping, paddling, and more. The Mountaineers also supports its mission through its publishing division, Mountaineers Books, and promotes environmental education and citizen engagement. For more information, visit The Mountaineers Program Center, 7700 Sand Point Way NE, Seattle, WA 98115-3996; phone 206-521-6001; www.mountaineers.org; or email info@mountaineers.org.

MOUNTAINEERS BOOKS

Our publications are made possible through the generosity of donors and through sales of more than 500 titles on outdoor recreation, sustainable lifestyle, and conservation. To donate, purchase books, or learn more, visit us online:

1001 SW Klickitat Way, Suite 201 • Seattle, WA 98134 • 800-553-4453
mbooks@mountaineersbooks.org • www.mountaineersbooks.org

Mountaineers Books is proud to be a corporate sponsor of the Leave No Trace Center for Outdoor Ethics, whose mission is to promote and inspire responsible outdoor recreation through education, research, and partnerships. The Leave No Trace program is focused specifically on human-powered (nonmotorized) recreation.

Leave No Trace strives to educate visitors about the nature of their recreational impacts and offers techniques to prevent and minimize such impacts. Leave No Trace is best understood as an educational and ethical program, not as a set of rules and regulations.

For more information, visit www.lnt.org or call 800-332-4100.

OTHER TITLES YOU MIGHT ENJOY FROM THE MOUNTAINEERS BOOKS

100 Classic Hikes in Washington
Ira Spring and Harvey Manning
Featuring Washington's finest trails, this is the all-time best-selling guidebook in the state

100 Classic Hikes in Oregon, 2nd Edition
Douglas Lorain
A full-color guide to the true hiking gems of Oregon

Day Hiking Columbia River Gorge
Craig Romano
Comprehensive hiking coverage of the Columbia River Gorge region

Waterfall Lover's Guide to Northern California: More than 300 Waterfalls from the North Coast to the Southern Sierra
Matt Danielsson and Krissi Danielsson
A comprehensive field guide to waterfalls from the Oregon border to the mountain ranges south of the Bay Area

---

Mountaineers Books has more than 500 outdoor recreation titles in print.
For more details, visit www.mountaineersbooks.org

MOUNTAINEERS
BOOKS